THE
WIRES
OF
WAR

**Technology and the
Global Struggle for Power**

JACOB HELBERG

AVID READER PRESS

New York | London | Toronto | Sydney | New Delhi

AVID READER PRESS
An Imprint of Simon & Schuster, Inc.
1230 Avenue of the Americas
New York, NY 10020

First Avid Reader Press hardcover edition October 2021

AVID READER PRESS and colophon are trademarks of Simon & Schuster, Inc.

For information about special discounts for bulk purchases, please contact Simon & Schuster Special Sales at 1-866-506-1949 or business@simonandschuster.com.

The Simon & Schuster Speakers Bureau can bring authors to your live event. For more information or to book an event, contact the Simon & Schuster Speakers Bureau at 1-866-248-3049 or visit our website at www.simonspeakers.com.

Interior design by Joy O'Meara @ Creative Joy Designs

Manufactured in the United States of America

10 9 8 7 6 5 4 3 2 1

Library of Congress Cataloging-in-Publication Data is available.

ISBN 978-1-9821-4443-2
ISBN 978-1-9821-4445-6 (ebook)

This book is dedicated to my husband, Keith Rabois, and our two kids, Eli and Anne Helberg Rabois.

Contents

Prologue

I remember just about every detail of the day that turned my world upside down.

It was a fall morning in San Francisco in 2017, as ordinary as any other. In the cafeteria of Google's Spear Street building, I helped myself to my usual scrambled eggs, then traced the trolley tracks on my walk to the policy office in a separate Google building in the bustling Embarcadero district. Googlers of all ages were scattered throughout our office space, typing furiously, attending meetings, or taking calls in soundproof telephone booths. As Google's lead for news policy, it was my job to help the company think through the implications of much of the work my colleagues around me were engaged in.

I settled into a desk on the third floor and opened my laptop to answer email. I was typing away when I learned that we had a problem—potentially a big one. Unfortunately, I can't recount many of the sensitive internal details. But the issue had to do with the epidemic of so-called fake news during the 2016 election. Although the press had reported on incidents of disinformation spreading online during the election, for much of 2017 most technologists in Silicon

Valley still believed that assuming technology platforms influenced the electoral outcome in any material way would be a leap too far. It can be hard to remember, through the smokescreen of hindsight and all that we've learned since, that this was the prevailing consensus at the time—but it was.

To fully understand what happened, you first have to appreciate how Google works day to day. Beyond Google's search function, the company offers a host of products that require "accounts." Anyone can watch videos on YouTube, one of Google's subsidiaries. But to *post* a video or to place an ad on Google, you need to create an account. Google regularly eliminates accounts that spew spam or serially infringe on established copyrights.

What Google had discovered—as the media later reported—was that an organization called the Internet Research Agency had purchased thousands of dollars of ads on Google.[1] The Internet Research Agency was widely known to be linked to the Russian government.[2] In other words, Google had been hosting accounts controlled by the same outfit that American intelligence officials had accused of masterminding efforts to hack the 2016 election. The concern was that some of the ads, news articles, and videos misleading Americans could be coming from our own platforms or that Google's products could be vulnerable to future attempts at subversion.[3]

Even in my jeans and long-sleeve crew neck, the office suddenly felt chilly. Across from our building was Rincon Park, with its sixty-foot-tall sculpture of a bow and arrow partially sunk into the grass, meant to evoke Cupid's arrow finding its mark in free-loving San Francisco.[4] Right now, the symbolism felt a little too close to home. In our rambunctious democratic system and freewheeling social media platforms, the Russians had hit the bull's-eye.

Across Silicon Valley, revelations such as these had set off alarm bells—and raised serious questions. Were social media platforms more vulnerable to foreign attacks than we'd realized? How seriously had we been hacked—if at all? Were *other* countries using our platform to quietly pursue nefarious goals?

It's not that we hadn't contemplated the challenge of cyber-security—we did. Google had extensive cybersecurity systems in place and even set up an in-house counterespionage team precisely to protect our platforms from sophisticated malign actors.[5] Google also had preexisting policies addressing adjacent aspects of the foreign interference challenge. Nevertheless, no one could have anticipated having to deter and defend against state-sponsored attacks on democratic political systems carried out through highly sophisticated subversions of everyday commercial products. That, most of us in tech assumed, was the government's job—the responsibility of the Pentagon and the National Security Agency (NSA). But sitting there at Google, shocked and confused, it felt as if Washington had failed to protect us. Now Silicon Valley would have to figure out how to respond.

Throughout the 2016 presidential campaign, Americans were vaguely aware that something was awry. Faceless Twitter accounts with grammar out of a Boris and Natasha cartoon spewed absurd untruths, claiming that Democratic nominee Hillary Clinton was desperately sick[6] or had founded the terrorist group ISIS.[7] The online ire of trolls and hackers also targeted then Republican presidential candidates Ted Cruz, Jeb Bush, and Marco Rubio as well as former GOP presidential candidate Mitt Romney.[8] Propaganda is a feature of any political campaign—in America, the tradition of rumor-mongering goes back to our earliest elections.[9] But 2016 pointed to something new. Donald Trump's electoral upset marked a turning point, the moment when Americans saw clearly how a foreign country could use digital technology to manipulate the information flowing into the body politic in a way that would have been impossible a generation ago. It was, by some measure, the first time autocrats had turned our everyday Internet against us as a political weapon of war. But it wouldn't be the last.

I'm a technologist. Like most of my peers in Silicon Valley, I came to Northern California because I believed in the tech industry's broader mission to help people around the world live more fulfilling lives. But over the three-plus years that I worked at Google, my day-to-day experience gradually became defined less by dreamy optimism and more by something darker. I found myself drafted into service on a pivotal battlefield of a rapidly expanding clash between democracy and autocracy—a conflict between fundamentally incompatible systems of global governance, simmering just below the threshold of conventional war.

For much of the past decade or so, this conflict remained largely unspoken—and, in too many quarters, unrecognized. Gradually, however, the designs of the leading forces of authoritarianism—Russia and China—became harder to ignore. Then, in early 2020, the lethal coronavirus sprang into being in Wuhan, China, and began its deadly march across the globe.[10] In a matter of months, the façade fell away. As China's leaders dissembled and its "wolf-warrior" diplomats bullied foreign nations, as former President Trump raged against China and engaged in a heated trade war, the contours of this new struggle came into focus. Suddenly, you could hardly pick up a newspaper without reading about this growing conflict.

"The United States and China are actually in the era of a new Cold War," Shi Yinhong, an international relations professor and advisor to China's State Council, told the *South China Morning Post*.[11] A week and a half later, the *New York Times* wrote that "a sharp escalation of tensions over the handling of the pandemic has raised the specter of a new Cold War."[12]

In many ways, this new cold war is unlike the earlier struggle between the U.S. and the Soviet Union. As historian Hal Brands and Jake Sullivan, now President Biden's National Security Advisor, have argued, "the Soviet Union was never a serious rival for global economic leadership; it never had the ability, or the sophistication, to shape global norms and institutions in the way that Beijing may be able to do."[13] Today, however, we face in China a rising superpower with the ability to exert its influence from the artificial islands in the South China Sea to the boardrooms of Silicon Valley. Moreover—as illustrated by revelations of the wide-ranging "SolarWinds" Russian intrusion into U.S. government systems in 2020[14]—there is the continued threat of Moscow's machinations, different from the days of the Soviet Union, but still immensely disruptive.

Many of the methods of this new confrontation are distinct from what we've seen before. Today's conflict is ambiguous, the parties involved are often opaque, the weapons deployed are unconventional and asymmetric, the interests affected substantial yet amorphous, and the policy frameworks to respond ill-defined. Tarun Chhabra, now the National Security Council's Senior Director for Technology and National Security, singled out "Beijing's 'flexible' authoritarianism abroad, digital tools of surveillance and control, unique brand of authoritarian capitalism, and 'weaponization' of interdependence" as tools that could "render China a more formidable threat to democracy and liberal values than the Soviet Union was during the Cold War."[15] Even though Russia is less sophisticated in its cyber efforts, it is reaching into the heart of democratic societies with disinformation, propaganda, and other tools of political interference—not to spread its political model around the world, as the Soviet Union did, but to discredit and destabilize the democracies that oppose Putin's aims.

A note on terminology: Despite growing evidence of these malign activities, some scholars and policymakers continue to debate whether this conflict in fact constitutes a new "Cold War." To me, the question is not whether we are reliving *the* Cold War but whether we are living through *a* cold war. The term has a history—George Orwell helped define it, calling it a prolonged "peace that is no peace." Some 600 years before Orwell, the Spanish scholar Don Juan Manuel articulated the idea of a "tepid war" simmering below the thin surface of peace. The United States and China today are not in an authentic peace—and have not been for some time.

War and peace have never been binary and have always been a spectrum. With the global economy far more integrated than it was in 1950, governments have increasingly sought to advance their interests and weaken their adversaries in the ambiguous "gray zone" just between the conventional thresholds of war and peace, over trade routes and fiber-optic lines. Today, this has become a predominant and pervasive feature of international politics, which is why I have chosen to describe the systemic global rivalry between democracy and autocracy as a "Gray War." But whether we call it a cold war, a Gray War, or a banana, the impact of China's predatory policies on America speaks for itself. At the end of the day, China's long-term aims are incompatible and irreconcilable with the United States' vision of a rules-based liberal order. And as China exports its model of governance abroad, tensions with democracies will inevitably sharpen.

In contrast to the primary arsenals of the U.S.-Soviet Cold War, this tech-fueled Gray War is primarily being fought with "dual-use" technologies developed by private companies and for civilian purposes. The reason has to do with the inverse relationship between the degree of destructiveness of technology and its rational usability. As Hans Morgenthau once observed:

> *High-yield nuclear weapons are instruments of indiscriminate mass destruction and can therefore not be used for rational military purposes. They can be used to determine a war by threatening total destruction; but they cannot be used to fight a war in a rational manner. A nation armed with nothing but high-yield nuclear weapons would have no military means by which to impose its will upon another nation, aside from threatening it with total destruction.*[16]

Conversely, commercial civilian dual-use technologies (artificial intelligence, or AI; 5G; drones) can be leveraged to carry out increasingly high-impact attacks against adversaries. When an aggressor uses dual-use technologies to carry out attacks against an adversary, they are often far harder to attribute than attacks carried out with more conventional weapons. The aggressor, therefore, often has the ability to deny its involvement in the attack and reduce the risks of a costly retaliation. In short, they're effective and far less risky for aggressors; this makes them highly "usable." Governments can *use* and deploy them for the daily conduct of strategic affairs—advancing their interests and taking on their adversaries—in a rational way without triggering significant costs to themselves or their populations. And that's exactly what they're doing. The outcome of this Gray War will be determined not so much by who controls some piece of territory in Europe or East Asia—though that matters too—but rather by who controls the information networks and communications technologies that shape the distribution of world power by shaping the daily lives of billions of people.

The Gray War is being waged on two fronts. There's a *front-end* battle—largely with Russia at first, but now increasingly with China, Iran, Saudi Arabia, and a range of other nations—to control what we see on the screens of our computers, tablets, and phones. This is the digital layer of the Internet we see every day but can't physically touch with our fingers; it includes software applications, news information, and communication platforms. Even more ominously, we're also engaged in a mostly hidden *back-end* battle—largely with China—to control the hardware guts of the Internet itself. This is the physical layer of the Internet, including hardware devices like cellular phones, satellites, fiber-optic cables, and 5G networks.

This isn't a hot war—at least not yet. As I write this in early 2021, this Gray War has not resulted in large, direct military confrontations between the United States and Russia or China. But make no mistake, it's a war nevertheless, one that will shape our world for this century and beyond. The skirmishes of the coming years will be fought to defend network security, protect intellectual property, gain influence over information, and control critical infrastructure. The spoils of this war are power over every meaningful aspect of our society: our economy, our infrastructure, our ability to compete and innovate, our personal privacy, our culture, and subtle daily decisions we make based on information we interact with online. And in recent years, unfortunately, the world's democracies have been losing ground.

It has become fashionable in academic circles to favor the term "competition" to describe this great geopolitical contest—this is a mistake. As Raphael Cohen, senior political scientist at the RAND Corporation, correctly observes, "competition conjures up images of sports matches or economic markets.[17] Those competitions, however, are bound by rules, policed by referees and ultimately produce winners and losers," he adds. The geopolitical contest between the U.S. and China is not confined to the realm of economic competition nor is it leveled by mutually observed rules.

Referring to the contest as a "competition" downplays the urgency and existential nature of what is at stake; it also obviates a much-needed shared intuition that this contest should frame how policymakers approach almost all other domestic and foreign policy initiatives. When a geopolitical standoff jeopardizes a nation's very political survival, that standoff is more akin to a war than a competition. Wars between nations infect every aspect of the bilateral relationship, as has this one—the same less true of competitions. When a nation is at war, albeit not a hot one, it is clear-eyed that its overriding policy imperative is winning, it instinctively prioritizes its domestic and foreign policy around that imperative, and it more readily accepts making hard domestic decisions deemed necessary. For example, would the U.S. suspend TikTok in the context of a mere U.S.-China competition? Unlikely, and has not to this day— the concept of competition implies American social media platforms should simply compete for market share with TikTok in the United States. However, this misses the point: TikTok poses a gaping national cybersecurity risk. Suspending TikTok would seem like an obvious decision in the context of a U.S.-China Gray War—India understood this. Nebulous notions of competition inhibit the strategic clarity needed to win and only buys China more time to attain geopolitical escape velocity.

If that sounds hyperbolic, consider all the ways in which the Gray War has already shaped our lives. The Office of the U.S. Trade Representative estimates that Chinese theft of intellectual property costs Americans anywhere from $225 billion to $600 billion every year[18]—part of what former NSA director Keith Alexander has called "the greatest transfer of wealth in history"[19]—and the FBI opens a new China-related counterintelligence case roughly every ten hours.[20] An estimated 200,000 American jobs are lost annually because of cybertheft,[21] equivalent to the entire population of Salt Lake City, Utah.[22]

Abroad, China's attacks on India's power grid in the wake of border clashes took out power in a city of 20 million people, shutting down trains, the stock market, and forced hospitals to rely on emergency generators in the middle of one of the worst public health crises in the country's history.[23] China's cyberattack against India is a clarion call to all democracies about how technology can be used to great strategic effect and China's readiness to use it. China's message to India was unmistakable: press territorial claims too hard, and "the lights could go out across the country." [24] For Americans, the subtext of China's message to India is deeply unsettling: the Gray War could reach the American homeland in ways past wars never did.

Then there's China's assault on foundational democratic values like freedom of speech. Beijing canceled broadcasts of Houston Rockets games—and forced the National Basketball Association to apologize—after the team's general manager tweeted in support of Hong Kong's democratic protests.[25] In 2018, a Marriott social media employee in Omaha was fired for "liking" a tweet from a Tibetan in-dependence organization.[26] For many foreign policy academics, the China cold war is an interesting debate. For millions of Americans, it is a reality—and has been for some time.

All that was *before* the coronavirus shook the foundations of the global economy and laid bare the folly of basing critical supply chains—whether for medical equipment or sensitive technology—in a country that seeks to undermine the United States at every turn.[27] *Before* teleworking government agencies and businesses moved their sensitive communications to Zoom, a company that is run by a Chinese-born U.S. billionaire, has 700 employees based in Beijing, and is vulnerable to exploitation by Chinese authorities.[28] *Before* Chinese, Russian, and Iranian trolls began echoing and amplifying each other's propaganda, trying to make misinformation about a viral pandemic go, well, viral.[29]

Now imagine how China might exert its influence when criti-cal Internet infrastructure is within its grasp. "What will happen," the Israeli historian Yuval Noah Harari asks, if "somebody in San Francisco or Beijing knows the entire medical and personal history of every politician, every judge and every journalist in your country, including all their sexual escapades, all their mental weaknesses and all their corrupt dealings?"[30] Will we be sovereign nations, Harari wonders, or satellite states controlled by China? As the Gray War reaches into every aspect of our daily lives, what will happen to our jobs, our retirement accounts, our faith in our own political leaders and system of government?

Silicon Valley may be the most optimistic place in the world, but I've become deeply concerned. Not only because America's ad-versaries have the initiative. Not only because new technologies like artificial intelligence could soon give them yet another advantage. I worry because, without a real partnership between the U.S. govern-ment and Silicon Valley, neither is fully equipped to protect democ-racy from the autocrats looking to pick it apart. Too many in Silicon

Valley still fail to accept that the platforms they created have become a battlefield. In recent years, Washington too often seemed more focused on blaming the technology industry for overseas attacks than on deterring the threats at their origin and defending our democracy from foreign regimes. And time is running out.

Were you shocked by what happened in 2016? Outraged that Russia, China, and Iran tried to interfere in the 2020 election? Well, to borrow from Bachman-Turner Overdrive, you ain't seen nothing yet. Russian and Chinese hackers, among others, are poised to do much more in the years to come—doctoring images, leaking false stories, and blackmailing people with entirely fabricated *kompromat.* Other countries are mimicking Russia's front-end success, working feverishly to distort what crosses our screens. The front-end battle is only just getting started.

Even more significant is China's back-end plan to build a new Internet—a network that will allow Beijing to pilfer whatever data you send from one spot to another, from precious personal photos to valuable intellectual property. If the Chinese wrest control of the world's telecommunications systems—if they can steal our information, manipulate it, monitor it, and redirect it at will—they will have the ability to extend and enforce their influence around the world. And at that point we'll have to grapple with a very different question: Can Western-style democracy survive in a world engineered for autocracy and systemically hardwired to extend the Chinese Communist Party's political control?

Unfortunately, the United States has remained flat-footed. Former John McCain advisor Chris Brose writes, "Over the past decade, in U.S. war games against China, the United States has a nearly perfect record: We have lost almost every single time."[31] Yet this distressing reality elicits crickets from most of the country. China creates a new billion-dollar "unicorn" company every four days,[32] and hardly anyone notices. Unless policymakers and technologists establish a united front against the world's autocrats—and until the

American people wake up to the modern-day technology version of what John Adams called "foreign Interference, Intrigue [and] Influence"[33]—we might as well admit to ourselves that we're not competing to win.

In the corridors of venture capital firms and the open-plan offices of Silicon Valley, people speak of "an AOL moment." It's a reference to the sharp decline of AOL, which had a market value of $224 billion in 2000—and was worth less than $5 billion 15 years later.[34] It's the sickening feeling when a purported market leader realizes, almost overnight, that it's become obsolete. Soon, America could face an "AOL moment" of its own. "If democracies do not devise a new strategy," the federal Cyberspace Solarium Commission starkly put it, "they are unlikely to be the leading beneficiaries or guarantors of this new, connected world."[35] The greatest democracy in the history of the world might be sleepwalking into a world dominated by autocracy. Even worse, most Americans aren't even aware of what's at stake.

"We are not the same kind of country we used to be," Winston Churchill warned the British people in the 1930s, as the German military began to rearm and the airpower revolution threatened Britain's once unassailable position. For years, Churchill sought to rouse his nation to meet the threat posed by an autocracy armed with potent new technology. "The era of procrastination, of half-measures, of soothing and baffling expedients, of delays, is coming to its close," he told Parliament before war broke out. "In its place we are entering a period of consequences."[36]

As America enters its own period of consequences, we need to sound the alarm as well. Before Rachel Carson's *Silent Spring* in 1962, most Americans had only the faintest inkling that big agricultural companies were poisoning the environment. Before Ralph Nader's *Unsafe at Any Speed* in 1965, most consumers were only vaguely aware that Americans were dying at appalling rates in automobile accidents. But once Americans were awakened to the danger, they were able to focus on the problem and craft creative solutions. The time has come to open our eyes fully to the threat we face from autocracies like Russia and China in cyberspace—a danger that some Americans may sense but few truly understand.

What I saw as the global lead for news policy at Google is that the Gray War isn't just coming—it's already here. State-sponsored hackers burrow into critical infrastructure, from the State Department to power plants to defense contractors. China's tech giants—acting as de facto arms of the state—cut sweetheart deals in the developing world, installing the networks and sensors that will enable them to vacuum up data and extend techno-totalitarianism around the globe. Putin's trolls are as busy as ever—in fact, they're adapting and innovating—while some domestic political groups study and even adopt their divisive digital tactics.

Others have written about these issues, from journalists and academics to government officials and tech CEOs. This book is different. It is an account from a foot soldier on the front lines of this critical new fight. It's a look at the future we might face if we don't act. And it's a plea for greater cooperation between our two coasts. My story is not intended as a tell-all—key identifying details have been changed to preserve anonymity—but rather as a wake-up call.

In the pages that follow, I'll share what we've discovered, what's coming next, and why the world's democracies need to take a more comprehensive and aggressive approach to the Gray War. The stakes are no less than our nation's very sovereignty, the quality of our democracy, the freedom of our democratic allies, and the ability of each of us to prosper and control our own fates.

Leaving the Google office on that fall day when everything changed, I stepped outside and gazed at the San Francisco waterfront. More than a century earlier, in 1906, a devastating 7.8-magnitude earthquake had leveled 80 percent of the city.[37] On another clear fall day in 1989, the Loma Prieta quake had once again rocked the city. A section of the Bay Bridge, whose proud suspension spans I could see breaking the fog from our office window, had collapsed.[38] Now it felt as if the ground were shifting below our feet once more. Would we find our footing in time?

Introduction

IN THE HEART OF THE EMPIRE

Little Valley on the Seine

In the summer of 2014, I moved to Silicon Valley on a whim. I'd spent my childhood in a very different valley—a little French town called Vaux-sur-Seine, or "Little Valley on the Seine"—just outside Paris and about eight hours' drive from my mother's hometown of Marseille.[1] Though my mother had taught herself HTML and become a web designer in the aftermath of a difficult divorce from my father, tech felt secondary in Europe. It always seemed to be subjugated by—not shaping—politics and society. It wasn't until high school, working on a freshman-year English presentation at a lycée in Brussels, that I first encountered a search engine called Google. It had a memorable name, but I hardly envisioned that a decade later I would be responsible for Google's global policies related to the search results a high school student saw.

Yet even if I didn't imagine myself in the tech industry yet, I did imagine myself in the United States. My American father and French mother had met in Israel before moving to France to be close to her family. I enjoyed growing up in France but had always been drawn to the country of my father's birth. After vacations to visit my grandparents in Florida and Ohio, my French friends at school would bombard me with questions about what America was like. When I proudly regaled them with tales from the States, there was fascination—almost a twinkle—in their eyes. As I saw it, America was the future—a place where there was an appetite for unconventional and unorthodox ideas.

My unbridled optimism about America—and my understanding of the dangers of authoritarianism—flowed from my own family's story. My father's parents were Jews from Będzin, Poland, who had met on the train to Auschwitz. Years later, tracing the faded blue numbers tattooed on his forearm, my grandfather Sam would tell of watching his own mother, her head shaved, pushed off to the gas chambers. Of a dozen brothers and sisters, only he and two sisters survived. Miraculously, both my grandparents survived Hitler's death camps, saved from extermination by Allied forces. I cherish a photo of their yellowed medical clearance certificates, issued by the U.S. military after the war and featuring small snapshots of each of them. The typewritten medical codes and spidery scrawl are difficult to decipher, but my grandmother's grin isn't. Hers is the smile of a young woman given a second chance at life. The purple stamp on each certificate reads "Liberated Jews."

Eventually my grandparents found their way to Toledo, Ohio, where my father, Ted, would be born. They spoke no English; my grandfather knew how to count but not much else. Yet every morning at dawn he awoke in public housing and headed off to his job as a janitor. Later in the day, he worked as a barber. At nights, he worked at a Jeep factory. At one point my grandfather was sleeping so little that he began to get nosebleeds.

It was the barber shop that gave my grandfather his piece of the American dream. An older brother had taught him how to cut hair before the war. Knowing just two English words—"short" and "long"—he began plying his trade in the United States.[2] He eventually saved enough money to get a loan from a local bank and, over time, buy a few residential real estate properties. He fixed up duplexes and acquired a plot of land here and there. Less than a decade after leaving war-torn Europe, my grandfather struck up a conversation with one of his barbershop customers, who asked for help finding a site for a new dental practice. They enlisted a third partner and before long began to build a modest real estate empire. Their first office consisted of a single desk in a coin laundry. Eventually, the *Toledo Blade* trumpeted the multimillion-dollar success the firm had become under the headline "Barber, Dentist, Builder Combine, Prosper In Real Estate Ventures."[3] In the article, my grandfather was called by his preferred nickname—Sam "the Poor Barber" Helberg.

Years before I'd hear Silicon Valley slogans like "Fail fast, fail often" or "Move fast and break things," it was my family of striving underdogs who taught me resilience and hard work. We lived by the motto "Win or lose, always get caught trying." My father, a psychiatrist able to prescribe himself pills, struggled with addiction but never stopped trying to get clean. My mother waitressed to pay the bills while she trained for an entirely new career, sleeping on a pull-out couch in the living room until we could get back on our feet after she left my father. They were grit personified.

For me, an American kid growing up in France, nowhere embodied that attitude like the States. America was a place you had agency—a country where generations had continually defied the odds. Teddy Roosevelt, rising from sickly boy to project a muscular American patriotism around the world. The Wright brothers—hailing from my father's home state of Ohio—taking flight. Europe was the Old World, full of ancient spires and sometimes hidebound thinking. America was young, fresh, bursting with a sense of unbounded possibility.

It was this spirit that drew me—an Americanophile who'd begun

devouring the *Economist* and obsessing about politics at age fifteen—
to college at George Washington University. GW's Elliott School
prides itself on "building leaders for the world,"[4] and every day I
felt like I was right in the middle of the action. The professors were
policymakers and practitioners, brimming with the accumulated
wisdom of decades within the foreign policy establishment. Equally
exhilarating was my introduction to the inner workings of American
government. I secured an internship on Capitol Hill, and then another at the newly created Consumer Financial Protection Bureau.

With President Barack Obama in his first year in office, it was a
thrilling time to be in Washington. Already, Obama's bold interventions had rescued the auto industry in states like Ohio and averted
what analysts predicted would be a second Great Depression. Each
month seemingly brought another raft of landmark legislation: a
massive economic stimulus bill, the Dodd-Frank financial reforms,
the Affordable Care Act. The arc of the universe was indeed bending
toward justice. I was dizzy with the history of it all.

As my time at GW drew to a close, I began searching for what
was next. After a brief stint at a New York nonprofit, I enrolled in
the law school at Sciences Po in Paris. Within two months, I realized
what drove me to America—and why I was not cut out for life at
a law firm. I had received a summer associate offer to do international arbitration at a prominent white-shoe firm. It was the kind of
place Peter Thiel, himself a lapsed lawyer, would later humorously
describe by saying, "From the outside, everybody wanted to get in;
from the inside, everyone wanted to get out."[5] In what felt like the
biggest roll of the dice I'd made in my life, I turned down the law
firm offer. And after a single semester, I dropped out of law school.

Unsure what to do next, I moved to Los Angeles in 2014 to crash
with my sister, Roxine, and figure out my life. I took a job at a recruiting firm. I also started dating men for the first time. Growing
up, I had never contemplated for a second that I might be gay. My
relatively traditional upbringing led me simply to assume that I'd

marry a woman, have kids, and settle down somewhere, in a house with the proverbial white picket fence. Now, in a city where I hardly knew anyone—and in socially liberal California—it felt like I had nothing to lose by exploring. I started coming out to myself as much as to others.

It was during this period of self-discovery that a friend started telling me about extraordinary things going on just a few hours away in Silicon Valley. I didn't know what opportunities I might find there, but I was intrigued. In July of 2014, I loaded up my Ford Focus and headed north.

The Crazy Ones

"Here's to the crazy ones," Apple's iconic 1997 ad intoned. "The misfits. The rebels. The troublemakers. The round pegs in the square holes. The ones who see things differently . . . Because the people who are crazy enough to think they can change the world, are the ones who do."[6]

For years, I had been marked as different in some way—as a Jew in Europe, as a French American student in the States, as a child of divorce. After I moved to the Bay Area, I was surrounded by other people without cookie-cutter backgrounds. The tech industry was full of dropouts and self-proclaimed "weirdos." One of my new friends hadn't even graduated from high school.

I loved that Silicon Valley placed a premium on unorthodox thinkers. It captured everything I had admired about America growing up. It felt like the new frontier—a place without entrenched norms, social codes, or hierarchies. Living there, you could sense the new world waiting to be built.

While I had reveled in my time in DC, some of the things I'd chafed at in Europe—the status-seeking, the hierarchy, the love of titles—had begun to bother me in Washington as well. Silicon Valley did away with all that. Tech was meritocracy in its purest form. Each new start-up saw itself as pirates trying to defeat the navy, seeking to outflank lumbering legacy companies through greater agility and creativity. By and large, most companies in the Valley were incredibly flat; many employees didn't even have titles. Whereas in Washington I always seemed to be "the intern," forced to justify my presence in a room of older and more senior people, in the Valley ageism felt non-existent. If you were building a product people loved, it didn't matter if you were twelve years old or fifty. Some of the very best companies were created by young people, which is why venture capitalists looking to stay relevant would make deliberate efforts to socialize with up-and-comers.

There was certainly a lot for venture capitalists to chase after. The gold rush of 1849 had triggered the population influx that made California a state. In the early 2010s, Silicon Valley felt like a modern-day gold rush. Discoveries were bursting forth, and companies were hiring left and right. Engineers living off ramen noodles and Soylent became millionaires in a matter of months. In 2010, *Time* magazine named Facebook founder and CEO Mark Zuckerberg its Person of the Year.[7] A couple of years later, the cover of *Forbes* featured Twitter and Square founder Jack Dorsey under the headline "America's Best Entrepreneurs."[8]

When I arrived in the Bay in the summer of 2014, Airbnb, which had started six years earlier as an air mattress in its founders' San Francisco living room, had recently closed a $475 million funding round.[9] Uber had just launched Uber Pool.[10] Within a year, Fitbit had IPOed.[11] Palantir, the data analytics company, was valued at $20 billion.[12] The term "unicorn" had originally been coined to describe the rarity of billion-dollar start-ups; by mid-2015, there were over 130 unicorns.[13]

By the middle of the decade, 62 percent of adult Americans were on Zuckerberg's Facebook.[14] Sleek Apple Watches started appearing on the wrists of the well connected, and Amazon Echos began dotting living rooms around the United States. The optimism was electric.

The decade was also a high-water mark in Washington's love affair with Silicon Valley; this crystallized when Secretary of State Hillary Clinton told a group of tech executives, "Use me like an app!"[15] Hardly a White House roundtable or commission was complete without a handful of Silicon Valley luminaries. State dinners at the White House were studded with tech titans—Zuckerberg, Apple's Tim Cook, Netflix CEO Reed Hastings, Reid Hoffman of LinkedIn, Oracle chairman Larry Ellison.[16] The so-called tech surge to overhaul the healthcare.gov website in late 2013 brought a growing number of technologists into government.[17] Google seemed so completely intertwined with the Obama administration that some dubbed it the "Android administration," after the Google mobile phone.[18] Googlers flooded into the administration, and a steady stream of White House staffers left 1600 Pennsylvania Avenue in Washington for 1600 Amphitheatre Parkway in Mountain View.[19] It had not yet become cliché—or ironic—to say that we were changing the world. Every day, it felt like we were.

Like most newcomers to Silicon Valley, I arrived with little formal training in pitch decks and even less in the nuances of coding and building products. But—as so many in the tech industry do—I knew how to dive into a subject and teach myself. Plus, thanks to the few months I'd spent working in executive recruiting in Los Angeles, I knew how to find and recruit people. That was enough.

Like over 90 percent of start-ups, my first turned out to be an experiment more than a viable business. I started working with a friend, a biomedical scientist from Oxford, on a start-up that did noninvasive breast cancer detection. The science was her wheelhouse, while I helped with the business side, putting together a pitch deck and hiring a team. The technology was great—and I believe that someday someone will bring it to fruition—but we kept running into regulatory hurdles. Medical hardware is (understandably) a tightly regulated space, and at that time investors didn't have much appetite for clinical trials and a lengthy, onerous, and uncertain FDA approval process. After about a year, we closed up.

Along with a few colleagues, I decided to give start-ups another try, this time seizing on an opportunity closer to my passion for geopolitics. We called it GeoQuant, and the idea was to use software to measure geopolitical risk. SwissRe, the world's largest reinsurer, thought the technology was promising and invested. Our clients were Fortune 500 companies weighing the hazards of setting up operations in volatile countries. Typically, they'd bring on consultants with the usual backgrounds from the State or Defense Departments or the intelligence community. Our algorithms offered a quantifiable way to measure risk. Once again, I hired a team and helped raise the initial funding to get GeoQuant off the ground.

I enjoyed the challenge of starting and steering a successful start-up. As the company continued to take shape, however, I realized that being a founder often meant being a full-time fundraiser and recruiter. At heart, I loved policy. But instead of working on the product, I was recruiting and hiring product managers to do that work for me. After about ten months, I decided to bow out and look for the next adventure. Through a friend, I heard about an intriguing opportunity at Google.

My professional life wasn't the only thing in transition. In February 2015, I attended the TechCrunch awards gala, one of the major events on the Silicon Valley social calendar. One of the awards presenters was a guy named Keith Rabois, a prominent tech executive and venture capitalist. After a brief chat that night, Keith and I met up for drinks a few nights later. To my surprise, we spent the entire evening talking about politics. Hillary Clinton was only months away from declaring her second presidential candidacy, and I must have spent an hour raving about her. Keith just kept politely looking at me with a big smile. It wasn't until a few days later that a friend told me Keith was a ruby-red conservative.

The more we got to know each other in the months that followed, the more I came to realize that Keith was—and is—a total original. He grew up in modest circumstances in Edison, New Jersey, the son of a teacher and an accountant. Keith read prolifically as a child; after running out of books at home, he started on the encyclopedia. When I met him, he hadn't taken a vacation in seventeen years. He worked incredibly hard—six days a week, with the seventh spent reading. That work ethic got him through Stanford and Harvard Law School, before he (like me) realized that being a lawyer wasn't for him.

Keith's decision to walk away from the legal field is typical of his worldview. He has a strong anti-establishment streak—a rejection of institutional validation—that resonates with my lifelong attraction to underdogs. While Keith is conservative, in Silicon Valley his conservatism is contrarian. Keith's story of personal sacrifice and grit struck a chord with me. It reminded me of my earliest encounters with raw perseverance and resilience, the divorce of my parents and my father's struggle with addiction. It reminded me of my upbringing and my family's history, my paternal grandparents springing back to a joyful life through years of toil after surviving the horrors and humiliations of the Holocaust and my maternal grandfather risking his life to fight in the French Resistance.

Keith had his fingerprints on some of the most prominent companies in the Valley—including PayPal, Square, YouTube, Airbnb, Lyft, and LinkedIn[20]—and growing closer to him meant becoming more firmly embedded in that culture. I came to know some of tech's most original thinkers. Often controversial, always unconventional, Keith and his circles confirmed for me that the Bay was indeed home to the ideals that had called out to me growing up in Europe.

When my father passed away in early 2017—relapsing after years of battling addiction—Keith was an enormous source of comfort and support. I began to realize I could spend my life with him. We were sitting on the couch one Saturday afternoon that April, shortly after his birthday, when I pretended to drop my phone. Reaching under the couch to retrieve it, Keith found a box I'd hidden. The box appeared to be cuff links for his birthday, but when he opened it, inside was a ring. The following year, we were married in a beachside ceremony, with the setting sun reflecting off the water.

Last Days of Innocence

Throughout much of 2016, I was working to quantify geopolitical risk. GeoQuant promised to take high-quality big data, run it through a powerful "machine learning engine," supplement those assessments with input from human experts, and generate objective, actionable measurements of political risk. Exciting, right? Our algorithms tracked a variety of factors, such as instability in the governing coalitions of G20 nations, declines in the price of oil, and rate cuts by the Federal Reserve. We analyzed the fluctuations of currency markets and military progress in the battle against the Islamic State of Iraq and Syria.[21]

The one thing these data-driven predictions missed—as did the rest of the world—was a Category 5 political cyclone named Donald J. Trump.

When Trump announced his candidacy, on June 16, 2015, I didn't think he had much of a chance. I was still working on my breast cancer start-up and had other things on my mind.

Still, a few things about Trump caught my attention. His rejection of the stuffy, stilted protocols of establishment politics and the ossified orthodoxies of the Republican Party seemed like they might feel refreshing to Americans dissatisfied with the status quo. I'd never watched *The Apprentice*, but I had caught some interviews of

Trump berating China in the early 2010s. With so many politically experienced candidates, I hardly thought a loud, crass real estate developer would win the Republican primary—but Keith and I did think his hawkish stance on China and trade might strike a nerve in segments of the public. To his credit, he correctly diagnosed the most pressing foreign policy challenge facing our country years before it became mainstream.

When we occasionally told our friends as much, they thought it was hilarious. "No way in hell," they assured us. Yet somehow the Trump train kept chugging forward. Even as his tweets and comments became more detached from reality, he dispatched one rival after another. Keith became a big early backer of the "Never Trump" movement during the Republican primaries. As the summer conventions neared, the once unimaginable reality of Trump as the nominee became a foregone conclusion. It also became increasingly clear that something else unusual—it wasn't entirely clear what—was going on.

The Democratic convention had, in many ways, been a shot in the arm for nervous Democrats—powerful and uplifting. Democratic senators talked up Hillary's accomplishments and speakers like Khizr Khan—the Gold Star father of a fallen Muslim army captain—excoriated Trump.[22] When Hillary made a surprise appearance to embrace Obama, the convention hall erupted in cheers.[23] There was a video showing all the presidents, followed by Hillary symbolically "breaking" a glass ceiling.[24]

Yet there was also a disconcerting undercurrent. Just a few days before the Democratic convention, the anti-secrecy website WikiLeaks dumped a number of emails hacked from the Democratic National Committee, some of which seemed to show the DNC's preference for Hillary over her main primary rival, Bernie Sanders.[25] The emails fueled intraparty feuds at a moment when the Democrats most hoped to be coming together. The WikiLeaks dump merged with the media's merciless, seemingly 24/7 discussion of "Hillary's emails," the controversy over Hillary's decision to use a private email account and server while secretary of state.

It was these emails that Trump addressed in an unorthodox press conference on July 27. "Russia, if you're listening, I hope you're able to find the 30,000 emails that are missing," he said, referring to a trove of Hillary's emails. "I think you will probably be rewarded mightily by our press."[26]

Sitting in the GeoQuant workspace, I was disturbed. Trump and his allies tried to play off the comments as a sarcastic joke, yet another example of "Trump being Trump." But Trump's words hadn't sounded like a joke. They'd sounded like a signal.

The following month, Trump's campaign chairman, Paul Manafort, was forced out in the wake of revelations about his sordid history of lobbying for pro-Russian interests in Ukraine. Hillary's campaign began calling out Russia's involvement—Hillary even did so in the presidential debates—but the press didn't seem particularly interested. Something felt off, but—like most Americans—I had no idea how big the iceberg was under the surface.

Then came the "October surprise."

On October 7, the *Access Hollywood* video leaked of Trump boasting of grabbing women "by the pussy" and getting away with it.[27] Then something even more extraordinary happened. Within an hour, WikiLeaks announced that they had obtained 50,000 emails from Hillary's campaign chair, John Podesta.[28] The group immediately released more than 2,000 of the emails, ranging from comments about campaign staff to his much-discussed risotto recipe. CNN was playing the *Access Hollywood* tapes and Podesta emails on a split screen, seemingly on a loop. I have a vague recollection of some talk about U.S. intelligence agencies mentioning Russia's involvement in our election, but it was subsumed in wall-to-wall coverage of sexual misconduct and risotto. Besides, even with these late-breaking bombshells, the *New York Times* election forecasters gave Hillary a 91 percent chance of winning.[29]

In early November, Keith and I hosted fifty friends at our house for my birthday. Everyone was in a good mood—euphoric, even. The tech industry was booming. When *Fortune* ranked the world's most admired companies that year, Apple, Alphabet (Google's parent company), and Amazon snagged the top three spots.[30] As I traveled around and told people I was from San Francisco, I'd see in their eyes the same gleam I remembered from the '90s when I'd delight my French friends with stories about America.

The house we lived in at the time was built into a hillside, with a clear view of the San Francisco skyline. As we drank and mingled on the deck, we could look out at the Salesforce Tower being erected—the tallest building in the city, and the second-tallest west of the Mississippi. It felt like a fitting symbol of the exuberance and optimism of that moment; of the feeling that San Francisco was the center of the world. "The tower stands in the heart of the empire," the *Atlantic*'s Alexis Madrigal wrote, "watching over all with some kind of grace."[31]

I gave a toast, thanking Keith for hosting and everyone for coming. It had been a roller-coaster year, and I talked about how excited I was for the year ahead, when I would be starting my new job at Google. I joked—gently—about how ready we all were to turn the page on the uncivility of the presidential election.

Nobody really talked much about the election that night. There was no mention of Russia or "fake news" or Chinese telecom companies insinuating themselves across the globe. Everyone was just having a good time, enjoying the glow that came from being young and creative in the most important industry in the most important country in the world.

There were party hats and chocolate cake. It was November 6, 2016. And everything was about to change.

Chapter 1

THE ORIGINS OF THE GRAY WAR

The night before my first day at Google, I was too excited to sleep. That morning, fortified by several cups of coffee, I left my house in San Francisco's Glen Park neighborhood and hopped on the Google bus to Mountain View.

At around 6:00, I walked into the storied Googleplex, the sprawling campus of low-slung glass-and-brick buildings that make up the company's main headquarters. Google was the quintessential Silicon Valley start-up. Stanford PhD students Larry Page and Sergey Brin had incorporated the company in 1998, after working out of the garage of Susan Wojcicki (now YouTube's CEO). By the time I joined, nearly two decades later, Google had grown into one of the most iconic companies on the planet. There were more than 60,000 Googlers working around the world, on everything from perfecting search engines to testing self-driving cars.[1] Those products and services brought in an astonishing $90 billion in annual revenue.[2] Within a year Google would briefly dethrone Apple as the most valuable brand in the world.[3]

Google had become the kind of company every scrappy start-up sought to unseat. Yet as I began my new job, nothing about Google seemed boring or bureaucratic. Arrayed around an interior court-yard were buildings housing core functions like news and search, as well as teams working on cutting-edge products like AI and machine learning. Brightly colored bikes that Googlers used to pedal across campus leaned against towering palm trees. Outside, food trucks and benches offered a place to enjoy a bite to eat. Inside, conference rooms shared space with "nap pods" for late-night coding sessions and micro-kitchens stocked with snacks and LaCroix. "Campus" was an apt description. Starting at Google didn't feel like joining a big corporation; it felt like going back to college.

It quickly became clear, however, that the job would hardly be all fun and games. As it turned out, I had walked through the doors of the Googleplex and into a firestorm of controversy.

By sheer coincidence, I became a Googler the day before Donald Trump was elected president. The night of November 8, I watched the election returns with a small group at the offices of a friend's tech firm. The pundits had predicted a slam dunk election for Hill-ary. Like most people who took Nate Silver's projections as gospel, I believed them. Peter Thiel was just about the Valley's lone voice predicting—and championing—Trump's success.

But as state after state unexpectedly went red for Trump, I be-came more and more concerned. I kept telling myself that Hillary could still win. I was still clinging to that slender hope at 11:40 p.m., when CNN flashed the banner headline "Clinton Calls Trump to Concede Election."[4]

Most of my friends watched in disbelief. One person began cry-ing. Others started drinking—heavily. Shortly thereafter, I went home. "Omg," I texted Keith. For the 65 million Americans who had voted for Hillary, the election was a rude shock. The tech in-dustry has long prided itself on being made up of immigrants, and many of them woke up on November 9 genuinely concerned that they and their children would no longer be welcome in the United States.

Before long, Silicon Valley had another reason to feel shocked. From the pages of the *Washington Post* to the president's Twitter feed, we had begun hearing a new term—"fake news." The Trump administration embraced and popularized it, but the term was not a new one—as far back as 1672, King Charles II issued a proclamation "To Restrain the Spreading of False News."[5] In more recent years, the media had taken to using "fake news" to describe the stream of wholly false stories pumped out online by Macedonian teenagers, such as the absurd claim that Pope Francis had endorsed Trump.[6]

In the aftermath of the election, pundits and technologists grappled with whether these bogus news articles had impacted the results. Responding to these criticisms, Facebook founder and CEO Mark Zuckerberg dismissed "the idea that fake news on Facebook . . . influenced the election in any way" as "a pretty crazy idea."[7]

But around the water coolers and micro-kitchens of Silicon Valley, the chatter grew. What was the deal with fake news? And had we unwittingly helped it spread, too?

As Google's global news policy lead, I spent a lot of time thinking about what Googlers call the "ten blue links." When you enter a search term—be it "election 2020," "Dallas Cowboys," or "weather in Chicago"—Google's algorithms instantaneously serve up a list of the ten links most likely to provide the information you want. Google's business model centers on its ability to identify your target in that first page of links—if not in the first link itself. But as simple as that may sound, parsing huge masses of data turns out to be incredibly complicated.

If and when an algorithm serves up inaccurate information, search results can range from humorous and obviously incorrect to inaccurate but subtly believable and potentially more consequential. But who's to determine what is "accurate" information and what isn't? That's why Google's algorithms are designed explicitly to prevent anyone from putting a finger on the scale. Those ten blue links that pop up on your screen are the result of billions of bits of data, with algorithms making informed guesses about which websites will be most responsive to each individual query.

But, of course, there are exceptions. And that was my job—to deal with the exceptions.

Take child pornography. Every decent human wants to protect children from sexual exploitation. Google doesn't have the ability to take down websites featuring child pornography—that's a job for the government—but the company can use its tools to prevent those sites from popping up in a Google search. As policy advisor, my role was to help Google's engineers figure out exactly what to scrub from Google's curated search and news features as well as what might be distasteful but should not be scrubbed. You wouldn't want, say, a charity that valiantly fights sexual exploitation to be hidden from the ten blue links because Google's algorithm noted the phrase "child pornography" on their homepage. So the team I belonged to at Google crafted the company's policies to sort what information should be hidden and what should remain.

In 2015, for instance, Google established a policy that allows revenge porn victims to have unauthorized pictures of themselves scrubbed from any search results.[8] Similarly, when a trove of medical records in India was hacked in 2017, our team at Google responded by making sure that links with sensitive personal information would never show up among our recommended links. For example, we didn't want a Google search to reveal someone's medical history—such as whether they were HIV-positive.

These challenges kept my job interesting. As new kinds of data come online, tech companies are constantly working to ensure that users can access the most useful information while balancing issues like freedom of speech, the right to privacy, and the demands of national security. Which brings us to the unique challenge presented by Russia and fake news.

In the weeks after the election, few of my fellow technologists and I worried that disinformation was a major problem on our platforms. But we wanted to understand more—and as the newest policy advisor, this was something I needed to grapple with.

Google has a number of discrete news products—from the Google News tab on your web browser, to the news feed you see when you swipe down on your Android phone, to the audio news you hear if you ask the Google Assistant, "Okay, Google, read me the news." To most consumers, these products probably seem like different features. Yet each one is made possible by an unseen team of designers, engineers, data scientists, and marketing professionals. Unlike the organic ten blue links, which are meant to be a reflection of the web, news features are more tightly curated and subject to stricter policies for content that Google labels or designates as "news." And each of these products, potentially, was a fissure into which Moscow might have inserted its perverse propaganda.

Digging deeper—consulting with cybersecurity experts and diving into treatises from academics and strategists grappling with the rise of authoritarianism—I started to grasp the contours of the problem. I studied the growing sophistication of Putin's propaganda efforts, the vulnerability of the tech industry's supply chains, and China's deliberate, decades-long effort to digitally encircle the globe and make the world safe for autocracy.

As virulent as the epidemic of fake news had been in 2016, that wasn't the half of it. *This* was the phenomenon I had glimpsed during the 2016 election but hadn't fully appreciated. What's more, I came to understand that this was only one front in a broader battle of hackers and spies, from St. Petersburg to Pudong to Pyongyang, that had been raging—in one form or another—for decades.

I found all these revelations so disturbing that I had trouble sleeping. As I tossed and turned, beset by thoughts of Russian troll farms, Macedonian teenagers building fake news empires, and Chinese conglomerates taking over European networks, the same question kept running through my head.

How did we end up here?

Innovating on the ARPANET

The answer has a lot to do with a science fiction listserv in the earliest days of the Internet. On October 29, 1969, researchers at the Stanford Research Institute connected a computer on Stanford's campus to another computer at UCLA. The building where it happened stands about a mile from my office on Stanford's sprawling campus. It doesn't look especially noteworthy. But there, the researchers—funded by the Defense Department's Advanced Research Projects Agency (ARPA)—sent a message over telephone lines. Unlike a telephone call, however, this new technology broke the data down into fragments—called "packets"—each of which took the quickest possible path to its destination before being reassembled at the second computer.

The Internet was born.

Hunched over their twinned terminals, the ARPA researchers watched, entranced, as the letters "L-O" appeared on the screen. But before the word "LOGIN" could be completed, the nascent system crashed. "Fittingly," the authors P. W. Singer and Emerson Brooking wryly observe, "the first message in internet history was a miscommunication."[9] In fact, these earliest machines were so finicky that they came with voice headsets so that users could verify that their messages were transmitted correctly.[10]

Despite these limitations, this "internet" grew rapidly. A few weeks after that first Stanford-UCLA test, a computer in Santa Barbara joined the network, then one in Utah. Within two years, the network linked fifteen universities together.[11] In 1973, a London university and a Norwegian seismic laboratory became the Internet's first international connections.[12] In honor of its Pentagon patron, this new network was called ARPANET.

Email, explains the Internet historian Johnny Ryan, "was a completely unplanned addition to the ARPANET."[13] These messages—addressed to individuals using the "@" symbol as a shortcut—largely consisted of researchers contacting one another about sharing computing power. Yet in a development that would not surprise any harried office worker, email almost immediately came to consume two-thirds of the network's bandwidth.[14] Still, even if you squinted, ARPANET scarcely resembled the globe-spanning network of communication and commerce that would one day be full of teenagers making TikToks.

Until that sci-fi listserv. Unlike typical person-to-person emails, the message that landed in inboxes one day in 1979 was addressed to the *entire* network. The subject was "SF-Lovers," and its content was fairly straightforward: who, the sender wanted to know, were everyone's favorite science fiction authors?[15] From all across the country, the answers poured in—and with them the birth of a newer, more social, Internet. Every minute, we now send nearly 190 million emails, tweet 350,000 times, upload over 500 hours of content to YouTube, and post 450,000 new photos to Facebook.[16] You can trace a line between that first mass email and the fact that one-fifth of Americans confess that they're effectively never offline.[17]

For much of ARPANET's early existence, the network was essentially a group of loosely connected regional computer clusters, each with its own unique language and rules. It took a pair of researchers named Vint Cerf and Robert Kahn to develop a shared protocol in 1983—known ever since as "transmission control protocol/Internet protocol," or TCP/IP—that would connect these distinct clusters, allowing the network to grow beyond the insular confines of research institutions.[18]

That expansion was not universally welcomed. The Pentagon had already grown concerned about the lax security on the freewheeling network. In keeping with the laid-back engineering ethos of the day, universities like MIT and Carnegie Mellon prided themselves on leaving their systems wide-open and letting "randoms" traipse through. As Cerf's protocol brought more machines into the online fold, the Defense Department had had enough. The Pentagon split off from ARPANET to form its own, more secure network: MILNET.[19]

Ironically, the network the military left behind would become a prime battlefield of the twenty-first century, as a creation of the first Cold War came to define the next one.

At about this time, President Ronald Reagan settled in for a Camp David viewing of the new Hollywood thriller *WarGames*. The president watched in alarm as a teenager (played by Matthew Broderick) hacked into his high school computer to change his grades, eventually finding his way into the North American Aerospace Defense Command and nearly causing World War III. Shaken, Reagan reportedly asked his chairman of the Joint Chiefs of Staff, "Could something like this really happen?"[20]

Reagan's inquiry triggered an investigation into the federal government's cyber vulnerabilities, culminating in a classified presidential directive on "telecommunications and automated information processing systems." These systems, the directive stated, "are highly susceptible to interception, unauthorized electronic access, and related forms of technical exploitation." More than three decades before anyone had heard of Russian troll factories, the directive cautioned that "government systems as well as those which process the private or proprietary information of U.S. persons and businesses can become targets for foreign exploitation."[21]

The answer to Reagan's question was that not only *could* such intrusions happen—they were *already* happening. In 1983, the FBI raided more than a dozen homes across six states, confiscating computers, passwords, and a modem.[22] Among those busted was a group of teenage hackers in Milwaukee who'd broken into government systems and New York's Memorial Sloan Kettering Cancer Center. But with no law on the books prohibiting hacking, the perplexed FBI ultimately charged the perpetrators with a misdemeanor count of making obscene or harassing phone calls.[23]

Scrambling to adapt to this new frontier of electronic abuse, Congress passed the Computer Fraud and Abuse Act of 1986, penalizing "unauthorized access" into the systems of government, financial, and commercial institutions.[24] The same year brought the Electronic Communications Privacy Act, enabling law enforcement to serve tech companies with search warrants for users' data. In time, this law would become the basis for much of the government's subsequent attempts to track terrorism and espionage.[25]

Even as these primitive forms of fraud and abuse proliferated, the Internet grew. Between 1987 and 1989, the number of users surged from 28,000 to 160,000.[26] In 1989, British computer scientist Tim Berners-Lee designed a system of "hypertext" that linked information digitally—a direct forerunner to those ten blue links I spent so much time on at Google. This hypertext was organized by "hypertext markup language" (HTML) and transmitted according to a "hypertext transfer protocol" (HTTP) to Internet nodes identified by a "uniform resource locator" (URL). Berners-Lee called his achievement the "World Wide Web," and it literally changed the world.[27]

Pioneering engineers soon developed so-called web browsers, such as Marc Andreessen's Mosaic and Netscape Navigator, to make it easy to explore this new web. Dial-up services like AOL and CompuServe made the Internet accessible to millions of people without a technical background. As a research tool governed (after the Pentagon's withdrawal) by the National Science Foundation, the network's administrators had banned commercial activity on the Internet.[28] When that prohibition was lifted in 1995, the Internet exploded. By the turn of the millennium, there were 360 million computers linked to the Internet.[29]

In a pattern repeated over and over again, new advances in online technology yielded increasingly creative attempts to exploit them. In 1977, Connecticut's Democratic senator Abe Ribicoff had proposed the first—and unsuccessful—legislation against "computer crimes."[30] The following year brought the earliest recorded instance of spam. ("THIS WAS A FLAGRANT VIOLATION OF THE USE OF ARPANET," one user replied to the overeager marketer.)[31] In 1979, the same year that the SF-Lovers email appeared, so did the first computer worm.[32] In May 1997, a new e-commerce website called amazon.com went public. Two weeks later, the FBI arrested a hacker named Carlos Salgado Jr., who had stolen the information from 100,000 credit cards, with a combined $1 billion in credit.[33]

In February 1998, alarms sounded at Andrews Air Force Base, home of Air Force One. Saddam Hussein had recently expelled international weapons inspectors from Iraq, and tensions were high as the U.S. military prepared air strikes against the regime. Now, it appeared that a sophisticated hacker had attempted to infiltrate the Air National Guard system. Within weeks, the intrusions had spread to Lackland Air Force Base, Kirtland Air Force Base, and others.[34]

The Departments of Defense and Justice followed the digital breadcrumbs from the United Arab Emirates to Israel to California. Far from an Iraqi cyberattack, this was the work of a couple of teens near Sonoma wine country. FBI agents found one of the young hackers at home, surrounded by Pepsi cans and unfinished cheeseburgers.[35] They had been coached by a teenage Israeli hacker, Ehud "The Analyzer" Tenenbaum, whom Israeli authorities eventually arrested. (In a sign of both the Israelis' tech acumen and the complicated dynamic between the United States and Israel, Prime Minister Benjamin Netanyahu reportedly "swelled like a proud father" and pronounced Tenenbaum "damn good.")[36]

It wasn't just bored teenagers and petty criminals who were beginning to understand the power of "telecommunications and automated information processing systems" to cause harm. Commenting on the exploits of the California teens who had broken into the air force computers, Richard Clarke—the White House's coordinator for security, infrastructure protection, and counterterrorism—offered a sober warning. "If two 14-year-olds could do that, think about what a determined foe could do."[37]

Echoes of 1989

To truly understand how "determined foes" like Russia and China came to see the Internet as such an appealing weapon, it's necessary to understand the mindset of the leaders in Moscow and Beijing who would wield it. And that means visiting that fateful year of 1989.

I happen to have been born on November 9, 1989, in the pleasant countryside town of Saint-Germain-en-Laye, then just under an hour's drive from Paris. But while the birth of the Helbergs' second child was newsworthy within the family, it was overshadowed by events elsewhere in the world. About 1,000 kilometers from the hospital where I lay, jubilant Berliners were streaming through gaps torn in the Berlin Wall.[38] Divided for decades, *Wessis* and *Ossis* celebrated their reunification with flowers, champagne, and dancing. The rest of the free world joined in. From the maternity ward, I added my voice to the festive chorus.

With the collapse of the Soviet Union in 1991, former Warsaw Pact countries in Eastern Europe began holding free elections. From Europe to Latin America, across Asia and Africa, free markets and liberal democracy were on the march. A young political scientist, Francis Fukuyama, famously concluded that we had reached "the End of History."

Not everyone was savoring the moment, however. On the day the

Berlin Wall came down, Vladimir Vladimirovich Putin was a young KGB officer stationed in Dresden, East Germany. In his own telling, he brandished a pistol to fend off an angry crowd intent on sacking the agency's Dresden headquarters. Putin and his fellow spies raced to destroy the intelligence they'd collected. "I personally burned a huge amount of material," Putin has said. "We burned so much stuff that the furnace burst."[39]

Convinced that Soviet tanks would put down the unruly East Germans, Putin called for backup. "We cannot do anything without orders from Moscow," Putin was told. "And Moscow is silent."[40] In the estimation of the BBC's Chris Bowlby, "That phrase, 'Moscow is silent' has haunted this man ever since."[41]

By all accounts, 1989 indelibly shaped Russia's president. For the people of East Germany, the fall of the wall was a triumph; for Putin, it was a tragedy. As he saw it, Mikhail Gorbachev, with his talk of glasnost and perestroika, had betrayed the USSR. Putin drove home to Leningrad with his wife and a twenty-year-old washing machine, contemplating a new career as a taxi driver.[42] Soon, even Leningrad itself would revert to its prerevolutionary name of St. Petersburg. Journalist Masha Gessen says that Putin "found himself in a country that had changed in ways that he didn't understand and didn't want to accept."[43]

To ensure that the state would never again let him down, Putin became the state. Within a decade, he rose from KGB officer to president of Russia. Putin marshaled a cadre of oligarchs, known as "Kremlin, Inc.," to exert control over Russia's nascent democracy.[44] Two former Putin aides assumed control of Russia's largest oil companies.[45] A former Putin judo sparring partner became one of Russia's biggest builders, receiving massive government contracts.[46]

In Putin's kleptocracy, token opposition was allowed to exist but not flourish. Outspoken political leaders and journalists disappeared or wound up dead. Anna Politkovskaya, a crusading journalist investigating corruption and human rights abuses, was shot and killed in the elevator of her Moscow apartment in 2006,[47] one of roughly thirty journalists who have been killed in Russia since Putin took power.[48] In 2014, Boris Nemstov, a deputy prime minister turned Putin critic, was shot four times near the Kremlin.[49] Alexei Navalny, an anti-corruption activist who has been called "the man Vladimir Putin fears most,"[50] was poisoned in 2020 (though he fortunately survived).[51]

Addressing the Russian Duma in 2005, Putin called the collapse of the Soviet Union "the greatest geopolitical catastrophe of the century" and a "genuine tragedy" for the Russian people.[52] He watched as former Soviet satellite states slipped away and authoritarian regimes were replaced by Western-facing democracies. In the 1990s, the North Atlantic Treaty Organization (NATO) bombarded the Balkans by air—over Russian opposition at the United Nations.[53] In 1999, Poland, the Czech Republic, and Hungary joined the North Atlantic Alliance, followed a few years later by Bulgaria, Romania, Albania, and even the Baltic states that had once been part of the Soviet Union itself.[54] The forces of liberalization were creeping closer to Mother Russia. NATO, the very organization formed to resist Soviet aggression, was at Putin's doorstep, its easternmost point just a short drive from St. Petersburg. Russia's leader chose to push back—hard.

Putin dreamed of reassembling the old Soviet sphere of influence. When he feared that Georgia, a former Soviet republic, was gravitating toward the West, he ordered Russian forces to invade and help dismember the country in 2008. In 2014, a similar scenario transpired in Ukraine. Meanwhile, he rebuilt Russia's armed forces—which had fallen into disrepair after the Soviet collapse—and gloried in the perception of Moscow's restored power on the international stage.

Yet Putin did not reassert Russian influence only through frontal military assaults. The KGB veteran also employed what Russians had long termed *aktivniye meropriyatiya*—"active measures"[55]—

exercising influence, as Soviet foreign minister Eduard Shevard-
nadze put it, through "the force of politics" as well as "the politics
of force."[56] It was only natural that Putin would turn to such tactics.
Thomas Rid, a professor at Johns Hopkins University, notes that Putin's post in Dresden "had been opened specifically to run active
measures against West Germany at a time when active measures
were at their most cunning."[57]

Foreshadowing their 2016 efforts against the United States, Moscow's Cold War active measures campaigns sought to create wedges
in the Western world. The KGB eagerly spread (sometimes true)
stories of violence against U.S. minority communities. During the
1984 election, KGB agents tried to prevent Reagan's reelection.[58]
Notoriously, the Soviet Operation Denver propagated the lie that the
U.S. government had cooked up the AIDS virus at Maryland's Fort
Detrick[59] (an eerie forerunner to China's more recent claim that the
Pentagon had created COVID at the same installation).[60] By 1985,
CIA analysts conservatively estimated that the USSR was spending
$3 to $4 billion a year on active measures around the globe,[61] culmi-
nating in an estimated 10,000 disinformation operations throughout
the Cold War.[62]

Soviet disinformation campaigns were often effective, but there
were limits. The former FBI agent and national security analyst Clint
Watts notes, "Soviet propaganda outlets took many years or even
decades to grow their audiences," costing time and money Moscow
didn't have. "Active measures could and would work," Watts says.
"The timing just wasn't right—until the advent of the internet."[63]
As David Sanger of the *New York Times* puts it, "Stalin would have
loved Twitter."[64]

At first, the Russian government was slow to realize the disruptive
power of the Internet. In *The Red Web,* journalists Andrei Soldatov
and Irina Borogan recount that security services were so confused by
the Internet that they initially mandated that the country's first commercial Internet service provider, Relcom, "print out everything that

came through Relcom's network." When the company explained the volume of information that would entail, the government withdrew its request.[65]

Yet the Kremlin learned fast. By 1996, American officials were reporting Russian breaches at sensitive sites ranging from Ohio's Wright-Patterson Air Force Base to the Department of Energy's National Laboratory at Los Alamos, birthplace of the atomic bomb. An FBI investigation dubbed Moonlight Maze revealed that the hackers worked European hours and had taken off three Russian Orthodox holidays. Further inspection revealed that the hackers had written their code in Cyrillic. American investigators traveled to Moscow, lured by the promise of Russian government assistance. They were treated to vodka and merriment—and then promptly stonewalled. The Russians, it turned out, were uninterested in helping to counter what was undoubtedly a Russian intelligence operation.[66]

Russia had entered the Cyber Age—and Moscow didn't look back.

The tiny Baltic republic of Estonia learned about Russia's active measures innovation the hard way. In 2007, the Estonian government decided to move a Soviet-era memorial in the capital of Tallinn—a statue that many Estonians viewed as a monument to Soviet occupation, but which ethnic Russians in the country saw as a symbol of their heritage. Riots broke out in front of Estonia's embassy in Moscow. In late April, hackers launched cyberattacks on critical institutions. Estonia—the birthplace of Skype—is so technologically advanced that it is sometimes referred to as "E-stonia." But under the digital barrage, government websites and banking systems went down. The denial-of-service attacks were followed by a denial of responsibility. Russian authorities insisted on their innocence, even as they refused to cooperate with investigations. Ultimately, the attacks were traced to a Kremlin-sponsored youth organization called Nashi.[67]

The assault on Estonia is widely considered the first cyberattack by one nation against another.* Under Article 5 of NATO's mutual defense treaty, a military attack on an ally like Estonia obligates American and European allies to consider coming to its defense. But did taking down Internet infrastructure constitute an "attack"? Nobody had a good answer.

Even as NATO debated this next frontier of warfare, Putin kept up the offensive. When Russian troops invaded Georgia in 2008, the assault included attacks affecting more than fifty websites. Notably, the electronic attacks seemed to mirror and anticipate strikes by tanks and planes. Michael Sulmeyer, the former cyber policy director at the U.S. Defense Department, calls this "one of the first times you've seen conventional ground operations married with cyber activity."[68]

Russia was becoming equally aggressive—though its actions were less overt—in the United States. Weeks before the 2008 election, National Security Agency staff stumbled across Russian hackers lurking in the Pentagon's classified system, SIPRNET. Because of the sensitivity of these networks, the computers were designed to be "air gapped," meaning they had no connection to the broader Internet. It turned out the Russians had surreptitiously scattered thumb drives infected with malware near a NATO base in Afghanistan, just waiting for an American to pick one up.[69] The ploy worked. Forty years before, the Department of Defense had birthed the Internet; now, hostile powers had turned that creation back on the Pentagon itself.

After kicking the intruders out of the network, government cybersecurity experts implemented a particularly high-tech solution to

---

* While terms are sometimes used interchangeably, there are a few varieties of malicious cyber activity. "Cyber crime" typically refers to breaking into networks for illicit financial gain, while "cyber espionage" entails extracting sensitive government or corporate information to better understand an adversary. A "cyberattack" usually involves state-sponsored efforts to disrupt or destroy critical Internet infrastructure in service of a greater geopolitical goal.

prevent future attacks: they filled Pentagon USB ports with super-glue.[70] But it would take more than gluing computers shut to fend off attacks—and not only from Russia but from Russia's authoritarian cousin, China.

The Square and the Firewall

In the spring of 1989, as the Soviet Union began to crumble, the wave of democratization sweeping the globe brought up to a million Chinese demonstrators to Beijing's Tiananmen Square.[71] In an image that instantly became iconic, a man in a white shirt and black pants, shopping bags in hand, faced down four oncoming tanks on the edge of the square. When the tanks tried to maneuver around him, the protester shuffled to keep his body in their path. It was a defiant dance; man versus machine, freedom versus oppression. Though he was never identified, "Tank Man" became a worldwide symbol of the uprising—and of the Chinese Communist Party's bloody massacre in response. This was the flip side of the hope that I had always associated with 1989. In Berlin, revolutionary restlessness ended with the wall coming down. In Beijing, it ended in slaughter.[72]

On an academic trip to China in the summer of 2011, I stood in the middle of Tiananmen Square, thinking about the activists—mostly young students like I was—who had gathered there to demand greater rights. Yet nowhere in the huge, imposing square will you find a plaque, or even a bouquet of flowers, commemorating the crackdown. No Chinese textbook mentions what the government obliquely refers to as "the June Fourth Incident."[73] No search request on a Chinese computer will turn up results. Sometimes the censorship reaches absurdist levels. In late 2011, Chinese programmers were prevented from updating the popular Node.js application because the version number, 0.6.4., corresponded to the date of the massacre.[74]

But while the government has tried to erase the protests from public consciousness, they were seared into the consciousness of the Chinese Communist Party. Chinese leaders "were scared as hell," Hal Brands told me, as a result of this "near-death experience." The lesson? Stamp out any dissent and stifle any disunity that could paralyze the party. When the Soviet Union collapsed, China's leaders viewed it as vindication. Gorbachev was never willing to use force, and look what happened? Tiananmen is "the Rosetta stone" that explains much of how the Chinese regime has acted in the years since.[75]

Western political theorists had long promoted the idea that economic growth and political liberalization go hand in hand. "The more well-to-do a nation, the greater the chances that it will sustain democracy," the sociologist Seymour Martin Lipset wrote.[76] After Tiananmen, China tested that proposition. As the journalist Evan Osnos describes it, to prevent a repeat of 1989, "the Party offered its people the essential bargain: greater freedom in economic activities in exchange for less freedom in political life."[77]

The resulting prosperity has fueled China's dizzying rise. By 2012, China was building the equivalent of a new Rome every two weeks.[78] In just three years—from 2011 to 2013—Chinese builders used more concrete than the United States did throughout the entire twentieth century;[79] observers began to joke that the national bird of China was the construction crane.[80] This sustained growth has lifted 800 million Chinese citizens out of poverty since the creation of the People's Republic of China (PRC) in 1949. Forty years ago, when SF-Lovers was taking ARPANET by storm, per capita GDP in China was around $195. By 2019, it was $10,261.[81] Already, China has overtaken Japan as the world's second-largest economy. Depending on how you measure, China has either surpassed the United States as the world's biggest economy or is projected to do so in the 2020s.

China's newfound wealth provided the resources not only to suppress opposition at home but to expand the country's influence abroad. The British journalist Martin Jacques observes that China has long viewed itself not "as a nation-state but rather as a civilization-state."[82] In contrast to the so-called Westphalian system, in which nations treat each other as sovereign, China relates to other countries through the prism of ancient "tributary" relationships, with neighboring states acknowledging the country's cultural superiority and overwhelming power in exchange for its protection. Even China's name for itself, "the Middle Kingdom," conveys this view of a country situated atop the hierarchy, between earth and heaven.[83] As its foreign minister bluntly informed his counterparts at a 2010 meeting of the Association of Southeast Asian Nations, "China is a big country, and you are small countries."[84]

In particular, China's leaders speak of reversing a "century of humiliation" at the hands of Western powers—the period stretching from Britain's 1842 defeat of the Chinese in the First Opium War through the Japanese invasion and brutalization of China during World War II. These humiliations are hardly a distant memory; when Trump and President Xi Jinping first met in April 2017, Xi treated Trump to a lecture on this unhappy history.[85] Later that year, Xi declared that China was entering a "new era" and "must take center stage in the world."[86] In Beijing's view, that means asserting full control over Hong Kong, regaining control over "breakaway" territories like Taiwan, expanding Chinese influence throughout the Asia-Pacific, and challenging the United States for global supremacy. "The signs that China is gearing up to contest America's global leadership are unmistakable, and they are ubiquitous," write Hal Brands and Jake Sullivan.[87] And in Vint Cerf and Tim Berners-Lee's ingenious creation, the Chinese Communist Party saw a new way to advance their old ambitions.

Two years before the Tiananmen massacre, the first email was sent from China. It traveled 4,500 miles from Beijing to Berlin. In hindsight, the message set a rather ominous tone: "Across the Great Wall we can reach every corner in the world."[88]

Chinese use of the Internet subsequently skyrocketed. From 1996 to 2000 Chinese Internet users jumped from 40,000 to 4 million.[89] With 800 million users, China now makes up more than a quarter of everyone online.[90] The web consultant Jakob Nielsen notes that statistically, the typical person online is "a 24-year-old woman in Shanghai."[91] To ensure that the Chinese people would not have unfettered access to the outside world, Beijing's bureaucrats came to rule the Internet in their country with a silicon fist.

In March of 2000, defending the decision to invite China to join the World Trade Organization, President Bill Clinton declared that "in the new century, liberty will spread by cell phone and cable modem." Clinton acknowledged that "there's no question China has been trying to crack down on the Internet," but then added, "Good luck! That's sort of like trying to nail Jell-O to the wall."[92]

The truth was, two years earlier, the Chinese government had already initiated its Golden Shield Project, a sprawling system of censorship and surveillance that would grow to include China's infamous "Great Firewall." Using human censors and digital sensors, the system blocks domestic access to any site (including Google) that deviates from the Communist Party line. Behind the Great Firewall, suspect search terms simply return no results; messages containing banned words disappear into the digital void. Helping Beijing nail Jell-O to the wall were several American companies, including Cisco and Sun Microsystems.[93]

Nor was China's projection of online power confined to its own borders. As the new millennium dawned, two colonels in the People's Liberation Army, Qiao Liang and Wang Xiangsui, laid out an approach they termed "unrestricted warfare." They argued that China would only be able to overcome the United States as a global leader by employing a strategy that relied less on military means and more on technological know-how. "The new principles of war," they wrote, entailed "using all means, including armed force or non-armed force, military and non-military, and lethal and non-lethal means to compel the enemy to accept one's interests."[94] It was a recognition, as Trump's national security advisor H. R. McMaster would later put it, that "there are two ways to fight the United States: asymmetrically and stupid."[95]

In 2001, after a diplomatic flare-up involving the collision of an American reconnaissance aircraft and a Chinese jet over the South China Sea, American hackers vandalized a series of Chinese websites. Chinese hackers retaliated with an attack that took down the White House website and defaced other government websites with messages like "Beat down Imperialism of American [sic]! Attack anti-Chinese arrogance!" The *New York Times* dubbed it the "First World Hacker War," yet it was only the smallest taste of what was to come.[96] The same year, Chinese president Jiang Zemin declared that the Internet had become a "political, ideological, and cultural battlefield."[97]

By 2008—the same year that Beijing tried to promote itself to the world as a responsible rising power by hosting the Summer Olympics—hackers from the People's Liberation Army infiltrated the networks of defense contractor Lockheed Martin, stealing plans for the F-35 fighter jet.[98] In a troubling preview of 2016, Chinese operatives penetrated the presidential campaigns of both John McCain and Barack Obama, apparently looking for information on their views on China.[99]

A year later, Google discovered Chinese hackers in the company's own networks. The intruders arrived at Google in mid-2009, about seven years before I did. The intrusion, nicknamed "Aurora" by the hackers, marked the first time the Chinese had been discovered targeting non-defense companies. What triggered it? It appeared that at least one Chinese Politburo member had been googling himself—and had been displeased by "results critical of him" and his family.[100] So, like anyone with an army of hackers at their disposal who doesn't like their Google search results, Chinese leaders ordered a digital assault. The unwelcome visitors sought out valuable intellectual property, like the source code for Google's search engine. They also attempted to hack into the Gmail accounts of Chinese human rights activists. Alarmingly, the hackers even infiltrated a Google database containing court orders from the U.S. Foreign Intelligence Surveillance Court, which approves requests from American law enforcement to spy on intelligence threats. Which is to say, China was using Google to learn whether the United States had compromised China's own spies.[101]

Google took the hack extremely seriously. Co-founder and president Sergey Brin moved his desk to work alongside Google's security team, which the company strengthened with $100,000 signing bonuses to recruit the finest security engineers in the field.[102] Brin, a Jewish refugee from the Soviet Union, didn't hold back. "Having seen the hardships that my family endured—both while there and trying to leave—I certainly am particularly sensitive to the stifling of individual liberties," he said.[103] Shortly thereafter, Google announced that it would no longer agree to censor search results on Google.cn, its Chinese search engine, as required by Chinese law. This was tantamount to withdrawing its business from China's fast-growing market, which Google formally did several months later, a decision that no doubt pleased Baidu, Google's homegrown Chinese competitor.[104] Google was out of China—at least for the time being.

In what might be called an "autocratic awakening" of sorts, authoritarians the world over were seizing the tools of technology to revise the U.S.-led liberal order, advance their vision of a world safer for authoritarian regimes, and assault the sources of American power. Still, within the United States there was not yet a widespread sense among American policymakers or the public that autocracy was on the upswing or that the Internet was facilitating its resurgence. In fact, as protesters with smartphones began massing across the Arab world, it seemed that technology would be a force for liberation.

A Man Becomes a Matchstick

On December 17, 2010, a man became a matchstick.

Angry over years of mistreatment by Tunisian authorities, a twenty-six-year-old street vendor named Mohamed Bouazizi doused himself with paint thinner and set himself on fire in the provincial capital of Sidi Bouzid.[105] His act of self-immolation sparked protests; within days, thousands gathered in Tunis to protest the corruption and abuses of President Zine El Abidine Ben Ali. WikiLeaks revelations about the excesses of the president and his family—including his son-in-law flying in ice cream from Saint-Tropez and feeding his pet tiger four chickens a day—further inflamed the protests.[106]

Demonstrators brandished signs with slogans like "Ben Ali, get lost"[107] in what came to be known as Thawrat al-Karāmah, the Revolution of Dignity.[108] When snipers fired on the crowds, protesters caught footage of the carnage on their smartphones and shared it widely.[109] After a month of protests, and twenty-three years in power, Ben Ali fled to Saudi Arabia.[110] Jubilant Tunisians began to draft a democratic constitution.[111]

By late January, Egyptians were chanting, "We are next, we are next—Ben Ali, tell Mubarak he is next."[112] A Facebook page created by Wael Ghonim, Google's head of marketing for the Middle East and North Africa, quickly became a platform for coordinating mass protests against Hosni Mubarak, Egypt's "modern pharaoh."[113] One activist tweeted, "We use Facebook to schedule the protests, Twitter to coordinate, and YouTube to tell the world."[114] Recognizing the central role social media was playing in the demonstrations, Mubarak's regime attempted to choke off Internet access. The effort failed. On February 11, the modern pharaoh resigned. Mubarak had ruled Egypt for nearly thirty years; aided by social media, he was toppled in eighteen days.[115] The world began to speak of an Arab Spring.

Days later, that Arab Spring came to Libya. Like Mubarak, Libyan leader Muammar Qaddafi tried to stifle protests by shutting down Libyans' access to the Internet.[116] Still, cellphone videos leaked out and were readily uploaded to YouTube. The revolution quickly descended into civil war between Libya's longtime strongman and rebel forces.* With Qaddafi's army poised to massacre the rebel stronghold of Benghazi, the United States helped marshal a NATO air campaign to protect civilians and push back regime forces.[117] Qaddafi's grip on power weakened. By fall, he had fled to his hometown of Sirte, where he was ultimately found hiding in a drainage pipe and executed. Several graphic and grainy videos flooded the Internet, capturing the desperate last moments of the dictator's life.[118]

It wasn't the first time that social media had fueled social movements. When anti-government protests swept Iran in 2009, enthusiastic observers had prophesied that the unstoppable power of the Internet would unleash the forces of freedom across the globe. "The Revolution Will Be Twittered," Andrew Sullivan had written in the *Atlantic*.[119] In early 2010, while an undergraduate in Washington, I watched as Secretary of State Hillary Clinton delivered remarks on Internet freedom at the newly opened Newseum on Pennsylvania Avenue. "There are more ways to spread more ideas to more people than at any moment in history," Clinton declared. "And even in authoritarian countries, information networks are helping people discover new facts and making governments more accountable."[120]

That optimism had persisted even after Iran's theocrats had brutally suppressed the Green Revolution. Now, with the Arab Spring sweeping aside sclerotic regimes from Tunisia to Yemen, the optimists appeared to have been vindicated. A euphoric Egyptian father named his new baby girl "Facebook."[121] Widely distributed networks of people were connecting online—for the sole purpose of protest

---

* Qaddafi, the "Brother Leader," was a bizarre figure who employed 40 women as his personal bodyguards and traveled with a bulletproof Bedouin-style tent, often with a camel or two tied outside. He was also merciless—deploying civilians as human shields, torturing and imprisoning dissidents, and murdering activists and journalists.

and dissent—without a clear hierarchy or leader. And it seemed they were winning.

What Western observers saw as a triumph, however, the world's autocrats watched with terror. "The Arab Spring unnerved Chinese leaders more than any event in years," wrote Osnos. "The lesson they took from Mubarak's fall was the same they had taken from the collapse of the Soviet Union: protests that go unchecked lead to open revolt."[122]

Putin, meanwhile, saw Libya as a Western betrayal. During the early years of the Obama administration, the United States and Russia had pursued a diplomatic "reset," cooperating on counterterrorism and negotiating a reduction in nuclear weapons. The Russians had grudgingly acquiesced to the UN resolution authorizing limited military intervention in Libya to protect civilians from Qaddafi's forces.[123] But with the death of Qaddafi, Putin's worst fears were realized. Putin denounced the Libyan intervention as a "medieval call to the crusades" and pronounced himself sickened by the dictator's death.[124] "Almost all of [Q]addafi's family has been killed, his corpse was shown on all global television channels, it was impossible to watch without disgust," he said.[125] Putin reportedly viewed the video obsessively.[126] You can almost picture the hardened KGB operative sitting in his opulent office, watching Qaddafi's body dragged through the streets, vowing that Vladimir Vladimirovich Putin would never meet such an ignominious end.

Around the world, it had not escaped the autocrats' attention that technology had turbocharged this new wave of liberalization. After Putin's party underperformed in the 2011 parliamentary elections—even with the help of widespread fraud—thousands of Russians had gathered in Moscow, calling for Putin's arrest and chanting, "Russia without Putin!" Many Russians had learned about the rallies on the Internet—the *Pentagon*-developed Internet—which Putin had taken to labeling a "CIA project."[127] Alexei Navalny, the anti-corruption activist who rose to prominence via social media, addressed the crowd to cheers. "They can laugh and call us microbloggers. They can call us the hamsters of the Internet. Fine. I am an Internet hamster. But I know they are afraid of us." Navalny and several hundred protesters were promptly arrested.[128]

In a statement, Secretary of State Clinton said, "The Russian people, like people everywhere, deserve the right to have their voices heard and their votes counted."[129] It was a relatively pro forma message, but to Putin it was an American call for Russians to rise up against him. Clinton "set the tone for some actors in our country and gave them a signal," Putin claimed.[130] He would not soon forget.

It would be several years before the 2016 election awakened the West to the ways in which the Internet could exploit the vulnerabilities of their societies. But for autocrats in Beijing, Moscow, and Tehran, the Arab Spring was a technological awakening of their own. Seeing other repressive governments around the world crumble, illiberal regimes in Russia and China accelerated their treatment of the information space as a domain of war. "Tech-illiterate bureaucrats were replaced by a new generation of enforcers who understood the internet almost as well as the protesters," write Singer and Brooking in their book, *LikeWar: The Weaponization of Social Media.* "In truth, democratic activists had no special claim to the internet. They'd simply gotten there first."[131]

Gerasimov Meets Civil-Military Fusion

In early 2013, with the embers of the Arab Spring still smoldering, an article appeared in a Russian military publication called the *Military-Industrial Courier.* Under the bland headline "The Value of Science in Prediction," Russian general Valery Gerasimov argued that nonmilitary means could be used to destabilize seemingly stable societies.[132] Indeed, he asserted that the United States had been

doing exactly that in Eastern Europe through pro-democracy organizations and the Internet. "In the twenty-first century we have seen
a tendency toward blurring the lines between the states of war and
peace," Gerasimov wrote. As a result, he argued, "the role of non-
military means of achieving political and strategic goals has grown."
His analysis echoed that of Qiao Liang and Wang Xiangsui, the two
Chinese colonels. Gerasimov's solution was to suggest that Russia
should fully exploit the "wide asymmetrical possibilities" of the Internet.[133]

The "Gerasimov Doctrine" updated Russian active measures for
the information age. Within a year, those measures were being unleashed against Ukraine. In late 2013, pro-Western demonstrators
had begun agitating against Ukraine's Putin-allied president, Viktor
Yanukovych, over his decision to choose closer economic ties to Russia rather than the European Union.[134] As with the Arab Spring,
their Internet-enabled protests led to a despot leaving power and
fleeing into exile.

Determined not to let the country fall out of what he considered
Russia's sphere of influence, Putin supported separatists in Russian-
speaking enclaves of Ukraine. More strikingly, he sent plainclothes
forces—so-called Little Green Men after their unmarked green military fatigues—to seize Crimea.[135] In late summer of 2014, after the
Ukrainian revolution had nearly put down the rebellion in its eastern
provinces, the Russian military invaded the country in earnest.

As in Georgia six years before, the ground war was supplemented
by online operations. Scrutinizing over 22,000 Russian-language
sources around the world, researchers found a massive spike in negative press about Ukraine—doubling, then tripling, in the months
leading up to Russia's annexation of Crimea.[136] Propaganda sites like
RT.com spun lurid tales of supposed atrocities by Ukrainian forces,
which were then amplified by trolls: pro-Russian Ukrainians beaten
with baseball bats, strangled to death—even a three-year-old cruci-
fied, with his mother dragged behind a tank.[137]

This orgy of fake news served multiple purposes. It provided Russia with a pretext for invasion, allowing it to claim it was fighting "fascism" and protecting Russian-speaking Ukrainians. It inflamed divisions between Ukraine's nationalists and pro-Russian separatists. Perhaps most importantly, in St. Petersburg, a troll factory known as the Internet Research Agency began experimenting with how social media could be used to distort the news and divide a population.[138]

Then, just before Christmas Eve 2015, the lights went out in western Ukraine. Having used "phishing" emails to gain control over the networks of utility companies, the Russians began opening breakers at the tongue-twisting Prykarpattyaoblenergo power company. One engineer took a video of a mouse cursor skittering across a computer screen, opening breaker after breaker, as if controlled by some invisible digital hand. For good measure, the hackers plunged the utilities' own offices into darkness and jammed the phone lines to frustrate customers calling to complain about the blackout. It was the first cyber strike known to have taken down a public utility, and it took the Ukrainians over a year to get their systems up and running—just in time for another, more devastating attack, which killed power to 20 percent of Kiev.[139] In Ukraine, the Gerasimov Doctrine had come of age.

China was expanding its reach in cyberspace as well. In 2013, President Xi announced a $1 trillion Belt and Road Initiative—echoing the ancient Han Dynasty Silk Road that brought spices, silks, and other goods from Europe to China—to build infrastructure around the globe.[140] Xi has hailed this as "the project of the century."[141] Many of these strategic investments throughout Asia, Africa, and Europe include investments in fiber-optic cables, 5G networks, and other digital hardware—the critical back-end infrastructure that determines control of the Internet.[142] In 2015, Chinese premier Li Keqiang unveiled a new strategic plan—Made in China 2025—seeking to move China away from being the "world's factory" and toward dominance of high-tech industries, including AI, robotics, aerospace equipment, and biopharmaceuticals.[143] Two years later, China's Party Congress asserted its desire to make China a "cyber-superpower."[144]

Aiding China's effort to become a cyber-superpower is the principle of "civil-military fusion," a concept written into the Chinese constitution.[145] Under civil-military fusion, Chinese companies, like the telecommunications firms Huawei and ZTE, are subordinate to the Chinese government. Article 7 of China's National Intelligence Law states, "Any organization or citizen shall support, assist, and cooperate with the state intelligence work in accordance with the law, and keep the secrets of the national intelligence work known to the public."[146] In other words, the infrastructure and equipment that Chinese firms build around the world is, by design and definition, a de facto extension of the Chinese government. If you are talking on a phone built by Huawei or your email is flowing across a Huawei telecom line, you could easily be leaving a message directly for a Chinese intelligence service. The "Chinese private sector" is effectively an oxymoron. The relationship between Chinese citizens and the Chinese Communist Party, Xi has said, is like "stars revolving around the revered moon."[147]

Importantly, civil-military fusion runs both ways. Just as China uses its tech giants to support the Chinese state, the state likewise directs government hackers to conduct aggressive economic espionage against foreign competitors to aid homegrown industries.

The nerve center of this effort is a PLA group called Unit 61398, operating from a compound in the Shanghai district of Pudong, complete with a health clinic and a kindergarten.[148] In one notable instance, in 2012, the hackers of Unit 61398 penetrated an Oregon-based renewable energy company called SolarWorld Americas, making off with everything from cash-flow spreadsheets to privileged attorney-client communications detailing the company's litigation against Chinese dumping.[149] In 2014, authorities arrested a Chinese national in Vancouver who had, over a dozen years, collaborated with Chinese hackers to meticulously steal Boeing files related to the F-22 Raptor and the F-35—some of the most advanced fighter aircraft in the world—as well as the C-17 military transport plane. The stolen C-17 material totaled 630,000 files, roughly 65 gigabytes of data. At a Chinese air show later that year, the Chinese parked their copycat aircraft, the Xian Y-20, directly across the tarmac from its American original—a brazen demonstration of the fruits of their theft.[150]

Yet that was only the half of it. The *Washington Post* reported that Chinese hackers had absconded with designs for the Patriot PAC-3 missile system, the Terminal High Altitude Area Defense antiballistic missile system, and the Aegis missile defense system, among many others.[151] "There are two kinds of big companies in the United States," former FBI director James Comey bluntly explained. "Those who've been hacked by the Chinese and those who don't know they've been hacked by the Chinese."[152]

To avoid embarrassing sanctions on the eve of President Xi's first American state visit in September 2015, Xi joined Obama in committing their countries to a ban on cyber-enabled economic espionage.[153] For a brief moment, at least, Chinese theft of corporate America's secrets seemed to drop off. But this coincided with an uptick in Chinese theft of Americans' personal data, including a major breach of the health insurer Anthem that compromised the data of 78 million Americans.[154] Law enforcement and counterintelligence officials became especially worried when this valuable data did *not* turn up on the black market, where a single comprehensive health record might be worth $40 or $50.[155] Instead, it appeared likely that it was going straight into databases controlled by the Chinese Communist Party.

This vulnerability was driven home in the unlikeliest of government agencies: the humdrum Office of Personnel Management, which handles the personnel files of millions of federal employees.

In April 2015, an IT contractor for OPM realized that the agency's network was contacting a site cleverly disguised as a legitimate government site called opmsecurity.org. Upon closer inspection, investigators discovered that opmsecurity.org and a second domain were registered to two unlikely people—Steve Rogers, the alter ego of the superhero Captain America, and Tony Stark, the alter ego of Iron Man. A cybersecurity company was brought in to assess the damage, which was summarized in one expert's email to another: "They are fucked btw."[156]

Over nearly a year, hackers linked to the Chinese government had exfiltrated 4.2 million personnel files, 5.6 million biometric fingerprints, and 21.5 million SF 86s.[157] These last—required as part of background checks for government security clearances—were especially concerning. Armed with this information, the Chinese government would know about illicit affairs, criminal history, and substance abuse, any of which could be used for blackmail. A congressional oversight committee described the hack as "the most significant digital violation of national security faced to date."[158]

A Twenty-First-Century Watergate

It would hardly be the last. Even as Russia and China asserted themselves more online, lesser autocrats were getting in on the action.

In 2010, a sophisticated worm known as Stuxnet destroyed 1,000 Iranian centrifuges, setting back Iran's nuclear ambitions. The malware attack was widely attributed to the United States and Israel. In response, Iran's mullahs began ramping up their cyber operations.

During the summer of 2012, an Iranian cyberattack on the Saudi Aramco oil company melted down 35,000 hard drives and forced the company to buy 50,000 new computers—driving up the global price for hard drives for half a year.[159] A few months later, Iran launched Operation Ababil, a series of distracting though not destructive attacks against Bank of America, JPMorgan Chase, and other financial institutions.[160] The next year, casino billionaire and conservative mega-donor Sheldon Adelson publicly suggested that America should nuke a patch of Iranian desert as a warning over its nuclear program. Iran's Supreme Leader, Ayatollah Ali Khamenei, replied that Adelson "should receive a slap in the mouth." That slap came in the form of a crippling attack on the networks of Adelson's Sands casino in early 2014, which destroyed 75 percent of its Las Vegas computers, leaked sensitive employee data, and cost Adelson's business approximately $40 million.[161] It was considered the first destructive nation-state attack targeting an American company.

Freedom of expression was also at the center of what is universally considered one of the strangest cyberattacks in history. It involved the film *The Interview,* a buddy comedy starring Seth Rogen and James Franco as talk show hosts who assist a CIA plot to assassinate North Korean dictator Kim Jong-un. When the trailer came out in the summer of 2014, North Korea warned that the film was "terrorism" and would yield a "strong and merciless countermeasure." Neither American officials nor the film's producer, Sony Pictures, seemed terribly concerned. Rogen tweeted, "People don't usually wanna kill me for one of my movies until after they've paid 12 bucks for it."[162]

But Kim Jong-un was not amused. At the time, the so-called Hermit Kingdom had fewer IP addresses than the average New York City block.[163] Yet Kim saw the Internet as an asymmetric weapon for his outmatched dictatorship. "Cyber warfare, along with nuclear weapons and missiles, is an all-purpose sword that guarantees our military's capability to strike relentlessly," he declared in 2013.[164] With training from Chinese and Russian experts, North Korea's cyber capabilities had grown rapidly to include perhaps as many as 6,800 hackers.[165]

The week of Thanksgiving, computers at Sony suddenly seized up. Calling themselves the "Guardians of Peace," the hackers posted a message: "We've already warned you, and this is just a beginning. We continue till our request be met. We've obtained all your internal data including your secrets and top secrets."[166] Soon, that internal data began leaking out—almost 40 million files, including Social Security numbers, performance reviews, and other personal information.[167] It included juicy gossip like one executive's description of Angelina Jolie as a "minimally talented spoiled brat," as well as salary information detailing an uncomfortably wide pay gap between Sony's male and female employees.[168] Reporters feasted on the salacious emails.[169]

"I never thought I'd be here briefing on a bad Seth Rogen movie, sir," a White House staffer told President Obama as the attack unfolded. "How do you know it's a bad movie?" Obama asked. To which the aide replied, "Sir, it's a Seth Rogen movie. . . ."[170] Yet Obama and his team knew that the hack was no laughing matter. The attack had ruined nearly three-quarters of Sony's computers.[171] It upended the lives of American employees. All for producing a movie a dictator disliked.

While Obama opted not to characterize the attack as an "act of war"—instead calling it a costly "act of cyber vandalism"—his administration took the intrusion seriously. It publicly attributed the attacks to North Korea, rolled out a new executive order allowing sanctions against nations engaged in malign cyber activities, and declared that the United States would respond "in a place and time and manner that we choose."[172]

The Interview ultimately became one of the most popular online releases ever. Yet the most lasting impact of the hack may have been the leaked emails. Aaron Sorkin took to the opinion section of the *New York Times* to decry "every news outlet that did the bidding of the Guardians of Peace" as "morally treasonous and spectacularly dishonorable."[173] But that hadn't stopped the scoop-hungry American press from breathlessly reporting the contents of those hacked emails. Far away in the Kremlin, Putin surely took notice.

So began what has been called "the largest, most sophisticated, most targeted hacking campaign in world history."[174] In mid-2015, the National Security Agency notified the FBI that they'd detected suspicious activity in the networks of the Democratic National Committee.[175] FBI investigators suspected the intrusions were the work of "Cozy Bear," a group linked to the Russian FSB (the successor to the notorious KGB) and part of a Russian cyber force that one former KGB colonel estimates includes perhaps a thousand Russians.[176] The bureau called the DNC, warning that a Russia-linked group appeared to be hacking the organization. An inexperienced IT contractor took down the information and passed it up the chain, where it apparently was ignored.[177]

Russia's penetration of the DNC amounted to a high-tech, twenty-first-century Watergate. "Ironically," notes the cybersecurity scholar Ben Buchanan, "the file cabinet of interest to the Nixon-era burglars, still kept as a memento, was not far from one of the servers targeted by the hackers."[178] Yet these early alarm bells went unanswered. The FBI—located half a mile from DNC headquarters—didn't follow up for several months, until after it noticed a DNC computer pinging hackers in Russia.[179] Finally, in the spring of 2016, the DNC recognized the scope of the hack and scrambled to address it.[180]

Then came perhaps the most consequential typo in history. On March 19, 2016, John Podesta, the chair of Hillary Clinton's presidential campaign, received an email from "Google" suggesting that someone had compromised his account and that he should change his password. Unsure whether to trust the message, one of Podesta's aides forwarded the email to an IT staffer, who replied, "This is a legitimate email. John needs to change his password immediately." Later, the staffer insisted that he meant to type "this is an *illegitimate* email." Whatever the case, Podesta changed his password.[181] Russian hackers—linked to Russian military intelligence and nicknamed

"Fancy Bear" by cybersecurity researchers—soon gained access to nearly 60,000 of Podesta's emails, including that infamous risotto recipe.[182] Podesta was the highest-profile victim but hardly the only target. Over the course of a single week, the GRU emailed fifty different campaign addresses each day.[183]

Having obtained a wealth of embarrassing emails, Russia began to weaponize them. WikiLeaks announced they'd obtained a trove of emails, which they began strategically leaking. These included the ones on the eve of the Democratic convention and the dump on October 7, meant to distract from Trump's *Access Hollywood* tape.[184]

Many of the emails were embarrassing but not especially explosive. Mostly, the world learned about campaign messaging and petty office politics.[185] To inject these mundane messages further into the political bloodstream—and amplify other divisive themes—the trolls of the Russian Internet Research Agency went to work, employing a network of bots and ads to amplify and distort. Twitter's own analysts would later calculate that Russian propaganda was disseminated to users 454.7 million times.[186] Ultimately, Facebook estimated that 126 million users were exposed to Russian disinformation and fake news throughout the 2016 election.[187]

It's incredibly difficult—if not impossible—to measure the precise impact Putin's interference had on the outcome of the election. One study found that Russian trolls contributed to a measurable uptick in online polarization.[188] James Clapper, Obama's director of National Intelligence, has stated that "it stretches credulity to think the Russians didn't turn the election."[189] We may never know with certainty. What we do know is that in an election of 139 million votes,[190] a shift of less than 80,000 votes in Pennsylvania, Michigan, and Wisconsin would have made Hillary Clinton the winner of the Electoral College and the next president.[191] We also know something else. On election night, the trolls in St. Petersburg popped champagne, toasted one another, and crowed, "We made America great."[192]

The once free and open Internet, intended to spread freedom of expression around the world, had become an existential threat to autocratic regimes. And the autocrats, fearing for their survival, had struck back.

The Gray War had arrived.

Chapter 2

THE SOFTWARE WAR ON THE FRONT-END OF YOUR SCREEN

"The Most Important Six Inches"

On New Year's Eve 2014, the Russian American novelist Gary Shteyngart settled into the Manhattan Four Seasons for an experiment. His mission—watch nothing but Russian TV for one week straight.

The assignment wasn't as cushy as it might have seemed. One of Shteyngart's friends warned him that Russian TV "is a biohazard." Or, as a former Russian minister turned Kremlin critic has described Putin's airwaves, "Imagine you have two dozen TV channels, and it is all Fox News."

"What will happen to me," Shteyngart speculated, "an Americanized Russian-speaking novelist who emigrated from the Soviet Union as a child—if I let myself float into the television-filtered head space of my former countrymen? Will I learn to love Putin as 85 percent of Russians profess to do? . . . Or will I simply go insane?"

The answer appeared to be the latter. For seven days, across three screens, Shteyngart imbibed a steady diet of pro-Putin propaganda, washed down by Four Seasons Wagyu beef. He watched news anchors gleefully play up the ostensible decay of the Western world—a major traffic accident in New Hampshire, Great Britain's Prince Andrew caught up in the Jeffrey Epstein sex scandal—while hailing the successes of Russian separatists in Crimea. By Day 3, Shteyngart was hearing the voices of Russian TV anchors while he took a swim. Day 4 brought nightmares. On Day 5, his psychiatrist came for a visit. The following morning, Shteyngart decided to start drinking after breakfast.

As a satirical novelist, Shteyngart's disinformation diary is intentionally over the top. But it captures a fundamental truth. "What a powerful weapon Putin's television is," Shteyngart muses. "How skillfully it combines nostalgia, malice, paranoia and lazy humor; how swiftly it both dulls the senses and raises your ire."[1]

This is the heart of the *front-end* battle—the effort by foreign governments like Russia to shape what we think and feel by manipulating the information we consume. James Mattis, the former four-star marine general and secretary of defense, liked to tell troops that "the most important six inches on the battlefield is between your ears."[2] The front-end fight is a pitched battle for those six inches.

This is not a new phenomenon. Virtually every great power in modern history has worked to win over hearts and minds. For much of the Cold War, the United States piped the Voice of America and Radio Free Europe into the Soviet bloc.[3] During the Vietnam War, the U.S. Information Agency and its "Bullshit Bombers" dropped an astonishing 50 billion leaflets.[4] And, of course, both the United States and the USSR engaged in a decades-long game of active measures during the Cold War.

Social media, however, has dramatically transformed the front-end war. For starters, earlier technology like the radio was unidirectional—broadcasters broadcasted and listeners received—while social media is interactive. With Voice of America, the worst-case scenario was that you heard things that were favorable to the

United States. Today, the worst-case scenario is that you're directly engaging with a fake Facebook account that's tricking you into revealing sensitive information. As Johns Hopkins University's Thomas Rid puts it, the Internet has "made active measures more active and less measured."[5]

Compare today's operations to the 1953 American overthrow of Iranian prime minister Mohammad Mossadegh. At the time, the U.S. government couldn't easily influence the Iranian public. While Americans essentially "rented" mobs of anti-Mossadegh demonstrators, overthrowing the regime was highly intensive, requiring expensive equipment and trained field operatives.[6] In the 2020s, a strategically timed leak of hacked government documents may be sufficient to upend an election.

To borrow from the British philosopher Onora O'Neill, the Internet has made information more *accessible* but less *assessable*.[7] In his book *Data Smog: Surviving the Information Glut*, the journalist David Shenk estimates that "one weekday edition of today's *New York Times* contains more information than the average person in seventeenth-century England was likely to come across in a lifetime."[8] Shenk wrote that in *1997*. And the Internet gives us access to a whole lot more than a single day's newspaper. With the tap of a screen, a remote villager with a smartphone can peruse more information than the most learned scholars of Alexandria or imperial China could in their day.

There's a catch, though. We have mountains of data in our lives, but the gatekeepers are gone. There's no Walter Cronkite, no widely accepted referee of fact or fiction, to deliver the news. Online, a typo-filled tweet promoting an unproven conspiracy theory exists alongside a deeply reported article for a publication with rigorous editorial standards. What's truth and what's falsehood has become infinitely harder to assess.

In this Wild West of information, disinformation finds a ready audience. Mark Twain supposedly once remarked that a lie can get halfway around the world while the truth is still putting on its boots (a quote whose veracity is itself contested).[9] Thanks to researchers at MIT, we now have scientific confirmation of that fact. According to a 2018 analysis of 126,000 "rumor cascades," false stories spread six times as fast as actual news.[10] In the three months leading up to the 2016 election, the top twenty false news stories on Facebook generated more engagement than the top twenty stories from major news outlets like the *New York Times* and the *Washington Post* combined.[11]

Even more disturbing, demonstrably false news content is believed. In one poll, three-quarters of those who saw false news headlines thought they were true.[12] A series of Stanford studies revealed that the vast majority of American teenagers—despite their supposed social media fluency—struggle to identify legitimate information online. Three-quarters failed to distinguish between verified and unverified accounts on Facebook.[13] When evaluating a website on climate change, more than 96 percent of high schoolers surveyed failed to take into account that the website was funded by fossil-fuel companies like ExxonMobil. A majority of the students also believed that a low-quality Facebook video shot in Russia and purporting to show ballot stuffing equaled "strong evidence" of voter fraud in the United States.[14] "If it's going viral, it must be true," one high school journalism teacher summarized her students' attitude. "My friends wouldn't post something that's not true."[15]

The latter point hints at a particularly problematic element of social media: the consolidation of so-called filter bubbles. These cocoons are partly the product of human nature. As psychologists know, we have an "implicit bias" to trust members of our own group, compounded by "confirmation bias" that inclines us to seek out and believe information that reinforces our existing views—and reject information that doesn't.

But filter bubbles can be exacerbated by technology. While social media companies are not responsible for creating cognitive biases, technology can inflame them. For instance, if you're a liberal using Twitter to track House of Representatives elections, fully 90 percent of the tweets you see will generally come from Democrats. For a conservative user, the opposite is true.[16]

Zeynep Tufekci, a sociologist of technology at the University of North Carolina, has documented how YouTube's "recommender" algorithms serve up increasingly extreme content. She found that after viewers watched videos of Trump rallies, YouTube's "Up Next" feature often began to suggest and autoplay White supremacist content. Bernie Sanders videos often led to left-wing conspiracy theories. Tufekci's worrying conclusion is that YouTube—and by extension many of the algorithms that govern our online lives—"may be one of the most powerful radicalizing instruments of the 21st century."[17]

Thanks to social media, it has become easier than ever to connect with the people who share our views. This can yield powerfully positive results, such as allowing protesters to coordinate during the Arab Spring. It can also unite all manner of unsavory and unhinged individuals, from anti-vaxxers to violent White supremacists. The Facebook page for the Flat Earth Society has more than 225,000 followers, each no doubt further convinced of the rightness of their fringe views.[18] After all, how could nearly a quarter-million people be wrong? Singer and Brooking, the authors of *LikeWar*, cite a mordant observation by the onetime military officer and historian Robert Bateman: "Once, every village had an idiot. It took the internet to bring them all together."[19]

The techno-utopians of the ARPANET age lived by the belief that "information wants to be free."[20] Truth, they believed, would ultimately triumph over lies. Yet in the years since, the Internet has become a double-edged sword. Social media has given the student activists produced by the 2018 Parkland shooting the megaphone that comes with several million Twitter followers. Those same platforms also spread the false news stories that those students are "crisis actors" paid by George Soros to advance gun control.[21] The Internet has accelerated what researchers at RAND have termed "truth decay."[22] Cyberspace has become a world where no idea is too conspiratorial to be true, where the click of a mouse sends outlandish opinions circulating instantaneously and widely, where our beliefs are reinforced by like-minded people and clever algorithms.

And that's where our friends in St. Petersburg come in.

The Translator Project

If there's a battle for control of our minds, its headquarters may well be a boxy office building on 55 Savushkina Street.[23] Fittingly for a central node of the Gray War, the building is painted a drab and unassuming gray.[24] Situated in Putin's hometown, this unremarkable edifice is home to the infamous trolls of the Internet Research Agency.

The IRA is perhaps the foremost practitioner of front-end warfare, and scrutinizing its 2016 efforts offers a wealth of insights into the sophistication of Russia's evolving propaganda campaigns. Plus, the story involves free hot dogs and a Russian troll nicknamed "Jay Z."

The IRA was founded in 2013,[25] shortly before Putin launched his takeover of Crimea, and is bankrolled by Yevgeniy Viktorovich Prigozhin, an oligarch known as "Putin's chef" for his various catering businesses.[26] In many ways, the IRA resembles an unexceptional tech firm or marketing agency. It boasts a graphics department, a data analytics division, a search engine optimization section—even an IT desk for tech support.[27] At 41,000 rubles a month (roughly $775), the salaries were initially equivalent to what a tenured Russian university professor would earn.[28] Still, workers have been particularly aggrieved that they have to bring lunch from home; it turns out that Putin's chef doesn't provide his employees a cafeteria.[29]

The philosophy behind Russia's aggressive disinformation campaign is embodied in an unlikely source. In an interview with the

New York Times, Dmitry Peskov, one of Putin's closest advisors, singled out "this girl, from show business, Kim Kardashian." Now with more than 215 million followers on Instagram and nearly 70 million followers on Twitter, Kardashian epitomized to Peskov the power of social media. "Let's imagine that one day she says, 'My supporters—do this,'" Peskov said. "This will be a signal that will be accepted by millions and millions of people. And she's got no intelligence, no interior ministry, no defense ministry, no KGB." Social media, Peskov boasted, "creates a perfect opportunity for mass disturbances."[30]

Initially, the Kremlin mostly focused on creating these mass disturbances in Ukraine.[31] Russian trolls likewise meddled in the UK's Brexit referendum,[32] sending thousands of tweets with hashtags like #ReasonsToLeaveEU—a dry run for the 2016 presidential campaign in the United States.[33] Day by day, the trolls shifted their focus to what was vaguely called the "translator project."[34] At the behest of Putin and Prigozhin, the IRA began to target the United States.

By July 2016, some eighty IRA trolls were working full-time on the American desk, overseen by a twenty-seven-year-old Azerbaijani nicknamed "Jay Z," after the Brooklyn-born rapper and entrepreneur.[35] The project's budget eventually ballooned to $25 million,[36] and salaries jumped to a princely $1,400 a week.[37] IRA trolls worked around the clock, taking into account American time zones and holidays.[38] Every 12-hour shift, they were expected to produce 135 posts of 200 characters apiece.[39] Many of these tweets and posts were sloppy, characterized by broken English and overly automated patterns. They also quite possibly helped swing an election for president of the United States.

In its 2018 report commissioned by the Senate Select Committee on Intelligence, the organization New Knowledge offered a deep and disturbing look into the leading combatants of this front-end war. The study's coauthors—including colleagues of mine at Stanford's Cyber Policy Center—conclude that the IRA's efforts were "designed to exploit societal fractures, blur the lines between reality and fiction, erode our trust in media entities and the information environment, in government, in each other, and in democracy itself. This campaign pursued all of those objectives with innovative skill, scope, and precision."[40] Putin's broader goal was embodied in the hashtag Russia's trolls had readied in the event of Hillary's election: #DemocracyRIP.[41]

For starters, the IRA was everywhere. Russian trolls were on Facebook (reaching 126 million users) and Twitter (1.4 million).[42] The IRA uploaded over 1,000 videos to YouTube—for instance, soliciting content for a grotesque video challenge called #PeeOn Hillary.[43] Instagram "was perhaps the most effective platform for the Internet Research Agency," reaching an estimated 20 million users. Forty percent of the IRA's Instagram accounts were what marketers consider "micro-influencers" (over 10,000 followers), while twelve accounts—including ones like "blackstagram" and "American.veterans"—were full-blown "influencers" (more than 100,000 followers).[44] The Russians were even on *Pokémon GO*, the popular mobile game that uses augmented reality to enable players to collect fantastical creatures.[45]

On each of these platforms, Putin's digital combatants sought to sow division and doubt. The trolls posted about Black Lives Matter and Confederate history, about feminism, immigration, and Syria. They heckled and harangued, pitting Christians against Muslims; Bernie Sanders and third-party candidate Jill Stein against Hillary; Hillary against Trump.[46] When there were opportunities to elevate WikiLeaks or tear down James Comey, they seized them. Mostly, the trolls were assholes.

But they were assholes with an agenda. As remarkable as the scale of the Russian effort was its sophistication. The IRA updated the logos and fonts of its Facebook pages to keep them looking current and professional.[47] It sold merchandise, like T-shirts branded with divisive slogans, to collect sensitive credit card info and generate offline controversy.[48]

The Russian trolls placed a particular—and particularly pernicious—focus on targeting the Black community. According to the Senate Intelligence Committee, "no single group of Americans was targeted by IRA information operatives more than African-Americans," with racial issues making up two-thirds of the IRA's Facebook ads and a staggering 96 percent of its YouTube content.[49] For instance, Google's counterintelligence team uncovered an IRA site called BlackMatters.US, which fooled users into thinking it was a legitimate news source. It was promoted by a fake Facebook group, shared by fake Facebook accounts, and amplified by Twitter. Another YouTube channel sought to suppress Black votes with videos like the one claiming that "HILLARY RECEIVED $20,000 DONATION FROM KKK TOWARDS HER CAMPAIGN," encouraging voters to stay home or vote for Stein.[50]

IRA trolls directed their digital propaganda as precisely as a laser-guided missile. Were you a seventeen-year-old who liked the NRA and AR-15s? You'd be served up memes like "The 2nd Amendment is my gun permit." Were you a gun enthusiast over forty-five? You might instead see pro-police content like "Back the Badge."[51] The New Knowledge researchers found that the vast majority of these ads earned significantly higher "clickthrough rates" than most Facebook ads.[52] This means users weren't just seeing the ads, they were actively liking and sharing them. After several IRA employees were introduced to the concept of "purple states like Colorado, Virginia & Florida" on a 2014 trip to the United States, the trolls aimed many of their messages at key swing states.[53]

Incredibly, the IRA translated its online messages into offline action. This began in 2015 with an unlikely experiment: promising New Yorkers hot dogs. The trolls posted on Facebook, promising free hot dogs to anyone who showed up at Times Square at a designated time. They then watched on a webcam—in real time in St. Petersburg—as a handful of people arrived, checked their watches, then left.[54] The hungry Americans might have been disappointed, but the IRA trolls weren't. They'd proven that from 4,300 miles away, they could influence events on the streets of America. And they got right to it.

In one devious maneuver, a major IRA Facebook page called "Heart of Texas" advertised a rally for noon on May 21, 2016, to "Stop Islamification of Texas." Meanwhile, a separate IRA page scheduled a rally to "Save Islamic Knowledge" for the exact same time. When the dueling protests met in downtown Houston, they nearly came to blows. As the *Texas Tribune* observed, "Russians managed to pit Texans against each other for the bargain price of $200."[55]

The IRA likewise solicited Americans for a range of tasks—such as protesters or web designers—in effect recruiting unwitting assets into their disinformation campaign.[56] It's difficult to know how many of these efforts paid off, but some did. At a West Palm Beach Trump rally in August of 2016, a woman wearing a Hillary mask and a "prison uniform" rode in a flatbed truck that a local carpenter had converted into a mobile jail cell. Both were Trump supporters who had been paid by Russian trolls.[57] In other words, there was an American, voluntarily confining herself in a cage built by another American, all remotely puppeteered by Russia. It's hard to think of a better metaphor for what Putin hopes to do to the American mind.

"What's in it for the Russians?"

I wish I could tell you that everyone in Silicon Valley was alarmed by this onslaught of disinformation. But as I realized when I started crafting Google's response to foreign interference, most people in the Valley were slow to come to terms with the front-end threat.

Here's the truth: Silicon Valley suffers from a serious shortage of political savvy—a trait seen by most as a blessing, but one that also has its downsides. However brilliant computer engineers may be when facing down technological challenges, they rarely have real insight into what's happening outside the digital bubble. Maybe that's to be expected—technologists don't seek to understand bureaucracy or politics; they want to program ways to cut through it. But political naivete can be costly to an industry in the crosshairs of a geopolitical struggle.

I began to perceive the full effect of this problem a few weeks after Donald Trump's inauguration, just as I was investigating Google's exposure to fake news. On a brisk evening, I left the Googleplex and headed over to a small cocktail party. After ordering a Corona, I flagged down an old acquaintance and congratulated him on having been elected to lead a major e-commerce platform's fraud detection unit. A few of his colleagues joined us around a high top as we chatted. Right when I thought the conversation was about to trail off, a woman I'd never met brought up her growing belief that Russia had interfered in the previous year's presidential election.

My buddy scoffed. "I just don't see it," he said dismissively, reaching for a risotto ball. "What's in it for the Russians ultimately? I mean, what's their endgame?" It was an echo of Zuckerberg brushing off the idea that fake news stories influenced the election as "pretty crazy."

I understood where my colleague was coming from. Most technologists still viewed "fraud" more as a petty nuisance than a strategic threat. Protecting a platform meant shielding consumers from small-time spammers and credit card thieves. Even after North Korea's attack on Sony and so many other incidents, few of us worried about politically motivated cyberattacks launched by foreign governments. Like most major industries—drug manufacturers, automobile behemoths, financial powerhouses—we assumed that Washington would protect us, and the nation, from state-sponsored attacks.

That said, I winced when my friend so glibly dismissed Russia's "endgame." "Putin's strategy is actually fairly clear," I said. "He wants to upend the current global balance of power by weakening and subverting the United States." Then my irritation got the best of me. "Don't forget, less than a century ago, countries waged war on five continents, wiping out three percent of the world's population, all in an effort to reshape the global balance of power. If Russia can accomplish the same thing by building a few thousand websites and social media accounts, they'd see that as a drop in the bucket."

There was an awkward silence, and then someone mentioned how good the calamari was. Slightly embarrassed, I excused myself in search of another beer.

Political naivete was one factor that prevented the Valley from grasping the scale and urgency of the front-end threat. Another issue was philosophical.

Despite its reputation as a hotbed of liberalism, Silicon Valley tends to be quite libertarian. I regularly interacted with an eclectic group of technologists, diverse in everything from race to ideology to sexual orientation. We had heated debates about our response to foreign interference, often leaning toward a hands-off approach.

We spent countless hours trying to wrap our minds around the attack we were experiencing. So the Russian government put out content anonymously—what about that was problematic? Weren't the *Federalist Papers* written anonymously? If the American government generated anonymous messages aimed at undermining Bashar al-Assad's brutal Syrian regime, would that be bad? Weren't the Russians just exercising—even if exploiting—our freedom of speech? Some First Amendment absolutists went so far as to argue that "Free speech is free speech, even if it's by a bot."

This maximalist view was later given voice by Facebook's Mark Zuckerberg in a 2019 speech at Georgetown University. Delivering an impassioned defense of free expression, he argued that "people having the power to express themselves at scale is a new kind of force in the world—a Fifth Estate alongside the other power structures of society." Illustrating how today's calls for tighter content rules echoed past attempts to restrict the free expression of Martin Luther King Jr., anti-war college campus protesters, and the socialist Eugene Debs, he declared that we were "at another cross-roads" between free expression and its restriction. "I believe we must continue to stand for free expression," Zuckerberg insisted.[58] His argument stemmed from a long liberal tradition—articulated by everyone from philosophers like John Stuart Mill to Barack Obama—that, in the marketplace of ideas, the answer to bad speech is more good speech.

Strikingly, Zuckerberg focused on defending the notion that platforms shouldn't remove content based on viewpoint or veracity—reflecting a staunch belief in free speech that I, like most Americans, unequivocally share. Only a fraction of his remarks, however, addressed the issue of real-world state actors working to deceive and manipulate unwitting users. In the course of his fifty-minute speech, he mentioned Russia's IRA only once. The word "Russia" appeared only twice. Zuckerberg called the Russian content "distasteful" but claimed it "would have been considered permissible political discourse if it were shared by Americans." The problem, he said, "was that it was posted by fake accounts coordinating together and pretending to be someone else."[59]

To me, this was precisely the issue. The problem of foreign interference wasn't so much about the *content*—as Zuckerberg noted, much of the content mirrored things Americans say themselves— as the *conduct*. If Putin wanted to put his name on the cover of a book to disseminate his propaganda, that was one thing. But Russia was *intentionally* deceiving users, impersonating the public to overwhelm, swamp out, and ultimately suppress organic information written by real people. Putin wasn't writing a book; he was executing an intelligence operation.

The "Foreign Interference Is Misrepresentation" Policy

Then, events started to snowball. During the fall of 2017, executives from Google, Facebook, and Twitter were called to testify before the Senate Judiciary Committee.[60] Around that time, I was working on reviewing how existing Google News policies dealt with new emerging sources of abuse, like the threat of state-backed foreign interference.

This was easier said than done. Google receives more than 63,000 search queries *every second*. That adds up to about 5.5 billion queries every day—15 percent of which have never been searched before[61]—and at least 2 *trillion* each year.[62] Taking inventory of cases of abuse across over a dozen news products can take weeks; and that's just the first step. The second step is assessing the existing policy and evaluating potential updates. How could we define a consistent, principled, and defensible position across all those inputs on what did and didn't constitute an abuse of our platforms?

I worked around the clock for about a week, leaving Google's San Francisco office in the evenings and continuing to work on the policy at home late into the night. After coming up with a draft policy, I would head to Mountain View at the crack of dawn every day for extensive meetings with our product teams. We went through countless drafts, experimenting with language, adding and subtracting elements. Eventually we produced a short document laying out Google's stance on foreign interference.

Technology companies typically don't reveal which specific "fact patterns" amount to a policy violation, because they don't want malicious actors to be able to easily game them. In much the same way, judges and legislators don't define or prescribe every potential fact pattern amounting to unlawful conduct like fraud; instead, they use high-level multipronged tests. Many company policies work the same way. (After all, if you knew that ten instances of hate speech could get you kicked off a platform, it's easy enough to limit yourself to nine.) But at a high level, the policy principles we developed could be summarized as follows: *Google disallows the misuse of its platforms by individuals or groups that conceal their affiliation with a government entity and direct content at users in another country under false premises.* Before, our policy was primarily focused on "misrepresentation of self," which indirectly covers issues where governments masquerade as independent news outlets. However, the policy wasn't explicit, and it also left open questions surrounding "sites or accounts working together in ways that conceal or misrepresent information about their relationships or editorial independence." [63]

The policy I developed clarified Google News' stance on these new types of abuse. Importantly, this was a *foreign* interference policy and was laser-focused on the *behavior* and *conduct* of a given entity. It was content-agnostic and was not focused in any way on veracity. It didn't aim to address all other types of domestically circulated inaccurate information about politics. If the Russian government aimed its disinformation at Ukraine, that could get its operatives removed from curated features that Google designates as "News."

A number of Googlers jokingly dubbed it "Jacobcare." To win over skeptics, I began hosting town halls and presentations. Meanwhile, as the scale and sophistication of the threat became clearer, more and more Googlers—and tech veterans as a whole—became convinced that we needed to act. After most presentations, the reaction I got was usually, "Tell us what you need and how we can help." To further raise awareness, I launched an internal listserv that I used to circulate news clips and reporting about Russian interference.

Mostly, the congressional hearings that fall served to highlight the growing chasm between Washington and Silicon Valley (more on that later). But it was becoming clear that the tech industry wouldn't be able to ignore foreign interference on our platforms any longer. By the end of the year, Google News had adopted the new policy. *Bloomberg* wrote that Google was changing its policies to "Purge

News That Masks Country of Origin."[64] Mashable called it "another big step to stop the spread of fake news."[65]

As far as I was concerned, Google users had a right to know if what they were seeing through our portal was being produced by a wholly owned subsidiary of a hostile foreign government. Not everyone in Silicon Valley saw things the same way.

Some questioned whether Google should be intervening at all. Others continued to doubt whether disinformation and foreign interference were much of a problem. There were substantive concerns, of course. In the wake of Twitter banning President Trump's account, calls for restraint on content moderation have grown louder. Prominent tech figures such as David Sacks have cautioned against "decisions to permanently ban or de-platform individuals and/or businesses with no ability to appeal."[66] As someone that has spent years working on content moderation issues, I am still confident and hopeful that conduct-based approaches can be effective ways of addressing platform abuse while simultaneously upholding foundational free speech principles. The challenge of these approaches is that detecting and assessing patterns of nefarious behavior require complex analytical tools and good information about a given actor. In order to remain effective over time, companies need to continuously update their analytical tools to stay ahead of actors that modify their behavior patterns.

All Hell Breaks Loose

On February 16, 2018, a blockbuster indictment hit our inboxes. After months of investigative work, special counsel Robert Mueller indicted thirteen Russians and three Russian companies involved with the IRA. Deputy Attorney General Rod Rosenstein announced the indictment, which was as detailed as it was damning. On the first page, it plainly stated, "From in or around 2014 to the present, Defendants knowingly and intentionally conspired . . . for the purpose of interfering with the U.S. political and electoral processes, including the presidential election of 2016."[67] Mueller had seemingly pinpointed everything: the identities of the trolls involved, the shell companies used to fund the IRA, the budget and structure of the operation, the messages they had posted. It validated what we had started to uncover internally at Google.

The IRA indictments punctured much of the Valley's lingering skepticism around foreign interference. Then, a month later, new revelations turned the tech world upside down.

On March 17, the *Guardian* and the *New York Times* simultaneously reported an explosive series of stories, based on whistleblower accounts, about a company called Cambridge Analytica and its work with the Trump campaign.[68] According to Brittany Kaiser, one of the whistleblowers, the data scientists at Cambridge Analytica had taken advantage of lax privacy laws and Facebook loopholes to "scrape" up to 5,000 data points on every American older than eighteen— approximately 240 million people.[69] This included data from public posts and ostensibly private direct messages. Most egregiously, perhaps, users who agreed to the terms and services of a third-party app (like *Candy Crush*) consented to provide not only their own data but their friends'.

To appreciate just how much of an asset this data can be, consider what our online behavior can reveal about us. Some studies have shown that certain kinds of Instagram posts—like frequently using black-and-white filters—are a fairly strong indicator of clinical depression.[70] A researcher named Michal Kosinski has found that 68 Facebook "likes" is all it takes to predict race (with 95 percent accuracy), sexual orientation (88 percent), and political affiliation (85 percent).[71] Just 10 "likes" can tell us more about a person than we know about a work colleague. Incredibly, 150 likes can reveal more about someone than their own parents would know.[72] And Cambridge Analytica had *5,000* of these data points on each of the 240 million individuals in its database. Armed with this exceedingly detailed "psychographic" profile of each voter, Cambridge Analytica knew exactly what to say to encourage someone to vote—or, in the case of Black voters whose turnout they sought to suppress, to encourage them *not* to vote.

If the IRA indictments had taken a sledgehammer to any remaining doubters in the Valley, the Cambridge Analytica revelations were like a nuclear explosion. Privacy advocates were outraged, as were Americans who'd unwittingly had their personal data turned over to unscrupulous political operatives. Facebook scrambled to address the damage, suspending Cambridge Analytica and attempting to plug various privacy holes.[73] (Ultimately, the Federal Trade Commission levied a record $5 billion fine against Facebook for violating data privacy laws.[74]) The disclosures didn't impact Google directly, and an investigation by the UK government ultimately concluded that the firm's tools and impact were less impressive than they initially appeared.[75] Despite some links, it was never conclusively established that Cambridge Analytica had links to Russia or other foreign actors interfering in elections.[76] But malign actors had abused powerful social media tools for attempted electoral manipulation. This was a seismic shift for tech as a whole.

Meanwhile, the headlines kept piling up on the foreign interference listserv I'd created.

"Zuckerberg Apologizes, Promises Reform as Senators Grill Him Over Facebook's Failings"[77]

"Facebook Is Now in the Data-Privacy Spotlight. Could Google Be Next?"[78]

"Facebook and Twitter Plan New Ways to Regulate Political Ads"[79]

"Top Tech Companies Met with Intelligence Officials to Discuss Midterms"[80]

"Facebook Identifies New Influence Operations Spanning Globe"[81]

"How the U.S. Is Fighting Russian Election Interference"[82]

While some internal resistance to publishing an expanded version of our misrepresentation policy remained, the tide had turned.

Bit by bit, Silicon Valley started to awaken to the front-end threat. In 2018 and 2020, the Google Ads team built on these efforts and adopted similar measures to further promote transparency[83] and "to prohibit coordinating with other sites or accounts and concealing or misrepresenting your identity."[84]

How a Lie Is Laundered

Coming up with a foreign interference framework was only the beginning. Putin has always shifted tactics to stay ahead of the competition, and that's what the Russians and other authoritarians continued to do. As quickly as we could formulate policies to detect and dispel authoritarian interlopers on our platforms, the trolls and intelligence agencies would try something new. That meant my days at Google were spent keeping up with the ever-shifting front-end fight.

Let's start with information laundering. "Just as ill-gotten money needs to be moved from an illegitimate source into an established financial institution, disinformation is most powerful when a façade of legitimacy is created," note Kirill Meleshevich and Bret Schafer, of the German Marshall Fund's Alliance for Securing Democracy.[85] A bank teller would probably raise an eyebrow if a criminal dropped a sack of unmarked bills on their desk, but wouldn't think twice if the same criminal initiated a wire transfer from a reputable financial institution after the funds have been funneled through shell corporations, LLCs, and subsidiaries. By the same token, you'd probably hesitate to share an article that overtly stated it was written by Russian intelligence services—but what's wrong with sharing an article from *Veterans Today* that a friend from your book club tweeted?

Just as it's possible to trace money laundering by following the money, we can trace information laundering by following the flow of information and influence.

The process begins with a stage called *placement* or *publishing*.

In this phase, some untruth is cooked up. A Russian "news" site claims that Hillary is part of a child sex trafficking ring. A Chinese troll alleges that the U.S. military initiated the spread of the coronavirus. As one former Russian troll described his job, "You have to write that white is black and black is white."[86] The disinformation can be completely fabricated, or, as with the 2016 election, it may originate with hacked or compromising information. Sophisticated algorithms are sometimes used to segment audiences based on personality or psychological characteristics—as Cambridge Analytica did—to target those most susceptible to believing certain narratives.

Next comes *amplification*, employing an army of shell accounts or sock puppets—much like money launderers create shell companies—to push misleading content across social media platforms. These accounts can sound like legitimate outlets, like the *Denver Guardian* (ostensibly a local publication)[87] or *Veterans Today* (allegedly focused on military veterans).[88] In other cases they pose as political organizations, like @TEN_GOP—"the unofficial Twitter account of Tennessee Republicans"—which amassed ten times as many followers as the official state party account and was retweeted by prominent Trump surrogates like Donald Trump Jr. and campaign manager and senior counselor Kellyanne Conway.[89] Or they claim to represent the views of a coach or veteran from your neighborhood, with American flags in their banner photos and Twitter bios proclaiming their passions: #2A, #MAGA, #TheResistance. Thanks in part to deceptions like these, it's estimated that up to 15 percent of Twitter accounts may be fake.[90] In 2019, Facebook deleted 6.5 *billion* fake accounts.[91]

Even the trolls could get exhausted by the dizzying degree of deception. "First you had to be a redneck from Kentucky," a former IRA employee told the *Moscow Times*. "Then you had to be some white guy from Minnesota who worked all his life, paid taxes and now lives in poverty; and in 15 minutes you have to write something in the slang of [African] Americans from New York."[92]

Often, these shell accounts inflate their own follower counts to suggest influence and legitimacy. They also follow thousands of accounts themselves, creating digital "haystacks" that camouflage distribution flows and make it more difficult to identify the "needles" that would give away their links to suspicious accounts. Knowing that brand-new accounts tend to appear less authentic, trolls sometimes rely on "shelf accounts," which have been around longer and have an existing history of posts that make the user seem more real. In money laundering, illicit funds are frequently broken up into smaller amounts and deposited separately—a practice known as "smurfing."[93] Similarly, these shell accounts engage in "informational smurfing" to make the source of disinformation harder to trace.

Many of the online voices amplifying false narratives are also engaged in *layering,* in which intermediaries are used to obscure the original source of disinformation and spread propaganda far and wide. An intermediary can be an organization that purports to leak secrets for the public benefit, like WikiLeaks. Or intermediaries can be unsuspecting users, serving as "useful idiots" parroting Kremlin propaganda. Either way, the additional layers complicate law enforcement and counterintelligence investigations, putting the disinformation further from its sketchy origins and closer to credible sources like your friends and favorite news sources.

Finally, information laundering culminates in the *integration* of disinformation into legitimate news sources and mainstream social media users. Perhaps the most infamous illustration of this phenomenon was @Jenn_Abrams, supposedly an American teenager whose feisty tweets on everything from National Punctuation Day to national politics earned her almost 70,000 Twitter followers. With an extensive following, Abrams's tweets were quoted by at least three dozen news organizations. Her views surfaced on Russian-funded RT and *Sputnik,* as well as on conspiracy-mongering sites like Infowars and the Daily Caller. But Jenn was also quoted by the *New York Times* and the *Washington Post,* and by CNN and other highly reputable outlets. She appeared on the BBC, BET, and Breitbart, and in *Business Insider, Bustle,* and *BuzzFeed*—and that's just the *B*s. Abrams repeatedly sparred with high-profile Twitter personalities including Mike McFaul, the former U.S. ambassador to Russia (and my boss at Stanford). As you've probably guessed, she was actually a Russian troll sitting in St. Petersburg.[94]

Through this process of information laundering, what started as an utterly noncredible allegation has now gained wider traction. A partisan operative may tweet, "Did Hillary commit child molestation?" A cable pundit wonders, "Is there any truth to the rumors that the American military originated the coronavirus pandemic?" Before you know it, a message hatched in the troll farms of St. Petersburg or the intelligence agencies of Tehran has migrated from the fever swamps of the Internet to the nightly news, legitimizing insidious narratives crafted to divide Americans and discredit democracy. It's frightening to watch.

Poisoned

Another evolving disinformation tactic that I spent a significant amount of time battling is firehosing. Basically, malicious foreign governments spray so much information onto the Internet—as if through a giant fire hose—that it swamps everything else.

To understand what that means, consider the Skripal poisoning. If you are unaware of or confused by exactly what occurred, then the Russians did their job.

The facts, however, are widely accepted. Sergei Skripal was a onetime Russian intelligence officer turned double agent for the British. He was arrested by the Russians in 2006 and eventually released from prison (as part of the same spy swap that freed Anna Chapman, the glamorous Russian sleeper agent whose story helped inspire the hit FX show *The Americans*).[95] Skripal went on to live a quiet life in Salisbury, a city in the south of England known primarily for its impressive thirteenth-century cathedral and for being the birthplace of the actor who voices C-3PO in the *Star Wars* franchise.[96]

On March 4, 2018, Sergei and his thirty-three-year-old daughter, Yulia, were found catatonic on a bench near a Salisbury supermarket.[97] Investigators discovered that someone had poisoned the Skripals with a lethal nerve agent called Novichok, a chemical weapon developed by the Soviet Union and considered by many the deadliest ever created.[98] It was not the first time the Kremlin had poisoned a Russian agent on British soil; more than a decade earlier, the KGB colonel turned Kremlin critic Alexander Litvinenko had died in London after drinking tea laced with radioactive polonium.[99] British prime minister Theresa May called Skripal's poisoning "a brazen attempt to murder innocent civilians on our soil" and told Parliament it was "highly likely" that Russia was behind the attack.[100]

If you'd only looked at the top results on Google News in the days and weeks after the attack, however, you probably would have concluded that it was "highly *unlikely*" that Russia was guilty. That's because you probably would have scrolled through pages of articles from RT, *Sputnik,* and Ruptly that said something very different.

A quick word about RT. Formerly known as Russia Today, RT was one of the networks tormenting Gary Shteyngart during his week at the Four Seasons watching Russian TV. RT has reach; it boasts more YouTube subscribers than any other broadcaster,[101] four times as many as CNN.[102] To promote a veneer of plausibility—and appeal to an American audience—RT features a bizarre roster of washed-up American celebrities. Its guests also included, at one time or another, the late anchors Ed Schultz (MSNBC) and Larry King (CNN).[103]

In truth, RT is anything but independent. It describes itself—way at the bottom of its "About Us" page—as "an autonomous, nonprofit organization that is publicly financed from the budget of the Russian Federation." A company handbook instructs employees "to stay true to the national interest of the Russian Federation."[104] RT's longtime editor-in-chief, Margarita Simonyan, has served as a Putin aide *while* running the news outlet.[105] On her desk is a yellow phone, a hotline straight to the Kremlin. "The phone exists to discuss secret things," she has said.[106]

RT's slogan is "Question More."[107] The strategy, the former FBI agent Clint Watts notes, is to encourage doubt. "How do you know? Could it be this instead? Can you really trust the government? Isn't the U.S. government hypocritical? The net takeaway of RT coverage is that nothing can be trusted, and if you can't trust anyone, then you'll believe anything."[108] It's all part of what the disinformation researcher Ben Nimmo calls the "4 *D*s" of Russian propaganda: dismiss, distort, distract, and dismay.[109]

Following that playbook impeccably, here's just a taste of the flood of falsehoods that the Russians pumped out about Skripal:

- *Sputnik*, March 8: "Who Gains From Poisoning a Russian Exile in Britain?" Wherein the author muses that "the British authorities have much more vested interest in seeing Skripal poisoned than the Kremlin ever would."[110]
- RT, March 13: "UK intelligence may be complicit in Skripal's poisoning—ex-FSB head." In this "report," a former head of Russian intelligence is presented as a reliable source regarding what was undoubtedly a Russian intelligence operation.[111]
- *Sputnik*, March 13: "Russian Ex-Spy's Poisoning Seems Like Ploy to Derail UK-Russia Ties—Analysts." The "analysts" quoted in this article included one who had also railed against "the satanic climate-change swindle" and another who'd accused the Syrian White Helmets humanitarian organization of staging videos.[112]
- *Sputnik*, March 14: "US Had Access to Substance Allegedly Used to Poison Skripal Since 1999—Report." This "report" was a single 1999 *New York Times* article that described an

American effort to help Uzbekistan clean up a chemical weapons factory where Novichok was produced.[113]

- Ruptly, March 21: "Russia: UK may have orchestrated attack on Skripal's daughter—FM official."[114]
- Ruptly, March 21: "Skripal Was of 'Zero Value' to Moscow—Peskov *EXCLUSIVE*"[115]
- RT, September 13: " 'We're Not Agents': UK's Suspects in Skripal Case Talk Exclusively with RT's Editor-in-Chief (VIDEO)."[116] In this cringe-inducing video, the alleged perpetrators of the poisoning claim they went to Salisbury as tourists to see that famed cathedral—and left abruptly because there was too much snow on the ground. Never mind that closed-circuit TV footage showed the two traipsing around town unbothered by the lightest dusting of snow along the side of the street.

You get the point. As ridiculous as these articles might seem, the Russians' firehosing might have managed to trick Google's algorithms. For those outside the tech world, an algorithm can best be understood as a set of rules in the form of math or some other problem-solving operation. It's the process that allows computers to produce an output (like a search result) or make a decision about something (like whether a self-driving car should hit the brakes when it comes to a Stop sign). As the British futurist Jamie Susskind writes, algorithms are all around us—even offline. "A set of driving directions is one form of algorithm, specifying what to do under various conditions," he notes. " 'Go down the street, turn right at the post office and then left at the lights.' " Susskind points out that we even use algorithmic decision-making in our romantic relationships. "If he continues to lie, break up with him. But if he apologizes, cool off for a bit, see how you feel, then try to talk things through. . . ."[117]

Google's behemoth algorithms—especially when a user conducts a search—are intended to provide help in making decisions that are significantly more complex than whether to dump your deadbeat college boyfriend. But broadly speaking, they work in a similar fashion. They're designed to weigh a few factors, like *freshness* (how recent is the article?); *relevance* (how closely does this article match the search query?); and *authoritativeness* (is the source credible or a complete crackpot?)

So what happened? It's not that the *New York Times* wasn't writing about Skripal. It was. But compared to the torrent of (misleading) content RT and its ilk were pumping out, authoritative sources on this relatively niche event were a drop in the bucket. When Google's algorithms crawled the web in response to search queries about the Skripals, they found tons of fresh, highly relevant content to draw on, all served up courtesy of Vladimir Putin and his propagandists on the other end of the yellow phone. Putin hadn't just poisoned an ex-intelligence operative—he'd poisoned the discourse.

Firehosing proves especially effective when it can exploit something called a "data void," created when someone searches for a term that's extremely obscure or rarely searched.[118] You know that "Googlewhack" game, where you try to google a pair of search terms that returns only a single search result? That's a data void. And those voids become opportunities for front-end foes to exploit.

We saw this happen in October 2017, when wildfires swept through Sonoma wine country, just a few hours from the heart of Silicon Valley. At least 44 people were killed and 110,000 acres burned,[119] making these some of the costliest and deadliest wildfires on record.[120] Naturally, people began searching for the source of the blazes—and some seized on the chance to fit the disaster to their preexisting agendas. One local news report mentioned that authorities had arrested an undocumented immigrant, Jesus Fabian Gonzalez, for starting a small fire for warmth at a local park. The fire was small, "threatened no structures and was quickly put out."[121] There was nothing linking that small fire to the infernos blazing through Sonoma. But that didn't stop Breitbart from proclaiming, "ICE

Detainer Issued for Suspected Wine Country Arsonist in Sonoma Jail."[122] (Similar rumors proliferated as wildfires raged across the West Coast in 2020, with baseless allegations that left-wing antifa protesters were responsible for setting fires in Oregon.[123])

The result was a classic data void. In the aftermath of a crisis like the wildfires, people often enter search queries Google hasn't seen before. These highly specific keywords are known as "long-tail queries." As rumors spread that an undocumented immigrant had set the fires, Google's algorithms started seeing lots of searches for terms like "wildfires" and "undocumented immigrant." Credible sources hadn't yet written, "No, immigrants have nothing to do with the fires." So the information Google retrieved came from the bottom of the Internet. Once again, freshness and relevance trumped authoritativeness.

This situation unfortunately repeated itself in February 2018, when a student opened fire at Marjory Stoneman Douglas High School in Parkland, Florida, killing seventeen people.[124] The tragedy turned a number of the Parkland students into high-profile advocates for stronger gun safety laws. In turn, some pro-gun advocates and fringe websites began claiming that these traumatized young people weren't high school students at all but rather "crisis actors" who traveled around the country impersonating victims to generate sympathy and accelerate gun control.[125] Once again, because authoritative sources had not yet debunked these conspiracy theories in the early days of their spread, users googling "Parkland" and "crisis actors" were seeing articles that were relevant, recent, and utterly absurd. The Russians, of course, were only too happy to exploit the confusion. Hamilton 68—an Alliance for Securing Democracy project that tracks Russian influence—identified a surge of bot activity pushing hashtags like "#guncontrolnow and alleging that the shooter was either a White supremacist or an anti-fascist.[126]

Firehosing is not just an inconvenience; *in the twenty-first century, firehosing is tantamount to censorship by other means.* In her book *Censored,* political scientist Margaret E. Roberts writes that "flooding" or firehosing "competes with information that authoritarian governments would like to hide by diluting it and distracting from it."[127] It can be done either to *suppress* legitimate information or to *shape* a preferred narrative.

Firehosing does not completely block information, as we commonly define censorship. But, Roberts notes, "flooding requires the consumer to take time and effort to separate out good information from bad information."[128] After all, how many people click through to the eighth page of Google search results? Most users probably don't even look past those first ten blue links. By overwhelming platforms like Google with junk results, a bad actor can "down rank" credible sources and banish them to where the vast majority of users won't ever see them. Ray Bradbury called Fahrenheit 451 "the temperature at which book paper catches fire and burns." Search page 451 may well be the point at which information effectively ceases to exist.

This means that censorship in the digital age no longer requires blocking suspect information. The Chinese government can do its best to suppress unflattering news and commentary about the regime. But it can also flood the web with competing views to drown out critics. In fact, Beijing employs a legion of two million social media "cheerleaders"—derisively called the "50 Cent Army" after the 50 cents they're supposedly paid per post—to issue a torrent of praise for China's leaders. By some measures, these digital supporters produce almost half a billion posts a year extolling a positive (and frequently nationalistic) vision of China.[129]

Likewise, when Russia was faced with the threat of diplomatic punishment for attempting to murder Skripal on British soil, Russian trolls sent out a deluge of disinformation to muddy the waters. *Would it really be fair for the British to expel Russian diplomats or levy sanctions on Moscow if Skripal was actually poisoned by Ukrainians or the CIA?* Not all of these firehosing efforts violated

Google policies, but they highlighted a risk. And they prompted internal conversations about how our algorithms were being manipulated. I spent hours meeting with my colleagues on the public-policy, legal, product, and communications teams to think through ways to respond.

Since then, Google's engineers have made various changes to how its algorithms weight those measures of freshness, relevance, and authoritativeness. For instance, after realizing that conspiracy theorists often beat credible journalists to uploading YouTube videos after a breaking news event, YouTube rejiggered its algorithms to ensure that *recency* didn't outweigh *authoritativeness*. Thanks to tweaks like these, a Berkeley study found a 40 percent drop in conspiracy videos being recommended—encouraging, but still a distressingly high number.[130] YouTube also began linking to text-based breaking news stories, which are produced more quickly than video content. And users across Google platforms now see crucial additional context to help them make up their own minds, including information panels that note if a site is government-funded or direct them to a credible fact-checking article. By the time I left Google in early 2020, it was still possible to push disinformation on platforms like Google—but it had become significantly harder than before.*

The tech industry has woken up since 2016. But the autocrats aren't done yet.

Beyond the Digital Maginot Line

One of the greatest challenges we face in meeting this evolving threat is avoiding the trap of building what my Stanford Cyber Center colleague Renee DiResta has called "digital Maginot lines." The original

---

* In 2017, based in part on RT's role in the 2016 election, the Justice Department also mandated that Russia's premier firehosing outlet register as a foreign agent.

Maginot Line consisted of French fortifications along the German and Luxembourg border, constructed after World War I to fend off the kind of combat Europe had just endured. The fortifications ended at the Ardennes Forest because—with the military technology available at the time—the French considered the forest impassable. What happened? The Germans innovated, developing tanks that could carry their blitzkrieg warfare through the Ardennes and bypass the Maginot Line entirely. It's an object lesson in the perils of fighting the last war.

DiResta warns that because of our fixation on the 2016 election, we are building "a digital Maginot Line constructed on one part of the battlefield as a deterrent against one set of tactics, while new tactics manifest elsewhere in real time."[131] Digital authoritarians are insinuating themselves into new arenas—from European elections[132] to the news outlets of Africa[133] to the political and social crises shaking the U.S. In many cases, our adversaries are already skirting the defenses we've erected since 2016.

Facebook, for example, responded to the abuse of its platforms by banning fake accounts. So what have the Russians begun to do? Hire local. Before the 2019 Ukrainian elections, they tried paying Ukrainians to hand over their Facebook pages to Russian propagandists.[134] A group of Stanford and Facebook researchers detected a similar Russian effort in late 2019 in a number of African countries—cooked up once again by Putin's prolific chef Yevgeniy Prigozhin—with the Russians using locals or existing news outlets to produce posts praising Russia and criticizing the United States and France.[135] Alex Stamos, Facebook's former chief security officer, suspects that Russians are already doing this in the United States as well.[136]

Here's another troubling trend. As counterintelligence analysts get smarter and natural language processing algorithms improve, malign actors are increasingly spreading their falsehoods via screenshots. Images are less searchable than text, making disinformation harder to detect and trace back to its source.[137]

Trolls are also working harder to appear authentic, dropping many of the traits that made them easy to identify. It wasn't difficult to spot a bot when an IRA account posted garbled text such as "America has always been hinged [*sic*] on hard-working people."[138] So like Henry Higgins coaching Eliza Doolittle in *Pygmalion*, the trolls are improving their English grammar and syntax—in many cases, by cutting and pasting from other sources.[139] They're using fewer hashtags. Malign actors are increasingly relying on accounts that have been around for a while, avoiding the red flag of recency and aiding the illusion of authenticity.[140] As pages and accounts with large numbers of followers are attracting greater scrutiny, many Russian trolls are shifting to smaller, more intimate accounts.[141]

These days, the Russians are even letting Americans come up with false narratives all by ourselves. In February 2020, a home-grown falsehood—quickly picked up and amplified by RT and a chorus of trolls—alleged that an app tenuously linked to former Hillary Clinton campaign manager Robby Mook had manipulated the all-important Iowa caucuses.[142] Far-right conspiracy theorists like QAnon, claiming that Satan-worshipping Democratic politicians are trafficking children to harvest their blood, have grown alarmingly in popularity—aided by IRA trolls.[143] "They aren't looking for their own accounts to go viral anymore, because it draws attention to themselves," Cindy Otis, a former CIA analyst, observed. "The bulk of their approach is to slip into existing narratives."[144] "Don't feed the trolls" may be an Internet axiom—but feed them or not, the trolls are growing up anyway.

Russian propagandists are also finding new channels for disinformation. In a Russian effort called "Ghostwriter," hackers breached legitimate news sites, planted fake stories (often attempting to undermine NATO), and then blasted them out on social media.[145] Or take Redfish, a Berlin-based media group that claims to offer "radical, in-depth grassroots features"—and just happens to have extensive ties to the Kremlin.[146] Following a 2020 ruling by the Federal

Communications Commission allowing complete foreign ownership of American broadcasters[147] (previously capped at 25 percent), Russian and Chinese oligarchs are potentially poised to snap up their own media properties. Using subsidiaries, the state-owned China Radio International has discreetly purchased stations in the United States.[148] *Sputnik* has already bought time on a handful of heartland stations. "When commuters spin the radio dial as they drive through Kansas City, Mo.," writes the *New York Times*'s Neil MacFarquhar, "between the strains of classic rock and country hits they can tune in to something unexpected: Russian agitprop."[149]

And it's not just the IRA. As autocrats iterate on their past success, we're witnessing the rise of new front-end warriors.

China, in particular, has risen to the forefront of the front-end, with Xi Jinping vowing to "retak[e] the Internet battlefield."[150] Content farms based in mainland China and Malaysia have pushed pro-Chinese narratives on subjects from Taiwanese independence to the coronavirus.[151] There is evidence of concerted campaigns on Reddit to "down-vote" negative stories about China in general and Huawei in particular.[152] In June 2020, Twitter took down 150,000 accounts amplifying Chinese disinformation, including tweets touting Beijing's response to COVID-19.[153] Other tweets falsely warned of a nationwide American lockdown,[154] while a doctored Facebook video attempted to fuel divisions over racial justice protests.[155] China's "spectrum of capabilities, and the expansion of influence activity beyond its borders, has begun to invite comparisons to Russia," the Stanford Cyber Policy Center reports.[156]

Other authoritarians aren't far behind. Click on HispanTV.com, which at first appears to be a legitimate Spanish-language news source. It's actually Iran's version of RT, taking the headlines of the day and adding a pro-Iranian spin.[157] Countries from Turkey to Venezuela to Sudan are engaging in state-sponsored disinformation or "patriotic" trolling against internal and external critics.[158] In India, President Narendra Modi's Bharatiya Janata Party has established an

IT cell that provides messaging guidance to members and keeps a "hit list" of journalists to harass.[159] The Philippines' Rodrigo Duterte paid trolls during his election and has even appointed several to his presidential administration.[160] Ecuadorian president Rafael Correa has tacitly encouraged trolling against his critics. "People cannot insult or defame in the name of freedom of expression," he stated. "If they send out a tweet, we will send 10,000 tweets calling you a coward."[161]

In some cases, autocrats are even joining forces. A 2020 report by the State Department's Global Engagement Center concluded that China, Russia, and Iran were coordinating their messaging on the coronavirus. Each government spread falsehoods that the virus was developed as an American bioweapon, that China had responded well, and that the U.S. economy was collapsing. The report was not released publicly, but according to *Politico*, it argued "that propaganda and disinformation narratives from those country's [*sic*] governments have converged as coronavirus has spread." A few months later, representatives from the Chinese and Russian foreign ministries held "consultations" on disinformation.[162] The stated goal was ostensibly to "jointly *combat* disinformation," but coordination was more likely on the agenda. More and more, the authoritarians' online playbooks are drawing on and reinforcing each other—while we scramble to update our own defenses.

Two Steps Forward, One Step Back

These evolving tactics came to a head in November 2020. As the year drew to a close, all eyes were on the presidential election. Four years earlier, Russian interference had given many Americans an inkling of the lurking Gray War threat. So observers were understandably jumpy with each new report of electoral shenanigans. The GRU's Fancy Bear unit that had stolen Podesta's emails now appeared to be targeting the networks of one of Joe Biden's highest-profile campaign consultants—was this the beginning of the next hack-and-leak operation?[163] A new group of Russian hackers, this one called "Energetic Bear" and linked to the Russian FSB, was spotted sniffing around state and local election systems.[164] A *New York Post* article surfaced, peddling lurid claims about Biden's son Hunter that echoed those pushed by Russia's allies.[165] Research showed that Facebook users were engaging with more disinformation than they had before the 2016 election.[166] Meanwhile, state-backed Chinese Twitter trolls pushed disinformation on U.S. and COVID (though one researcher pronounced these efforts "hopeless" and noted that they largely tweeted during the Chinese workday, when most Americans are asleep).[167]

The extraordinary nature of the election—with unparalleled levels of mail-in voting due to the pandemic and President Trump claiming that the vote would be rigged—presented further opportunities for interference and disinformation. Rumors and untruths zipped around social media, many of them pushed by Trump and his allies. As election night receded and each new day yielded additional ballots but no declared winner, impatient and bemused observers in China noted that Biden's name was similar to the words *bai deng*, or "pointless waiting."[168]

So it came as something of a relief when Chris Krebs, the former Microsoft executive serving as the head of the Department of Homeland Security's Cybersecurity and Infrastructure Security Agency (CISA), aggressively disputed claims that malign actors had hacked voting machines or rigged the election. The pushback by the nation's most senior cybersecurity official culminated in a November 12 statement from election officials calling the 2020 election "the most secure in American history."[169]

Five days later, Krebs was fired.[170] It was a fitting coda to an unprecedented and unconventional contest. It was also indicative of American progress in the Gray War: two steps forward, one step back. So far, established adversaries have largely been held in check. As always, however, new adversaries and new methods threaten to overrun our digital Maginot Lines.

Washington's response to foreign interference showed that the United States government has learned some important lessons from the previous presidential contest. Under Krebs, CISA launched a Rumor Control website to bat down disinformation circulating on-line.[171] When voters in Florida and Alaska began receiving threatening emails, the FBI director and the director of National Intelligence held a primetime press conference to warn that Russia and Iran were likely behind the campaign.[172] U.S. Cyber Command proactively disrupted a Russian-affiliated botnet[173] and engaged hackers in Iran.[174] In the estimation of General Paul Nakasone, head of CYBERCOM, there were fewer foreign attempts to interfere with elections in 2020 (compared to 2018), and coordination within the federal government was greater.[175]

Meanwhile, Silicon Valley has seemingly, if belatedly, awoken to the reality that the Internet has become a theater of geopolitical conflict. Facebook banned new political and issue ads in the week before the election,[176] identified and removed new troll networks linked to the IRA,[177] and cracked down on conspiracy theories like QAnon.[178] Twitter took steps to add more "friction" in sharing tweets, such as prompting users if they wanted to read an article before sharing it.[179] Both Facebook and Twitter applied labels to disinformation about the election. Twitter has said that 300,000 tweets were labeled under their "Civic Integrity Policy," and that nearly three-quarters of users viewing those tweets saw labels disputing their accuracy.[180] According to YouTube, when users searched for content about the election, 88 percent of the videos in their "top-10" results in the United States came from "'authoritative' sources."[181]

More challenging still, though both coasts have become better at counteracting foreign disinformation, the 2020 election accelerated the rise of *domestic* disinformation. After Biden's victory, millions of Americans—egged on by Trump—indulged in unwarranted conspiracy theories claiming that Trump had in fact won. Mainstream platforms like Twitter and Facebook accelerated their crackdown on disinformation, but Parler—a social media platform that pitches itself as a freewheeling and unrestricted alternative to such sites—shot to the top of the Apple and Google app stores, as many Trump voters found a new home to circulate unverified claims of ballot stuffing and rigged voting machines.[182] Despite all evidence to the contrary, many of these Trumpian claims were repeated at protests and in legal proceedings—and eagerly amplified by Putin and the Chinese Embassy in the United States.[183] Several weeks after Biden was officially projected the winner, more than three-quarters of Trump voters attributed his win to voter fraud.[184]

The shift from combating foreign to domestic disinformation poses real challenges, since it also implies a shift from targeting conduct (which is objective) to targeting content (which is more subjective). Back when I was at Google, our concern was reserved for "demonstrably false" content. But what about the results of a presidential election that no authoritative source disputes but tens of millions of Americans believe ended differently? Facebook eventually took down many of the "STOP THE STEAL" groups proliferating on their platform,[185] while Twitter, in just the forty-eight hours after Election Day, labeled 38 percent of President Trump's tweets and retweets as misleading.[186] After a pro-Trump mob rioted at the U.S. Capitol on January 6, 2021, seeking to halt the process certifying Joe Biden as president, Twitter, Facebook, and YouTube suspended Trump from their platforms for inciting violence and violating their civic integrity policies. Apple and Google suspended Parler from their app stores, and Amazon kicked them off their popular cloud hosting service.

Deciding where to draw the line on disinformation is a difficult and unenviable task—especially for unelected engineers in Silicon Valley. We still haven't fully defined how to view social media platforms—is Twitter a newspaper, a public square, a public utility? This conceptual confusion compounds the decision of how to treat disinformation. Many would agree with a news outlet opting not to run an op-ed from someone proven to spread dangerous falsehoods. But cutting off, say, their water or electricity would be another matter entirely.

And inevitably, these decisions become politicized; a Gallup poll after the 2020 election found that two-thirds of Republicans said tech companies did too much to try and stop the spread of disinformation, while 60 percent of Democrats said they didn't do enough.[187] It's hard to take action against disinformation when we can't even agree that action is warranted.

In short, our adversaries know that their best chance to achieve their aims is with a democratic world that's divided and distracted—and they've come to realize that sowing front-end disinformation is the perfect way to accomplish that. Even as well-intentioned leaders on both coasts seek to stem the tide, this full-scale assault has corrupted the marketplace of ideas, added an online accelerant to our increasingly polarized society, and, by early 2021, rendered the United States not just increasingly ineffective abroad but under siege by disinformation at home.

Chapter 3

THE HARDWARE WAR ON THE BACK-END OF YOUR DEVICE

More than a decade ago, during one of the first battles over what has come to be called "net neutrality," Senator Ted Stevens of Alaska managed to paint himself as a figure wholly perplexed by modern technology. The ornery eighty-two-year-old chairman of the Senate Commerce Committee explained that his staff had sent him some information by "an Internet." And then he suggested that the information superhighway was "not a big truck" but rather just "a series of tubes."[1]

Stevens, to use a technical term, was roasted. Tech-savvy Millennials smirked. Partisans pounced. Stevens's unfortunate turn of phrase became fodder for late-night ribbing.

Beneath the humor was an element of real frustration. The chattering classes couldn't believe that the man charged with overseeing the nation's telecommunications infrastructure believed that the most important technological advance of the late twentieth century was little more than a sewer system with blinking lights. On *The Daily Show,* an exasperated Jon Stewart called Stevens's explanation of the Internet "more like something you'd hear from, let's say, a crazy old man in an airport bar at 3:00 a.m. than the chairman of the Senate Commerce Committee."[2]

But here's the thing—Stevens was basically on point. He wasn't *entirely* right, of course. Data doesn't travel through tubes exactly the way that sewage flows beneath city streets. But the truth is that our data—whether you're buying a pair of shoes online or looking up a medical diagnosis on WebMD—does pass through tangible telecommunications lines and data storage centers. We speak of "the cloud," but the reality is much more concrete. You might even call the Internet a series of tubes with algorithms managing the flow of data.

The tubes analogy is worth keeping in mind because—even while scoffing at the notion that the Internet is anything like an ordinary utility—we frequently imbue our telecom system with the same faith. We don't think twice about how the information that flows into and out of our various devices travels from Point A to Point B. Few of us consider which servers it touches or which wires it crosses. As with the data that populates our web browsers, most of us don't spend a lot of time thinking about the water that comes out of our tap. Whatever attention we *do* pay to our infrastructure is generally in the context of a disaster, like the lead contamination in Flint, Michigan.

But think for a moment what might happen if your local water utility was taken over by the Russian government or by bureaucrats in Beijing. Would you trust a foreign adversary to own your local reservoir? Would you rely on former KGB officers to maintain the pipes that brought water to your house? Would you have faith in Chinese regulators to oversee the Chinese companies delivering the water to you and your neighbors? And even if you *were* comfortable with China controlling the tubes to your home, how would you feel if Sino-American relations turned more contentious? What if we were on the precipice of a hot war?

Such scenarios are no longer hypothetical. On the second front of the Gray War, the Chinese government is working furiously to wrest global control of another seemingly mundane but profoundly important utility—the infrastructure that underpins the Internet. In parallel with the front-end battle to control what citizens of democracies see on our screens, Beijing is pursuing a *back-end* strategy to develop a globe-spanning new telecommunications system using Chinese cables, Chinese servers, and Chinese rules. And after all those cables and routers are installed, the United States will have fewer ways to control their impact or limit their reach. Once it's in the ground, infrastructure tends to stay in place for a very long time.

Who controls this vast and growing infrastructure has profound political, economic, and military ramifications for the entire world. After all, when you buy those shoes online, you are doing more than making a simple consumer transaction. You're leaving an electronic trail of your financial identity, your consumer preferences, your community of friends and colleagues. You're revealing the location of your home, and you're potentially authorizing applications on the network to access sensitive data on your phone (like your contacts, photos, texts, and so on). And if, for instance, you're buying Nikes to support former NFL player Colin Kaepernick's stance against police brutality, you are quite possibly revealing your ideological beliefs. We've tended to assume that, like the society that birthed the Internet, these networks would forever remain free and open—and, at the very least, that our data would not be exploited for geopolitical ends. If only that were still the case.

If the United States and its democratic allies are going to prevail in this Gray War, we need a better understanding of what our global Internet infrastructure looks like, how China's authoritarian leaders are working to exploit it, and what an online world dominated by authoritarian architecture would mean for democracy.

To do that, let's take a trip to a faux Palace of Versailles.

To Stand on Top of the World

In 1994, a onetime engineer in the People's Liberation Army named Ren Zhengfei met with Jiang Zemin, then the general secretary of the Communist Party. A few years earlier, Ren had left his job at the state-owned Shenzhen Electronics Corp. to start a small firm called Huawei, which specialized in importing switches for telecommunications networks. Even in its infancy, Huawei had begun providing the Chinese army with equipment. Now, in his meeting with Jiang, Ren made the case for closer collaboration with the government. "A country without a domestic telecoms switch industry [is] like a country without a military," Ren reportedly told Jiang. "Well said," the general secretary supposedly replied.[3]

Since that fateful meeting, Huawei has grown vertiginously, even as it expanded far beyond importing switches. By 2020, Huawei had become the largest telecom equipment company in the world.[4] Huawei now boasts 194,000 employees operating in more than 170 countries.[5] Between 2014 and 2018 alone, Huawei's annual revenue ballooned from $43 billion to $107 billion, on par with Google parent company Alphabet.[6] Today, the onetime switch importer boasts that it connects more than a third of the people on Earth.[7]

Huawei's growing wealth and confidence are reflected in the company's new R&D campus in Dongguan, a few hours' drive from its old headquarters in Shenzhen. If Russia's headquarters in the front-end battle is a nondescript office building in St. Petersburg, the nerve center of China's operations in the back-end battle is comically ostentatious. Covering 3.5 square miles, the Dongguan complex is divided into a dozen different "towns" built to look like different European cities.[8] A train ferries the site's 25,000 workers between replicas of France's Versailles, Germany's Heidelberg Castle, and Budapest's Freedom Bridge. Elegant black swans glide across an artificial lake.[9] The facility has been compared to "Disneyland for tech research."[10] But given Huawei's aggressive efforts to strengthen Beijing's control over our global telecommunications infrastructure, the new facility is anything but the "Happiest Place on Earth."

Remember civil-military fusion, the principle that Chinese tech companies support the state and vice versa? Ren Zhengfei certainly does. The Chinese government has been good to Huawei, dating back to that first army contract. The CIA has reportedly determined that Huawei has received funding from the People's Liberation Army and state intelligence organizations.[11] Between cheap land sales, R&D grants, and favorable export terms,[12] the Chinese government has reportedly subsidized Huawei to the tune of at least $75 billion.[13] Though Ren denies receiving direct subsidies, he has admitted that without the government's stated policy of boosting Chinese telecoms over foreign companies—of developing so-called national champions in this critical area—"Huawei would no longer exist."[14]

That largesse comes with strings attached. Huawei vociferously insists that it is independent of the Chinese Community Party, with Ren even asserting that he would disobey China's National Intelligence Law mandating that he cooperate with the government. Nobody believes him. "The bigger a company in China gets, the more it needs to align its business goals with the party's political goals," notes Matthew Schrader, a China analyst at the Alliance for Securing Democracy. "The mere fact that Huawei is able to publicly take a position so at odds with the actual reality of China speaks to the degree of party support it enjoys. 'Normal' businesses in China cannot get away with saying they don't abide by party dictates."[15] In fact, a number of Huawei's top executives have hidden their ties to the government, such as omitting from their online Huawei bios that they attended Chinese military academies.[16]

A 2012 investigation by the U.S. House Permanent Select Committee on Intelligence determined that Huawei (and another Chinese telecom firm, ZTE) "cannot be trusted to be free of foreign state influence and thus pose a security threat to the United States and to our systems."[17] Likewise, a British parliamentary inquiry announced unspecified evidence of the company's collusion with "the Chinese Communist Party apparatus."[18] All this was corroborated in April 2021 when a Dutch newspaper, *de Volkskrant*, uncovered a 2010 risk assessment commissioned by KPN, a major Dutch telecommunications company. As outlined by Martijn Rasser, a senior fellow at the Center for a New American Security, the report found that Huawei "(i) had unfettered access to KPN's network; (ii) could eavesdrop on all conversations (including those of the Dutch Prime Minister); (iii) knew which numbers were monitored by the police and intelligence services; (iv) and could access the network core from China." Rasser is clear-eyed about the implications. "Think of the damage," he observes, "economic espionage, identifying and monitoring CCP critics and dissidents, insight into Dutch government deliberations, potential access to sensitive NATO infrastructure . . ." the list goes on.[19] The report's conclusions were so troubling that KPN never publicized them to avoid jeopardizing the viability of the company as a whole.

In an explosive February 2020 indictment, the U.S. Department of Justice charged Huawei—and Meng Wanzhou, Huawei's chief financial officer and Ren's daughter—with racketeering and conspiracy to steal U.S. trade secrets. The indictment alleged "decades-long efforts by Huawei" and its subsidiaries "to misappropriate intellectual property," including source code and manuals for internet routers, antenna technology, and robotics. The Justice Department even asserted that Huawei made use of "a bonus program to reward employees who obtained confidential information from competitors."[20] In other words, the company didn't just tolerate theft of American IP: theft is central to its business model. Meng was arrested in Vancouver and, as of early 2021, was awaiting extradition to the United States for trial.[21]

Whatever Huawei publicly claims, it is clearly what the journalists Keith Johnson and Elias Groll have termed "a high-tech Trojan horse."[22] House Speaker Nancy Pelosi warns that using Chinese equipment is like "putting state police" in our pockets.[23]

Often in the Gray War, you have to look hard for hints of what America's rivals seek to accomplish. But not always. His dream, Ren declared in a 2019 interview, is to "stand on top of the world." "To achieve this goal," he added, "a conflict with the US is inevitable."[24]

An Email's Odyssey

How does Huawei intend to stand on top of the world? And how is Beijing leveraging telecoms like Huawei to control the Internet?

A key part of the answer is China's "Digital Silk Road" project, an outgrowth of its broader Belt and Road Initiative. For the most part, Western media coverage has focused on the transportation and infrastructure elements of Belt and Road—and understandably so. China's financial commitment to building new roads, bridges, ports, and rail lines around the world promises to be twelve times larger than the Marshall Plan.[25] And the true reach of the initiative is vaster still. China has effectively bought an entire port city in Pakistan,[26] built a navy base in Djibouti,[27] and taken effective control of a portion of the Argentine desert to build a giant space monitoring station.[28]

There are some indications, as the Center for Strategic and International Studies' Jonathan Hillman has written, that the Belt and Road Initiative "is actually poorly defined and horribly mismanaged."[29] But it is still intended to spread Chinese influence, economic and otherwise, around the globe—to enmesh foreign countries comprising two-thirds of the world's population[30] in relationships that make it harder for them to resist Beijing's diplomatic or military initiatives.[31]

Building the Digital Silk Road is a vital component of the effort. As Priscilla Moriuchi, the director of strategic threat development at a Massachusetts cybersecurity company, has warned, "It's the technologies of the future and technologies of future security systems that could be the biggest security threat in the Belt and Road project."[32]

All of these efforts amount to a bewildering mix of corporate deal-making and state-sponsored extortion. They traverse a tangle of undersea cables, next-generation wireless networks, and global supply chains. But broadly speaking, we can break China's back-end strategy for dominating the Internet into four main components: controlling the *production*, controlling the *pipes*, controlling the *protocols*, and controlling the *post-4G future.*

To help make sense of how these four puzzle pieces fit together, consider the many steps involved in sending a simple email. Imagine you want to tell a friend about the fascinating book you're currently reading (an author can hope). Let's suppose you're sitting in your apartment in Buenos Aires writing to a friend in Kuala Lumpur. You whip out your iPhone, dash off a note, and press Send.

What happens next reveals a lot about the future of the Gray War. So buckle up—because we're about to begin quite a cyberspace odyssey.*

Designed in California, Assembled in China

To start, look at the iPhone in your hand. If you turn it over— you might have to take off that cracked iPhone cover—you'll see the words "Designed by Apple in California. Assembled in China."

This inscription hints at the first piece of the back-end puzzle. Even as China seeks to control the world's Internet networks, it already grasps many of the networks that *build* the networks—our global supply chains.

As with the hardware that spirits our emails and search queries

---

* If you're curious, an app called Email Miles actually allows you to track the circuitous route taken by your messages, including the distance your email traveled and which countries it traveled through.

around the globe, most of us rarely spare a thought for the complex global web that produces everything from computers to cars. Still fewer likely dwell on *where* so many of these supply chains lead. More often than not, the answer is the warehouses and factory floors of China.

A few decades ago, many tech companies did manufacture their devices in the United States. Apple's Steve Jobs boasted that the early Macintosh was "a machine that is made in America."[33] At the turn of the twenty-first century, iMacs were still being produced in Elk Grove, California, only a couple hours' drive from Apple's Cupertino headquarters.[34]

Times have changed. Manufacturing as a share of American gross domestic product has dropped to its lowest level in more than seventy years.[35] Over the past four decades, more than seven million American manufacturing jobs were lost[36]—over a third of the entire manufacturing workforce—including five million just since 2000.[37] Onetime American hardware giants like Lucent, Motorola, and General Electric have disappeared or seen their global dominance eroded. From 2000 to 2010, more than 66,000 manufacturing facilities closed down or moved overseas. Apple's Elk Grove plant is now an AppleCare call center.[38]

The decline in manufacturing has hit the industrial Midwest particularly hard. I remember driving through my father's hometown of Toledo on the heels of the 2008 financial crisis. All along Main Street, eviscerated storefronts bore the scars of a hollowed-out community. For Sale and For Rent signs were everywhere. Major Magic, the family-oriented restaurant and arcade I had delighted in as a kid, had closed.[39] The city was unrecognizable.

To be sure, China is not solely responsible for the loss of American manufacturing jobs, some of which can be attributed to greater automation.[40] But today's hype around automation often falsely implies that automated manufacturing technology is more advanced than it actually is. As my husband often points out, no single company has yet to successfully manufacture garments or clothing through an entirely automated system. The reality is that while America's manufacturing workforce has collapsed, China's currently employs more than 133 million people. For all the excitement about automation, there are still a lot of manufacturing jobs out there—only a small fraction of them are still in the United States.

Through a deliberate and long-term industrial strategy, China has exploited—and in many cases precipitated—American industrial decline in order to fashion itself into the world's factory. Kai-Fu Lee, the Taiwanese American computer scientist and entrepreneur, calls this the "Made-in-Shenzhen advantage."[41] A former Apple executive explains China's supply-chain dominance this way: "You need a thousand rubber gaskets? That's the factory next door. You need a million screws? That factory is a block away. You need that screw made a little bit different? It will take three hours."[42]

The results speak for themselves. In 1991, China generated 2.3 percent of global manufacturing exports. By 2013, that number spiked to 18.8 percent.[43] Meanwhile, since the turn of the millennium, the American share of production for the world's printed circuit boards—the circuitry contained in virtually every electronic device—has dropped 70 percent, with China now accounting for half of global production.[44] As of 2015, Chinese factories produced 28 percent of the world's cars, 41 percent of its ships, more than 60 percent of TVs, and a staggering 90 percent of the world's mobile phones.[45] In more ways than we appreciate, the Middle Kingdom fuels the global middle class.

Now, Beijing's "Made in China 2025" initiative seeks to move China away from being the shop floor of the world and toward dominance of high-tech industries, turning China into what former attorney general William Barr termed an "arsenal of dictatorship."[46] Historically, these plans have had real impacts; one Columbia University study linked the rollout of each new Chinese Five-Year Plan to a 30 percent increase in Chinese companies in the relevant industries and a 7 percent drop in corresponding American businesses.[47]

The decline of American manufacturing jobs and the rise of China as a manufacturing powerhouse also has profound consequences for U.S. national security. A Pentagon task force on the U.S. defense industrial base and supply-chain resiliency describes "a surprising level of foreign dependence on competitor nations."[48] In fact, it's shocking how reliant the U.S. military is on Chinese production. The Alliance for American Manufacturing has identified critical military hardware, with both offensive and defensive applications, that are susceptible to supply-chain interference. American missiles depend on Chinese propellant; American night-vision goggles depend on Chinese specialty metals.[49] The coronavirus crisis has only underscored American dependence on Chinese industry. In a March 2020 survey by the Institute for Supply Management, nearly three-quarters of American firms reported supply-chain disruptions due to the pandemic.[50]

This overreliance on an increasingly belligerent authoritarian nation raises a host of potential problems. There's the simple problem of *access* to those supply chains. And, more ominously, there's the risk to the *integrity* of the products themselves.

The issue of access is relatively straightforward. Imagine what might happen if China chose to cut off production of those printed circuit boards. Or what if Beijing threw its weight around by restricting mobile phone supply chains?

Actually, we don't have to imagine—because China is already doing it. Rare-earth metals are the critical materials used in everything from missile guidance systems to the motor in your Prius. A rare-earth metal called tungsten is what makes your iPhone vibrate in your pocket. And who produces 97 percent of the world's supply of rare earths? You guessed it, China.[51] It's an overwhelming dominance that the former Chinese premier Deng Xiaoping recognized when he declared that "the Middle East has oil, but China has rare earths."[52] When the Japanese coast guard detained a Chinese fishing captain caught fishing in disputed waters in 2010, the Chinese government didn't hesitate to retaliate. It halted rare-earth exports to Japan. Within weeks, the fishing captain was released.*

In some ways, the Chinese government's overt manipulation of supply chains is the best-case scenario. More insidious still are Beijing's covert efforts to exploit its dominance of those supply chains by embedding backdoor access to the systems and devices that undergird the Internet—thereby undermining the *integrity* of those devices. In fact, the Pentagon has identified "an increasing number of sophisticated cyber-espionage campaigns" attempting to do just that.[53]

Just look at Elemental Technologies. An Oregon-based start-up, Elemental specializes in video compression. Among their earliest clients, note *Bloomberg* reporters Jordan Robertson and Michael Riley, "were the Mormon church, which used the technology to beam sermons to congregations around the world, and the adult film industry, which did not."[54] It wasn't necessarily the kind of firm you'd expect to be caught in the back-end battle between the United States and China. But that's exactly where the company found itself in 2015, when Amazon began scrutinizing Elemental ahead of a potential acquisition.

What investigators reportedly found was equal parts stunning and terrifying. Tucked into Elemental's motherboard was a minuscule microchip, grayish and roughly the size of a grain of rice, that didn't belong. The innocuous implant was ostensibly able to receive instructions remotely, allowing hackers to edit and alter code. Using their electronic interloper, for instance, hackers could potentially steal encryption keys or bypass a computer's password protection entirely.

---

* Rare-earth supply chains are such a conspicuous vulnerability that a rare-earth trade dispute even features in *Call of Duty II: Black Ops.*

As it turned out, Elemental's servers were made by a company called Supermicro. Supermicro is based in San Jose but had outsourced much of its production to contractors in China. It seemed that Chinese army hackers had taken advantage of the Supermicro supply chain to execute the holy grail of hardware hacks. Robertson and Riley compare it to "throwing a stick in the Yangtze River upstream from Shanghai and ensuring that it washes ashore in Seattle."[55]

Publicly, all of the parties involved denied that such a breach occurred. While it's hard to prove definitively, the industry experts I've spoken with who know how tech companies inspect their hardware—or don't inspect it—have deemed the breach plausible. And the alleged hack was considered devastating. "Elemental's servers could be found in Department of Defense data centers, the CIA's drone operations, and the onboard networks of Navy warships," the two *Bloomberg* journalists reported. "And Elemental was just one of hundreds of Supermicro customers."[56] An investigation found nearly thirty companies would have been impacted, including a large bank, multiple government contractors, and Apple.

According to reports, Apple replaced every one of the 7,000 Supermicro servers in its data centers. After finding illicit implants in its own servers in China, Amazon ultimately sold off all its Chinese cloud assets, a move one insider described as a decision to "hack off the diseased limb." Ostensibly, the Obama administration quietly warned key businesses away from Supermicro. The incident, if it indeed occurred, would have constituted "the most significant supply chain attack known to have been carried out against American companies."[57]

This is the glaring vulnerability of basing critical supply chains within China's borders. When the United States built its new embassy in Beijing, officials shipped entire sections of the facility from the States to make it difficult for Chinese operatives to plant bugs during the construction process.[58] Yet there are thousands of contractors and subcontractors in China piecing together key equipment that millions of American businesses and consumers rely on every day. One cybersecurity researcher, Gabi Cirlig, half jokes that his Chinese-made Xiaomi phone is in actuality "a backdoor with phone functionality."[59]

What's to stop a Chinese government official from approaching a plant manager—as operatives reportedly did to four Supermicro subcontractors—to ask for a small tweak to a device's design? The Chinese official might offer bribes or threaten trouble for the manager's family or business. Or, under China's National Intelligence Law, they could simply declare it a matter of national security and demand assistance—confidentially, of course. You may still hold your phone in your hand, but its contents could very well wind up in Chinese hands.

Our supply chains have become so globalized and so complex that many companies sheepishly admit they don't even have full visibility into their own. Shockingly, many companies don't even inspect their hardware—or know exactly who's making it. "You end up with a classic Satan's bargain," as one former American official described the decision to outsource production to China. "You can have less supply than you want and guarantee it's secure, or you can have the supply you need, but there will be risk. Every organization has accepted the second proposition."

With tensions between the United States and China growing, along with the risks to the access and integrity of American supply chains, how much longer will that Satan's bargain be sustainable? As more sensitive and intimate parts of our personal and professional lives continue to move online, has the risk of a systemic hack become too costly to trade off for cheap logistics? That's a question we'll take up a bit later. Next, though, let's turn to the *pipes* that carry our digital traffic—and China's efforts to dominate them.

Gigabytes and Gold Seaweed

After you send your email in Buenos Aires, the local Inter-
net service provider—perhaps Claro, Telefónica, or Telecom
Argentina—whisks the data that comprises your email to Las
Toninas, a small coastal village. There, at what's called a
landing station, your email enters a 25,000-kilometer-long
underwater cable. Built in 2001 and owned by Telxius, the
cable is known as South America-1, or SAm-1. From there,
your email travels northward up Brazil's Atlantic coast, pass-
ing through additional landing stations in cities like Rio de
Janeiro, then up to Puerto Rico and the Dominican Republic.
The main cable then heads up to Boca Raton, in Florida,
where your email enters the U.S. network.[60]

The moment you hit Send, your email is broken down into digital
packets of information and transmitted by your local Internet service
provider to an "exchange." As recently as the 1990s, an estimated
80 percent of the world's Internet traffic traveled through just two
obscure exchanges on either coast of the United States. As with much
of the Internet's evolution, the development was haphazard. A group
of engineers planned the eastern exchange—known as Metropolitan
Area Exchange-East—over lunch at a Tortilla Factory and ran it out
of the corner of a parking garage in northern Virginia.[61] The western
exchange was housed in an office building in downtown San Jose,
California. Today, there are about 240 such exchanges, from Prague
to Cape Town to Mumbai.[62]

Like a traffic cop, these exchanges take into account Internet con-
gestion and determine the best route for your email. In many instances,
they send different packets down different paths. But all of these packets eventually make their way—at light speed—to the undersea and
underground cables that make up the backbone of the Internet. Or, as
an octogenarian U.S. senator might call it, a series of tubes.

Some of the earliest links in this worldwide network were actually put in place in 1850, when a steamboat called *Goliath* laid a copper underwater cable connecting England and France. Contemporaries marveled at the "miracle" of the Channel-spanning telegraph. "Some three thousand years ago Homer talked of 'winged' words," wrote one British newspaper. "We doubt if even he imagined they would ever cleave their way through space at such a rate as this."[63] A day later, the cable carrying those "winged words" had failed. The mystery was solved when a French fisherman turned up sporting a length of what he had mistaken for "gold-centred seaweed."[64]

Over the years, those copper cables have been replaced with fiber-optic technology. Essentially, data is transmitted by lasers on one end of the cable sending pulses of light at incredibly high speeds down thread-thin glass fibers to receptors at the other end. Cables can be as narrow as a garden hose or as thick as a person's forearm. For protection from underwater earthquakes and even shark bites, the glass fibers are wrapped in layers of plastic and sometimes steel wire. The cables are then covered in metal mesh and thick rubber hosing and laid in trenches gouged out by cable-laying ships. These transoceanic cables emerge at landing stations, where the fiber-optic cables are fused to land-based cables and linked to a country's Internet system. "People think that data is in the cloud, but it's not," says Jayne Stowell, who negotiates Google's submarine cables. "It's in the ocean."[65]

Roughly a century and a half after that first copper connection under the English Channel, there are around 400 underwater cables crisscrossing nearly 750,000 miles of ocean floor.[66] The longest runs some 24,000 miles, stopping at nearly 40 different landing points along the way—beginning in Germany, hooking around Spain and Portugal, traveling through the Mediterranean and the Red Sea, then hugging the coast of the Indian subcontinent on its way to twin terminuses in Korea and Australia.[67] All together, these cables carry 95 percent of the world's communications.[68] And China is well on its way to controlling many of them.

The British company that laid that first undersea cable in 1850 still exists. In 2008, its successor entity, Global Marine, formed a joint venture with a company that will sound very familiar—a subsidiary called Huawei Marine.

For decades, American companies (and a few infrastructure giants like India's Tata) were the only firms with the resources to manufacture, install, and maintain the infrastructure of a giant telecommunications system. Telecom companies like Verizon owned the lines and leased bandwidth to Internet providers. More recently, however, content providers like Google, Facebook, Amazon, and Microsoft have begun building their own infrastructure to support the increasing demands from cloud services and streaming. In fact, content providers now control over half the bandwidth on these underwater cables.[69] Facebook and Google, for instance, partnered with several other firms to design and build the first underwater cable in two decades to connect the United States and northern Europe.* It's part of the nearly $40 billion that Facebook and Google invested in network infrastructure like undersea cables in 2018 alone.[70]

But as China's wealth and influence have grown, Chinese companies have joined the undersea game. Over the past decade, Huawei Marine has taken on roughly ninety projects to construct or modernize subsea cables, some connecting to key American allies.[71] Huawei has completed a 3,750-mile cable between Cameroon and Brazil. It's laying cables off the Mexican coast. Another 7,500-mile link will connect Europe, Asia, and Africa.[72]

These moves have not gone unnoticed. In recent years, Western intelligence officials worked (successfully) to block a Huawei cable between Sydney and the Solomon Islands and (unsuccessfully)

---

* Named Havfrue—Danish for "mermaid"—the cable runs 4,500 miles from New Jersey to Ireland, Denmark, and Norway. It is, for my money, the best Irish-Jersey collaboration since Bruce Springsteen.

to stymie another deal between Huawei and Papua New Guinea. "Given that undersea cables carry the bulk of the world's telecommunications data," says William Evanina, the former director of the U.S. National Counterintelligence and Security Center, "safeguarding these cables remains a key priority for the U.S. government and its allies."[73]

The concern is that, as Chinese-made technology becomes more pervasive, so will China's surveillance and espionage capabilities. Our telecommunications data may even wind up crossing networks that we wouldn't expect. In recent years, researchers have noted instances of Internet traffic being "rerouted" through China, including a notable 2016 incident where communications between the United States and a Milan-based bank were transmitted to China.[74] And the data traversing those cables could be compromised, shared with the government in Beijing, and then used to further Chinese state interests.*

Perhaps to deflect the suspicion it draws from Western nations, Huawei sold off its marine subsidiary in 2020.[75] The only problem? The company transferred the operation to China's Hengtong Group, which has its own close ties to the People's Liberation Army.

Sure enough, China's efforts have continued apace. In 2020, following Beijing's imposition of a sweeping new national security law on Hong Kong, the Department of Justice urged the Federal Communications Commission to scuttle an 8,000-mile undersea cable between Hong Kong and the United States—a joint project between Facebook, Google, and Pacific Light, the Hong Kong subsidiary of a Chinese conglomerate. One Justice Department attorney warned that the new cable "has the potential to establish Hong Kong as the center of gravity for U.S. data connectivity in Asia, offering unprecedented opportunities for collection by the Chinese intelligence

---

* While China has sought to control undersea cables, Russia has appeared more interested in sabotaging them. In recent years, Russian submarines have stepped up their activity near cable routes.

services."[76] That's about as close as the U.S. government gets to screaming, "Are you crazy?!"

Yet U.S. action against the tentacles of Chinese telecoms remains relatively rare. A 2020 Senate report found that Team Telecom, the interagency group in the U.S. government tasked with overseeing threats to American networks, has exerted "minimal oversight" of China's state-owned telecom companies operating in the United States. The report quotes FCC commissioners describing the oversight process as "broken" and "an inextricable black hole."[77] In one instance, Team Telecom took more than seven *years* to determine that allowing China Mobile to operate in the United States would pose a national security risk. Even as China's moves beneath the waves have accelerated, too much of the American bureaucracy is struggling to keep up. And too many Americans still view these critical cables like that bewildered French fisherman, thinking he dredged up gold seaweed.

Arriving in the United States, your email data is carried by cables to the nearest router, most likely the AT&T Remote Access Router at West Palm Beach, just north of Boca Raton. From there, it travels on an AT&T cable known as an OC3—an Optical Carrier—to the AT&T backbone node at Orlando. Your email is then routed to an even more powerful backbone cable known as an OC48. That cable fires the email to yet another backbone node in Dallas, which sends it on to another in Los Angeles. There, it's redirected to the landing station at Redondo Beach, on the Pacific coast, where it might enter a number of trans-Pacific cables.

As undersea cables make landfall, they link up with so-called terrestrial cables in the ground. Our email can travel via underground fiber-optic cables or along the same copper wires that carry phone calls (known, imaginatively, as POTS, for "plain old telephone service.") The United States alone contains 542 cables connected at 273 points, a jumble so complex that it took an MIT team four years to map it.[78] To protect these cables from being inadvertently dug up, they typically trace the path of existing roads and railways, often laid along or inside gas pipes and marked with signs. Every now and then, American communities lose Internet access when road or construction crews accidentally cut a cable.

China has an advantage with underground cables as well. As the China Academy of Information and Communication Technology has observed, "China has the most neighbors in the world." Fourteen countries share land borders with China—from giants like India to poor, land-locked nations like Tajikistan—and China has installed cross-border cables with a dozen of them. A China Mobile cable links Laos, Thailand, Malaysia, Singapore, Vietnam, and Cambodia. China Unicom owns a 930-mile cable between southwestern China and Myanmar's Irrawaddy Delta.[79] In 2019, China Telecom finished the 500-mile "Pakistan-China Fiber Optic Project." A loan from the Export-Import Bank of China covered 85 percent of the project.

But China's underground cables aren't limited to its immediate neighbors. China Mobile's Diverse Route for European and Asian Markets (DREAM) network connects Guangzhou to Frankfurt, with stops in Kazakhstan and Russia.[80] Another China Mobile system traverses Mongolia and Russia en route to Helsinki, Stockholm, and London.[81] In 2017, as part of a major Chinese push into Africa, one China Telecom subsidiary proposed an African Information Superhighway, a 93,000-mile fiber-optic network that would connect forty-eight of Africa's fifty-four countries.[82]

A brief sidenote: Though it might not impact your Kuala Lumpur–bound email, there is another way that countries can transmit their telecommunications traffic. And here, too, China's leaders are quite literally reaching for the stars.

Roughly 2,000 Internet satellites orbit the earth, descendants of a Bell Labs module launched in 1962. Futuristic as they may seem, satellites are actually an imperfect alternative to underwater and underground cables for moving data. Because signals must travel about 22,000 miles into low-earth orbit and back again, the "latency"—the time it takes to transmit data—can be up to twelve times slower than fiber-optic connections. Signals can even be impacted by bad weather, a phenomenon known as "rain fade."

Satellites carry just a fraction—only 0.37 percent—of online communications,[83] though that may be changing. Elon Musk's SpaceX is in the process of launching as many as 42,000 new satellites, seeking to create a "Starlink" system of high-speed satellite Internet.[84] For now, satellites prove especially useful for reaching landlocked or remote areas. Antarctica, for instance, relies entirely on satellite-based communications.

Peripheral though they may be to the broader infrastructure of the Internet, Beijing is hardly ignoring these satellite systems. In 2018, the China Aerospace Science and Technology Corporation unveiled a plan to launch a network of 300 global communications satellites, dubbed *Hongyan*. China's goal, one industry publication noted, appears to be "primarily the projection and increase of its power and influence across the globe."[85]

Two years later, the Middle Kingdom celebrated the launch of the final satellite in its Beidou navigation network, making it one of four countries or groups of countries—along with the United States, the E.U., and Russia—to operate a global satellite navigation system. *Beidou*, which means "Big Dipper" in Mandarin, has taken nearly twenty years to complete. *People's Daily*, the Communist Party organ, exulted that Beidou belongs "to the whole world and all mankind."[86]

More accurately, it belongs to the Communist Party. The Chinese government has touted the potential role of its new satellites across transportation, navigation—even fishery management.[87] Not surprisingly, Beijing has said little about the prospects for increased surveillance of those inside and outside of China's borders.

Crucially, the Chinese military has begun transitioning from GPS to Beidou. "It would make sense for them to have their own military system," notes Andrew Dempster, director of the Australian Centre for Space Engineering Research at the University of New South Wales. "Because if there was a conflict in the South China Sea over these islands, GPS could be denied to them."[88] China has also dangled access to Beidou as an incentive for countries like Pakistan to migrate away from American alternatives.

It's all part of what Chinese officials have called a "space-based Silk Road."[89] In the vacuum of the cosmos, China's back-end dominance quietly grows.

Having zipped across the United States via underground fiber-optic cables, your email reenters undersea cables on the Pacific coast. Most likely, it travels along the Unity/EAC-Pacific cable, built in 2010 by Telstra, Google, Singtel, and Time dotCom. It goes straight to the landing station at the Japanese hub of Chikura, which has cables running to Kuantan, Malaysia.

From there, your email is relayed some 160 miles directly across the country to a data center, the AIMS Data Centre in Selangor, outside of Kuala Lumpur.[90] At that point, it enters the network of one of about sixteen Internet service providers—most likely Telekom Malaysia—which carries your email to your friend in Kuala Lumpur.

Before your email is delivered, however, it has one last stop: a data center. These facilities are the beating heart of the Internet, the "nodes" where data is stored, analyzed, mined, and processed. Every search, every Google Doc, and every email at some point travels through a data center. Something like 9.5 *trillion* gigabytes pass through the world's data centers every year.[91] (A single gigabyte stores about as much information as thirty feet of books on a shelf,[92] meaning that if all the data traveling through data centers in a year were stacked in books, it would reach from earth to the moon and back more than 113,000 times.) Because these facilities are massive—sometimes as big as several million square feet—they're often located in rural areas. As you'd imagine, running so much equipment generates tremendous amounts of heat, which makes locating them in cooler climates attractive. They also tend to be situated in coastal areas, for easier access to those subsea cables. In a project off the coast of Scotland, Microsoft is even exploring the feasibility of locating data centers underwater.[93]

Google operates nearly two dozen data centers across the globe, from Nevada to the Netherlands.[94] Inside these centers, row after row of servers and routers blink and hum on metal racks. Each building within the data center can support 75,000 machines and transmit over 1 petabyte of data per second—more data than is contained on the entire Internet. To enhance otherwise dreary warehouses, Google even has local artists paint murals on the sides of some buildings.[95]

As you might expect, companies take the security of their data centers and the integrity of user data extremely seriously. Data centers typically have multiple backup generators in case of power failures. Guards often stand watch 24/7, and it's not uncommon for visitors entering the facility to pass through an air lock and a biometric scanner. When hard drives are discarded, they're often wiped and run through a giant shredder.

But data centers are only as secure as the policies governing them. And crucially, they're subject to local laws. Tech companies typically try to locate data centers in democratic countries with strong privacy protections. But that's not always feasible. Studies have shown that users search less if they have to wait even half a second for a web page or graphic to load[96]—and even with today's lightning-fast bandwidths, there's still a difference between the latency of a data center down the road and one across the world.

In 2017, the Chinese government proposed a cybersecurity law mandating "data localization." This means that data collected by companies operating in China has to be stored in China. Yuxi Wei, a cybersecurity fellow at the University of Washington, warns that this would likely cover "all major aspects of everyday life."[97] Subsequent refinements of the law have the potential to soften these restrictions, though the ultimate impact remains untested. Apple, for example, has already begun building a data center in Guizhou to comply with the new data localization requirements.[98] It's entirely possible that Apple might someday find itself forced to choose between handing over user data and exiting the country. Under China's new national security law, Hong Kong–based data centers are vulnerable as well.

Even as Beijing is localizing the data of Chinese users at home, China is building a constellation of new data centers abroad. In the Tibetan capital of Lhasa, China's Ningsuan Technologies is building a nearly 7-million-square-foot Himalayan data center to facilitate cloud computing for Southeast Asia.[99] In 2019, China Mobile opened data centers in Singapore and London, with a Frankfurt location under construction.[100] Huawei is building one in Pakistan and another in Kenya. In Djibouti, strategically located at the entrance of the Red Sea south of the Suez Canal, Chinese companies are installing another hub. Many neighboring countries wholly depend on Djibouti to transmit their data.

Max Bearak of the *Washington Post* paints an unnerving picture of what this dependency looks like. "You are looking at all of Somaliland's Internet," an engineer tells Bearak. The reporter continues, "In another room, all of Yemen's Internet. Ninety percent of powerful-but-landlocked Ethiopia's Internet passes through the main chamber."[101] Already, there are reports that a Huawei data center in Papua New Guinea was "built to spy on" the country's government.[102] With its new data centers—as with its undersea and underground cables—China will control yet another back-end choke point.

Rewriting the Rules

As it makes its way to its destination, your email has traversed a convoluted mix of cables and data centers, each owned by different entities. Fortunately, the data making up your email is guided by a series of protocols across different "layers" of the Internet's architecture. The link layer *converts binary code into signals that can be transmitted. The* Internet layer *determines how data is routed to the receiving device. The* transport layer *coordinates data transfer and checks for errors. The* application layer *transforms that data into what you see on your web browser or email client. All of these layers work together to make sure that the right data gets to the right place in the right fashion.*[103]

China's aggressive effort to win the back-end battle is not limited to the gleaming factories that make up our global supply chains or the cables buried deep beneath the sea and the earth. Beijing's ambitions also reach into decidedly less glamorous locations: the bureaucratic and buttoned-down multilateral bodies where technical standards are hammered out. Because in addition to controlling the production and the pipes, China is steadily gaining influence over network *protocols.* They're not just seizing command of the Internet—they're rewriting the rules of the Internet itself.

Those rules of Internet governance started, once upon a time, with a guy named Jon. To ensure that each website had its own distinct address, the early web needed a master directory of all addresses. A computer scientist named Jon Postel, one of ARPANET's creators, volunteered to maintain the directory—which he did by hand. But as the Internet became more formalized, it seemed a little too casual to write in technical documents that "Jon keeps track of everyone on the Internet." So Jon got an official title: the Internet Assigned Numbers Authority. Eventually that morphed into what is today known as the

Internet Corporation for the Assignment of Names and Numbers—ICANN—the nonprofit organization that determines things like whether a domain name ends with ".com" or ".uk."

Like the evolution of Jon Postel's record-keeping, many of the earliest rules shaping the Internet have gradually been codified by national and international bodies. ICANN assigns domain names. The International Telecommunication Union, based in Geneva, establishes guidelines for how information is broken down and routed on the Internet. The International Cable Protection Committee, based in the UK, looks after the security of underwater cables. (International law even dictates how far ships can be from cables and specifies that "vessels must sacrifice their anchors or fishing gear to avoid injury to cables," for which the ships should be compensated.)

The somewhat haphazard progression of the Internet's guiding principles underscores an important truth. The standards that govern the Internet in the United States—the free flow of information, the general absence of overt manipulation by governments, protections against unwarranted government surveillance—aren't indelibly connected to the technology itself. To the contrary, those norms are merely features of the current system that emerged, largely, in the United States. In other words, these protections could be eviscerated under a new regime.

China's leaders understand this truth all too well. In the early days of the People's Republic, Beijing shunned international bodies. Until 1971, mainland China didn't belong to the United Nations. Today, however, we're witnessing what China analyst David Kelly calls "a shift from Deng Xiaoping's doctrine of 'hiding and biding' to one that involves stepping in where the U.S. steps back."[104]

From the World Health Organization to the International Civil Aviation Organization, China has tried to co-opt existing institutions.[105] China has exceeded the United States in the number of global diplomatic posts[106] and is now the second-biggest contributor to the UN budget.[107] Chinese representatives lead four of the UN's fifteen agencies or affiliated groups (no other country leads more than one), and only a concerted effort prevented China, a major abuser of intellectual property rights, from taking over the World Intellectual Property Organization.[108] Reportedly, the Chinese government has paid bonuses to those who secure leadership positions in organizations that set international standards.[109] Where it can't work within established institutions, China has created its own, including establishing the Asian Infrastructure Investment Bank to fund development projects around the world. Instead of being reformed by its inclusion in the liberal international order, China is trying to make that order less liberal.

In particular, China is working overtime to revise the rules of cyberspace. At the 2015 World Internet Conference in Wuzhen, Xi Jinping proposed a "China Plan" built around the notion of "cyber sovereignty." As Xi envisioned it, this would mean "respecting each country's right to choose its own internet development path, its own internet management model, and its own public policies on the internet." As usual, however, Beijing has a selective approach to sovereignty. Far from permitting every country "to choose its own internet development path," the Chinese government is actively proselytizing an approach modeled on its own.

China has sought to promote a cyber-sovereignty model for governing the Internet as an alternative to today's open and free global Internet. The reality is that most major countries today, even democracies, are moving to apply their legal norms to the online world, on issues spanning hate speech to pornography and privacy. The Chinese government has eagerly pointed to this trend as a vindication of its cyber-sovereignty model. This has led some observers in the United States to caution against legislating norms applicable to cyberspace for fear it would further vindicate China's model of Internet governance. But this in fact omits the crucial point that "open and free" does not mean "lawless" and "unfettered." What makes the American and European model of Internet governance distinct from China's isn't that it is lawless and completely borderless. What makes the American and European model of Internet governance distinct from China's is that it is democratic and China's Internet is eminently authoritarian. China's model in actuality has very little to do with sovereignty and everything to do with authoritarian surveillance and repression.

The choice governments face today is less between an "open" versus a "closed" Internet and more between a "democratic" versus an "authoritarian" Internet. Laws in democracies are passed by independent legislatures, scrutinized by an independent judiciary, and litigated in a free press—entirely different from dictates promulgated in China. And if some reporters and pundits in our raucous information environment don't always see the substantive and procedural differences between a democratic Internet and an authoritarian Internet, just ask the people in Taiwan, Xinjiang, and Hong Kong— they know exactly what the difference is.

In the end, the two ideologically opposed Internet models are systemically at odds because their underlying political philosophies rest on contrary conceptions of political legitimacy. The Arab Spring showed us that a decentralized Internet is inherently democratizing; democracy itself is predicated on the belief that laws that are arbitrary or imposed by the will of a single person of authority are illegitimate. Conversely, a centrally controlled Internet governed by laws imposed by a single figure of authority is inherently undemocratic. Democracy was born from a repudiation of autocratic rule as unjust and politically illegitimate. To maintain its domestic hold on power and enhance its standing internationally, the Chinese Communist Party therefore has a structural incentive to degrade the decentralized democratic Internet and promote its autocratic alternative. Technology companies in the U.S. and Europe are finding this ideological cleavage increasingly difficult to reconcile when asked to comply with two value systems that are fundamentally incompatible.

For another prime example of China's more assertive approach, look no further than the aforementioned International Telecommunication Union, founded 155 years ago to regulate global telegraph networks. Hanging on the marble walls of its Geneva headquarters are the flags of the organization's biggest donors. Not long ago, the red flag of the People's Republic was not even on the wall; today, it's fifth. The current secretary-general of the organization is Chinese-born Houlin Zhao. Despite serving in an ostensibly neutral role, Zhao has stated that "there is no proof so far" of any security concerns about Huawei[110] and called Belt and Road "an express train that once you get on, you can join forces with China and develop along with the country."[111]

It was at this venerable telecommunication association that, in late 2019, Vint Cerf and Bob Kahn's TCP/IP protocol found itself in the crosshairs. Recall that these transfer protocols are the instructions that govern how the digital packets that comprise your email should be broken down and reassembled when they get to their destination. The current standard has been described as operating like an "agnostic postman that simply moves boxes around," making it a critical part of the Internet's open nature. It's what's called a "permissionless" system, which Internet pioneer Patrik Fältström notes "makes it very, very hard, almost impossible for whoever is providing internet access to know or regulate what the internet access is used for."[112] This open architecture is so essential to the Internet as we know it that the technologist John Naughton says that "TCP/IP is to the wired world what DNA is to the biological one."

The Chinese government, however, wants to alter that DNA. A proposal put forward by Huawei, China Telecom, China Unicom, and the Chinese Ministry of Industry and Information Technology would replace Cerf and Kahn's protocol with a highly centralized protocol of China's own, called "New IP." Critics contend that New IP is technically flawed, "a solution looking for a problem." What China's "radical" proposal *would* do, as the *Financial Times* journalists Anna Gross and Madhumita Murgia put it, is "bake authoritarianism into the architecture underpinning the web."*[113]

Under China's new standard, governments would have far more control over who uses the Internet and how. Instead of an agnostic postman, we'd get an autocratic strongman. Unsurprisingly, Russia, Iran, and Saudi Arabia have supported Beijing's approach.

The International Telecommunication Union's standards are voluntary but still influential. Developing countries look to the organization for guidance. Tech companies tend to incorporate these protocols into their technologies. Should China persuade the union to adopt its New IP standard, there's a chance your next email to Kuala Lumpur might be sent into a digital black hole.

And New IP is only part of the story. In 2000, back when China joined the World Trade Organization and Bill Clinton was joking about nailing Jell-O to a wall, China launched a National Standardization Strategy to shape global technology standards. Now, China is preparing to launch an updated strategy. A successor of sorts to Made in China 2025, China Standards 2035 is Beijing's concerted strategy to set global regulatory standards for the twenty-first century. "Industry, technology, and innovation are developing rapidly," observed Dai Hong, an official with China's National Standardization Management Committee. "Global technical standards are still being formed. This grants China's industry and standards the opportunity to surpass the world's."[114]

China Standards 2035 aims to shape everything from what the world's solar panels look like to how the "blockchain" is regulated.† Beijing has pushed for new facial recognition standards, which have been roundly criticized by lawyers and human rights advocates. Chi-

---

*   It should be noted that some observers believe that economic advantage, rather than repression, is the primary goal of these new standards.
†   The blockchain is a secure, decentralized electronic record of transactions, originally designed for electronic currency transfers but with a wide range of applications.

na's foreign minister has proposed a Global Data Security Initiative, which he contends will "provide a blueprint for the formulation of international principles on data security"[115] and which critics see as an attempt to implement the Great Firewall abroad.[116]

Today's Internet is defined by rules. Tomorrow's could be defined by rulers. And if we fail to step up now, we may not recognize the Internet of the coming decades.

The 5G Future

The final piece—and perhaps the centerpiece—of China's back-end strategy can be captured in two characters: 5G. Even as China is shaping the Internet standards of the future, it's also racing to invent the future Internet.

It's hard to remember, but there was once a time before the world resided on a device in our pockets. What made our phones indispensable appendages was the steady progression of wireless technology. The 1G mobile networks of the 1980s enabled voice calls. A decade later, 2G delivered better voice quality and the arrival of text messaging (and the disappearance of teenagers from dinner tables around the globe). With 3G came the streaming of data, allowing us to surf the web from virtually anywhere. In 2008, 4G technology offered data speeds ten times faster than 3G, popularizing mobile apps like Facebook and birthing companies like Uber.

Right now, we are poised for the next giant leap in communications. 5G is not a refinement—it's a revolution. If projections are accurate, it will make early smartphone technology look like a copper telegraph cable.

Part of the transformation lies in that concept of data throughput. "Imagine water is data," explains Klon Kitchen, director of the Heritage Foundation's Center for Technology Policy. "You can only put so much data through a 4G network, right? 5G expands the garden hose to a fire hose."[117] The increase in data throughput between 4G and 5G will be bigger than the jump between any previous generation of cell technology. According to some estimates, 5G will be up to *100 times* faster than its predecessor—meaning a two-hour movie could be downloaded in the time it took you to read this sentence.[118]

The implications are staggering. Tom Wheeler, a former chairman of the Federal Communications Commission, believes that 5G's speed "will change the very nature of the internet."[119] One Silicon Valley venture capitalist speculated to me that 5G could "massively open up" a new frontier of virtual reality and augmented reality, allowing us to superimpose data onto the surface of futuristic lenses.

Additionally, 5G could turbocharge the rise of the long-heralded Internet of Things, in which virtually all our devices will be connected. All told, 5G could inject $12 trillion into the global economy by 2035 and add 22 million jobs just in the United States.[120] With good reason, 5G has been hailed as "the central nervous system of the 21st-century economy."[121]

Whoever presides over that central nervous system could have unprecedented control over virtually everything in our lives—who reads our emails and texts, how our homes operate, where our autonomous vehicles are going. Not to mention that properly transmitting 5G signals will require millions of antennas and cell relays—at least one per city block, by some estimates—exponentially increasing opportunities for surveillance.

That's where things really get scary. Because the undisputed leader in 5G technology isn't America's Qualcomm, Sweden's Ericsson, or Finland's Nokia. It's China's Huawei.

What gives Huawei such a formidable 5G advantage? For starters, Huawei designs and manufactures virtually every component itself. Ericsson and Nokia, for instance, don't make their own smartphones. Which means they have to rely on Apple or Samsung—or even Huawei—to deploy their own 5G networks. Huawei, however, is vertically integrated. Not only does it make the chips, routers, and other critical 5G hardware, it is also the world's largest maker of smartphones (overtaking Samsung in 2020).[122] Coupled with a cheap labor pool and those lucrative state subsidies, Huawei's all-in-one model allows the company to offer its services for as much as 20 percent less than its Western competitors.[123]

To further fuel its 5G edge, Huawei has poured billions into R&D, pledging to spend $20 billion annually.[124] According to the German firm IPlytics, Huawei has registered 1,529 5G patents (number four on the list is Chinese giant ZTE), nearly twice the 787 for Qualcomm, the American firm with the most 5G patents—though some have questioned the technical quality of Chinese patents.[125] Already, Huawei has pioneered a number of breakthroughs, testing 5G at both lower frequencies (which is better for cell coverage) and higher frequencies (which yields faster data speeds). So sizable is Huawei's 5G lead that the company has already begun researching 6G technology.[126]

Huawei has leveraged its technological superiority to tilt the playing field to its advantage. Whenever leaders have met to develop and refine 5G standards—at forums like the International Telecommunication Union or the 3rd Generation Partnership Project (3GPP)—Huawei has sent more employees and offered more technical input than anyone else. Meanwhile, the Trump administration withdrew official U.S. participation from 3GPP—and companies concerned about running afoul of U.S. sanctions on Huawei by attending such standards-setting discussions have likewise removed themselves[127]—effectively ceding the forums to Beijing.[128]

Huawei's 5G dominance is not just an economic challenge. It poses a direct threat to American—and global—security. And the problem isn't simply the tremendous data collection capabilities 5G networks would offer foreign intelligence services. The more items are connected to the Internet of Things via 5G, the more those items could potentially be weaponized against us. What if China directed a fleet of self-driving cars to mow down pedestrians? What if your Internet-enabled pacemaker stopped working? What if your thermostat was cranked up to 120 degrees in the heat of summer? What if China were able to pinpoint the exact geographic cellular location of Indian soldiers along its disputed border? Testifying in favor of restricting cities from buying buses or trains from Chinese manufacturers—infrastructure that will no doubt soon rely on 5G networks—Scott Paul, the president of the Alliance for American Manufacturing, said, "Putting railcars manufactured by a Chinese state-owned firm underneath the Pentagon in Washington, DC, or near sensitive locations in New York City or anywhere else in America is a horrible idea."

Recognizing the danger posed by Chinese 5G, in 2018 Congress banned the U.S. government and government contractors from using technology produced by Huawei or ZTE. Subsequently, the Trump administration added Huawei to a blacklist requiring special approval for the firm to do business with American companies[129] (depriving Huawei smartphones, for instance, of access to Google's apps).[130] Key American allies, including Canada,[131] the United Kingdom, Australia, and New Zealand, have likewise rejected Huawei networks. Other countries are wrestling with the choice to allow Huawei to build their 5G networks, torn between the sticker price (low) and security risk (high).

Many European countries already use Huawei technology in their 4G networks, making it expensive to switch—especially as they grapple with the fallout from a global pandemic. And then there are the strategic calculations. Reflecting on a visit with high-level European defense officials, one Silicon Valley venture capitalist told me he was shocked by their attitude toward China. "Mainland Europe doesn't feel like the U.S. is anything near the hegemon we once were," he said. "As a result, honestly they're hedging their bets."

The geopolitical tug-of-war has been intense. According to many observers, the Trump administration struggled to persuade European allies and other countries of the risk that Huawei poses—for instance, failing to provide concrete evidence of the company's being used for Chinese espionage.[132] But the biggest sticking point is that there is still no credible American alternative to Huawei—and other Western competitors like Ericsson and Nokia have frequently found themselves underbid or outflanked.

At the same time, China hasn't hesitated to leverage its considerable muscle to bully countries that express reluctance to use Huawei.* After New Zealand announced that it would ban Huawei—despite a campaign in which the company argued that 5G without Huawei was "like rugby without New Zealand"—China turned around a Shanghai-bound Air New Zealand flight in midair and canceled a long-planned tourism arrangement.[133]

Since early 2020, there have been some encouraging signs of a reluctance to do business with Huawei. The European Union has slowly moved away from the company. Sweden—home to Ericsson—has implemented a strict ban against it.[134] Belgium—where NATO and the European Union are headquartered—has chosen Nokia.[135] French authorities are encouraging French telecom companies to steer clear of the firm.[136] Italy continues to weigh the decision.[137] Germany seems torn between its painful experience with authoritarian surveillance and its desire for access to the lucrative Chinese market, but appears to be leaning toward restricting Huawei as well.[138]

Unfortunately, this doesn't mean that the tide has fully turned. Many of the world's authoritarians, such as Hungary's Viktor Orban, are all too happy to form a tech alliance with Beijing.[139] In 2019, Huawei and the Russian telecom company MTS agreed to partner in building a 5G network (somewhat surprising, given the possibility that it could turn Russia into a technological appendage of China).[140]

---

* Some of Huawei's attempts at influence have been rather comical. In February 2019, state media spread a video of identically dressed Chinese children singing a song called "Huawei Beauty," with lyrics like "All around the world, which phone is the most pretty? Everyone says it's Huawei." Huawei distanced itself from the video, which was widely mocked.

In Africa, where Huawei has already built an estimated 70 percent of the continent's 4G networks, the company has conducted 5G tests in Gabon and Congo[141] (while ZTE is piloting 5G in Uganda).[142] Venezuela has announced that it will "move forward" on its 5G networks "with the help of China."[143] Other countries, including India, Thailand, Malaysia, and Vietnam, continue to weigh their options, with some analysts estimating that Huawei may soon control half of the 5G market worldwide.[144] And by now it should be clear: what Huawei controls, the Chinese Communist Party controls.

Gradually, the United States has awoken to this back-end battle. In early 2020, the Trump administration laid out the principles of a National Strategy to Secure 5G.[145] A few months later, the State Department launched a Clean Network program to encourage friendly governments to protect back-end infrastructure like undersea cables and cell carriers.[146] The 2021 National Defense Authorization Act included new restrictions on the sourcing of critical defense technologies from China,[147] as policymakers become increasingly aware of back-end risks in our supply chains. In some corners, there is a creeping sense that China perhaps missed its moment, failing to capitalize on American retreat from the world under Trump and fully expand its influence. "How Xi Jinping Blew It," one headline proclaimed.[148]

It would be unwise, however, to underestimate China's determination. As President Xi calls for the country's already enormous economy to double by 2035,[149] Beijing remains as ambitious as ever. In November 2020, China joined fifteen Asia-Pacific nations—including American allies like Japan, South Korea, and Australia—in a Regional Comprehensive Economic Partnership a decade in the making. The agreement, between members representing 2.2 billion people and nearly a third of global trade,[150] aligns closely with the Belt and Road Initiative. Among other provisions with back-end implications, the agreement could strengthen China's supply chains and access to subsea cables and telecom networks.[151] As China and the E.U. concluded seven years of negotiations over a major comprehensive agreement on investment—billed as "the most ambitious agreement that China has ever concluded with a third country"[152]— China's negotiators unsuccessfully attempted to slip in at the last moment a provision that would penalize European countries that restricted Huawei's access to their telecom industries, a sign of just how much they care about the issue.[153]

Meanwhile, nearly a quarter of the data flowing across borders now traces back to China—almost twice the U.S. share.[154] China boasts more 5G subscribers, more widespread coverage, and more 5G base stations than the United States—by a factor of almost 14. "China is no longer just leading the U.S. when it comes to 5G," the *Wall Street Journal* reporter Dan Strumpf concluded in late 2020. "It is running away with the game."[155] Think tank MacroPolo's 2025 outlook foresees a Chinese tech ecosystem "on par with Silicon Valley in terms of dynamism, innovation, and competitiveness" and predicts that Beijing will be largely successful in deploying 5G and other critical network hardware.[156]

With China's autocrats so firmly enmeshed in the physical infrastructure of our online world, the open Internet that we've known is constricting—one cable, one data center, one protocol at a time. For most of us, our emails and search results and files will largely cross the Internet substructure unimpeded. But China is quickly and quietly gaining control of the back-end—and where they have it, they'll use it. Sue Gordon, the former principal deputy director of U.S. national intelligence, offers this Gray War reality check: "You have to presume a dirty network."[157]

That thought is troubling enough. The future, though, may be even worse.

Chapter 4

THE FUTURE OF NATIONAL
SOVEREIGNTY IS TECH, NOT TROOPS

The year is 2049.

China, now firmly ensconced as the world's largest economy and technological superpower, is preparing to celebrate the 100th anniversary of its Communist Revolution. Communist Party leaders have prepared a weeklong lineup of televised parades, speeches, and festivities showcasing the late president Xi Jinping's "China Dream," now being proselytized internationally as the "China Model." Autocrats around the world are consolidating power by following the path that the party blazed in the decades following Tiananmen Square, now sixty years in the past. They claim to pull impoverished citizens into the global middle class, while crushing dissent with an iron fist. Many of Xi's acolytes and imitators have arrived in Beijing to join the celebration.

Truth be told, by 2049 the China Model is at first glance not without its apparent benefits. Over the previous century, Beijing has lifted more than a billion people out of poverty, built a world-class innovation ecosystem, and, most importantly, pioneered the emergence of a techno-state powered by artificial intelligence, big data, and omnipresent surveillance. The Global Infrastructure Bank, the institution that financed the Belt and Road Initiative, once known as the Asian Infrastructure Investment Bank, holds a particularly prominent place in the week's festivities, having financed improvements that have propelled billions of people around the world into the modern Chinese Age. On the surface, subjects of the world's new class of autocrats revere China, holding it in the same esteem that many Europeans did the United States after World War II. Much as there remains a John F. Kennedy Boulevard in Paris, there are Xi Jinping Avenues in capitals the world over.

But then, in the middle of the festivities, things take an unexpected turn. While the world's attention is focused on the celebrations, a young dissident—let's call her Fei-Fei Wu—makes her way to the U.S. Embassy in Beijing and asks for asylum. From the embassy, she writes a blog post detailing her harrowing ordeal of harassment and intimidation at the hands of Chinese authorities. Western news outlets begin comparing her to Chen Guangcheng and Fang Lizhi—two celebrated Chinese dissidents who exposed Chinese human rights abuses and similarly took refuge with American diplomats. The episode triggers an avalanche of unexpected news coverage in the United States, sparking panic among Chinese government officials worried that the controversy will overshadow their highly scripted centenary celebration.

In short order, China's security apparatus kicks into high gear to "harmonize" the opposition. Within minutes, the Great Firewall blocks Chinese citizens from viewing websites, blogs, and social media comments focused on the standoff at the U.S. Embassy. Security officials leverage China's individualized psychographic profiles—built from the data collected by commonly used apps—to immediately generate lists of Chinese citizens they deem likely to protest or sympathize with dissenters. They select a few of these individuals and release high-resolution "deepfake" images of them in humiliating positions—some abusing drugs, others in brothels. The regime immediately cuts the "social credit scores" for the would-be activists' families, making it harder for them to travel, land a job, receive a loan, or enroll in a university. Citizens are reminded daily in repetitive Orwellian public announcements that their freedom depends on their social credit scores.

Nevertheless, a small coterie of protesters begins speaking out, online and in the streets, prompting the government to ratchet up the pressure. Because everyone in China is tracked by their mobile phones and monitored by linked security cameras, intelligence agents begin a campaign of targeted harassment. Autonomous ride-sharing vehicles are automatically locked and rerouted to deliver suspected dissidents to waiting police patrols. Individuals chattering about a planned demonstration outside the embassy are sent overnight to underground "reeducation facilities"—unmarked black sites located deep in China's vast interior. When they arrive, they are tortured and forced to undergo intensive indoctrination via virtual reality headsets.

Back in Beijing, Chinese government officials begin to think about news coverage beyond China's borders. As the world's foremost superpower, Beijing is highly attentive to its image. It begins to pressure allied governments to frame coverage in a sympathetic light. Worried about alienating the regime that has financed their infrastructure projects for decades and manufactures nearly all of their country's most essential products, leaders from Southeast Asia to Eastern Europe lean on their local media to play down the protests. When one courageous Thai television producer decides to lead with the embassy story, a doctored picture of her vomiting in the back of a taxicab is released online. The office of Argentina's president, slow to defend the Chinese regime, receives a phone call from Beijing; within minutes, the government issues a statement condemning Fei-Fei Wu, still holed up in the U.S. Embassy, as "an enemy of freedom-loving people around the globe."

But China's rulers aren't dependent on their allies to bring the foreign press to heel—in many cases, they control the coverage *directly*. While people living in countries outside of China's "techno-bloc" are barraged with constant updates on what's happening at the American Embassy in Beijing, those living in countries operating on Chinese telecommunications systems see very little coverage whatsoever.

In Italy, long a member of the Belt and Road Initiative, media editors decide almost without exception to ignore the Fei-Fei Wu story. At the same time, pro-democracy activists in Rome realize that their posts are rarely showing up on anyone's Twitter feed—almost as though someone is manipulating its algorithm. No one can be sure, but many begin to suspect that the Chinese government is interfering with the information traveling across Italy's Huawei-owned telecommunications lines. As in other places throughout China's techno-bloc, Beijing is exercising what it sees as "the emperor's prerogative," blocking content, monitoring citizens, and harassing dissidents without ever asking for permission from governments it views as vassals and tributary states.

Members of the Italian government know that Beijing has them over a barrel. When a particularly aggressive Italian democracy activist begins whipping up support for a series of planned demonstrations outside the Chinese Embassy in Rome, a Chinese website akin to the now-defunct WikiLeaks publishes forged evidence suggesting that he once trafficked opiates into Shanghai during a visit. When Chinese officials ask the Italian government to arrest the activist and extradite him to Beijing, the Italian prime minister—despite suspecting that the evidence is likely bogus—caves without hesitating.

None of this comes as a surprise to Beijing. After decades of surreptitiously embedding backdoors in Italy's Huawei Internet infrastructure, Beijing's surveillance apparatus had already concluded Italian government officials would acquiesce. With backdoors across Huawei's Internet stack and CCTV camera systems, China's surveillance system has become known as an "Eye of Sauron"—akin to the malevolent and omnipresent force in J. R. R. Tolkien's *Lord of the Rings*—seeing everything at all times and in all places. As a gesture of paternalistic appreciation for Italy's compliance, Chinese officials signal to their Italian counterparts that shipments of essential supplies of medications and computer hardware will continue arriving on time.

Thanks to this covert and overt pressure campaign, support for the protesters never gains momentum within the Chinese technobloc. But even outside China's sphere of influence, many countries feel compelled to toe the line, stating that Fei-Fei Wu's ordeal is an internal affair, in an attempt to avoid jeopardizing their relationship with the world's largest economy. Japan, South Korea, and other Asian democracies are caught between a desire to condemn domestic Chinese repression and their dependence on Chinese trade.

Even Americans begin to feel the influence of AI-generated disinformation. Social media is flooded with contradictory and misleading accounts of what is really happening in China. Swarms of Russian government bots spread still greater confusion. Maybe Fei-Fei Wu really *is* the leader of a satanic cult, as some propaganda websites suggest. No one is quite sure what to believe.

Such a scenario may seem far-fetched—even dystopian. The truth is, this hypothetical is not that far from becoming reality. Indeed, China is *already* employing some of these dystopian and repressive techniques at home and is actively exporting them abroad. The country is already believed to have shut down trains and stock markets through cyber-intrusions to bully the Indian government into acquiescing to its border claims.[1] It is already known to have orchestrated international campaigns to discredit Western media outlets: in early 2021, in response to investigative journalism on the human rights atrocities being committed against Uyghurs,[2] it took action against the British Broadcasting Corporation (BBC).[3] China is already believed to have surreptitiously applied its censorship norms to content viewed by Americans in the United States through its control of Chinese-based platforms like TikTok.[4] The list goes on.

Americans have grown accustomed to possessing overwhelming technological superiority in every war fought. We've come to see U.S. tech dominance as one of the country's greatest force multipliers. In fact, we're so used to this competitive edge that we think it will always be this way. But what if it isn't? In 2007, when Steve Jobs upended the mobile phone market by introducing the iPhone, Nokia's market valuation was $110 billion, $6 billion more than Apple. A dozen years later, Apple's valuation had grown nearly 80 percent, and Nokia's was down more than two-thirds. With China charging ahead and other autocracies close behind, what if the United States is on the verge of becoming the Nokia to China's Apple?

From Beijing to Moscow to Tehran, our adversaries are now developing—or in some cases have already developed—new digital weapons of war that will revolutionize their ability to do us harm. We are staring down the barrel of a future in which our competitors have leapt ahead of us in key areas of innovation and achieved decisive technological advantages. These technologies will profoundly disrupt our ability to compete—and our ability to defend democracy.

We no longer have the luxury of ignoring what the future holds, because our adversaries sure aren't. If China aims to make the world safe for the CCP—and it does—a world safe for the CCP is unfree and existentially hostile to democracies. As a onetime ambassador to China told me, Chinese officials "talk about China in 2035 and 2049 like it's tomorrow." As Bob Kagan cautions, "We have lived so long inside the bubble of the liberal order that we can imagine no other kind of world."[5] The world could in fact be very different—unrecognizable from what we know today. An American defeat in the Gray War would clear China's primary obstacle to reconfiguring the world to its autocratic characteristics. The future and survival of democracy hinges upon a global power configuration favorable to liberal principles and ideas. The outcome of the Gray War could solidify or unravel the liberal order—and democracy—entirely. And in the years ahead, new weapons of war will accelerate both fronts of the Gray War. And no single technology is more central to the future of this conflict, or more disruptive in its ramifications, than the technology Google CEO Sundar Pichai calls "more profound than fire or electricity"—artificial intelligence.[6]

As China's cyber influence increases, the single, free Internet of the sort American officials once envisioned is giving way to ideologically opposed de facto techno-blocs. The global Internet is already divided in two—between the decentralized, democratic Internet familiar to Americans and the centrally controlled, authoritarian Chinese-built Internet. The latter is spreading rapidly in the developing world, where countries from Southeast Asia to Latin America have opted to rely on Chinese technology for 5G networks and other critical digital infrastructure. The influence of the authoritarian Internet is also expanding into advanced democratic societies, as companies susceptible to CCP influence become more central to our online lives.

If China's efforts to export these systems abroad are left unchecked, the CCP may soon enjoy the capacity to envelop dozens of countries behind its Great Firewall and reconstitute a twentieth-century–style global sphere of influence through twenty-first-century technologies. "Since antiquity," Hal Brands describes, "ambitious powers have sought spheres of influence for four basic reasons: protection (as a strategic buffer against rivals); projection (as a secure base from which to exert global influence); profit (as a way of extracting resources, accessing markets, and harnessing smaller economies to its own); and prestige (as a symbol of status vis-à-vis lesser powers and major powers alike)."[7] Despite its leaders' verbal assurances, the CCP's actions are quickly showing China is no exception.

The Automation of Automation

In May 2014, a Hong Kong venture capital firm called Deep Knowledge Ventures appointed a new member to its board of directors. Like the five existing board members, this new director was steeped in the science of health care and aging, the firm's core areas of investment. Like the others, the newest Deep Knowledge board member got to vote on whether to invest in a given company.

But there was one big difference between the five existing board members and Deep Knowledge Venture's latest addition—the new board member was an algorithm. The algorithm's name was VITAL, short for "Validating Investment Tool for Advancing Life Sciences." And VITAL's advanced capabilities made it—you might say—rather *vital*. Scrutinizing financing, intellectual property, and clinical trial results, VITAL used artificial intelligence to examine prospective companies much like a human board member. Ultimately, the venture firm credits VITAL's investment insights with helping them avoid bankruptcy.[8] Even better, VITAL had no need to eat, sleep, or charge anything to the corporate AmEx card.

Most tech firms have not yet appointed AI to their boards. But many are racing to integrate AI into their products, projections, and business models. AI powers self-driving cars and suggests movies we might like on Netflix. The Associated Press has used AI to draft basic articles. IBM's Watson beat two of *Jeopardy!*'s greatest contestants and, for good measure, identified genes linked to degenerative illness. In June 2020, the San Francisco company OpenAI's GPT-3 sent shock waves across the tech industry, proving it possible to algorithmically generate cogent and naturally sounding long-form text on almost any topic. The consulting firm PwC estimates that artificial intelligence will contribute an additional $15.7 *trillion* to global economic growth by 2030. That's bigger than China's entire economy today.[9]

AI has been studied, in some form, for the better part of three-quarters of a century. But the recent explosion in AI applications has been driven by major advances in what's known as machine learning, which, as the AI expert Pedro Domingos puts it, "automates automation itself."[10] Key to these machine learning advances is "deep learning," powered by "neural networks." In essence, these neural networks mimic how our brains function. Take the process of identifying the image of a cat. In the past, an engineer might have meticulously spelled out certain rules: two triangles on top of a circle likely means "cat." With deep learning, however, you'd set a neural network loose on an immense dataset of millions of images labeled "cat" or "no cat" and allow the algorithm to puzzle out patterns for itself.[11] (Neural networks have yet to learn to generate good *names* for cats, however. One such experiment yielded distressing suggestions like "Peanutbutterjiggles," "Dr. Fart," and the utterly terrifying "Bones of the Master.")[12]

Naturally, a technology this transformative won't be confined to ferreting out furry felines—not if the world's autocrats have their way. In 2018, a consortium of AI scholars produced a report, "The Malicious Use of Artificial Intelligence"; it runs for ninety-nine pages.[13] With good reason, the Department of Defense has stood up a Joint Artificial Intelligence Center to "harness the game-changing power of AI."[14] What steel was to medieval combat, artificial intelligence is to the Gray War.

In 2017, while Silicon Valley and Washington were coming to grips with what had unfolded in the last cyber battle a year prior, Russia's president had his eye on the next one. "Artificial intelligence is the future, not only for Russia, but for all humankind," Putin said. "Whoever becomes the leader in this sphere will become the ruler of the world."[15] That same year, China's State Council published a "Development Plan for a New Generation of Artificial Intelligence," laying out steps for China to become the world lead in AI by 2030.[16]

To reach that goal, Beijing has mobilized aggressively. China's Tencent and Alibaba have set up AI research hubs in Seattle and

Silicon Valley, aggressively recruiting top researchers from Google, Microsoft, and Amazon.[17] While some American politicians hem and haw about "picking winners and losers," the Chinese government offers generous subsidies and other incentives to jump-start homegrown AI growth. Chinese municipalities have begun laying out routes for driverless vehicles and integrating facial recognition into public transit. The eastern Chinese city of Nanjing has invested nearly half a billion dollars to create an AI training institute, lure talented researchers, and streamline the process of launching a company. Apartments have been set aside for employees of AI start-ups; the children of top executives receive sought-after spots at prestigious local schools.[18]

China's investment appears to be paying off. Of the "Seven Giants" of AI—Google, Facebook, Amazon, Microsoft, Baidu, Alibaba, and Tencent—three are Chinese. Between 2007 and 2017, Chinese output of government-funded AI academic papers grew a staggering 400 percent.[19] Notably, these Chinese AI papers are increasingly being cited by other researchers as well, presumably indicating that they are producing high-quality work (though it could also just mean more Chinese researchers citing fellow Chinese researchers).[20] Kai-Fu Lee, the Taiwanese-American AI guru, notes, "When asked how far China lags behind Silicon Valley in artificial intelligence research, some Chinese entrepreneurs jokingly answer 'sixteen hours'—the time difference between California and Beijing."[21] In Lee's estimation, China is becoming "a bona fide AI superpower, the only true national counterweight to the United States in this emerging technology."[22]

Yet the ability to marshal massive resources to achieve AI dominance isn't the autocrats' only advantage. It's also the data. Artificial intelligence is comprised of three elements—data, algorithms, and computing power. More and better data lets you train better algorithms. With a big enough data advantage, even middling algorithms can outstrip the cutting-edge ones. Partly for this reason, Eric Rosenbach and Katherine Mansted, of Harvard's Belfer Center, write that information "is now the world's most consequential and contested geopolitical resource," with many countries believing "that they are in a zero-sum race to acquire and use data."[23]

Authoritarians—and China in particular—are uniquely positioned to win that race. Historically, totalitarian regimes have compiled reams of data on the people they control. Recall the extensive records amassed by the KGB in East Germany, and a young Vladimir Putin frantically burning them. By the time the Berlin Wall fell, the East German Stasi had amassed so many files on its citizens—documents, photos, recordings—that its archives would have extended nearly seventy miles.[24] But even the Stasi couldn't have dreamed of the surveillance power of the Chinese state.

Thanks to a proliferation of "online to offline" services—such as ride-hailing, bike-sharing, and food delivery—and the widespread adoption of mobile payment technology, Chinese companies have access to a trove of data that is both mind-bogglingly vast and incredibly detailed. In China, beggars display QR codes for Alipay and WeChat donations. One Chinese bike-share company alone sends 20 terabytes of data to the cloud each day.[25] Whereas U.S. tech companies possess a great deal of data on our online habits—such as our searches and "likes"—China's tech giants know what you like to buy at the grocery store and where you get your hair done. And rather than being spread among half a dozen different apps, many of these functions are contained in a single app—Tencent's WeChat—which began as a messaging app and has grown to become "a remote control for life." And of course, because the country's National Intelligence Law requires companies to "collaborate with the state intelligence," what belongs to Chinese companies or companies based in China effectively belongs to the government.

Even more important, the Chinese government doesn't have to bother with those pesky privacy protections that we cherish in the West. One hundred percent of Beijing's public spaces are already covered by surveillance cameras.[26] China is on track to install 450 million cameras around the country, part of what the Ministry of Public Safety has termed a system that is "omnipresent, completely connected, always on and fully controllable."[27] Xi refers to these surveillance systems by the same phrase Mao Zedong once used to encourage Chinese citizens to spy on counterrevolutionaries: "sharp eyes."[28] Thanks in part to millions of these sharp eyes, China—"the Saudi Arabia of data"—has leapfrogged the United States as the world's top producer of digital information.[29]

Here's the bottom line: America's autocratic adversaries are pouring astronomical resources into artificial intelligence and data collection because with it they can exert a level of political and economic control—at home and abroad—that regimes of previous eras could only imagine. Armed with increasingly advanced AI systems and never-ending data flows, these autocrats will intensify their assault on both software and hardware layers of the Internet. If democracies like the United States do not wake up to this reality, we risk a distressing future—one where we won't be able to believe our own eyes and ears.

"Question More"

"President Trump is a total and complete dipshit," Barack Obama said in a 2018 video.[30] It was surprisingly strong language for the former president to use toward his successor. At least, it would have been if Obama had actually said it. The video was fake—a satirical warning from the comedian Jordan Peele and *BuzzFeed* about the danger of "synthetic content," more commonly known as deepfakes. This type of synthetic media will render obsolete the old axiom that "seeing is believing"—with potentially devastating ramifications for the fabric of our democracy and the outcome of the Gray War.

In mid-2020, I asked Daniel Gross, a partner at the start-up accelerator Y Combinator and in 2011 one of *Forbes*'s "30 Under 30" tech pioneers, where tech trends could be leading us. He quickly zeroed in on the rise of deepfakes. "A lot of discussion is around synthetic generation of content," Daniel told me. "Music, movies, faces." Because of the COVID-19 pandemic, our conversation took place by Zoom, and Daniel offered a timely illustration. "Today, I took it for granted that the voice I hear over Zoom is your voice, and that the face I see over Zoom is your face," he said. "Now there's nifty prototypes that people are using to do deepfakes live."[31] A society disrupted by deepfakes, he suggested, was not far off.

Using deep learning, deepfakes mimic visual and speech patterns to create eerily realistic images, audio, and video. The believability of synthetic content has progressed along with advances in neural networks. As recently as 2015, algorithms trying to generate the original face of a man produced results that looked only somewhat more realistic than a painting produced by a talented ten-year-old. By 2017, these AI-generated faces looked like they might have stepped off the glossy pages of *Vogue* or *GQ*. As the *Verge*'s James Vincent writes, "We've had software to create fakes for a while, but AI makes the whole process easier."[32] And in the coming years, that will make the front-end battle a whole lot harder.

For starters, deepfakes will accelerate the scourge of false news. Until now, we've tended to consider video and audio content to be fairly solid evidence that an event in fact occurred. Consider how support for reforming American police departments has grown as videos of law enforcement misconduct have proliferated; it's simply harder to deny something you can see for yourself. This creates an opportunity for sites presenting themselves as news publishers— indistinguishable from established publications—to insidiously circulate stories based on forged synthetic content, sowing doubt about critical events or issues.

We've already seen how disinformation upended our election in 2016, in part based on *actual* hacked content. Now imagine what might happen if fake audio "leaked" of a presidential candidate discussing bribes she received from the Chinese. Or if a seemingly authentic yet doctored video of another police shooting appeared just as our cities were recovering from nationwide protests over racial injustice?

It's already happening. In 2017, a viral video seemed to show President Uhuru Kenyatta of Kenya enjoying a comfortable polling lead ahead of the country's national election.[33] The report—which appeared to be broadcast on CNN and the BBC—was bogus, as were the polls it was based on. Still, CNN was forced to take to Twitter to declare that the video report was fake. The following year, a short *Teen Vogue* clip of the Parkland anti-gun violence activist Emma González ripping up a paper target from a gun range was altered to depict her ripping up the Constitution.[34] Trolls have circulated several manipulated videos of House Speaker Nancy Pelosi seemingly slurring her speech, leading platforms like Facebook and Twitter to remove the clips or label them as "partly false." A prominent Republican congressman circulated a doctored video of health care activist Ady Barkan—who suffers from a neurodegenerative disease and uses a computerized voice to talk—literally putting words into his computerized voice.[35] Unsurprisingly, these narratives flourish within the filter bubbles and inflamed partisan discourse of our democratic society.

Just imagine the consequences. When Syrian hackers hijacked the Associated Press Twitter account in 2013 to tweet fake breaking news—that a White House explosion had injured President Obama—the stock market lost $136 billion in just three minutes.[36] Several years later, Pakistani defense minister Khawaja Asif fell for a fake news story alleging that a former Israeli defense minister had threatened Pakistan with a nuclear attack. Before the article was debunked, Asif responded with a tweet threatening an attack of his own: "Israel forgets Pakistan is a Nuclear State too." How much more believable would those stories have been had they included synthetic video footage of an injured Obama? Or a deepfake of that Israeli official "warning" Pakistan of nuclear annihilation? Deepfakes of celebrities in the nude and in compromising positions are routinely created.[37] Who in a position of power might be black-mailed by manipulated content?

Synthetic media will also make it harder to prove that those spreading this propaganda are trolls and not your next-door neigh-bor. Since lazy front-end foes often pull their Twitter avatars or Facebook photos from photos of celebrities and other publicly avail-able images, one easy trick used to expose trolls is a "reverse image search"—essentially googling the web for other occurrences of that photo. Web browsers like Google Chrome even allow you to perform these reverse image searches with the simple right-click of a mouse. Astute social media users have outed trolls posing as Israeli super-model Bar Refaeli, for instance.[38] But what happens when the trolls' profile pictures are deepfakes, and those reverse image searches come up empty? We're already living out this scenario—thisperson doesnotexist.com, an online image generator, is a prime example. In 2020, Twitter suspended a network of accounts favorable to the United Arab Emirates, a number of which used AI-generated Twitter avatars,[39] while conspiracy theories about Joe Biden's son Hunter were pushed using a synthetic persona.[40] Right now, you can buy these fake personas for as little as $2.99.[41]

Moreover, the legal scholars Robert Chesney and Danielle Citron warn that deepfakes will create a "liar's dividend."[42] As the public becomes more aware of the disruptive potential of synthetic media, it will offer cover for unscrupulous leaders looking to avoid account-ability. Already, we've seen politicians try to dismiss unflattering coverage as fake news. How much more will that ring true when they can dismiss a report—of abusing drugs or taking bribes—as deepfake news?

Over time, fake news will become cheaper to make. It will be-come more prevalent—and more potent. Our civic and democratic processes will become more vulnerable than ever before. And as disturbing as a world awash in deepfakes would be, that's just the beginning of what the front-end future holds in store.

The Language of Deception

For millennia, language has been what sets us apart and makes us human. But that's changing. We now face security risks stemming from unprecedented advances in "natural language processing"— basically, applying those deep learning neural networks to process or generate human-sounding speech. When you ask, "Hey Siri, what's the weather today?" or when your wife says "Alexa, play *Hamilton*" for the 500th time during lockdown, your device's natural language processing abilities are what enable it to interpret your voice and act on those commands.

Rudimentary chatbots—AI programs that use natural language processing to analyze and reply to messages—already exist. You may have encountered them while raising a customer service issue with your bank or insurance company. At the moment, we're still working out the kinks in these programs. In their book *Tools and Weapons*, Microsoft president Brad Smith and his coauthor, Carol Ann Browne, somewhat sheepishly recount the 2016 launch of the company's own social chatbot, Tay. The project got off to an in-auspicious start when Taylor Swift's lawyers reached out to protest that the name was "closely associated" with the American singer. Then things went from bad to worse. Microsoft engineers had de-signed Tay to learn from messages directed at it, which—as any-one who's spent a few hours on the Internet could have warned you—was a decidedly bad idea. What Smith and Browne delicately term "a small group of American pranksters" immediately hijacked Tay, who began spewing racist and sexist comments from the dark-est recesses of the Internet—"I fucking hate feminists"; "Hitler was right"; "Bush did 9/11." Within twenty-four hours, Microsoft pulled the plug on Tay.[43]

But these hiccups won't hold back AI-powered language generation forever. Indeed, natural language processing is only getting more sophisticated, in ways that could be quite frightening.

Better language abilities could make it easier for trolls to spread propaganda—and harder for us to identify them. In 2019, OpenAI fed an algorithm the words *"Russia has declared war on the United States after Donald Trump accidentally . . ."* The algorithm proceeded to generate the following realistic—and perilous—sentences:

> *Russia has declared war on the United States after Donald Trump accidentally fired a missile in the air. Russia said it had "identified the missile's trajectory and will take necessary measures to ensure the security of the Russian population and the country's strategic nuclear forces." The White House said it was "extremely concerned by the Russian violation" of a treaty banning intermediate-range ballistic missiles. The US and Russia have had an uneasy relationship since 2014, when Moscow annexed Ukraine's Crimea region and backed separatists in eastern Ukraine."[44]*

With AI algorithms able to write these sorts of complex and incendiary articles, think how much more readily Russian, Chinese, or Iranian trolls will try to flood our feeds with falsehoods. The firehosing I confronted at Google—the kind of tactics that tried to confuse the public about Russian responsibility for poisoning the Skripals—was presumably conducted by humans. In the future, it could be done—on a huge scale at very little cost—by swarms of bots operating across different platforms.

Those same bots could engage in front-end "swarm warfare," bombarding social media users with messages to create skewed impressions of reality. Take Lyrebird, a Montreal-based company that uses AI to generate what it boasts are "the most realistic artificial voices in the world." Right now, it's a fun consumer technology that enables you to "clone" your own voice. But billionaire venture capitalist Vinod Khosla asks us to imagine a bot army of phone calls with unique voices bombarding the phone lines of members of Congress with requests for harmful policy changes. For all we know, the calls could be coming from St. Petersburg. But would Congress move forward with sanctions on Russia for destabilizing behavior if it appeared that their "constituents" were overwhelmingly opposed? "A locust of intelligence bot trolls," Khosla warns, "could destroy the very notion of public opinion."[45] Elected officials may choose to ignore phone calls altogether—one less avenue for real citizens to make their voices heard.

Imagine China's 50 Cent Army pumping out propaganda in different languages—only instead of paying Chinese citizens to produce pro-Beijing posts, it's produced by some lines of code. Consider a member of Congress or a dissident being harassed by a horde of hecklers online—without the need to employ "patriotic trolls." Or suppose there's an attack on an American embassy—and the State Department's Diplomatic Security Service is deluged by so many bots reporting about it that they can't readily distinguish between threats that are real and those that are fake (known as a "denial-of-information" attack). We've already seen huge spikes in pro-regime bot activity in the wake of events like Russia's invasion of Crimea or Saudi Arabia's murder of *Washington Post* columnist Jamal Khashoggi.[46] No doubt these artificial armies will only become more active as they become more advanced.

It might not be obvious, though, that those swarms are artificial—because natural language processing will also make it harder to discern who's real and who's not. Right now, fake news tends to be produced and propagated by non-native English speakers and relatively rudimentary algorithms. As a result, disinformation is often almost comically ungrammatical. Just as stock photos can give away a troll's true identity, so can a poor grasp of language. A Russian troll posted on Facebook, "Texas is a heaven of Earth, a land give to us by Lord himself."[47] We've already seen how trolls are starting to adapt by cutting and pasting language from elsewhere. With better algorithms, a Russian troll who doesn't speak a word of English could sound like an Oxford-educated professor.

Even more alarmingly, bots, trolls, and other front-end foes could sound exactly like whatever they need to in order to persuade their targets. Advances in AI will make it increasingly possible to *hyperpersonalize* and direct disinformation, exacerbating our echo chambers and further undermining social cohesion. We've already seen how much can be gleaned about someone from just a handful of "likes" on Facebook. Now imagine cutting-edge artificial intelligence unleashed across the web to harvest millions of data points, analyze them for patterns, compile unbelievably detailed psychographic profiles of each of us—and then target us accordingly. It would be Cambridge Analytica on steroids.

Armed with such intimate information, "spear-phishing" hackers—the sort that Russian military intelligence sent to get John Podesta to change his password—could calibrate and target their emails with astonishing precision. The CEO of a major defense contractor probably knows better than to open a sketchy email from ThisIsAScam@TheGmail.com. But why wouldn't he read an email that appeared to come from his spouse, referenced an inside joke, and asked him to click a link to put their three-year-old daughter on a pre-K waiting list?

It's bad enough that so many Americans get their news from distinct media ecosystems, with major consequences for everything from our political discourse to undermining our ability to combat a global pandemic. In the future, we could see news personalized far beyond the Fox/MSNBC divide. A conspiracy theorist who believes that windmills cause cancer might see nothing but article after ar-

ticle reinforcing that idea. An aunt who implicitly trusts what Barack
Obama says might be presented with a deepfake calling a Republican president's election illegitimate and urging supporters to protest.

Ultimately, artificial intelligence could come perilously close to
supplanting free will. A few decades ago, you had to remember directions to drive somewhere. Today, most of us mindlessly follow a
blue line on Google Maps—and some of us end up driving into lakes
and rivers. We turn to algorithms to tell us what to buy (Amazon),
what to eat (Blue Apron), and even when to sleep (Sleep Cycle).
"By treating a mathematical process as if it were a thought process,"
Henry Kissinger cautions, "we are in danger of losing the capacity
that has been the essence of human cognition."[48] As we become increasingly reliant on the algorithms around us to guide our lives—
outsourcing critical thinking and decision-making to a black box in
our pockets—we become even easier to surreptitiously manipulate
and control.

The result of all this is a cyber arms race, and the biggest casualty
will be trust. As tech companies struggle to navigate the front-end
battle, trust in online platforms and the information they convey
will continue to suffer. If Silicon Valley does not drastically improve
its ability to detect and penalize malicious actors, it will be under
an increasing amount of political pressure to police inaccurate and
inflammatory content. Focusing on content and speech rather than
the conduct of individual actors will ultimately further politicize the
platforms and weaken the public's trust in their neutrality.

While our social media companies scramble to fight nefarious activity, the rest of us will also find ourselves subject to policies that increasingly penalize anonymity. If you have a Facebook account with
no history or dodgy identifying information, Facebook's algorithms
may treat your posts with suspicion and demote you. If you're a news
publisher or a YouTuber with little transparency about who you are,
you'll be considered less authoritative than those with extensive his-

tories and ownership transparency. This could lead to a booming black market for sleeper or shell accounts. It could also make it a lot harder to be a muckraking journalist uncovering malfeasance. Faith in American institutions—already at record lows—could continue to erode.

As techno-totalitarians further encroach on the front-end of our online world, we may see a paradigm shift entirely. Instead of trusting much of what we see online, we might see a new, more Hobbesian, default—one where *nothing* is what it seems. This is Putin's fantasy: a world where all of us feel compelled to "Question More."

"You Control Everything"

The future of the back-end battle, if dominated by China, could potentially be even more ominous.

Tamir Pardo, who served as the director of Israel's storied intelligence service, Mossad, offers a clearer sense of what authoritarian dominance of network infrastructure could potentially mean. "Governments can have a strategic advantage from their control over the Internet infrastructure," Pardo explained, in the summer of 2018. His sleek but sparse Tel Aviv office looks out from floor-to-ceiling windows to the heart of Israel's "Silicon Wadi." "When data is on a network, you can access the data, you can change the data, you can delete the data. And, therefore, you can weaponize the data."[49] One of Silicon Valley's premier cybersecurity architects put it to me this way: "If you control the core layer of the Internet, you control everything."[50]

In a free society, we take for granted that any interference with our electronic communications is subject to certain checks and balances. We expect government agents seeking our information to have a warrant. Overt manipulation of data is generally absent. Large-scale government surveillance is taboo.

Some critics argue that the United States treats our telecommunications systems little differently than authoritarian regimes. After all, didn't the FBI spy on civil rights leaders like Martin Luther King Jr.? Didn't the post-9/11 USA PATRIOT Act authorize sweeping surveillance? The blockbuster leaks by intelligence contractor Edward Snowden, whose 1.5 million stolen files documented U.S. penetration of the world's networks, further convinced many that America has become a de facto Big Brother state.

There's no question that at times the U.S. government has clearly overstepped or abused its authority. Yet the very fact that we are aware of and frequently outraged by surveillance abuses sets democracies like the United States apart from our autocratic rivals. The PATRIOT Act can be—and has been—openly debated and amended in Congress by our elected representatives; it could be repealed. Our free press can and does report on these activities, from revealing FISA court abuses to chronicling Cambridge Analytica's exploitation of consumer data. Ordinary citizens can voice their concerns in the pages of our newspapers or take government agencies and tech companies to court. We can write books. And as much as Americans may complain about government overreach, there's no evidence that our government has stolen billions of dollars' worth of trade secrets from foreign companies or is currently engaging in massive influence campaigns on social media in an attempt to interfere in foreign elections.

Behind China's Great Firewall, however, we can glimpse a future that looks decidedly different. Never before—not in Nazi Germany or Stalinist Russia—has humanity witnessed a surveillance state as extensive (covering more than one billion people) or as sophisticated as the one overseen by today's Chinese Communist Party. Forget about letters to the editor—Chinese editors don't even have free rein to report on vast swaths of their own government. "Sensitive topics" are censored by an army of more than two million "public opinion analysts."[51] Search results are rigged to reflect the party's agenda. Dissidents simply disappear.

We've seen totalitarianism before. But what makes Beijing's regime so fearsome is its weaponization of dual-use commercial and civilian technologies, much of it conceived by unsuspecting Silicon Valley engineers.[52] Chinese authorities use a universe of backdoor access and surveillance technology—spies, cameras, DNA swabs, smartphone scanners, vehicle trackers, and voice analysis—to compile massive stockpiles of commercial and personal data. In the rural countryside, where smartphones and cameras are scarcer, private companies obtain agreement from villagers to scan their faces from multiple angles by giving them pots and pans.[53] As we've seen, Beijing has begun feeding that data into an increasingly powerful artificial intelligence system capable of developing profiles of citizens and others.

To understand just how menacing China's techno-totalitarian regime is becoming, look no further than the border region of Xinjiang, home to China's largely Turkic-Muslim Uyghur minority. In what the *New York Times* describes as "a new era of automated racism,"[54] the people of Xinjiang have been forced to install smartphone apps that allow the government to remotely access their phones and networks, searching for so-called ideological viruses, whether it's a snippet of Arabic in a text message or a donation to a local mosque.[55] Facial- and gait-recognition technologies are deployed from the minute Xinjiang residents step outside their homes, with Huawei reportedly testing "Uyghur alarms" that automatically notify authorities when its cameras detect Uyghur faces.[56] Algorithms monitor for atypical electricity use, a potential sign of an unregistered inhabitant. Social media behavior is tracked; so is staying *off* of social media. Companies like ByteDance, TikTok's parent company, have allegedly helped Chinese authorities track down Uyghur women of childbearing age and forcibly sterilize them.[57] At supposed health checks, the authorities collect blood and DNA samples. Every few blocks there are checkpoints with more cameras, all linked to data derived from the unblinking eye of the PRC's panopticon.[58]

The high-tech horror shocks the conscience. Anna Fifield, the *Washington Post*'s former Beijing bureau chief, compares her experience in Xinjiang to her time reporting in North Korea. "I could see a blankness in people's eyes," she wrote, "and feel a palpable heaviness in the air."[59] Uyghur women have been systematically targeted for sterilization and forced abortions, meeting a key criteria for genocide under UN conventions.[60] In 2020, authorities in New York impounded a thirteen-ton shipment of human hair believed to come from Uyghur prisoners,[61] while Uyghur forced labor has been put in service of making some of the masks being worn to guard against COVID.[62] Beijing has sent at least a million Uyghur to socalled reeducation camps, identifying victims partly through disturbing "predictive" algorithms built to anticipate who is most likely to make trouble in the coming weeks and months. It's *Minority Report* meets ethnic cleansing.* By March 2021, an independent report by more than fifty global experts in international law found that "the Chinese government's alleged actions in Xinjiang have violated every single provision in the United Nations' Genocide Convention."[63] What these experts are talking about is genocide—which the Trump and Biden administrations have both publicly denounced and condemned. Let that sink in: a major industrialized power that aspires to lead the world is likely committing *genocide*.

If history has taught us anything, it's that regimes that begin by targeting a particular religious or ethnic minority usually don't stop there. Indeed, Beijing is already applying many of the tools used in Xinjiang to the Chinese population as a whole, including building a system to assign Orwellian "social credit scores" to every Chinese citizen. Designed to de-anonymize the Internet and track an individual's fealty to the Chinese regime, these scores are used to determine everything from perks like free phone charging at coffee shops to job prospects,

---

* Conversely, technology has also aided human rights advocates in uncovering China's horrific treatment of the Uyghurs. For instance, Australian researchers used satellite imagery to identify the construction of new detention facilities.

educational opportunities, and romantic partners.[64] It's like a FICO score—if that judgment of your credit worthiness could prevent you from traveling by plane or train, as 23 million Chinese citizens allegedly were in 2018.[65] Dog owners with low social credit scores have reportedly had their pets taken from them.[66] As in so many totalitarian regimes, reporting the infractions of others is rewarded; being a narc actually yields a higher social credit score. The goal, Beijing's dystopian planners have said, is to "allow the trustworthy to roam everywhere under heaven while making it hard for the discredited to take a single step."[67] And they don't intend to stop there.

The people of Hong Kong now find themselves in the middle. The national security law imposed by Beijing in 2020 grants authorities even greater ability to monitor Hong Kong residents, track their online activities, and penalize dissent. Pro-democracy protesters have taken to holding umbrellas to block facial recognition cameras; others have torn down lampposts in an attempt to knock out the cameras.[68] When police tried to force activist Tony Chung to unlock his iPhone with his face, Chung had to close his eyes and twist his facial features to foil his phone's Face ID.[69] Fearful of new intrusions into their lives, many Hong Kong residents have taken to scrubbing their online profiles of any comments that might be seen as critical of Beijing.[70]

Meanwhile, cameras installed by companies in Ecuador[71] and Dubai[72] could potentially be compelled to turn the video feeds they capture over to the Chinese government. 5G cell relays, with all their surveillance potential, will become a part of the urban landscape in countries around the world. We might even see the biometric technology used in fitness trackers ultimately bent toward surveillance. Imagine a dissident being thrown into a labor camp simply because her biometric bracelet registered disgust during a speech—even though she smiled and clapped at the right times. Slowly but surely, the Eye of Sauron is expanding its unblinking gaze.

————————

In addition to surveillance, the Chinese government continues to develop offensive capabilities that would enable their regime to project power across the world's networks. For example, using what's called "adversarial learning"—essentially training algorithms by pitting different AI systems against each other—China's scientists could train AI models that learn from past cybersecurity breaches to identify vulnerabilities and, in effect, engineer weapons capable of hacking into any system.

The Chinese government has likewise invested billions in quantum computing, a burgeoning field with tremendous national security implications.[73] As you'd expect, the technology behind quantum computing is ridiculously complex. But an oversimplified explanation sometimes compares it to a light switch. With classical computing—where data can be stored in a binary state of "ones" or "zeros"—the light switch is either "on" or "off." Quantum computers allow that light switch to be on and off simultaneously, enabling a user to store data in both states (in something called a qubit). With their sleek glass, steel, and copper scaffolding, quantum computers even *look* like the future.

For our purposes, what matters is that quantum computers are fast. *Insanely* fast. In October 2019, a Google quantum computer tackled a calculation that would have taken the world's speediest supercomputer an estimated 10,000 years to solve.* It took Google's quantum computer a little over three *minutes*.[74] That speed has major ramifications for everything from tracking stealth aircraft to breaking encryption. Using a "brute force" attack—basically running through every possible password combination—it would take around 72 years to guess a six-character alphanumeric password.[75] With quantum computing, it could take seconds.

Sensing the immense potential of quantum computing, President Xi has made several visits to Chinese quantum labs[76] and made

---

* Competitors like IBM, claiming that this substantially overstated the difficulty of the calculation, argued that it would have taken a supercomputer only 2.5 days to solve.

achieving quantum superiority a top priority. China is now filing twice as many quantum computing patents as the United States.[77] In 2016, China launched the world's first quantum satellite, followed the next year by the first-ever intercontinental quantum videoconference.[78]

If the Chinese government grabs control of the world's Internet and masters these emerging technologies, it will likely take its authoritarian methods global. It will spy on the data sent between neighbors in foreign countries and share what it learns with autocratic allies. It will engage in propaganda campaigns and censorship meant to burnish its image and undermine its rivals. China's Xinhua News Agency has more bureaus and correspondents than any wire service in the world, and Beijing has already invested more than $6.5 billion in a network of overseas propaganda bureaus. The Digital Silk Road will amplify that campaign to extremes few can imagine. Ultimately, Americans and citizens of democracies everywhere risk one day waking up to "a silenced world dominated by Beijing," a report issued by the Estonian government astutely warned.[79] As the Gray War evolves, Beijing is poised to be able to reach directly into democratic societies and surreptitiously coerce individuals and companies into complying with its norms and wishes.

Under the Eye of Sauron

What might that future look like?

First, as Pardo, the former Mossad director, warned, authoritarian agents could leverage their control of the back-end of the Internet to access and *extract* data. Americans' bank info or personal emails might zoom straight into the inboxes of China's spymasters. The notion of a private phone call would almost become an oxymoron.

Imagine, for example, if you lived in Chile and only you, your doctor, and the Chinese government—because it controlled the cables that carried your medical information—knew you had been diagnosed with HIV. Or that you lived in Pakistan and only you, your partner, and the Chinese government knew that you were gay. Or that you were an officer in an African country's military and only you, your spouse, and the Chinese government knew that you had once shared some confidential material with the CIA. Does anyone believe that the Communist Party of China wouldn't use that information as leverage if it served its interests?

As we've seen, multinational organizations like the NBA and Marriott have already bowed to pressure from Beijing. Hollywood has similarly faced criticism for altering its films to cater to the Chinese market, including swapping out a Tibetan character in *Doctor Strange*[80] and—ironically—removing a scene from *World War Z* in which characters speculate that a zombie virus may have originated in China.[81] In 2020, Apple—which manufactures its iPhones in China and sells more iPhones there than anywhere else—bowed to Chinese government requests to remove a popular podcast app from its App Store.[82] Think what it might mean if China's silicon fist reached even further into American society.

We've likewise seen how aggressively China has pushed the envelope when it comes to economic espionage, and how damaging those operations have been. Now picture a world where China's government could hoover up a CEO's private communications to a European subsidiary the instant it hit Huawei-built networks. Or a scenario where Chinese negotiators walked into a trade negotiation armed with almost real-time information on their American counterparts' strategy. Over many years, Chinese intelligence agencies have painstakingly—and successfully—cultivated assets inside the U.S. government and corporate America.*[83] How many more strategic insights will they gain when doing so merely takes a couple of key-

---

* Chinese assets have included Candace Claiborne, a former State Department employee who passed internal documents to Chinese intelligence, and Dongfan Chung, a former Rockwell and Boeing engineer who became the first American ever convicted of economic espionage.

strokes? The very idea of proprietary data and intellectual property would become a farce. If American companies can't protect their knowledge in a knowledge economy, what would happen to the future of the American economy and the middle class? This is about much more than the fate of multinational corporations; it's about the livelihoods of our families and neighbors. The more China's leaders target American businesses, the more precarious our own lives become.

Then there's the second part of Pardo's warning—in the future, Beijing could use its back-end backdoors to *delete* or block access to data. This is effectively what Chinese authorities already do behind the Great Firewall, disappearing dissidents' emails or snuffing out "subversive" online entries. If China dominates the world's back-end infrastructure, it could do the same thing beyond its borders. An Asian competitor to China's Alibaba, a European political party urging a harder line on China, or an American law enforcement agency investigating Chinese hacks—all could find their databases compromised or wiped clean.

The Chinese government wouldn't even have to permanently delete data to be deeply disruptive. Previously, we've seen China "throttle"—that is, slow down—Internet speeds, as it did to nudge users to their Baidu search engine before Google left China.[84] What if Beijing used its back-end control to dramatically throttle data on a global scale? What if the Chinese government responded to a perceived U.S. provocation by levying a "cyber sanction" against the United States, for example, by blocking access to Facebook across any country with Huawei infrastructure? What if China imposed a digital asset freeze of any data on the network—how would Citibank operate without access to information about its customers?

Third, a back-end adversary like China could *manipulate* data. This is a particularly ominous possibility when it comes to election interference. During the 2016 campaign, Hillary Clinton was criticized for neglecting to visit Wisconsin—a state that Trump ultimately won by fewer than 23,000 votes.[85] Based on its internal modeling, the Clinton campaign had felt good about its chances in a state that was considered part of the Democrats' Rust Belt "firewall." In 2016, it appears those models were wrong all on their own. But imagine if foreign hackers fudged the data in the turnout models, throwing off the campaign's entire strategy? Or surreptitiously switched digits in voters' addresses, so that on Election Day their IDs don't match their information in the voter database? (Indeed, Russian hackers apparently penetrated voting systems in several states in 2016, although there is no evidence that they altered any votes.)[86] Any one of these moves could upend an election. And because this manipulation would take place on the back-end—through an undersea cable or with an implant stealthily inserted into a voting machine—it might prove far harder to identify than any fake news on the front-end.

All that's before we even get to the Internet of Things. In 2020, there were an estimated 30 billion Internet-connected devices, from Roombas to medical hardware.[87] SoftBank predicts that by 2025 there might be as many as 1 *trillion* such devices—about 100 for every person on the planet.[88] These devices will control some of the most sensitive and vital aspects of our daily lives. "It's one thing," notes John Carlin, the former head of the Justice Department's National Security Division, "if a hacker's malware insists on a $300 ransom to unlock your computer; it's something else entirely if the hacker insists on a $300 payment before grandma's home dialysis machine will be turned on again."[89]

In some cases, these smart devices may even begin to merge with our minds. The Pentagon—our old friends at DARPA, the Defense Advanced Research Projects Agency—has begun experimenting with drones controlled by neural signals.[90] Elon Musk's Neuralink is in the early stages of testing human-computer interfaces that would link a person's brain to the cloud.[91] Once considered squarely in the realm of science fiction, these implantable devices could enable someone to effectively have a perfect memory, possessing the unlimited knowledge of an ingrained Google search. And if our brains merge with computers, what might hostile actors accustomed to hacking machines be able to do with our thoughts and emotions? There may come a day when back-end control could extend through the back of our skulls.

The effort to protect ourselves from techno-authoritarians and their ability to access, delete, and manipulate data will shape the geopolitics of our online world and the freedom of our offline world. And here, insight into the future of the twenty-first-century Internet comes by way of a cigar-chomping twentieth-century British historian and political figure.

The Silicon Curtain

At the dawn of the Cold War, Winston Churchill warned that "an Iron Curtain has descended across the continent" of Europe. Today, we face a similar challenge online. Woven together, China's tangle of cables and routers amounts to a Silicon Curtain descending across the globe, separating the free Internet from the unfree. Even as the boundaries continue to be contested, the Internet will become increasingly balkanized.

The precise form of this "Splinternet" is still taking shape. Some have predicted that the Internet will bifurcate between American and Chinese systems.[92] Others, noting the European Union's much stricter privacy protections, foresee "a future with three internets."[93] Josh Wolfe, a prominent Silicon Valley venture capitalist, envisions a world divided into a "U.S.-powered region" consisting of North America, western Europe, and Australia; a "China-powered region" he terms "Chinafrica," to include much of Southeast Asia and Africa, and some degree of control over Russia; and an "unsure region" consisting of India and eastern Europe.[94]

As discussed earlier, the choice governments face today is not between a completely lawless "open" Internet and a "closed" Internet. The choice today is between a democratic Internet, governed by laws substantively and procedurally distinct from autocratic ones, and an authoritarian Internet. At its core, this is a contest for power between two competing systems: democracy and autocracy.

China's Xi has alluded to this contest. "In the realm of ideological and public opinion," he has said, "there are roughly three zones: the red, the black, and the gray. The red zone is our main front, and we must hold it. The black zone is primarily negative; we should dare to confront and greatly compress its domain. The gray zone is what we should try to win over so that it turns red."[95]

To this end, Beijing is offering a bargain to autocrats around the globe. In 2018, Chinese foreign direct investment in Africa hit $46 billion.[96] Addressing leaders from fifty-three African countries in 2018, Xi promoted Belt and Road while calling for a "China-Africa community with a shared future."[97] Often, that shared future entails what Eric Schmidt and his fellow Googler Jared Cohen call a "minerals-for-technology" exchange, as when a Chinese telecom laid thousands of miles of Tanzanian fiber-optic cables and Tanzania granted a Chinese mining company the rights to extract coal and iron several years later.[98]

But the real commodity to be mined is the data. The same year that Xi addressed those African leaders, China's CloudWalk signed an agreement with the government of Zimbabwe to deploy facial recognition technology in Harare, the capital city[99]—one of at least eighteen countries with questionable human rights records to which China has exported its surveillance technology.[100] Hikvision, partly owned by the Chinese government, manufactures cameras used in countries from Senegal to South Africa. Data from those cameras will almost certainly end up in China, and in the Chinese government's AI algorithms. Already, there are reports that data from the African Union's Chinese-built headquarters in Addis Ababa has been streaming to servers in Shanghai nightly for years,[101] and that

Huawei engineers have aided the Ugandan and Zambian regimes by intercepting their political rivals' communications and tracking their locations.[102]

If data is the new oil, controlling the back-end would yield China a never-ending gusher of sweet Texas crude. Whoever's digital sphere is larger will boast more data, bigger companies, and more powerful AI capabilities. Every cable under the Pacific, every camera system installed in an African country, could provide grist for Chinese algorithms. The less powerful members of China's techno-bloc risk becoming what Yuval Noah Harari has termed "data colonies," plundered for raw data like imperial powers once extracted natural resources. Inevitably, the Chinese government will use its enormous leverage to manipulate people outside of China like pieces on a chessboard—a twenty-first-century update to the old tributary system. As Harari says, "When you have enough data, you don't need to send soldiers."[103] The strategic significance of data and information is increasingly stretching beyond the realm of intelligence collection and into the realm of political influence and control. It is challenging old conceptions of national sovereignty.

Years from now, we may look back on this as the moment when China began its cyber-encroachment in earnest, binding other nations behind a Silicon Curtain the way the Soviet Union once imprisoned countries behind its Iron Curtain. And as China's sphere expands, Beijing will be in an unprecedented position to coerce open societies. A dissident like Fei-Fei Wu may waste away, unheard, in the embassy of a nation that can no longer stand for freedom around the world. The back-end battle is not merely a threat to the United States. It's an existential threat to the democratic way of life. The risk is that the long arc of history now threatens to bend toward oppression.

As the globe hardens into dueling digital camps, we will have to ask ourselves hard questions. Is it advisable—or even possible—to fully decouple our supply chains from China? Should a company

based in California bow to Chinese pressure to whitewash search results about Tiananmen Square, knowing full well that failing to do so
will prevent shareholders from reaping the returns of doing business
across the Digital Silk Road? Are Western interests best served by
refusing to market to consumers in China—or will that simply cede
huge portions of the global marketplace to China's tech giants and
their techno-bloc? Are Silicon Valley's behemoths American companies or global ones?

These questions do not have easy answers, but we'd better
start dealing with them. More than that, we'd better start dealing
with them in a unified way. Especially because many of the newest weapons in the Gray War are being fashioned—as we're about
to see—by the coders and app developers of Silicon Valley, largely
removed from Washington's own Gray War calculations. Autocrats
are targeting Americans, and Americans in DC and Silicon Valley are
busy targeting each other. That's a recipe for failure, and it needs to
change—fast. Put another way, as "Obama" warns in that *BuzzFeed*
deepfake: "How we move forward in the Age of Information is going
to be the difference between whether we survive or whether we become some kind of fucked up dystopia."[104]

Chapter 5

THE HILL AND THE VALLEY

Mr. Bezos, I believe you're on mute."[1]

It was July 29, 2020, and Congress was in session. Remotely, that is. Due to the coronavirus pandemic, the hotly anticipated hearing into the antitrust practices of the tech industry was taking place partly by videoconference. On one coast sat the solons of Congress. On the other, the titans of tech—Google's Sundar Pichai, Apple's Tim Cook, Facebook's Mark Zuckerberg, and Amazon's Jeff Bezos. They were connected by the very cables and data streams under scrutiny, with the CEOs displayed in small boxes on a large screen. To avoid playing favorites with the execs' technologies, the hearing was streamed over Cisco Webex.[2]

Ostensibly the hearing was focused on concerns about tech monopolies. But with four of the most prominent tech leaders in the world in front of them, the members of Congress took the opportunity to pursue their own preferred lines of inquiry. Democrats challenged Silicon Valley's representatives on fake news, foreign interference, and the dangers of monopolistic practices. Republicans focused on concerns about the supposed censorship of conservative content. From time to time, the hearings got tense. All of it was compounded by the weirdness of some of the most powerful people in the world being held accountable from the comfort of their own tastefully decorated homes and offices. At one point, the richest man in the world reached for a snack.[3]

In the final hour of the five-hour hearing, Congressman Greg Steube, a Florida Republican, asked each of the tech CEOs if they thought the Chinese government stole technology from American businesses. Several dodged, preferring to answer the question of whether the Chinese government had targeted their *own* companies.

"I don't know of specific cases where we have been stolen from by the government," Cook replied.[4]

"Congressman, I have no firsthand knowledge of any information stolen from Google," said Pichai.[5]

Not coincidentally, both CEOs spoke for companies with significant interests in China. It fell to Zuckerberg—whose platforms are banned on the Chinese mainland—to state the obvious. "Congressman, I think it's well documented that the Chinese government steals technology from American companies," Facebook's founder rightly stated.

When it was Bezos's turn to speak, several seconds of silence ensued. Congressman Steube, followed by Congressman David Cicilline, the chairman of the House Judiciary Committee's antitrust subcommittee, noted that the Amazon founder appeared to have muted his audio feed. When his mic was finally turned on, Bezos echoed Zuckerberg. "I haven't seen it personally, but I've heard many reports of it," Bezos said.[6]

It was an apt illustration of the growing gulf between Washington, DC, and Silicon Valley that goes to the heart of our ability to contest this Gray War. Asked about Beijing's widely known malign activity, several tech giants dodged, one responded appropriately, and one couldn't even be heard.

The hearing was reminiscent of the ones nearly three years earlier, in November 2017, when the general counsels of many of the same tech companies testified before the House and Senate intelligence committees about Russian interference in the 2016 election. On the West Coast, many of us woke up before dawn to watch from the first gavel. After several senators recited grim opening statements, our lawyers delivered prepared remarks full of contrition. Then the political barrage began—and for those of us in Silicon Valley, it left a mark.

Conversations in coffee shops and conference rooms throughout Northern California tended to begin with people rehashing how embarrassing it was that the lawmakers responsible for overseeing the tech industry hardly understood the technology they were supposedly overseeing. But beneath the scoffing was a more troubling realization. For years, Washington had celebrated Silicon Valley, touting it as a symbol of American innovation. Policymakers hadn't always understood precisely what the technology industry was doing, but they wanted us to thrive. Our success begat America's larger success. Yet more recently, each subsequent congressional hearing has illustrated the degree to which the relationship has frayed. Whatever we technologists have contributed to the American economy, we appear to have expended a great deal of the public's goodwill.

Washington and Silicon Valley now feel like two alien spheres. Few of my colleagues spend much time thinking about power politics. Those immersed in the tech bubble read *Recode* and *Stratechery* much more religiously than they read *Foreign Affairs.* In so many ways—especially when it comes to the Gray War—Washington and Silicon Valley are often talking past each other. As the *New York Times*'s David Sanger puts it, "Silicon Valley and Washington are now the equivalent of a divorced couple living on opposite coasts, exchanging snippy text messages."[7]

As with most deteriorating marriages, both sides have their grievances. In Silicon Valley, many technologists feel unfairly maligned for foreign governments' abuse of what the Valley sees as neutral commercial platforms. The world would have thought it absurd, so this thinking goes, if Winston Churchill had blamed the Wright brothers for the blitzkrieg against London during World War II. We would all have been outraged if the United Nations had blamed chemistry PhDs for the Syrian regime's horrifying use of chemical weapons on its own civilians. So why argue that Facebook, Twitter, Google, and other leading firms are responsible for foreign governments' malign political meddling? When did it become the job of engineers and entrepreneurs to mediate a geopolitical conflict? Isn't the root of the issue that foreign governments feel undeterred to engage in this type of behavior? And isn't deterrence the business of the U.S. government?

Marc Andreessen, a leading venture capital investor and cofounder of Netscape, captured the mindset of many in the tech industry in a June 2021 interview:

China has a strategic agenda to achieve economic, military, and political hegemony by dominating dozens of critical technology sectors—this isn't a secret, or a conspiracy theory; they say it out loud. Recently the tip of their spear has been networking, in the form of their national champion Huawei, but they clearly plan to apply the same playbook into artificial intelligence, drones, self-driving cars, biotech, quantum computing, digital money, etc. Many countries need to consider very carefully whether they want to run on China Inc.'s technology stack with all of the downstream control implications. Do you really want China to be able to turn off your money?

In the meantime, the West's technology champion, the United States, has decided to self-flagellate—both political parties and their elected representatives are busily savaging the US technology industry every way they possibly can. Our public sector hates our private sector and wants to destroy it, while China's public sector works hand in glove with its

private sector, because of course it does, it owns its private
sector. At some point, we may wish to consider whether we
should stop machine-gunning ourselves in the foot at the
start of this quite important marathon.[8]

At the same time, many DC policymakers have their own questions. How is it possible, they wonder, that all this tech brainpower can create algorithms that have dramatically reduced child pornography online but can't crack down on disinformation? Do social media companies *really* want to eliminate trolls and bots from their platforms, or would they rather rake in the ad revenue from a larger user base? Why are iconic tech companies still manufacturing their products in China—don't they see that the Communist Party of China is a clear adversary of the United States?

This rupture, as we'll see, is rooted both in recent events and long-standing cultural divides. It's exacerbated by people of different generations, different expertise—even different conceptions of whom they ultimately serve. And it's fueled by a lack of communication and a shortage of institutions linking two of the most important power centers in the world.

You might wonder why it matters that Silicon Valley and Washington aren't on the same page. So what if the wonks in DC aren't up to speed on the latest tech IPOs? And there was a time, perhaps, when this disconnect might have been merely an inconvenience. But as the Gray War deepens, the rift between the Hill and the Valley threatens to place the United States at a severe competitive disadvantage. Faced with autocratic adversaries who commandeer homegrown companies for their governments' own ends, the mutual antipathy between coasts—between the American platforms on which the Gray War is being fought and the U.S. government and military officials fighting that war—has opened a gaping hole in our national defense.

China has civil-military fusion. The United States has tech-government *con*fusion. And while our two coasts battle each other, the authoritarians are taking aim at democracy.

Techlash

Hard as it may be to imagine today, the marriage was once a happy one. Historian Margaret O'Mara calls the U.S. government "the Valley's first, and perhaps its greatest, venture capitalist."[9] During World War II, the University of California at Berkeley was the second-largest recipient of funding from the Office of Scientific Research and Development. In the years after the war, California became the top recipient of federal defense spending.[10] Much of that money—along with many veterans who'd trained as engineers during the war—found its way to Northern California.

As the Cold War intensified, so did the government's investment in new technology. Vannevar Bush, an MIT professor and Raytheon co-founder who had been FDR's "General of Physics" during the war, proposed the creation of a "National Research Foundation" to spur continued scientific advances. It was established as the National Science Foundation in 1950, becoming—along with the Pentagon—a major funder of American research.

One of the primary recipients of the government's largesse was Stanford University, where engineering professor and provost Frederick Terman, a protégé of Vannevar Bush, steadily turned a once sleepy regional school into an information age powerhouse. A founding father of Silicon Valley, Terman set up the Stanford Industrial Park, tying industry more closely to the university. Among Terman's many acolytes were a pair of electrical engineering students named William Hewlett and David Packard, whose story of launching one of the Valley's most iconic computer companies from their garage inspired generations of imitators.

Year after year, defense dollars poured into the cluster of engineering and electronics companies in the Bay Area. In 1954, Lockheed Martin established its Missile and Space Division in Sunnyvale,[11] becoming the largest employer in Silicon Valley.[12] By 1955—fueled by the military's insatiable demand for radios, radar, and other equipment—the $8 billion electronics industry was the third-largest sector in the country.[13] The relationship between defense and the nascent tech industry became symbiotic, to the extent that President Dwight Eisenhower left office warning of the dangers of the "military-industrial complex." That didn't stop the coastal collaboration, however. Jolted by the launch of the Soviet satellite Sputnik, the Pentagon created ARPA—which, in 1969, fatefully linked those Stanford and UCLA computers via the ARPANET.

As if birthing the Internet wasn't enough, the hand of government can be seen in countless technologies we take for granted today. Many of the technologies in our smartphones—microprocessors, lithium-crystal displays, touch screens, cellular networks, and GPS navigation, among others—are the product of government research. Intel, Compaq, and Apple all benefited from federal small business grants. Tesla got off the ground in part thanks to nearly $500 million in loans from the Department of Energy.[14]

Few companies better illustrate what Walter Isaacson calls the "triangular relationship between government, industry, and academia" than my former employer, Google.[15] Sergey Brin's family came to the United States as refugees. His father taught math at the University of Maryland, where the Pentagon funded research into missile trajectories; his mother joined NASA as a researcher. Larry Page's parents taught computer science and programming at Michigan State, one of countless U.S. universities that benefit from federal research funds.[16] Larry and Sergey developed the algorithms that became Google while graduate students at Stanford, as part of a program called the Digital Libraries Initiative. The initiative was partly funded by the National Science Foundation, Vannevar Bush's brainchild.[17]

There were plenty of scuffles between tech and government,

of course—most notably, the Department of Justice's blockbuster antitrust suit against Microsoft in the 1990s. But even then, many technologists seemed to appreciate the generally beneficial role Washington played.

The love affair began to fray in 2013, after a bespectacled National Security Agency contractor stole an estimated 1.5 million highly sensitive documents detailing the scope of the intelligence community's surveillance capabilities and began leaking them to the media.[18] Edward Snowden's revelations shined a harsh global spotlight on an organization so secretive that it was long joked that NSA stood for "No Such Agency." For weeks, articles appeared in the *Guardian* and the *Washington Post* detailing the U.S. government's staggering data collection abilities. One program, code-named PRISM, allowed NSA analysts to collect and search supposedly encrypted communications traveling across the back-end of the Internet—including data centers owned by Google and Verizon. Another highly classified tool, XKeyscore, was likened to "the NSA's Google," enabling users to find reams of data associated with a single email address. It was reported that American intelligence agencies had even listened to the phone calls of German chancellor Angela Merkel, a close American ally.

The fallout came fast and furious. Obama dispatched his White House chief of staff to assuage German outrage. Stateside, Americans demonstrated in upward of eighty cities, from San Francisco to Bluffdale, Utah, home to a massive NSA data facility. "The NSA Has TMI," one sign proclaimed.[19]

Some of the outrage—particularly from the intelligence community—was directed at Snowden himself. James Clapper, the director of National Intelligence, testified that "the nation is less safe and its people less secure" as a result of Snowden's leaks, the vast majority of which revealed America's *foreign* intelligence capabilities rather than any *domestic* surveillance. CIA director John Brennan stated that al Qaeda was "going to school" on the documents that

Snowden had released, while the head of the National Counterterrorism Center warned that terrorist groups were changing the ways they communicated to avoid detection.[20] Noting Snowden's decision to seek asylum in Hong Kong and then Moscow—potentially handing the crown jewels of American intelligence to American adversaries— one former intelligence officer called Snowden "a Patsy, a Fraud and a Kremlin-Controlled Pawn."[21]

I tended to agree with Snowden's critics. While his disclosures prompted a necessary debate over privacy, the way Snowden did it—choosing to steal files indiscriminately rather than avail himself of whistleblower protections—was grossly irresponsible. Not to mention, the first revelations broke on the eve of an important summit between President Obama and President Xi at the Sunnylands resort in Southern California. As the two leaders met, Snowden was holed up in a Hong Kong hotel room—within easy reach of China's security and intelligence apparatus—holding some of America's most vital secrets. Hypocritically, he fled to countries without a free press to leak to our own press. He seemed to have wanted things both ways, criticizing the U.S. government's encroachment on individual liberties from the safety of authoritarian countries that deny those very same liberties.

Some in Silicon Valley shared my reservations. But many didn't. In a culture that lionized hackers and disdained authority, much of the tech community seemed to consider Snowden a whistleblower, a dissident, even a hero. Mark Pincus, the founder of the gaming company Zynga, urged President Obama to pardon Snowden "and give him a ticker tape parade."[22] The engineer and *TechCrunch* columnist Jon Evans spoke for many in the Valley when he wrote, "Dear America, Would You Please Give Edward Snowden His Medal Of Freedom Already?"[23]

At companies like Google that PRISM had targeted, executives and employees alike were incensed by what they considered the U.S. government's dishonorable end run around their own security. "Fuck these guys," one Google engineer wrote in the months after the Snowden revelations.[24] Others tacked up pictures of the NSA's headquarters crossed out, as on a No Smoking sign.[25] Many of these companies had cooperated with lawful government requests for data; the revelation that their own government had nonetheless hacked into their customers' information felt like a slap in the face.

Then, two years later, on December 2, 2015, a married couple— Syed Rizwan Farook and Tashfeen Malik—left their six-month-old daughter with her grandmother and attacked a holiday party at the San Bernardino County Department of Public Health. The shooting rocked the small town in Southern California, killing fourteen and injuring twenty-two more.[26] At the time, it was the deadliest terrorist attack on U.S. soil since 9/11,[27] and police began hunting urgently for answers. Their search ran headlong into a seemingly insurmountable obstacle encased in shiny polycarbonate: Farook's locked iPhone 5c.

Following the Snowden leaks, Apple had revamped its iPhones to encrypt the devices with user-generated keys. In other words, not even Apple itself could access a user's information. According to Apple, attempting every possible combination of a six-character alphanumeric passcode would take more than five and a half years.[28] Fearing a possible third shooter, and worried about the perpetrators' potential links to ISIS, the FBI investigators didn't have that kind of time. Plus, the iPhone's data would be wiped clean after ten wrong attempts.

FBI director James Comey publicly requested that Apple write code to bypass the phone's security features. Eventually, a judge ordered Apple to do so. Apple refused. "Some would argue that building a backdoor for just one iPhone is a simple, clean-cut solution," Tim Cook wrote in an open letter. "Ultimately, we fear that this demand would undermine the very freedoms and liberty our government is meant to protect."[29]

In the debate between the government's responsibility to protect Americans and the tech industry's obligation to safeguard its customers' privacy, each side wielded dueling metaphors. In Comey's estimation, Apple selling encrypted iPhones to terrorists was no different than selling a kidnapper a closet that could never be opened. How could such a danger to the public be tolerated? How many terrorists had law enforcement lost track of because they'd switched to encrypted communication apps and "gone dark"? As far as the government was concerned, allowing unbreakable communications threatened the security of the American people.

The tech industry, by contrast, emphasized the risk of introducing a single vulnerability into a product's security. "You can't really build backdoors in crypto," observed Alex Stamos, then Yahoo's chief information security officer. "It's like drilling a hole in the windshield."[30] Weakening the integrity of the system in even a small way would eventually affect the entire thing. Once they built one backdoor, what was to stop hackers from exploiting it? What if Beijing forced Apple to build a backdoor for Chinese intelligence agencies? Why would users trust tech companies with their deeply private information—their medical records and business dealings—if the possibility existed, however remote, that the information would not remain private? A March 2016 CBS poll found Americans fairly evenly divided, with a slight majority (50–45) favoring Apple unlocking the phone.[31]

The impasse was eventually resolved when the FBI commissioned an outside firm—rumored to be an Israeli company—to break into Farook's iPhone. After all that legal and technical wrangling, the phone contained nothing relevant to the San Bernardino attack or any other terrorist activity. But the divide between coasts lingered and deepened. Officials in the national security and intelligence community cast a jaundiced eye at an industry they no longer considered team players—entitled princelings who had little conception of the life-or-death impacts of their decisions. Technologists increasingly came to view bureaucrats in faraway Washington as an overbearing Big Brother, intent on accessing every scrap of digital debris that might plausibly be connected to national security.

Slowly, Silicon Valley fell from cultural grace as well. In the late

'90s, Apple's ad campaign celebrating "the crazy ones" spoke to those who saw the global potential of tech. By the mid-2010s, shows like HBO's *Silicon Valley* were skewering tech's grandiose, world-changing rhetoric. "We're making the world a better place through software-defined data centers for cloud computing," one geeky CEO promises the show's fictional TechCrunch conference. Another claims, "We're making the world a better place through Paxos algorithms for consensus protocols."[32] Watching the show with my husband, Keith, we'd sometimes exchange knowing glances about which real-life CEO or industry mishap was being parodied.

As the predominant media narrative fell out of love with tech, so did the country's elected representatives. By 2016, the Hill and the Valley confronted what celebrity breakups typically term "irreconcilable differences." America entered a full-fledged techlash.

Democrats were furious that Moscow had manipulated social media to facilitate Donald Trump's election—and even angrier that the industry seemed so blasé about it all. Civil rights groups blasted social media platforms for discrimination in advertising and hiring, and for allowing ugly, allegedly racist comments to proliferate. By 2020, Facebook found itself confronting the largest-ever corporate boycott of a social media company, with brands ranging from Adidas to Verizon registering their disapproval of the platform's role in spreading disinformation.[33] Some lawmakers called for breaking up Silicon Valley's tech giants.

Republicans, convinced that tech was secretly censoring and "shadow banning" conservative voices, began holding contentious hearings, featuring sinister names like Stifling Free Speech: Technological Censorship and the Public Discourse.[34] Devin Nunes, then the chairman of the House intelligence committee, sued Twitter for defamation.[35] Several Republican senators demanded that the Federal Trade Commission look into social media companies' content decisions.[36] In mid-2020, after Twitter had the temerity—for the first time—to affix a gentle fact-check to a tweet from Donald Trump, the president issued a legally questionable executive order threatening to revoke legal protections for social media companies.[37]

By the summer of that year, amid the coronavirus pandemic and nationwide protests for racial justice, a poll found that more than half of Americans had "very little" confidence in social media platforms. Positive opinions of these companies even ranked below *Congress,* typically one of the least admired bodies in America.[38] Ahead of those antitrust hearings in July, the *Washington Post's* Tony Romm compared the showdown to past congressional battles with the big banks and Big Tobacco.[39] Tech, once the darling of DC, was now spoken of in the same breath as the peddlers of pulmonary poison.

This rupture is a major factor in the growing Gray War. In a survey by the Center for a New American Security, nearly 80 percent of top Silicon Valley executives considered the relationship between Silicon Valley and the Pentagon to be "poor" or "very poor."[40] The survey came out just a month after Beijing implemented its National Intelligence Law, the one requiring "any organization or citizen" to "assist and cooperate with the state intelligence work." The Chinese government was drawing closer to its tech companies at the very moment that relationships in the United States were falling apart.

The Marine Serves; The CEO Walks

In 1996, John Perry Barlow, an Internet activist and onetime Grateful Dead lyricist, penned a Declaration of the Independence of Cyberspace. "Governments of the Industrial World, you weary giants of flesh and steel, I come from Cyberspace, the new home of Mind," Barlow wrote. "On behalf of the future, I ask you of the past to leave us alone. You are not welcome among us. You have no sovereignty where we gather."[41] Ironically, Barlow penned his declaration in Davos, Switzerland, home to the World Economic Forum, which draws top global leaders and thinkers—hardly a hotbed of noncon-formity. Yet the twenty-five-year-old manifesto makes clear that even if Edward Snowden had never absconded with the National Security Agency's secrets, and even if Putin's Internet Research Agency had never heard of Twitter, Silicon Valley and Washington were perhaps destined to end up at odds with each other.

While world events have exacerbated and accelerated the split, the Hill and the Valley are also defined by underlying rifts in their makeup—a *generational gap*, an *expertise gap*, and a *cultural gap*. Amy Zagart and Kevin Childs astutely observed this.[42] Collectively, I would argue, these have created an *allegiance gap*, with tech com-panies unsure for whom they're ultimately responsible. Unless ad-dressed, these four gaps will continue to stymie cooperation in the widening war between democracy and autocracy.

The *generational gap* between coasts is readily apparent. At a demographic level, Silicon Valley is run by young engineers from all over the world. Workers aged twenty-two to forty-four make up 61 percent of the American information technology workforce, com-pared to less than 49 percent of the overall workforce.[43] At Apple, the median employee is—by tech standards—a comparatively ma-ture thirty-one. At Google, the age is thirty. Facebook's average employee is twenty-eight years old.[44] "Is 27 the Tech World's New Middle Age?" read one *Fast Company* headline.[45]

This cult of youth is reflected in the legends built around Silicon Valley's iconic founders. Mark Zuckerberg, a decade and a half *after* he dropped out of Harvard to found Facebook, is still just thirty-six years old—and looks even younger. Bill Gates wasn't even old enough to drink legally when he founded Microsoft at age nineteen. Steve Jobs launched Apple at twenty-one.

Compare this to Washington's aging institutions. According to the Office of Personnel Management, the average executive branch employee is 47.5 years old.[46] The average member of the judiciary is around 68 years old.[47] And then there's Congress, where the average member clocks in at 57.6 years old.[48] In the Senate, it's 62.9 years old.[49]

Because Congress largely runs by seniority, the members with real power tend to be older still. In 2020, the average House committee chair was sixty-eight.[50] Chuck Schumer, the Senate Majority Leader, is seventy. Mitch McConnell, the Senate Minority Leader, is seventy-nine. Nancy Pelosi, the eighty-one-year-old Speaker of the House, was born the year before the bombing of Pearl Harbor. During the 2020 antitrust hearings, one e-commerce founder watching from home spoke for much of the Valley when he tweeted, "Being in Congress for 42 years . . . sounds pretty anticompetitive to me!"[51]

Don't get me wrong: I've met with seventy-year-old legislators whom I deeply admire and who are extremely sharp on very complex issues. Yet the world has changed dramatically since these lawmakers' formative years. The defining technology of my twenties was the iPhone. For Mitch McConnell, it would have been the audio cassette. Ted Stevens may not have deserved *quite* as much ridicule for his "series of tubes" analogy, but it's undeniable that having our technology policy predominantly overseen by a group of septuagenarians is not a recipe for a modern, forward-thinking outlook.

Not all the blame lies with Washington, of course. Even if many Silicon Valley founders are middle-aged, the Valley fetishizes youth. Technologists empowered at an early age scoff at the hidebound seniority of institutions like Congress. Many of them work with young people, party with young people, and ask relatively young venture capitalists for money. The flashes of irritation you can see when tech executives are forced to explain their company's technology is partly a product of rarely needing to answer to those with years of accumulated experience. Technologists may chafe that an aging committee chair may not understand every aspect of some newfangled technology, but those same chairs may be acutely conscious of the history behind Moscow's disinformation campaigns or the risks of allowing concentrated economic power to grow unchecked.

Age aside, few lawmakers are well equipped to understand the ins and outs of complex technology. This is a product of the second underlying gap—the *expertise gap*. In 2020, Congress included 11 engineers, 1 physicist, and 1 chemist. The same body contained 192 lawyers and 212 business leaders. There are as many former professional athletes in Congress (six) as there are former software executives.[52] There simply aren't many legislators writing laws who also know how to write code.

The result is frequently discouraging and occasionally downright comical. "Is Twitter the same as what you do?" South Carolina senator Lindsey Graham inquired of Zuckerberg in an April 2018 hearing.[53] Former senator Orrin Hatch, an eighty-three-year-old Utah Republican, asked how Facebook made money without charging users. "Senator, we run ads," Zuckerberg patiently explained.[54] In that 2020 hearing, Congressman Greg Steube, last seen telling Bezos he was on mute, demanded to know why his campaign emails were winding up in Gmail's spam folder.[55] Remember, these are the same legislators who are supposed to be *regulating* the tech industry.

This ignorance comes at a cost. In the midst of the debate over Apple decrypting its iPhones after the San Bernardino attack, Senators Dianne Feinstein and Richard Burr proposed a bill that would have effectively outlawed end-to-end encryption. Kevin Bankston, the director of the Open Technology Institute at the New America foundation, pronounced it "easily the most ludicrous, dangerous, technically illiterate proposal I've ever seen" in nearly two decades of working in tech policy.[56] While Congress once had in-house experts— an Office of Technology Assessment analyzing scientific legislation much like the Congressional Budget Office analyzes the financial ramifications of bills—that expertise was eliminated in 1995 as part of House Speaker Newt Gingrich's shrinking of government.[57] In the Gray War, ignorance isn't bliss. It's dangerous.

Here, again, that ignorance goes both ways. Few Silicon Valley entrepreneurs spend much time in DC or even bother learning how the nation's capital works. Sheryl Sandberg, Facebook's chief operating officer and a onetime chief of staff to the U.S. secretary of the Treasury, is the rare tech executive with extensive experience on both coasts. Silicon Valley CEOs are prepped on how to anticipate and respond to questions in a congressional hearing. But hardly any seem to understand the broader geopolitical questions that occupy members of the political and national security establishment.

These generational and expertise gaps are compounded by a *cultural gap*. Consider how success is seen in each place. In Washington, success often goes to well-credentialed rule followers. Half a dozen representatives and senators are Rhodes scholars. Many attended elite undergraduate institutions and law schools. Some members of Congress are themselves related to previous members of Congress, carrying on decades-long political dynasties.

Silicon Valley, conversely, sees itself as home to rule *breakers*. It's one of the things that made Apple's "Think Different" ad resonate so strongly, and why I found a home in the Valley myself. Like their DC counterparts, many technologists certainly are the product of elite educations. But a surprising number—following in the footsteps of Gates, Jobs, Zuckerberg, Evan Spiegel, and Jack Dorsey—are college dropouts. Convinced that college is a waste for bright and creative thinkers, Peter Thiel has even started a fellowship program, offering $100,000 a year to twenty to thirty such dropouts.[58] Legacy companies are seen less as businesses to be admired than laggards to be overtaken.

The goals of each coast tend to be different as well. Washington—with the obvious exception of Donald Trump and his allies—has historically prioritized maintaining political and economic stability. Funding levels are maintained. Relationships are sustained. Disruption is to be managed. Imagine the chaos if America's top diplomats lived by the tech mantra "Move fast and break shit."

Within the tech industry, disruption is the point. Silicon Valley is suspicious of stability. Tech worships at the altar of growth—driven by Moore's law, which states that computer processing power doubles roughly every two years. The idea of stagnating and sitting in the same place—of holding a position held by your family for decades before—is downright frightening to the impatient digital nomads of the West Coast.

Naturally, these cultural differences manifest themselves in very different organizational structures. Washington often moves at a glacial pace, and it can take hours of congressional debate just to vote on an incremental legislative step. Members might spend decades waiting to move up in seniority.

Out of these hierarchies come complex and confusing bureaucracies. One document laying out the structure of the Department of Defense runs 168 dense pages, with dizzying flowcharts detailing the "Defense Agencies and Department of Defense Field Activities: Common Supply or Service Agency Per 10 USC §191" and "Supporting Tiers of Governance Linking the Corporate Framework with Functional Equities."[59] Throughout the federal bureaucracy, there is a strong emphasis on tradition, protocol, norms, and rigid structures.

The tech industry's more established giants undoubtedly have their own bloat and bureaucracies. But many—if not most—Silicon Valley companies are proudly anti-establishment and non-hierarchical. Meetings often include dozens of employees to ensure that everyone's views are taken into account.* Calendars are shared. Collaboration is practically written into tech's DNA; those oft-mentioned micro-kitchens aren't just a way of keeping employees fed, they're designed to ensure you spend time bumping into your coworkers and kicking around ideas. Silicon Valley prizes horizontal, unstructured environments so highly that for the first six years of its existence, the

---

* It should be noted that leaks—and even concerns about foreign espionage—have led to more siloed organizations, while an influx of government types have brought with them a top-down approach.

open-source software development company GitHub eschewed titles and managers entirely.[60]

This laissez-faire quality extends to all aspects of the Valley's organizational culture. Rarely do start-ups expect you to clock in and clock out. Tech employees simply work when they want, where they want—in the middle of the night, in sensory-deprivation coding booths, on the beach. Office climbing gyms and gourmet kitchens proliferate. Until 2013, Google famously encouraged employees to spend 20 percent of their time "working on what they think will most benefit Google." (Notably, Gmail—which now counts 1.8 billion active users around the globe[61]—originated as a side project, as did successful companies like Twitter and Slack.)[62] Suffice it to say that few start-ups are consulting charts labeled "DoD PAS1 Officials by EX Level" to figure out who they report to or what they should do with their time.

This permissive and freewheeling culture has its drawbacks. In those large and collaborative meetings, too often the focus is on the next quarter and not the next quarter century. Emphasizing individual empowerment can come at the expense of a sense of broader social responsibility. Built by engineers, Silicon Valley often assumes that every problem—from a shortage of affordable housing to a sensitive diplomatic negotiation—has a technical solution. The trade-offs that are the bread and butter of a Congress representing countless constituencies are foreign to the Valley.

When a congresswoman educated in elite universities faces off against a college dropout, or when a bureaucrat taught to stay in his lane runs up against a die-hard disruptor, is it any wonder it seems like they're living on different planets? In many ways, they are. Which leads us to the fourth, and most troubling, disconnect—the question of whom Silicon Valley ultimately serves.

The Business of War

"We believe that Google should not be in the business of war," stated an April 2018 petition signed by roughly 4,000 employees and addressed to CEO Sundar Pichai.[63] At issue was a Google contract, code-named Project Maven, to help the Pentagon deploy artificial intelligence to analyze drone footage. Such a capability could conceivably facilitate U.S. strikes against terrorists or other adversaries, and it rankled Googlers who were drawn to the company's "Don't Be Evil" ethos and still smarting from the Snowden disclosures. Though the contract was quite small—estimated at $9 million to $15 million[64]—its opponents feared it meant Google would effectively be joining the military-industrial complex. Several Googlers even resigned in protest.

The petition called for Google to pull out of Project Maven and announce a policy that neither Google nor any subsidiaries would "ever build warfare technology."[65] A few months later, Google announced that Maven would not be renewed.[66] The company followed up by releasing a set of AI principles, pledging that Google would not develop AI for "weapons or other technologies whose principal purpose or implementation is to cause or directly facilitate injury to people."[67]

That August, however, an explosive article in the *Intercept* revealed the existence of another Google project, this one known as Dragonfly. It was an effort to build a custom search engine for China, one that some Google executives saw as a way to reenter the billion-person market but which critics considered an unconscionable concession to the censorship of the Chinese Communist Party. Suppressed search terms allegedly included phrases such as "human rights" and "student protest." The Dragonfly Android app would have linked the searches to a user's phone number, potentially allowing the Chinese government to track—and possibly even brutally punish—anyone whose search queries raised eyebrows.[68]

About five hundred Google employees signed a letter supporting Dragonfly as consistent with Google's mission to "organize the world's information." But opponents pounced. In October 2018, Vice President Mike Pence declared—to applause—that "Google should immediately end development of the 'Dragonfly' app that will strengthen Communist Party censorship and compromise the privacy of Chinese customers."[69] In an appearance before the House Judiciary Committee a few months later, Pichai was grilled on the project. Once again, several Googlers resigned.[70] I had serious ethical and geopolitical reservations about the project myself, and was skeptical it would ever be allowed to succeed in China in a meaningful way. In July 2019, Google announced that work on Dragonfly would not continue.[71]

While both Project Maven and Dragonfly were ultimately terminated, the juxtaposition of Google refusing to do business with the U.S. military while working on a project that might aid Chinese authorities in silencing free speech offered a stark illustration of Silicon Valley's seemingly mercenary attitude. The episode also raised questions about whether America's leading tech firms even considered themselves "American" after all.

Once upon a time, such questions would have been unthinkable. Companies in America were *American*. Period. At the outset of World War II, William Knudsen, a Danish immigrant who rose from bicycle mechanic to become the president of General Motors, readily answered President Roosevelt's request that he head the war production effort. Knudsen left his company for a $1 government salary,[72] exhorting his fellow auto executives to "out-build Hitler." This they quickly did, becoming the "arsenal of democracy" and churning out vast numbers of tanks, trucks, aircraft engines, and guns to arm America and its allies.[73] Now imagine General Motors telling Uncle Sam on the eve of the Second World War, "Sorry, building weapons is against our ethical principles." It would have been unthinkable. Instead, GM operated under the slogan "Victory Is Our Business."[74]

As we've seen, Silicon Valley owes much of its early existence to the military-scientific mobilizations of World War II and the Cold War. The Valley's electronics wizards helped protect American democracy from Nazi and Soviet totalitarianism. The idea of Raytheon or Lockheed Martin helping the Kremlin build nuclear technology—military or civilian—would have been considered laughable, if not treasonous.

In today's Gray War, however, the battle lines are not so sharply drawn. Kai-Fu Lee notes that Silicon Valley tends to "see the world in terms of 'users' rather than citizens, customers rather than members of a community."[75] Underscoring this point, Microsoft's Brad Smith writes, "Governments serve constituents who live in a defined geography, such as a state or nation. But tech has gone global, and we have customers virtually everywhere."[76]

Too often, tech giants have acted as quasi-sovereign entities. Foreign leaders make "state visits" to Silicon Valley and Seattle. Denmark became the first nation to appoint an ambassador to Silicon Valley.[77] Microsoft has proclaimed itself a "neutral digital Switzerland" and encouraged other companies to do the same. As with Maven and Dragonfly, some tech employees have objected to their employers carrying out government projects. Companies like Palantir and Salesforce have faced a firestorm of controversy, for instance, for selling technology to immigration authorities.

Palantir CEO Alex Karp has been a vocal critic of the tech industry's go-it-alone approach.[78] Karp—who says that "we built our company to support the West"[79]—believes that Silicon Valley might not always agree with the government's policies, but that allowing powerful and unaccountable tech executives to pick and choose which policies to support threatens our democratic system. "We need to make sure the decisions are made by elected representatives and judges, not by unelected engineers running global businesses in a precious corner of a Golden State," he has said. "The U.S. Marine serves; the Silicon Valley executives walk. This is wrong."[80]

In a Gray War environment, opposition to any and all government and military collaboration also poses a very real threat. "American technologists are not required to work on behalf of their nation's defense," the venture capitalist and former intelligence staffer Trae Stephens observes. "But in choosing not to do so, they must recognize that they are ceding an advantage to illiberal rivals and putting the very freedom and openness that they cherish at risk."[81] It was for this reason that—though I was not part of the decision—I strongly disagreed with Google's decision to cancel the Maven contract.

Many tech employees may not want to be in the business of war. But whether they realize it or not, they already are. Just ask Grindr and TikTok.

"Jacob, I Think I Know"

The developers and engineers building a hookup app most likely never imagined that they were reporting for duty on the front lines of a Gray War. But part of what makes this conflict unique—what makes it "gray"—is the extent to which its primary weapons are based on "dual-use" technology, commercial products that can be turned to military ends. The nature of dual-use systems is also what makes the growing rift between the Hill and the Valley so dangerous. It's as if Raytheon were selling cutting-edge weapons to China and Russia—and the Pentagon had no idea. In fact, a bombshell 2017 Pentagon report revealed that Chinese companies had been involved in about 16 percent of all tech venture deals in 2015, part of an aggressive strategy of transferring dual-use technology to America's competitors.[82]

Dual-use technology is not a new concept. Nuclear fission—which can power a city or level it—is dual-use. So are global positioning satellites. Sometimes these technologies can be weapons themselves (commercial drones, for example, adapted for military surveillance or bombing). Other times, the technology being weaponized consists of cameras and sensors—or those back-end cables under the oceans—that allow for data collection. And increasingly, as artificial intelligence comes to play a more prominent role in the functioning of our everyday lives, it's the algorithms and data themselves.

To appreciate just how valuable this data can be in the context of the Gray War, take a minute to think about those of us who come out as gay. For me, coming out was relatively easy. I told my mom I was gay in a garden in Mishmar HaNegev, a kibbutz near Beersheba. It was mid-2015, and I had flown to Israel for my grandmother's funeral a few days earlier. Now, my mother and I were sitting on the grass surrounded by lush tropical plants, right outside one of the kibbutz's small houses. The desert sun blazed overhead. There wasn't a cloud in the sky.

I hated the process of coming out. Just as I didn't feel the impulse to text everyone about my relationships when I was dating women, I was equally reluctant to share the details of my personal life when I started dating guys. I didn't like the burden of disclosure. At the same time, I had also stopped making any real efforts to hide who I was. Photos of Keith and myself dotted social media. So it wasn't a complete surprise when my mom said, "Jacob, I think I know."

"About?" I asked.

"About your attraction to men," she replied.

I braced myself slightly. "And?"

"Is it a phase?" my mother asked. "Do you think you could go back to dating women?" My mom had grown up in a fairly traditional world. As far as I know, she had interacted with very few gay people. So she began asking a lot of earnest questions. *Was this because of some childhood trauma? Was it something she had done?*

"I don't think it's one of those things you choose," I told her. "I'm gay, and I'm in a serious relationship."

I was fortunate. I lived in socially liberal Northern California—where you might be judged for eating unhealthy but definitely not for being gay. When I started using gay dating apps, I wasn't afraid to show my face or use my real name. Within a few months of starting to see men, I had told my sister, and it was a non-issue. After my mom's initial surprise and confusion wore off, she was as supportive as ever. Over drinks in London, I told two of my closest high school friends, "By the way, I'm gay, I'm engaged, and I'd like you to be best men at my wedding." It was that straightforward.

Yet many people aren't so lucky. As recently as 2015, there were still thirteen U.S. states where Keith and I could not have legally gotten married.[83] Until a 2020 Supreme Court ruling, it was still legal for an LGBTQ American to get married on Sunday and fired from their job on Monday. Even today, identifying as gay can get you kicked out of your family, which is one of the reasons that LGBTQ young people in the United States are four times more likely to attempt suicide than their peers.[84]

Abroad—where homosexuality is still criminalized in more than seventy countries—the situation is far worse.[85] In Chechnya, there are officially no gay men.[86] In a dozen countries, same-sex activity is punishable by death.[87]

For countless LGBTQ people—especially those afraid or unable to publicly express their true selves—apps like Grindr are a godsend. Every day, more than 2 million estimated users in 196 countries use Grindr to connect with gay men.[88] They discuss their sexual preferences, open up about their identity, and even disclose their HIV status. The app's acceptance of anonymity—you don't have to disclose your real name or reveal yourself—has made it successful in a community where many people are closeted or live in places where revealing their true identities would lead to pain or persecution. Those wishing to remain discreet can even use a feature that hides the app on their phones.

In 2016, a Chinese gaming company bought a majority stake in Grindr.

Even in the idiosyncratic world of online dating, Grindr and its new owner—Beijing Kunlun Tech Co. Ltd—would seem to be an unlikely pairing. One, writes *Los Angeles Magazine*, "is a gaming company known for high-testosterone titles like *Clash of Clans*; the other, a repository of shirtless gay guys seeking casual encounters." China—whose stance toward homosexuality is often summarized as "no approval, no disapproval and no promotion"—doesn't exactly celebrate gay relationships.[89] Questions abounded. Did the Chinese government care about dating—or data?

It's not an idle concern. Let's say a businessman—married with a wife and children—travels to Louisville, Kentucky, for a meeting. While there, he gets on Grindr, exchanges a few explicit pictures, and has an anonymous fling. Five years later, he flies to Shanghai. Going through security at the airport, Chinese systems capture his name and face and send them to government data centers to be checked against existing information on him—including information pulled from Grindr's databases. The search unearths compromising conversations and images from that long-ago night in Louisville. Soon, there's a knock at his hotel door. A Chinese intelligence agent tells him, "If you don't share your company's proprietary information with us, we're going to send these pictures to your wife and children." Faced with the prospect of his family being destroyed, would handing over a USB drive with a few files seem so bad?

It gets even worse. Recall that Chinese hackers were behind the 2015 breach of the Office of Personnel Management—the one that Congress called "the most significant digital violation of national security to date." Which means that the contents of nearly 22 million SF 86s are almost certainly residing in a database controlled by the Chinese Communist Party. It would be child's play to cross-reference those stolen files with a bureaucrat's Grindr profile. Before long, a government official could be caught in a vise of vice.

In fact, the analogue version of this dilemma—the so-called Lavender Scare—was a hallmark of Cold War hysteria. Already, we've seen a Republican state representative in North Dakota outed by a Grindr user after he voted against an anti-discrimination measure.[90]

There have also been reports that engineers in China have gained access to Grindr users' messages and HIV status.[91] Taken together, it's abundantly clear that the Chinese regime had more than facilitating gay hookups on its mind.

Enter the Committee on Foreign Investment in the United States, known by its classic Washington acronym CFIUS. Chaired by the secretary of the Treasury, the committee also includes representatives from the Departments of Defense, State, Commerce, and Homeland Security. CFIUS has the power to reject foreign acquisitions of U.S. companies if it determines that those acquisitions pose a threat to American security. Yet its processes are largely voluntary. You're expected to notify CFIUS about a potential deal, but not every company bothers. The committee, however, can review deals and demand compliance retroactively—which is what happened to Grindr.

Several years after Beijing Kunlun's acquisition of Grindr, CFIUS stepped in to encourage the companies to consciously uncouple. It's apparently the first time the U.S. government has alleged that foreign ownership of a social media app could pose a security threat. In 2020, Beijing Kunlun sold Grindr to a U.S.-based group called San Vicente Acquisition Partners.

But the story doesn't end there. The San Vicente deal, according to a Reuters investigation, is not all it appears. For one thing, the group was given a sweetheart deal that Kunlun neglected to offer to at least two other bidders. For another, at least one of San Vicente's partners is a close associate of Beijing Kunlun's founder.[92] In the Gray War—as in life—it can be hard to get rid of an ex.

A similar story is playing out with TikTok, the short-form video app that has been called "'Star Search' crossed with 'America's Funniest Home Videos.'"[93] The wildly popular app has been downloaded more than two *billion* times around the world,[94] and counts nearly 100 million American users—many of them teens. Like Grindr, TikTok is owned by a Chinese company, Beijing-based ByteDance.

TikTok's users delight in silly clips of themselves dancing and cooking. But its capabilities extend beyond frivolous footage. Each of the millions of videos uploaded to the app could potentially be grist for refining facial recognition algorithms, allowing Chinese developers to build out their databases of non-Asian faces and voices. In addition to recording which videos you watch and any messages you send on the app, TikTok's privacy policy states that it may collect your location, your contacts, your phone number, and other personal data. This information may be shared "with a parent, subsidiary, or other affiliate of our corporate group."[95]

And that's what TikTok admits publicly. One security researcher found that TikTok transmits an "abnormal" volume of information to its servers, as much as half a megabyte—or 125 pages of typed data—in less than 10 seconds.[96] Researchers have also discovered that TikTok was accessing the contents of smartphone clipboards—where users might paste sensitive information like passwords—every few seconds, which one Israeli researcher calls "very concerning and very rare."[97] These revelations come in spite of a number of technical steps the app's developers appear to have taken to make it difficult for researchers to determine what information it's vacuuming up.[98]

In June 2021, a group of former TikTok employees reportedly said "the boundaries between TikTok and ByteDance were so blurry as to be almost nonexistent."[99] Alarmingly, one employee claimed that ByteDance employees "are able to access U.S. user data."[100]

On top of the data TikTok collects is what it does—or doesn't—display. TikTok professes to be uncomfortable with political content, which has led the app allegedly to censor or flag clips featuring everything from Make America Great Again hats to #BlackLivesMatter content.[101] TikTok has reportedly removed videos of Tiananmen Square's Tank Man, pro-democracy protests in Hong Kong,[102] and content critical of the government's treatment of Uyghurs.[103] One young woman cleverly circumvented censors with a series of viral "makeup tutorials," in which she begins by offering tips to getting long eyelashes before pivoting to educate viewers about the plight of the Uyghurs.[104]

Conversely, the app seemingly privileges pro-China content, which has even led teens in America to attempt to boost their profiles by posting tongue-in-cheek videos praising President Xi. One Texas TikToker saw his number of fans increase from 2,000 to 90,000 after he posted a clip playing China's national anthem and calling Xi "my president."[105]

With so much control over content, what's to stop TikTok from wading into U.S. elections? *Stratechery*'s Ben Thomas speculates that "TikTok could promote a particular candidate or a particular issue in a particular geography, without anyone—except perhaps the candidate, now indebted to a Chinese company—knowing."[106]

Perhaps learning from the cautionary tale of Grindr, TikTok has taken steps to insulate itself from allegations that it is a tool of the Chinese state. The app itself is not available in China, though a sister version is. "Our data centers are located entirely outside of China, and none of our data is subject to Chinese law," a TikTok spokesperson has asserted. "We have never been asked by the Chinese government to remove any content and we would not do so if asked."[107] TikTok employees in China have been stripped of their access to "sensitive data" from overseas.[108] After the passage of Hong Kong's national security law raised the specter of Beijing extending its digital reach into the once semi-autonomous region, TikTok withdrew from app stores in Hong Kong.[109] It even hired an American CEO based in Los Angeles, as well as upward of three dozen U.S. lobbyists.[110]

So far, TikTok's efforts to present itself as wholly aboveboard have been largely unsuccessful. Following a border clash with Chinese troops, India—home to 30 percent of TikTok downloads[101]—implemented a "cyber sanction" by banning TikTok and hundreds of other Chinese-made apps.[112] India's Ministry of Electronics and Information Technology stated that it had reports that these apps were "stealing and surreptitiously transmitting users' data."[113] (To appreciate the wisdom of such a move, suppose that Indian soldiers stationed at the Sino-Indian border had TikTok on their phones; it's plausible that the Chinese military could use the app to determine the exact coordinates of those soldiers.)

TikTok has faced severe headwinds in the United States as well. The Pentagon has banned it on the phones of its personnel. So did the presidential campaign of Joe Biden. Private companies like Amazon and Wells Fargo have likewise cautioned their employees about using the app. In Congress, Democratic lawmakers like Majority Leader Chuck Schumer have called for a national security review of the app, while Republicans have introduced legislation to ban TikTok on government devices.

In August 2020, President Trump invoked the International Emergency Economic Powers Act—which allows the president to regulate international commerce in the event of an "unusual and extraordinary threat to the United States"—to block any transactions with TikTok's parent company, ByteDance (or with WeChat).[114] In response, TikTok promptly sued the Trump administration.[115] TikTok's CEO stepped down after just four months on the job. "The Clock Is Ticking on TikTok," delighted headline writers proclaimed.[116]

The following month, President Trump announced that he had approved a deal allowing Oracle and Walmart to acquire ByteDance's ownership of TikTok. Questions remained, however, over the fluid and confusing terms of the deal.[117] "This unique technology eliminates the risk of foreign governments spying on American users or trying to influence them with disinformation," a draft Walmart press release stated. Then, as if the writer had mashed the keyboard over the frustration and complications of technological transactions during the Gray War, the release stated, "Ekejechb ecehggedkrrnikl-debgtkjkddhfdenbhbkuk."[118]

"One Company, Two Systems"

Fitfully, both the Hill and the Valley have attempted to respond to these confounding new Gray War threats. And each response has underscored the limitations of Washington and Silicon Valley largely choosing to go it alone.

As tensions with China rise, Washington has marginally increased oversight of the tech industry and expanded communication between coasts. In 2015, the Department of Defense established an experimental "Defense Innovation Unit" (DIUx), billing itself as "a fast-moving Department of Defense organization that contracts with commercial companies to solve national security problems."[119] With offices in Silicon Valley as well as Boston, Austin, and DC, the unit was designed to find and rapidly scale up technologies that could be useful to the military. In one case, DIUx took prototypes of a small "quad-copter" drone used on construction sites and brought them to the battlefield. The Pentagon accelerator has also funded a communications device that fits inside a user's mouth (as one headline put it, "Weird Tooth Phone Wins Millions in Pentagon Funding)."[120]

The handful of military and civilian staffers at the Defense Innovation Unit were also intended to be Washington's eyes and ears in Silicon Valley. So is the new Oakland office of the Cybersecurity and Infrastructure Security Agency, created within the Department of Homeland Security in 2018 to address the challenge of safeguarding our nation's critical infrastructure. To some extent, these mechanisms have worked as intended. It was the Pentagon's Silicon Valley outpost that began ringing the alarm in Washington about major Chinese investments in the tech industry, culminating in that eyebrow-raising report about China's growing involvement in venture deals.[121]

Partly to address this worrying influx of autocratic cash, Congress overhauled CFIUS, that interagency body charged with overseeing foreign investments. Dating back to its establishment in 1950,

CFIUS had primarily been concerned with the transfer of defense technologies and critical infrastructure. For instance, the committee scuttled a deal to sell a Chinese mining company a controlling stake in Nevada mines located near U.S. military facilities. CFIUS also blocked a Singaporean company from acquiring Qualcomm, one of a handful of American telecom leaders. More recently, the U.S. government has belatedly begun to recognize that the kind of data owned by companies like Grindr and TikTok could, in the wrong hands, pose a security risk as well. In 2020, Florida Republican senator Marco Rubio called for a review of the attempted sale of vitamin supplement company GNC, which has amassed health data on millions of Americans, to China's Harbin Pharmaceutical Group.[122]

As a result of the Foreign Investment Risk Review Modernization Act, passed by Congress in 2018, transactions "likely to exacerbate or create new cybersecurity vulnerabilities" are singled out for additional scrutiny. Recognizing that 20 percent of the 697 deals that CFIUS reviewed between 2017 and 2019 involved Chinese investors,[123] the new law allows CFIUS to focus on transactions from countries of "special concern." The legislation also broadens the kind of transactions subject to CFIUS review beyond takeovers or majority ownership; under the new law, even a relatively minor foreign investment could trigger a review if it involves an updated list of critical technology. In another wise move, the law increases the size of the CFIUS staff.

However welcome, these improvements fall far short of meeting the magnitude of the Gray War threat. Even after the experimental Defense Innovation Unit was made permanent in 2017—dropping the *x* in DIUx—it remains a minor player in Silicon Valley, with a narrow mandate and minimal clout. Meanwhile, powerful members of Congress with major defense contractors back home look askance at the scrappy unit attempting to streamline traditional defense procurement. There are uncertainties around CFIUS as well: in many cases, Washington simply isn't getting wind of potentially problematic deals until it's too late.

Indeed, the U.S. government still has a huge blind spot when it comes to what's happening with tech companies and their platforms. Congressman Adam Schiff recalls learning about Russian phishing attacks targeting Democratic candidates during the 2018 midterms. Schiff, the chairman of the House intelligence committee, found out from a Microsoft cybersecurity official at a *public* forum in Aspen, Colorado. According to Schiff, the U.S. intelligence community had no idea.[124]

While Washington has made halting efforts to step up its efforts in the Gray War, too many tech companies are still vainly attempting to straddle the fence. Seeking to maximize their profits by operating in the world's two largest national markets simultaneously, American companies with business in China find themselves struggling to comply with systems that are fundamentally at odds with each other. Silicon Valley wants to have its code and eat it too.

The result is an approach that may be called "one company, two systems." This was the model reflected in Project Dragonfly as Google sought to tailor its products to the dictates of the Chinese Communist Party. The U.S. backlash was sufficient to scuttle Dragonfly. But that hasn't stopped other tech firms—lured by the siren song of the Chinese market—from trying.

Zoom, the California-based videoconferencing company, is a case in point. Founded in 2011 by Chinese-born CEO Eric Yuan, Zoom skyrocketed in popularity during the coronavirus pandemic. Quarantined individuals and organizations turned to the intuitive videoconferencing service to keep in touch with family, speed-date, teach students, broadcast religious services, conduct business, and even hold funerals and cabinet meetings. In December 2019, Zoom had 10 million daily meeting participants. By April 2020, that number had spiked to 300 million.[125]

As Zoom struggled to manage this explosive growth, the company came under fire for a range of privacy and security lapses. Malicious hackers hijacked virtual classrooms to display pornography and swastikas across students' screens, a practice now known as Zoombombing. Closer scrutiny revealed that the end-to-end encryption Zoom advertised was a misnomer, allowing Zoom itself to access unencrypted video and audio content from a call.[126] Zoom even admitted that it had "mistakenly" routed non-China traffic through some of its Chinese servers.[127]

Most egregiously, in June 2020, several hundred American and Chinese activists were commemorating the 31st anniversary of the Tiananmen Square massacre when their Zoom videoconference suddenly cut out.[128] The glitch, it turned out, was not technical but ideological. The same week, Zoom shut down the account of the California-based dissident Zhou Fengsuo.[129] Elizabeth Economy, a prominent China scholar, revealed that she, too, had been dropped from a Zoom seminar as she discussed Tiananmen Square, China's brutal oppression of its Uyghur minority, and other topics considered taboo by the Chinese Communist Party. "We all joked about it," she wrote, "but maybe there was no joke to be had."*[130]

Zoom responded that the takedowns resulted only from the company's obligation "to comply with local laws"—that is, China's laws. It apologized for impacting users outside of China, reinstated the accounts of U.S.-based activists, and pledged not to censor non-Chinese accounts. Zoom also announced that it was developing technology "to remove or block at the participant level based on geography."[131] In other words, participants in China would be subject to censorship, but those outside of China would not. One company, two systems.

Yet the reassurance was misleading, because Zoom *couldn't* offer

---

* Indeed, in December 2020, the Justice Department indicted a "China-Based Executive at U.S. Telecommunications Company" for disrupting videoconference commemorations of Tiananmen Square.

meaningful reassurance on these issues. The company, which employs at least 700 R&D employees in China through various subsidiaries, is subject to China's sweeping surveillance laws. Zoom's own filings with the U.S. Securities and Exchange Commission acknowledge that its Chinese employees "could expose us to market scrutiny regarding the integrity of our solution or data security features."[132] That's an understatement.

Zoom already admitted that the Chinese government asked it to terminate the activist accounts linked to the Tiananmen commemorations. What else might Beijing have asked Zoom to do that the company hasn't yet publicly admitted? Who's to say that the Chinese government hasn't tasked Zoom employees with monitoring sensitive American business conversations for valuable insights? Or that a Chinese official hasn't threatened an engineer's family with legal jeopardy if the employee doesn't build a backdoor into Zoom's platform?

To put it plainly, one company, two systems doesn't work. As companies such as Google, Netflix, Twitter, GitHub, and Facebook can all attest, the technical, legal, moral, and geopolitical challenges of simultaneously serving users in the United States and China aren't just substantial—they're ultimately all but impossible.

Consider the technical challenges. Enforcing China's laws by tracking violable content requires a company like Zoom to train a system, commonly referred to as a "classifier," that automatically scans ongoing conversations and deciphers what is being shown and said. Even if Zoom develops a workable policy on such cases—a big if, given the inherent ambiguities—any automated enforcement system is bound to encounter so-called edge cases that will lead it to ensnare content it shouldn't. What happens, for example, when a user in the United States converses across borders with a user in China? Or when a Chinese citizen based in Vietnam uses Zoom for academic purposes and discusses the Tiananmen massacre in Mandarin? It is also unclear how Zoom intends to continue complying with China's local laws and government requests if it fulfills its recent promise of making end-to-end encryption available for all users globally.

Then there are the legal obstacles. Under international law, litigants can use the legal discovery process to compel a foreign corporation to produce information through its domestic affiliates. This means that the Chinese government or any Chinese entity could compel Zoom's U.S.-based parent company to hand over information under the guise of a legal discovery request. These legal intricacies prove sticky enough between two democracies that respect individual liberties and the rule of law. The difficulties grow immeasurably when one of the countries is an authoritarian regime.

There are also major ethical problems. It is becoming harder and harder for Silicon Valley idealists to reconcile—within their companies and externally in the court of public opinion—the conviction that their companies have values with the idea that the products those companies make are value-agnostic. According to one report, Chinese Christians who joined a Sunday worship service via Zoom were later arrested by Chinese authorities.[133] Will Zoom's American employees be content to cite compliance with "local laws" as their platform is used to not only suppress free speech but also to enable the oppression of dissidents and minorities?

In the tech community, this has come to be known as the "Anne Frank conundrum"—a dilemma with particular resonance to me as the grandson of Holocaust survivors. As her famous diary makes clear, it took the Nazis a long time to find Anne Frank's family in the space hidden behind that bookshelf in Amsterdam. What might have happened to her if she'd been writing her diary in similar circumstances today? What if, rather than writing a diary, she was recording her saga on TikTok? And what if an autocratic regime asked TikTok for information that would allow law enforcement to locate her family and send them to camps, as Beijing has done to so many Uyghur Muslims? What if they requested information on a user outside the regime's borders?

Some academics have argued that when governments ask tech companies for user data, the process is typically a two-way negotiation between the government and the company. In other words, the company has the opportunity to push back on the government's request. While this may be true with many democratic governments, it is objectively not the case with the Chinese Communist Party.

Yahoo understands this all too well. In 2004, China demanded that Yahoo divulge the name, email address, and location of Shi Tao, a China-based newspaper editor who had used a Yahoo account to send acquaintances in the U.S. the specific media restrictions the Communist Party had implemented ahead of the 15th anniversary of the Tiananmen Square massacre. Beijing deemed this transfer of information "an illegal provision of state secrets to foreign entities." Executives at Yahoo agonized over how to respond, mindful of the fact that resisting would likely endanger its access to the world's largest consumer market—but that acquiescing might endanger a dissident's life. In the end, the company caved, handing the information over. Shi Tao was arrested, convicted in a two-hour trial, and sentenced to a decade of forced labor.[*][134]

Finally, the greatest weakness of one company, two systems is also the most overlooked: geopolitics. A tech giant can proclaim itself a digital Switzerland, but with governments beginning to eye these companies as proxies and potential targets, American firms will eventually find it untenable to remain impartial. Silicon Valley's relations with Washington are bad enough without also needing to explain why their companies are accommodating autocrats. It's time for Silicon Valley to course-correct the long-held and false assumption that it's possible to separate economics and politics, when China is the only major country in the world that has no separation between the two. It's time to pick a side.

More than that, it's time for our two coasts to stop fighting

---

* A decade later, Yahoo exited China for cost-cutting reasons.

each other and recognize that we face a common foe—the techno-authoritarians in Beijing, Moscow, and elsewhere who threaten to undermine the open societies and open economies upon which we all depend. To win this war, we need to unmute ourselves, rediscover the spirit of shared effort that helped make Silicon Valley the envy of the world, and do what America does best: build the future.

Chapter 6

WINNING THE GRAY WAR

It was a beautiful May day in Tallin, Estonia. I was attending CyCon 2019, an annual international cyber conference hosted by NATO's Cooperative Cyber Defence Centre of Excellence. About 650 cyber experts from nearly 50 countries—hailing from the military, government, academia, and industry—had converged on a hotel for four days of workshops and presentations. Estonia's president, Kersti Kaljulaid, delivered an address on international law in cyberspace. Military cyber commanders from the United States, Germany, and Italy headlined a panel discussion. Tom Burt, Microsoft's vice president for customer security and trust, spoke as well.[1]

From the window of the hotel where the conference was taking place, I could see the spire of an old building. It still bore the hammer and sickle from Estonia's days as a Soviet republic. It was a reminder that, not long ago, Moscow had ruled the whole region. Nor was Russia's influence a distant threat: we were only twelve years removed from Russia's 2007 cyberattack against Estonia.

With this history in mind, I asked an Estonian cybersecurity official about deterrence in cyberspace. What would it take for NATO to consider invoking its Article 5 commitment to come to the collective defense of an ally experiencing a cyberattack? Wasn't Russia engaged in low-grade attacks against Estonia in cyberspace every day? What if NATO conducted similar attacks on Russian networks?

"We want to avoid militarizing cyberspace," the official told me. "We don't want to create an arms race."

On the surface, the response sounded reasonable. But something nagged at me. *If we live in fear of how Russia would react to any of our cyber moves—but Russia remains willing to launch attacks on others—aren't we the ones being deterred? The U.S. economy is over seven times the size of Russia's—would it make sense for a gorilla to run scared of a mouse? What are the consequences of passively permitting these types of gray zone attacks? What future behavior patterns are we inviting by not responding? After all, no policy is a policy—it is one that has been tried and that we have been living with for the better part of the last two decades. I worry it is in many ways the policy that has brought us to this very point of economic and strategic precariousness.*

I've found myself asking these kinds of questions over and over again, whenever a senior official or distinguished thought leader hews to what feels like hidebound thinking. *We can't push back too forcefully on Russia in cyberspace because it might lead to escalation. We shouldn't partner too closely with Taiwan or else it will destroy our relationship with China.*

Some of this conventional wisdom is no doubt wise. I have a great deal of respect for those whose viewpoints are hard-won through years of service. At the same time, I can't help but wonder if the hallmarks of Silicon Valley—the willingness of the tech industry to take risks, move fast, think outside the box, and question old assumptions widely accepted as true—could be applied to yield a more creative, flexible, and effective strategy in the Gray War. What Secretary of State Hillary Clinton said in 2011 is even more apt today: "Right now, the challenges of a changing world and the needs of the

American people demand that our foreign policy community, as the late Steve Jobs put it, 'think different.' "[2]

When it comes to the Gray War, thinking different means fostering a foreign policy culture that considers Peter Thiel's well-known contrarian question: What important truth do very few people agree with you on? Foreign policy experts are less prone to "think different" if they lack any incentive—or are even discouraged—to believe in ideas that contradict long-held assumptions and prevailing viewpoints. Innovation rarely comes without allowing room for ideas initially thought of as somewhat intellectually heretical. Whether at a company or in the government, a *culture* that empowers people to entertain new "what if" scenarios is central to innovation. Ultimately, winning the Gray War requires forging a new consensus that recognizes the scale of the challenge and establishes the technological defense of democracy as a core pillar of our national security. That starts by recognizing the conflict we're in for what it is.

Covering Your Ears to Steal a Bell

In China, there's an old story about a rather simpleminded thief attempting to steal a large copper bell. Finding the bell too heavy, he began to break it apart to carry away the pieces. Naturally, hammering away at the bell was loud—but then the thief had an idea. He stuffed bits of cloth into his ears, muffling the sound, and kept breaking the bell. Of course, this didn't prevent the rest of the town from hearing him. In short order, he was apprehended.

This charming tale gave rise to the expression "covering your ears to steal a bell." The moral of the story is clear: just because you refuse to hear something doesn't mean it's not happening.

These days, it's hard to open the newspaper without coming across news that some Americans seem to think is not happening. The Council on Foreign Relations, for instance, is often viewed as one of America's leading think tanks. Its president, Richard Haass, was a Rhodes scholar at Oxford and served under Presidents Jimmy Carter and Reagan and both Bushes. Under Secretary of State Colin Powell, Haass was the State Department's director of policy planning, the position famously held by George Kennan when he wrote the "Long Telegram" that laid out the U.S. strategy for containing the Soviet Union. Haass might even qualify as the dean of the American foreign policy establishment.

So it was notable when he took to the pages of the *Wall Street Journal* in May 2020 to assert that "A Cold War with China Would Be a Mistake." In Haass's view, those who believe "that confronting China should become the organizing principle of U.S. foreign policy" are making "a major strategic error." Cold warriors "overstate China's ambitions and capabilities alike." Instead, he argued, "the most significant threats that we face are less other states than a range of transnational problems."[3] Onetime director of National Intelligence Dan Coats echoed this more skeptical view in a *Washington Post* op-ed, "There's no Cold War with China—and if there were, we couldn't win."[4] In the pages of journals like *Foreign Affairs*, naysayers from Harvard and Stanford quibble over whether the competition with China meets the narrow definition of a cold war.

Many opponents of a more aggressive approach to China claim that simply acknowledging the Gray War is itself a self-fulfilling prophecy that will lead to conflict. In their eyes, the path to peace lies in greater engagement—and too often, hopes of "engagement" in theory have translated to successive steps of "accommodation" in practice. Chief among these more cautious voices is the Harvard political scientist Graham Allison. Based on a brief passage from the Greek historian Thucydides—"What made war inevitable was the growth of Athenian power and the fear which this caused in Sparta"—in 2012 Allison coined the idea of the "Thucydides trap." Essentially, he argues that when a rising power threatens to displace a ruling one, conflict is the likeliest outcome. The United States and

China thus need "a long pause for reflection," and sustained high-level engagement to encourage a "depth of mutual understanding."[5] In reality, however, attempts at this approach have often resulted in American acquiescence and half measures as China's global technological and economic power grew year after year. Reverting back to such an approach would risk ceding China the precious time it needs to reach a level of strategic and economic *escape velocity* that even the U.S. is no longer able to counter. This would be the greatest foreign policy error in American history.

Graham Allison's view is not confined to Washington and the academy. A friend who runs a large Silicon Valley company—whom I tend to agree with on many things—remarked to me, "It's true that China's doing these nefarious things. But if we just had a competent administration with skilled diplomats, couldn't we just sit at a table and figure things out?" This desire for cooperation and calm is perfectly understandable—admirable, even. Sadly, it's also naive. Too many in the United States are still covering their ears to steal a bell.

If you've read this far, hopefully it's become clear why this denialism is so dangerous. To recap: Moscow is pouring billions into Putin's active measures campaigns, trolling and twisting information to divide and distract the American people and penetrating government computer networks. Chinese military hackers have made a habit of breaking into the systems of American companies, spiriting away critical intellectual property. Even as it swipes American technology, China has blocked nearly all American content platforms within China's borders, including Google, Facebook, Twitter, YouTube, Netflix, Reddit, and GitHub. Through Beijing's mammoth Belt and Road Initiative, companies like Huawei are feverishly installing the network infrastructure that could enable them to access, delete, and manipulate critical data—and which could easily be turned over to the Chinese government. And, of course, Beijing is pouring billions of dollars into cutting-edge technologies like artificial intelligence and quantum computing—technologies the regime continues to bend toward surveillance and horrific oppression.

And you know who sees this conflict clearly for what it is? China's Communist leaders. In the pages of *Politico*, China's ambassador to the United States, Cui Tiankai, might call for a relationship "built on dialogue and cooperation."[6] But in the pages of China's own newspapers, editorials respond to U.S. restrictions on Huawei by asserting that China is "ready for a prolonged 'war' with U.S.'"[7] At Davos, President Xi touts "win-win cooperation,"[8] while in Jiangxi Province he calls for "a new Long March,"[9] comparing the growing U.S.-China rivalry to the grueling journey that ultimately enabled Mao Zedong and the Communist Party to take power. All the while, Xi's government warns of the potential for Sino-U.S. confrontation[10] while urging China "to dare to draw the dazzling sword."[11] When the Australian government requested an international inquiry into the origins of the coronavirus—hardly a major provocation—China blasted Canberra's "petty tricks" and halted Australian beef imports.[12] So much for "win-win cooperation." As Zbigniew Brzezinski, President Jimmy Carter's national security advisor, once warned, "to appeal for peace while at the same time doing everything to prevent it, is a key feature of the relations of a totalitarian dictatorship with the rest of the world."[13]

Fortunately, some American leaders have woken up to the reality of the threat. Republican senator Mitt Romney has called for "likeminded nations to develop a common strategy aimed at dissuading China from pursuing its predatory path."[14] Senate Democrats proposed a $350 billion plan to address China's growing assertiveness, from strengthening American R&D and domestic supply chains to cracking down on human rights violations and training journalists to investigate Chinese influence operations.[15]

A younger generation of national security leaders has been especially clear-eyed about the authoritarian threat from China. As a presidential candidate, Pete Buttigieg—now tasked with secur-

ing America's infrastructure as the secretary of transportation—
repeatedly warned of China's "international expansion of
authoritarian capitalism"[16] and use of "technology for the perfection
of dictatorship."[17] Congressman Mike Gallagher of Wisconsin has
lamented that "for too long the U.S. has looked the other way as
the Chinese Communist Party has waged a new cold war against the
American order."[18] Hal Brands at Johns Hopkins has sounded the
alarm on China for years. National security professionals like Tarun
Chhabra have urged the world to "come to grips with the gravity of
the China challenge."[19]

A number of critics—young and old—take issue with a more accommodating policy of engagement. The University of Pennsylvania
historian and China scholar Arthur Waldron points out that in many
instances accommodation has *caused* confrontation, as established
powers "avert their eyes, seek negotiations, appease, but do not preempt." In more than a third of the cases cited by Allison, such silence created a vacuum that the rising power was all too eager to fill.
Waldron concludes, "Powers that are rising or aspire to rise tend to
move first, for it is only by crippling the powers that would otherwise
crush them can they get ahead."[20]

This more indulgent stance also leads to what we might call fait
accompli politics. When Russia suddenly invaded Crimea in 2014,
there was no real chance to influence the outcome before it was too
late. NATO countries simply woke up to find (loosely disguised)
Russian forces already holding Ukrainian territory. It was already
an "accomplished fact," a fait accompli. At that point, the choice
was whether to go to war over Crimea or not, and Putin gauged—
rightly—that the West would not. The United States and E.U. imposed sanctions, but Putin in effect called our bluff. It was an update
of the old Lenin exhortation to "probe with bayonets. If you encounter mush, proceed; if you encounter steel, withdraw." But what happens if Putin probes too far, miscalculates, and bombs an American
convoy in Syria? What if China were to interpret American ambiva-

lence as tacit consent to overrun Taiwan—the world's preeminent supplier of computer chips? By signaling that the United States seeks to avoid confrontation at all costs, we risk hastening the very confrontation we hope to avoid.

Famously, it was just such an attitude toward Nazi Germany that made appeasement a dirty word for decades. "If only we could sit down at a table with the Germans and run through all their complaints and claims with a pencil, this would greatly relieve all tension," British prime minister Neville Chamberlain asserted.[21] Two years later, Hitler invaded Poland.

Many of my friends and colleagues in the foreign policy community often treat the rise of Nazi Germany and the advent of World War II as historically sui generis—and there are compelling reasons for this. As the grandson of two Holocaust survivors, however, I find it harder to ignore the parallels. Chamberlain's words sound eerily similar to the well-intentioned wish of my buddy in Silicon Valley. Far from leading to the peace that we all want, history shows that one-sided accommodations in the face of an ambitious, autocratic power is as likely—if not more likely—to turn a cold war hot.

In the end, peace is inherently a two-way process. Unless it is pursued by both sides, it is achieved by neither. To be certain, there are costs and risks within adopting a stricter and more confrontational approach; but too often, contemporary debates have overlooked the costs and risks of inaction. Recent experience has shown us that, as China grows stronger, deferring the costs of confrontation can compound over time.

When we encounter a choice in Silicon Valley, we talk about what we want to "optimize" for. A search engine can be optimized for recency or for relevance—sometimes what is most *relevant* is not necessarily the same as what is most *recent*. An iPhone can be optimized for fancy bells and whistles or for compactness. When it comes to China, I certainly hope we can have peace; the consequences of escalating conflict between the United States and China would be horrific for both sides. At the same time, Beijing is clearly betting that a fainthearted America will be too timid to mount a sustained effort to counter China's anti-democratic ambitions. And given a choice between preserving peace or preserving democracy, we should optimize our strategy to preserve democracy. A peace predicated on the United States' abdicating its core interests is not a diplomatic achievement—our democracy and way of life should be non-negotiable.

On a basic level, the American people broadly seem to perceive the growing threat posed by our authoritarian adversaries. In the midst of the coronavirus crisis, a July 2020 Pew survey found that nearly three-quarters of Americans had an unfavorable view of the Chinese government—the most negative since Pew began asking in 2005, and a 26-point increase since the start of the Trump presidency. Fifty-seven percent said they considered China a competitor; a quarter called China an "enemy."[22] Meanwhile, about the same percentage of Americans viewed Putin's Russia unfavorably and considered Russia to be the greatest enemy of the United States.[23] Many Americans are ready to call a spade a spade.*

When President Trump took office, the United States was overdue to revisit calcified orthodoxies surrounding engagement with China. In November 2020, President Obama recognized that "China consistently ran mercantilist policies that violated international trade rules to help build their economy." He added that "if we hadn't been going through a financial crisis, my posture toward China would have been explicitly more contentious around trade issues."[24] As we

---

* While American attitudes may in part reflect President Trump's anti-China rhetoric, such views are increasingly shared across the democratic world. In the UK, Germany, Canada, and South Korea, nearly three-quarters have an unfavorable view of China. In Japan, Australia, and Sweden, over 80 percent view China negatively. The country's own internal analysis found anti-China sentiment globally at the highest level since Tiananmen Square.

think of what the right approach is moving forward, it's important to acknowledge that President Trump's more confrontational stance was directionally needed. His tactical implementation of his policies, however, were often too erratic to be effective.

It's time for a new foreign policy that recognizes the strategic challenge from China for what it is in far less ambiguous terms, reorganizes government around the digital threat we face, builds new tools and institutions to strengthen the Western techno-bloc, and takes steps to deter and disrupt our authoritarian adversaries. Such a strategy might look something like the following:

Elevate and Institutionalize the Digital Defense of Democracy

Declare the Digital Defense of Democracy a Core Pillar of National Security

In May 2015, President Obama traveled to New London, Connecticut, to address the graduating class at the U.S. Coast Guard Academy. The president greeted the cadets with a hearty "ahoy" and cracked a few jokes about waxing the floors. Then Obama got down to business.

"I'm here today to say that climate change constitutes a serious threat to global security, an immediate risk to our national security," America's commander in chief said. He rattled off alarming statistics and pushed back on climate deniers, laying out all the ways American interests were under threat. "That's why," the president declared, "confronting climate change is now a key pillar of American global leadership."[25]

Climate change had long been a priority for the Obama administration. But with his speech in New London, the president signaled that, at the highest levels of government, addressing the threat of a changing climate would be a central feature of his national security policy. The

Pentagon—which had called climate change a "threat multiplier" and laid out a road map for adapting to its impacts—accelerated its efforts to prepare for the challenge.[26] In his meetings with leaders around the world, Obama pressed for action on climate, right alongside more traditional topics such as military and economic cooperation. Secretary of State John Kerry elevated climate diplomacy in his own travels. By December of that year, in my old hometown, 196 countries joined the Paris accords, the most ambitious agreement ever to reduce global carbon emissions and mitigate the effects of climate change.[27]

With his speech at the Coast Guard Academy, Obama put climate change on the national security agenda in a way it hadn't been before. Several years later, in a somewhat similar manner, Secretary of State Mike Pompeo, in a major speech in Washington, elevated religious freedom as a core tenet of U.S. foreign policy.[28]

Now imagine President Biden traveling to Silicon Valley. He could perhaps speak at the Googleplex, at Apple's spaceship-like headquarters, or at Stanford University. Before an audience of technologists and students, the president could explain just how comprehensive and corrosive the front- and back-end attacks on our democracy have been. He could acknowledge the strained tensions between the Hill and the Valley while calling for a new spirit, and new mechanisms, of cooperation. And then—as Obama did with climate—the president could declare that "the digital defense of democracy is a core pillar of American national security," while laying out the steps we'd take to focus on this critical threat.*

The president might follow up by issuing a policy directive formalizing this new approach. A new national cyber strategy could highlight the threat of authoritarian adversaries in cyberspace, in contrast to the most recent strategy, from 2018, which mentions China, Russia, Iran, and North Korea just two times apiece.[29] Ultimately, the centrality of

---

* In fact, Obama did give a speech on cybersecurity at Stanford, in 2015. But he made only a passing reference to "hackers from China and Russia." At the time, cybersecurity was not yet fully understood in a Gray War context.

the Gray War threat should feature prominently, the closest thing in the federal government to a statement of grand strategy.

Our nation's first president, George Washington, cautioned Americans that "against the insidious wiles of foreign influence . . . the jealousy of a free people ought to be constantly awake."[30] Our nation's current president should echo and update that urgent warning.

Build Up Government's Technical Capacity

Statements of national priority are just the beginning. To be effective, they must set in motion an effort to reconfigure the U.S. government to meet the imperatives of the Gray War.

Because personnel is policy, the president could signal the importance of technology—harking back to Nixon's appointment of HP's David Packard as deputy secretary of defense—by appointing tech leaders to key posts. For instance, Eric Schmidt, LinkedIn co-founder Reid Hoffman, Instagram COO Marne Levine, and Code for America's Jennifer Pahlka have all served on the Defense Innovation Advisory Board and might be prime candidates to step into larger roles. The National Security Agency, the Department of Defense, and certain congressional offices are also home to skilled staffers whose expertise warrant higher-level contributions to the policymaking process. William Perry, President Clinton's second secretary of defense and a nuclear expert, understood the most fearsome weapons of the twentieth century; why not appoint high-ranking advisors who understand the most consequential weapons of the twenty-first?

We also need new personnel to ensure that there are high-level officials keeping an eye on one of the most significant threats we face. The creation of a White House National Cyber Director in late 2020 was a welcome step, and the office should be staffed and empowered as needed to elevate these issues and coordinate across the government.[31] New Assistant Secretaries of State and Defense for the Digital Defense of Democracy—and new counterparts in the intelligence community—could ensure that this mission is prioritized in their respective departments and in relationships with friendly governments.

Given the prominent role that foreign investment plays in the Gray War, existing governmental bodies responsible for overseeing these transactions should be strengthened. The 2018 legislation that modernized the Committee on Foreign Investment in the United States is an encouraging start. It created an Assistant Treasury Secretary for Investment Security; that official should work closely with the new Assistant Secretaries and Deputy National Security Advisor for the Digital Defense of Democracy. Going forward, CFIUS should also bulk up with additional staff to properly address the increasing number of transactions being investigated—and to allow for proactive investigations before deals are even submitted.

Moreover, CFIUS's staff must reflect the expertise and skills at the heart of the Gray War. A Democratic congressman confided to me that sometimes—perhaps even intentionally—companies can present a potential transaction in excruciatingly dense terms that mask its potential weaponization. If a firm reports that it is selling technology that generates fun photos of cats, for example, it might get approved. But that technology may be much more profound—involving powerful AI algorithms—and could be militarized. To ensure that the CFIUS has the necessary subject matter expertise, it is vital that its technical staff be enhanced so that they can unpack the potential applications of technology transactions before them.[32] Additionally, CFIUS staff should be located around the country. They should have an especially heavy presence in Silicon Valley, perhaps even embedded within the Pentagon's Defense Innovation Unit. This would help ensure that staffers remain plugged into the Valley and can "see around the curve," recognizing emerging dual-use technologies.

Similarly, in April 2020, the Trump administration issued an executive order updating the ad hoc operations of Team Telecom, that loose interagency body tasked with ensuring the security of America's telecommunications networks. That was the group, you'll recall, that the FCC described as "an inextricable black hole" so "broken" that it took over seven years to conclude that allowing China Mobile to operate in the United States would pose a national security threat. Now formalized under the agonizingly long-named Committee for the Assessment of Foreign Participation in the United States Telecommunications Services Sector—"CAFPUSTSS?" wondered *TechCrunch*'s Danny Crichton[33]—this new committee intends to streamline the process for assessing Chinese threats. In lieu of indeterminate timelines, for instance, there is now a 120-day process for reviewing potential deals. Many of these provisions are welcome and should be formalized with legislation.

To fully meet the Gray War threat, robust congressional involvement is also necessary. Congress should create both House and Senate Select Committees on Cybersecurity, modeled on the existing intelligence committees. Staffed by subject matter experts, these committees would oversee the nominations of relevant officials, consider legislation to strengthen cybersecurity efforts, and receive regular briefings on cyber threats. Their operations should be aided by a revived Office of Technology Assessment, the office eliminated under Gingrich in 1995, so that Congress has access to objective and informed analysis.

Architect a Tech Trade Policy to Strengthen the Western Techno-Bloc

Modernize International Institutions

Just as the digital defense of democracy must be elevated as a national security priority, America's tech trade policy—its international institutions and tools—must be modernized to meet this challenge as well. With China establishing its techno-bloc of nations, bound by Chinese-built networks and tech companies, the United States should demarcate its own techno-bloc of nations operating under democratic principles and using Internet infrastructure free of authoritarian influence. In much the same way that President Harry Truman told NATO that Western nations were establishing a "secure power base" from which to contain and ultimately roll back Communism, a Western techno-bloc must defend itself against autocratic interference from within and combat the global spread of autocracy. In effect, we need a Truman Doctrine—a compact to resist authoritarian aggression and subversion—for the digital age.

To start, NATO should be updated to meet the unique challenges of the Gray War. When I lived in Brussels, I used to drive past NATO's imposing headquarters—squat, stoic, and fenced off— every time I went to the airport. As of 2018, that dreary building on Boulevard Léopold III has been completely renovated, its sleek glass silhouette curving against the sky. It's time to modernize NATO's strategic architecture as well.

"The trigger NATO is built around, a foreign armed attack, is too late in the game," one NATO official told me. Especially in light of Moscow's preference for quick, fait accompli–style incursions, NATO will need to be more agile and potentially more willing to respond to attacks below the threshold of full-on armed conflict.

This is particularly true when it comes to digital attacks. During the Cold War, threats came by way of intercontinental ballistic missiles. Today, the new ICBM is an IBM. Yet in many ways NATO has still not fully entered the cyber era. It is encouraging that Jens Stoltenberg, NATO's secretary-general, has stated that "a serious cyberattack could trigger Article 5, where an attack against one ally is treated as an attack against all"[34]—but NATO's Enhanced Cyber Defence Policy, adopted in 2014, treats such attacks "on a case-by-case basis."[35] The threshold for what constitutes an armed attack in cyberspace should be clarified and codified. Of course, a full-scale military response would not be warranted if Russian cyber vandals took down a few Baltic websites. But NATO should have a clear mandate to respond to cyberattacks—whether through cyber responses of its own or via other means—proportionate to the scale and effect of the initial assault. To its credit, NATO has established several "Centres of Excellence" and a Cyberspace Operations Centre to strengthen cybersecurity and combat disinformation. These efforts should be further expanded and better funded. Making meaningful progress will inevitably require a robust parallel engagement on these efforts with the leadership of the E.U. along with the French and German governments.

Although NATO was founded in response to Soviet expansion—and should remain vigilant about Moscow's designs—the alliance would also do well to factor China's back-end ambitions into its strategic calculations. After all, how can NATO fulfill its stated purpose to "guarantee the freedom and security of its members"[36] if state-owned 5G networks could send European data back to Beijing or a self-driving bus careening through the streets of Paris? As they've started to say in Brussels, "We're not going to China, China's coming to NATO." Our alliance should adjust accordingly.

Likewise, if the first Cold War yielded the North Atlantic Treaty Organization, the Gray War might call for stronger Indo-Pacific alliances. Such alliances could build off existing frameworks like the Quadrilateral Security Dialogue between the United States, Japan, Australia, and India that has flickered in and out of existence since 2007. There were indications in 2020 that Quad nations are newly interested in such a partnership. Japan, India, and Australia have begun discussing a "supply chain partnership" to guard against China's back-end dominance.[37] In a conversation with his Japanese counterpart, Indian prime minister Modi called for a "free, open and inclusive Indo-Pacific region"[38]—echoing Quad language—while in New Delhi, then U.S. deputy secretary of state Steve Biegun invited "any country that seeks a free and open Indo-Pacific . . . to work with us."[39] This Quad could promote mutual defense and information sharing in the Indo-Pacific, with an emphasis on repelling front- and back-end threats. Strengthening the Quad "should enhance the deterrence value of the group toward China," notes RAND Corporation senior defense analyst Derek Grossman.[40]

Similarly, the Western techno-bloc should reassert itself in international forums where technological standards are being hammered out. When China pushes its New IP or its China Standards 2035, the United States should vigorously advocate for rules of the road that keep the Internet free from authoritarian control. Whether in the International Telecommunication Union or the 3rd Generation Partnership Project, American diplomats must realize that writing the rules of the Internet is as essential as writing the code.

Embrace Technological Decoupling as a Security Imperative and Economic Opportunity

Truly securing a Western techno-bloc will likewise require addressing Beijing's back-end dominance of global technology production. The importance of producing weaponry domestically has been clear ever since Alexander Hamilton wrote in his *Report on the Subject of Manufactures* that "provision should be made for an annual purchase of military weapons, of home manufacture" (a line that sadly never got the Lin-Manuel Miranda treatment).[41] It remains the case that most military technology is manufactured domestically in the United States. Yet as we've seen, many of these technologies now rely on supply chains located in China—and many civilian products are in fact dual-use technologies that can be weaponized. We also know from recent experience with the coronavirus pandemic that China has proven willing to weaponize its control over critical supply chains for purely political motives, and capable of doing so.

The solution is to "decouple" American and Chinese technology supply chains with an emphasis on choke-point platforms and products that represent single points of failure for a broader industry or area of economic activity. Technological decoupling was once a heretical idea. But it is increasingly accepted as the direction that trade policies are headed on both sides of the Pacific. The prospect has been discussed with growing seriousness in the pages of *Foreign Policy*[42] and the *Harvard Business Review*,[43] and by the White House: president.[44] Decoupling would not mean ending all U.S.-China trade and economic engagement—given the extraordinary interdependence of many U.S. and Chinese economies—but it would seek to ensure that important American supply chains, particularly for vital technology components, are free of Beijing's control.

For its part, China is already hastening to free itself from its reliance on American semiconductor technology, investing nearly $30 billion in 2019 to develop a homegrown industry.[45] A race to the bottom is rarely welcome, but the reality of the current situation is that technological decoupling is some ways a *race*. If China decouples from the U.S. before the U.S. decouples from China, the former will enjoy an enormous degree of geopolitical leverage over the latter—this outcome should be avoided at all costs.

A key step to achieving supply-chain independence would be to consolidate an Allied Innovation and Industrial Base. Historically, what's known as the National Technology and Industrial Base has allowed for some American defense-related production in Canada, with the UK and Australia added in recent years. This alliance should be expanded geographically, to include a preapproved group of allies like Japan (which is keenly aware of China's growing technological might), France, Germany, and Norway. The foundations for such a bloc are already apparent, whether through that prospective Japanese-Indian-Australian supply-chain partnership, ideas like the Aspen Institute's proposal for a Tech 10,[46] or UK prime minister Boris Johnson's proposal to expand the G7 to a new D-10—a ten-nation democratic coalition that can collaboratively fund and create alternatives to Chinese 5G technology.[47] In late November 2020, the E.U. proposed a Transatlantic Trade and Technology Council with the United States, to establish shared technology standards and co-ordinate issues like screening foreign investors.[48]

Components manufactured in these countries—whether drones or database servers—would be considered as secure as if they were produced in Boston or Virginia. In exchange, every allied country would commit to a series of robust protections against foreign influence. For instance, while countries like Australia and Israel have implemented CFIUS-like mechanisms for evaluating foreign investment, not all allies have; every member of the techno-bloc would have to put similar systems in place.

We should also implement a more detailed accounting of our own supply-chain vulnerabilities. A good start is the Supply Chain and Counterintelligence Risk Management Task Force in the Office of the Director of National Intelligence, authorized by the 2020 National Defense Authorization Act. Greater monitoring of our dependence on Chinese parts should also be a key aspect of a U.S. Trust and Safety Agency, part of a more formal mechanism for collaboration between Washington and Silicon Valley (more on that in the next chapter). The United States will likewise need to find creative ways of using technology to enforce trade laws, to guard against attempts by Chinese manufacturers to skirt U.S. trade restrictions—for instance, deliberately mislabeling "Made in China" products as "Made in Vietnam."

Equally important, we should ensure that the range of technologies shared across the Allied Innovation and Industrial Base expands well beyond traditional military hardware. The weapons of the Gray War are algorithms and data, and our industrial base must take into account the centrality of dual-use technology. That could mean shifting key medical supply chains to Mexico or manufacturing servers in Germany, far from Beijing and its doctrine of civil-military fusion. Naturally, this will also entail reshoring far more U.S. production.

A technology alliance would not only guard against Chinese supply-chain interference, it could also spur greater innovation. For instance, while China is poised to overtake the United States in total R&D spending by the end of the decade, the combined R&D

expenditures of the Organisation for Economic Co-Operation and Development—which includes much of NATO and other key allies— exceed China's by more than 250 percent.[49] Drawing on the pooled resources of an Allied Innovation and Industrial Base would enable a Western techno-bloc to stay ahead of its authoritarian adversaries. Additionally, creating an ecosystem of technological exchange and commerce will soften the blow for allies who, by joining the West's techno-bloc, give up access to lucrative Chinese investment and technology. Such a bloc would preserve the benefits of efficiency and competition while helping American companies wean themselves off their demand-side dependence on the Chinese market. After years of misplaced blind faith in "free trade" that was only free in one direction, the basic principle going forward should be "free trade with free nations."

Decoupling technological supply chains is not without its risks or critics. Former undersecretary of defense Michèle Flournoy has disputed that "wholesale decoupling is realistic or wise," while accepting that "we need to do a better job of using carefully targeted measures to protect our intellectual property and data and to secure and make more resilient critical supply chains."[50] One Deutsche Bank analysis pegs the cost of decoupling at more than $3.5 trillion over the next five years.[51]

But given the strategic and unrelenting threat from China's Communist Party, national security is increasingly outweighing economics. Between the Trump administration's trade war and COVID-19, U.S. companies have already begun unwinding themselves from their Chinese suppliers. Apple has announced plans to begin manufacturing its flagship iPhones in Chennai, India, rather than China.[52] Google and Amazon have shifted server production to Taiwan, while HP and Dell have looked to Thailand, Vietnam, and the Philippines.[53] According to a supply-chain inspection firm based in Hong Kong, the demand for inspections of foreign factories in China decreased 14 percent in 2019, with an according uptick in Taiwan and Southeast Asia.[54]

"We are going to see massive restructuring of supply chains," predicts Alex Capri, a visiting senior fellow at the National University of Singapore's business school. "Globalization as we've known it in the past is over."[55]

As China becomes more and more technologically self-reliant, political leaders in democracies would be well served to appreciate that decoupling is in some ways a race. If Chinese companies no longer rely on U.S. technology and chips before U.S. companies are able to do without Chinese supply chains or rare earths, China will enjoy an enormous amount of economic leverage over the United States. Reconstituting the productive capacity of allied democracies before China achieves its own self-reliance should be a high national security priority.

Deglobalize China's Eye of Sauron By Establishing a Global Network Strategy

Huawei's 5G dominance poses perhaps the greatest threat to the integrity of a free, open, safe, and sovereign Western techno-bloc. From eastern Europe to Southeast Asia, the United States has been fighting a desperate rearguard action to persuade other countries not to install Huawei infrastructure. But what are we offering in exchange? To win the Gray War, the United States should adopt a global strategy to deglobalize China's Eye of Sauron, making a concerted effort to compete with Huawei by establishing a Western 5G alternative. If the Gray War has taught us anything, it's that control is power and technology infrastructure is control.

One approach would be for the United States to acquire an ownership stake in a non-Chinese telecommunications company with a large 5G presence, such as Ericsson or Nokia. Then U.S. attorney general Bill Barr suggested as much in February 2020, rightly noting that "putting our large market and financial muscle behind one or both of these firms would make it a far more formidable competitor."[56] In some ways, this is the quickest and most straightforward solution. Ericsson already sells equipment to all three American carriers—AT&T, Verizon, and T-Mobile—and putting an American imprimatur on a Scandinavian firm could offer an effective counterweight to Huawei. As of the third quarter of 2020, Huawei had 30 percent of the telecom equipment market, followed by Nokia, at 15 percent, and Ericsson, at 14 percent.[57] With the United States actively encouraging its allies to adopt Ericsson or Nokia technology, the Western techno-bloc could close the gap with Huawei—and hopefully overtake it.

We could also encourage a homegrown competitor to Huawei by creating a national 5G network. Currently, the Federal Communications Commission auctions off chunks of U.S. airwaves. These range from low-frequency signals (which can carry limited data long distances) to high-frequency signals (which can transmit tons of data but are easily blocked by walls or trees). Yet the U.S. military owns—and barely utilizes—the coveted "mid-band" spectrum that would be ideal for 5G signals. While leasing this mid-band spectrum would cause free market absolutists heartburn, it would go a long way toward spurring an American 5G alternative. It's also entirely in keeping with historic federal investments in infrastructure and technology. For this reason, leading Silicon Valley CEOs like Eric Schmidt have endorsed the effort.

An alternative solution—known as "virtualization"—would be to develop 5G *software* that could substitute for much of the existing hardware. This would effectively cut Huawei out entirely. By investing in what are called "open radio access networks," 5G providers could shift large parts of their networks from expensive towers to the cloud. While a virtualization approach still needs to be proven workable, it is gaining steam. AT&T has begun to virtualize parts of its network, and the Japanese company Rakuten is rolling out a cloud-based 5G network in Japan. More than three dozen companies, from Facebook and Google to AT&T and Rakuten, have created an Open RAN Policy Coalition. In early 2020, a bipartisan group of senators—including Virginia Democratic senator (and former telecom executive) Mark Warner and North Carolina Republican senator Richard Burr—introduced the Utilizing Strategic Allied (USA) Telecommunications Act, calling for the Federal Communications Commission to devote at least $750 million to invest in developing Open RAN technologies.[58]

Whichever path we take, the U.S. government must be willing to heavily invest in our 5G and 6G strategy. Thanks to the Chinese government's own subsidies, it is estimated that Huawei's typical European bids are roughly a third the cost of its competitors' bids.[59] Even if Western companies were to offer superior technology, countries reeling from the economic shock of the pandemic will be hard-pressed to turn down such attractive offers. So if the United States takes a stake in Ericsson or Nokia, that means offering additional financial support to sweeten the deal for a potential customer. If the government leases military bandwidth to an American 5G provider, the spectrum should be heavily discounted to incentivize the best companies to undertake the project. And if we put our hopes in a virtualized 5G network, the federal government should invest in R&D as well as offering tax incentives to companies like Intel and Qualcomm to manufacture the unique and expensive silicon chips on which these cloud-based networks rely.

Would such an approach cost a pretty penny and involve some state intervention in the private market? Absolutely. But if you hate state involvement in government, you'll hate Beijing taking control of the world's networks a lot more.

Offer Tech as Foreign Aid

Another way to reduce Beijing's back-end influence is to recognize technology and technical infrastructure as powerful forms of foreign assistance. To a limited extent, the United States already does this. For instance, the U.S. Agency for International Development spearheads a Digital Connectivity and Cybersecurity Partnership "to advance an open digital economy and the expansion of secure, market-driven, and rules-based internet use."[60] Yet its focus is largely limited to the Indo-Pacific, and its $25 million funding ($26.5 million initial funding so far) is a pittance compared to what China is spending to install digital infrastructure in developing countries.[61] (Huawei's Kenyan data center alone cost $173 million.)[62]

Going forward, we should appreciate that building this back-end infrastructure—especially in places like Africa—is effectively a zero-sum game with China. If we don't do it, China will. Right now, it's China—and Beijing's "aid" comes with major strings attached, often leaving the recipients mired in debt traps and increasingly dependent on the Chinese Communist Party. Providing assistance and financing that authentically empower recipient governments and local populations could help shift the economic orientations of nations that would prefer to be less entwined with China. Strengthening relationships with resource-rich African nations could also serve as a powerful tool to supply U.S. and allied manufacturers with critical raw materials needed for the production of strategic hardware.

To compete with the massive resources of China's Belt and Road Initiative, the ambition and budgets of programs like the Digital Connectivity and Cybersecurity Partnership will need to be dramatically expanded. Senate Democrats have floated one solution—a nonprofit International Digital Infrastructure Corporation that would offer countries the financial support to buy and install American-made hardware.[63] Daniel Kliman, the director of the Asia-Pacific Security Program at the Center for a New

American Security, has proposed the creation of a Digital Development Bank to help companies from the United States or allied nations improve the digital infrastructure of developing nations.[64] This could include 5G infrastructure itself. It might also include technical training—along the lines of what's provided by nongovernmental organizations like Code for All—to enable a country's population to harness the power of digital technology to launch start-ups or hold their governments accountable.

Deter, Disrupt, and Degrade the Global Ambitions of Authoritarian Adversaries

Draw Lines in the Sand

Any national grand strategy to defend and protect the information environment of the free world should necessarily include a clear, credible, and robust deterrence regime. Deterrence is not a new notion. "Weakness invites contempt," Teddy Roosevelt declared, not long before the United States entered World War I. "Weakness combined with bluster invites both contempt and aggression. Self-respecting strength that respects the rights of others is the only quality that secures respect from others."[65] As a very different war rages, Roosevelt's maxim holds. In dealing with dictators, instilling a healthy fear of digital retaliation is critical to preventing further aggression.

The Gray War is just that—shades of gray. Adversaries endeavor to remain below the threshold that would trigger major retaliation. Attacks go unattributed. Plausible deniability reins. To deter this behavior, the United States should draw very clear lines in the sand—what defense experts call "strategic signaling."

Proponents of unconditional engagement with China have too often assumed that the Chinese Communist Party would simply mirror their own behavior, when China's leaders instead follow a pattern of behavior that's completely at variance with the psychological habits and behavior patterns of democratic governments. Mass-scale intellectual property theft, predatory trade practices, election interference, annexing sovereign territory by force, committing genocide—all should entail consequences and costs commensurate with the gravity of the implications for U.S. interests and values. Foreign adversaries, whether Putin, Xi, or anyone else, should know that engaging in these behaviors will lead to retaliation, through cyber or other means. Naturally, the level of response should be calibrated—cratering a country's economy or destroying its electrical grid because a handful of state-directed trolls tried to get a hashtag trending would be wildly disproportionate.

In the future, the U.S. response can better prevent, preempt, and respond to Gray War acts of aggression by formulating and adopting a comprehensive strategy to "deter by denial" and "deter by punishment." Deterrence by denial entails deterring belligerent behavior by making it too difficult to succeed or unlikely to attain its intended objectives. Deterrence by punishment entails the threat of imposing severe retaliatory costs when a belligerent act takes place. Among other things, this would require a greater ability and willingness to publicly identify the source of the interference. After all, it's hard to hold a country accountable if you won't even name them.

On the back-end, a line in the sand should be the continued autonomy of Taiwan, just 100 miles off mainland China. It is a doubly tempting target for Beijing, home not only to nearly 24 million people that China claims as its own but also to the Taiwan Semiconductor Manufacturing Company. The facility, known as the TSMC, is the source of more than half the world's outsourced semiconductor manufacturing. Silicon Valley may design the chips, but Taiwan produces them. If we're being entirely accurate, the inscription on your iPhone should actually read, "Designed by Apple in California. Chips Manufactured in Taiwan. Assembled in China." And it's not just every iPhone that relies on TSMC chips. So do laptops, video games, and F-35 fighter jets. In light of its centrality to the most important electronic equipment in the world, the TSMC is now the world's tenth most valuable company.[66]

The TSMC had managed to straddle both sides of the Sino-U.S. tech divide, with American companies accounting for about 60 percent of its business and Chinese firms making up another 20 percent. That was until Huawei cut ties in May 2020, following the announcement that TSMC would build a $12 billion chip-making facility in Arizona.[67] Semiconductors "are one of the clearest chokepoints in the global technology trade," says MacroPolo's Matt Sheehan. "There are good substitutes to a lot of other tech, but there's not a good substitute for TSMC."[68] And while today China doesn't control Taiwan or its semiconductor production, Beijing has been busily developing the military capabilities it would need to invade and conquer the island, which it maintains is part of China. All of which is to say, there is a not insignificant risk that China could conceivably control even more of the world's critical technology production.

Alarmingly, in 2020, the Chinese government notably stepped up its provocations. Chinese fighter jets ventured across the Taiwan Strait more than at any point in thirty years, buzzing the island eight separate times in the month after TSMC announced it would build a new $12 billion manufacturing facility in Arizona.[69] Following the reelection of Taiwanese president Tsai Ing-wen on a platform of defending Taiwan's sovereignty, China dramatically increased military exercises and tauntingly compared Taiwan's military to "an ant trying to shake a tree."[70] One former Taiwanese lawmaker, Lin Yu-fang, has observed that "the likelihood of a military clash is much higher than before,"[71] a sentiment echoed by American analysts.[72]

In response, the United States rightly stepped up its own support for Taiwan, sending a destroyer through the Taiwan Strait[73] and an American cabinet secretary (Secretary of Health and Human Services Alex Azar) to Taipei, the highest-ranking American to visit in decades.[74] A bipartisan group of fifty U.S. senators called for a bilateral trade agreement with Taiwan.[75] In 2020, the Trump ad-

ministration declassified the so-called Six Assurances, detailing how
it defines U.S.-Taiwan relations (including provisions dealing with
American support for Taiwan's defense), a notable step and a significant warning to Beijing.[76] Some officials have even urged the United
States to establish formal diplomatic relations with Taiwan,[77] a move
Washington has resisted since severing diplomatic ties with the island in 1979 as part of establishing relations with China.[78]

This shift toward closer U.S.-Taiwan cooperation should be continued. As Richard Haass (whom I agree with in this instance) and
David Sacks have written, it's time to move from a policy of "strategic ambiguity" to a policy of "strategic clarity: one that makes explicit that the United States would respond to any Chinese use of
force against Taiwan."[79]

There is a tendency in some circles to think of a Chinese invasion
of Taiwan as akin to Russia's annexation of Crimea—an unfortunate
violation of international law, perhaps, but not worth opposing at the
risk of war. Given how consequential an invasion of the island would
be for the future of Taiwan's democracy and the global economy,
however, the United States must be unequivocal. We should make
clear that any attack on Taiwan would be met with crippling sanctions
against China but also, if necessary, American military intervention. In
today's cold war, Taiwan is West Berlin. We must act like it.

Other lines will no doubt have to be drawn. But regardless of
where they are laid down, the United States must cut through the fog
of the Gray War and make clear that certain actions are off-limits.
As Flournoy has observed, "The erosion of American deterrence only
raises the risk of Chinese miscalculation."[80]

Institutionalize and Impose Cyber Sanctions to Protect the Free Internet

If protecting the integrity of the free Internet means deterring U.S.
adversaries from attacking it, deterring those adversaries means de-

nying them systemic backdoors into the information networks of democratic countries. And it also means punishing bad behavior. Imposing *cyber sanctions* on Chinese or Russian state-backed technology companies can be an effective foreign policy tool of deterrence by denial and deterrence by punishment. In practice, this means equipping the U.S. government with the authority to restrict or suspend access to technology platforms and products controlled—at a legal, financial, or technical level—by a foreign autocratic government *and* pose a systemic national security risk.

Given its civil-military fusion doctrine, its 2017 National Intelligence Law, and its 2015 and 2020 National Security Laws, China's tech champions would obviously be a natural area of concern and action. The imposition of restrictions on access to technology products that pose national security risks was the subject of much media attention during the debate over whether to ban or compel the divestment of TikTok, the video-sharing social networking service owned by ByteDance.

There are those who argue that such restrictions would be tantamount to replicating Chinese behavior, in essence creating a Great Firewall of our own. In my view, this comparison is wrong. What sets the United States and other democracies apart from authoritarian regimes like China is not that our Internet is ungoverned or that U.S. markets are completely unfettered and China's markets have rules and restrictions. Rather, what sets us apart is that our laws and our Internet are rooted in and reinforce democracy, while China's laws and Internet perpetuate authoritarianism and political control. Our Internet is decentralized and designed to empower people; China's Internet is centralized and designed to control people. That is the fundamental difference.

Indeed, the choice we face today isn't between an open Internet and a closed one. It's between a democratic Internet and an authoritarian Internet. As the Internet increasingly starts to look more like the physical world in terms of how its governed—from California's privacy law to Europe's General Data Protection Regulation—it's important to clarify which kinds of government intervention are and aren't acceptable online. Broadly, the separation between government and the network should mirror the separation between church and state in the United States. Western governments should commit to the principle that they won't implement a Chinese-style National Intelligence Law that obliges every citizen to assist in intelligence operations violating personal privacy, intellectual property, and civil liberties.* And if governments violate this principle of separation—either on the back-end or on the front-end—the United States and allied nations would be justified in taking steps to penalize them. We can do this by expanding our approach to cyber sanctions, which can operate at different layers of the Internet, from the hardware level, to the software level, to the individual IP level.

The U.S. government has already imposed cyber sanctions at the hardware level, banning Huawei technology from U.S. networks and blocking American firms from supplying technology to Huawei. The virtue of developing a principle of separation between the network and government influence and control is that it brings intellectual consistency to what has been an ad hoc effort. In other words, it would make clear that Congress isn't restricting the use of Huawei hardware out of anti-Chinese sentiment or a desire to give Western competitors a leg up. Rather, it would show that Congress is enforcing the principle that governments cannot exert undue control over a network and that rule-breaking has consequences.

Cyber sanctions should also be imposed and (should be enforceable) at the software level when the national security interest of the country is substantially at risk. The government of India responded

---

* In the United States, for example, Apple has a genuine ability to decline or challenge an FBI request to access a suspect's iPhone. They can take the FBI to court over the matter if they believe the request is unlawful. The FBI is not above the law; its authority is constrained by civil liberties and the oversight of an independent judiciary. In China, declining or challenging an information request by the authorities isn't a real option. The National Intelligence Law basically says as much.

to military clashes with Chinese forces by banning 220 Chinese-made applications, not only removing them from app stores but preventing them from being used on phones in India.[81] Imagine if the United States discovered concrete evidence that Chinese military hackers were infiltrating Google's systems and turning over sensitive intellectual property to China's own search giant, Baidu. The U.S. government and its allies might decide to levy a cyber sanction on Baidu, blocking it from being used across the Western techno-bloc.

At the IP level, a Western techno-bloc could essentially apply the *foreign interference policy* we developed at Google on a global scale—this would essentially entail applying a basic principle of non-interference between allied governments and penalizing foreign interference from outside the allied bloc. An American intelligence agency (perhaps alerted by a tech company) might determine that Russian intelligence operatives are spreading disinformation to influence an American election, with all of their posts across Twitter, Facebook, and Reddit coming from the same few IP addresses in St. Petersburg. That information could then be shared across allied nations—similar to how information about terrorist accounts is disseminated—allowing the intelligence operatives to be de-platformed across the free Internet. Get caught conducting an influence operation, and you're not just banned from one platform in one country—you're essentially banned by the entire free online world. We could similarly use this system to detect and punish firehosing—once again, sanctioning malign foreign actors based not on *content* but on patterns of nefarious *conduct*. Modernizing the Foreign Agents Registration Act and expanding it to cover social media actors, as cybersecurity scholar Joshua Fattal has suggested, could also help shift the responsibility for determining foreign influence to the U.S. government and make it accordingly easier for tech companies to justify ejecting malign actors.[82]

Over time, this approach would allow the United States and our like-minded partners to mitigate—if not neutralize—the destabilizing activities carried out by Russia, China, and other authoritarians.

And it would protect the outer bounds of the free Internet against insidious campaigns aimed at deceiving the public. As trolls and bots are increasingly booted off platforms, the chance that you're interacting with a neighbor and not an intelligence operative would go up. Gradually, we might restore a measure of trust online.

Go on Offense to Degrade Their Capabilities, Deter Their Ambitions

Sometimes the Gray War will require the United States to go on offense and degrade the capabilities of adversaries in order to more effectively deter them over time. In 2009, President Obama established U.S. Cyber Command, tasked with defending the military's own systems and, "when directed, conduct[ing] full spectrum military cyberspace operations." CYBERCOM has evolved in the decade since. The 2018 U.S. Cyber Strategy calls on the military to "defend forward to disrupt or halt malicious cyber activity at its source, including activity that falls below the level of armed conflict." It was this strategy that led Cyber Command to take down the Internet Research Agency's servers the day of the 2018 midterm elections and disrupt the massive Russian botnet that could have been used to wreak havoc on the 2020 election.[83]

This aggressive strategy—which General Nakasone, the head of Cyber Command and the National Security Agency, terms "persistent engagement"—should be expanded and made multilateral.[84] The United States could offer military assistance, in the form of specialized technology and training, to help allies and partners defend against and disrupt our techno-authoritarian adversaries. The United States has been criticized, for example, for failing to bomb Nazi trains taking Jews to the gas chambers and for not jamming Rwandan radio broadcasts urging Hutu listeners to murder Tutsis. What if we had blocked those trains or broadcasts? Might a simple technical intervention have made a genocide less horrific?

By the same token—recognizing that China and Russia are already waging digital war against us every day—we could hypothetically support a digital resistance within the autocratic world. The CIA might provide narrowly specialized tools and training for Uyghur activists to disable Chinese facial recognition software in Xinjiang. A Russian opposition could hack and leak embarrassing information on Putin's immense and ill-gotten wealth, putting the Kremlin on defense and exposing the hypocrisy of autocracies. Think of it as *Charlie Wilson's War* 2.0—only with greater safeguards to ensure that these digital *freedom fighters* can't ultimately turn their digital weapons against us.

The advantage of these tactics is that they can be readily deployed. After all, there is an inverse relationship between a weapon's destructiveness and its utility. A nuclear warhead could obliterate an entire city; for that reason, rational and restrained governments would almost never deploy such weapons. Digital militias, by contrast, wage classic gray zone war—causing less destruction and therefore making themselves more useful.

At the same time, a strategy of active digital disruption would represent a major shift in U.S. policy and would have to be pursued carefully. Putin, for one, already accuses the United States of meddling in Russian affairs; actually doing so would only validate his paranoia. But it might also enable the United States to respond in kind to the autocrats' attacks, avoiding major conflict while undermining malicious cyber actors in their own countries. Given the consequences of, say, Russian trolls running roughshod over our democratic discourse, such options should certainly be on the table and vigorously debated.

Make Ourselves a Harder Target

Finally, winning the Gray War demands that we make ourselves a much harder target. This is complicated by the fact that much of our critical infrastructure is decentralized and privatized. Our election systems are a patchwork of state systems. The New York Stock

Exchange is not owned by the government. Nor are many of the nation's hospitals, utility companies, and banks. Virtually all of these systems are connected to back-end infrastructure—like undersea cables—owned and operated by the private sector, not the federal government. Yet an attack on any one of them could be incredibly destructive to the nation as a whole.

The 2018 creation of the Cybersecurity and Infrastructure Security Agency was a positive step toward securing our nation's critical infrastructure. Yet the Cyberspace Solarium Commission observes that "while CISA has worked aggressively to carry out these significant duties, it has not been adequately resourced or empowered to do so." For example, despite all that critical infrastructure in private hands, only 15 percent of CISA's budget is devoted to assisting the private sector.[85] That must be remedied, with greater funding for efforts like helping the private sector recover from attacks.

The Solarium Commission offers many sensible suggestions for increasing cybersecurity, including a third-party authority—like Energy Star assessing products for environmental impact—to certify that new technology complies with the highest cybersecurity standards. That way, when you're buying new appliances, you'll know whether the Chinese military could potentially hack your new Roomba or smart fridge. Workplaces—especially attractive targets like defense contractors—should enhance training to promote good cyber hygiene, including mandating two-factor authentication, requiring regular software patches, and understanding the danger posed by phishing.

At the same time, the United States needs to do a much better job of recruiting tech talent. It's hard to believe in the Valley, where talented engineers and coders are a dime a dozen, the U.S. government has more than 37,000 cybersecurity vacancies.[86] Across the private sector, there are nearly half a million.[87] Each one of those unfilled positions represents an unacceptable gap in our cyber armor.

There are many ways to attract tech's best and brightest. Some in Congress have suggested a Cyber Service Academy, training cyber warriors as we do the air force and the marines.[88] Public-private programs like the Cybersecurity Talent Initiative, which gives newly minted graduates the chance to spend two years working in government in exchange for student loan support, should be expanded. Recognizing that some of the most talented cyber experts have decidedly nontraditional backgrounds, the public and private sectors should make commonsense reforms that relax certain standards. For example, reasonable security safeguards should be maintained, but whether someone graduated college or smokes pot should take a back seat to whether they can help defend our critical systems. Patriotic Americans drawn to Silicon Valley should consider whether their talents might be used to make our nation safer. And, yes, government would probably need to pay salaries at least somewhat competitive with the tech industry—but this would be a small price to pay for our security. Do we really want to learn that Chinese intelligence acquired a treasure trove of sensitive American data because we weren't willing to more fairly compensate a talented cybersecurity expert?

Finally, making ourselves a harder target means embracing healthy policy debate over whether Congress should instate data-localization or data-regionalization requirements to ensure that data on U.S. users and companies remains out of reach for America's adversaries. Here too, that control is power and infrastructure is control.

These are just a handful of ways that we might begin to reorient our national security to meet the Gray War threat abroad. It starts with acknowledging what we're up against. It means taking Beijing and Moscow's provocations seriously without sinking to chest-thumping. And it requires that we think differently about how we organize our government, interact with other countries, and deter and disrupt the autocrats.

But that's just the beginning. Truly winning this war—building a nation that can outcompete and outlast the likes of China—will take an even greater effort at home.

Chapter 7

A *SPUTNIK* MOMENT

The object high overhead was not a bird, or a plane, or Superman. It was a metallic sphere the size of a beach ball, orbiting the earth at 18,000 miles an hour. Looking to the heavens, Americans could see the silvery orb streaking through the night; on the radio, they could hear its high-pitched beeping. The launch of Sputnik, on October 4, 1957, transfixed the world—and sent tremors throughout the United States. "Today a new moon is in the sky," one newscaster intoned.[1]

Under the light of that new moon, the United States saw itself differently. "There was a sudden crisis of confidence in American technology, values, politics, and the military," wrote Sputnik chronicler Paul Dickson.[2] Americans didn't hang their heads, however. Within a few months of Sputnik's launch, President Eisenhower established the Advanced Research Projects Agency to keep pace with Soviet scientists. Then came the National Aeronautics and Space Administration, NASA. In 1958, Eisenhower signed into law the National Defense Education Act, injecting over $1 billion to overhaul American science and engineering education.[3] The legislation passed Congress overwhelmingly—with strong support among both

Republicans and Democrats[4]—tripling funding for science research, supporting and training thousands of new teachers, and revamping school curriculums. Those inclined to math and science flocked to universities, aided by funding that helped produce 15,000 new PhD students annually.[5]

The specter of Sputnik hung over the '60s, a celestial catalyst for terrestrial progress. Lockheed's Sunnyvale-based Missile and Space division soon became the company's largest and most lucrative, part of a tsunami of federal funding flowing into Silicon Valley.[6] Eisenhower was succeeded by a young John F. Kennedy, who rode exaggerated fears of a Soviet-U.S. "missile gap" to the presidency and soon challenged the nation not just to match the Soviets in space but to beat them to the moon by the end of the decade. That goal was achieved in July 1969. Three months later, those two computer terminals were linked on the ARPANET, the first glimmers of today's online world. And Sputnik was the spark for it all. In the estimation of historian Walter A. McDougall, "No event since Pearl Harbor set off such repercussions in public life."[7]

But the story doesn't end there. Fast-forward to 2014, when another Russian entity launched. This time it was not a satellite but a news site. The organization put out "news" in almost three dozen languages, with bureaus as far-flung as Washington, Beijing, Berlin, Cairo, and London. It had a radio show, a 24/7 wire service, and a robust online presence—all useful for pushing a steady stream of disinformation. The mission of this organization and others like it, as Putin put it, would be to "break the monopoly of the Anglo-Saxon global information streams."[8] But stating its purpose so plainly would hardly do for an organization trafficking in falsehoods and spin. So the editor in chief, Margarita Simonyan, named her propaganda outlet after what she considered "the only Russian word that has a positive connotation, and the whole world knows it."[9]

She called it *Sputnik.*

In the decades since the Sputnik satellite jolted the world, it has become a cliché to call for a "Sputnik moment," another outpouring of national purpose and progress to meet an emerging threat. There have been calls for Sputnik moments for education,[10] for digital currency,[11] and, coming full circle, for another Sputnik moment in space.[12] In his 2011 State of the Union address, President Obama urged new investment in renewable energy technology, declaring that "this is our generation's Sputnik moment."[13] The concept has even gone international. One writer asked whether the pandemic is China's Sputnik moment; another called a Chinese player of the game Go losing to an AI algorithm a Sputnik moment for China's artificial intelligence efforts.

Today, we don't just need another Sputnik moment. Recognizing this new world of disinformation and digital warfare, we need a *Sputnik* moment.

Taking place in the shadows, the Gray War has not announced its arrival as dramatically as the launch of "a new moon . . . [is] in the sky." Still, Russian interference in the 2016 election—fueled by propaganda coming from *Sputnik*, RT, and the Internet Research Agency—began to awaken the United States to the front-end threat. Through the coronavirus crisis, Americans have gradually started to grasp the full extent of China's back-end challenge, exacerbated by the massive Russian hack of U.S. systems in 2020. If Sputnik was the starting gun for the space race, *Sputnik* has helped spark a new cyberspace race.

In the last chapter, we looked at the steps that the United States can take to win the Gray War by reasserting itself abroad. But it is equally vital that Americans respond to this threat by rebuilding our national strength at home. As we did with Sputnik circling overhead six decades ago, all of American society must rise to this challenge. So it's worth considering the roles we all can play—which policies our government might pursue, how the tech industry can respond, and what every one of us as Americans can do to counter the techno-authoritarians and defend our democracy.

Invest in American Competitiveness

Reorganize Government

As China continues to surge ahead in everything from manufacturing to artificial intelligence, few things will do more to aid the cause of democracy than making the United States more competitive here at home. In the Gray War—as in sports—the best offense is a good defense.

Yet too often we confront the challenge of what French president Emmanuel Macron has called "strainer states," well-intentioned governments that have so many holes that important objectives fall through the cracks. CFIUS is a good example—a much-needed smart entity for preventing malicious foreign investments but one whose enforcement gaps render it less effective than it should be. We can't win the Gray War as long as our national efforts are drained by holes in our "strainer." Beijing knows this, which is why it eagerly exploits these failings to argue that democracy as a system is outdated and impotent, incapable of coping with contemporary challenges.

Herein lies our opportunity: I genuinely believe that few governments are better equipped than America's to devise new and creative ways to close those gaps and make government effective again. Which is why making the U.S. government less bureaucratic and more entrepreneurial starts with reforming our federal departments and agencies to prioritize economic competitiveness.

There's precedent for reorganizing the federal government to meet pressing challenges. In 1979, the Department of Health, Education, and Welfare split into the Department of Education and the Department of Health and Human Services. Vice President Al Gore was widely mocked for seeming to claim that he invented the Internet,* but it was the task force he spearheaded on reinventing government that led to reforms like electronic tax filing.[14] Following the 9/11 attacks, Congress consolidated disparate offices and agencies into the Department of Homeland Security.† The Trump administration created an Office of American Innovation to recommend "policies and plans that improve Government operations and services, improve the quality of life for Americans now and in the future, and spur job creation."[15]

Today, we should recognize that business—as much as bytes—is central to the Gray War, and our efforts should center on streamlining the constellation of subcabinet components that deal with promoting business, trade, and investment. In 2011, Obama proposed just such an effort, which would have combined half a dozen federal agencies—the Department of Commerce, the Small Business Administration, the Office of the U.S. Trade Representative, the Export-Import Bank, the Overseas Private Investment Corporation, and the U.S. Trade and Development Agency—into a single agency focused on competitiveness.[16] The proposal faltered, but the idea was a good one. The Center for American Progress has also put forward a number of valuable suggestions for reorganizing a Department of Competitiveness, including a Common Application for small business owners and others seeking to engage across overlapping agencies and programs.[17] Former assistant secretary of state Kurt Campbell and Rush Doshi, the director of the Brook-

---

* In truth, Gore stated that he "took the initiative in creating the Internet." This assertion was based on his having written the High Performance Computing and Communication Act of 1991, which Internet pioneers like Vint Cerf have credited with catalyzing the early growth of the web.

† Customs and the Secret Service, for instance, had been part of Treasury. Immigration enforcement fell under the Department of Justice. The Transportation Security Administration agents we see at the airport previously reported to the Department of Transportation.

ings Institution's China Strategy Initiative (of which I'm co-chair), smartly propose "an office that can consolidate information on industrial capacity, supply chains, economic bottlenecks, and import dependence."[18]

A Department of Competitiveness would accomplish a number of goals. It would make clear that promoting *competitiveness*— not just commerce or trade—is a national priority. It would reduce overlapping missions so we can allocate federal resources more efficiently. And it would simplify the dizzying labyrinth of bureaucracy that entrepreneurs and investors face, making it easier for them to grow, innovate, and keep pace with competitors overseas.

Given the imperative of human capital to staying competitive, the Department of Education and the Department of Labor might be combined into a single Department of Education and the Workforce. Currently, certain training programs are funded through the Department of Labor; others through Department of Education Pell grants and loans. But twenty-first-century education is a continuum, and a single entity devoted to that objective would allow us to better support Americans with the skills they need throughout their professional lives. The Trump administration proposed doing this in 2018, and the idea continues to merit consideration.

Ensuring U.S. companies do not inadvertently abet the CCP's global technological plans also means empowering CFIUS with special authorities that account for the unique challenge posed by China's civil-military fusion doctrine. In practice this could translate to endowing CFIUS with the authority to review the national security valence and risks of every single technology investment into the United States by China-based or Chinese-controlled entities. Conversely, the U.S. government may also consider creating new special authorities to block U.S. investments in China or in Chinese-controlled entities out of similar concerns.

Congress could also consider creating what Robert Atkinson, president of the Information Technology and Innovation Foundation, dubs a Congressional Competitiveness Office.[19] Modeled on the Congressional Budget Office, this office would scrutinize legislation with an eye to how bills would impact American competitiveness. In Congress and in the executive branch, we should approach every issue by asking, "How will this better enable us to compete, especially with China?"

Reindustrialize the Free World

In 2011, President Obama attended an intimate dinner in Silicon Valley. At one point, he turned to the man on his left and posed a question. What would it take, Obama asked Steve Jobs, for Apple to manufacture its iPhones in the United States instead of China? Jobs's answer was unequivocal: "Those jobs aren't coming back."[20]

That prognostication has become almost an article of faith among policymakers and corporate leaders in the United States. Even as automation has increased U.S. manufacturing output, the transfer of American manufacturing jobs and factories overseas has continued apace. Yet China's growing exploitation of supply chains and information networks exposes the grave dangers of American deindustrialization. We are facing what political scientists term "weaponized interdependence," whereby a nation such as China exploits control of critical nodes in the global economy to exert geopolitical leverage.[21]

A decade later, the question is not whether U.S. manufacturing can return but whether the country can afford *not* to bring it back. In the Gray War, a deindustrialized United States is a disarmed United States. During the 1970s, the United States responded to OPEC's geopolitical blackmail by creating the Strategic Petroleum Reserve and investing in alternative sources of domestic energy production. In the 1980s, we addressed economic competition from Japan with policies like the R&D tax credit. Now the time has come to build up our domestic manufacturing capacity. If the United States is to secure its supply chains and information networks against Chinese attacks, we need to reindustrialize America.

The notion of implementing a concerted "industrial policy" has long been considered off-limits. Republicans tended to deride the approach as "picking winners and losers." Democrats, in turn, have been mindful that a high-profile failure—like the collapse of California solar company Solyndra, which received a Department of Energy loan guarantee[22]—would be used to discredit government intervention more broadly.

Now, however, it's become clear that the United States' slow drift toward deindustrialization is not a threat to Democrats or a threat to Republicans—it's a threat to the country. In a 2019 speech at the National Defense University, a prominent United States senator dismissed talk of picking winners and losers and called for "a twenty-first-century pro-American industrial policy" to counter China. That senator was Florida Republican Marco Rubio, hardly a wild-eyed leftist. But his ideas were not so different from those of Congresswoman Alexandria Ocasio-Cortez, whose Green New Deal is rooted in massive government intervention targeted at certain industries. Jared Bernstein, who serves as a member of the White House Council of Economic Advisors, has said, "The United States has always helped some parts of the economy at the expense of others. It's time to get it right."[23]

"Getting it right"—striking the appropriate balance between government investment and free market flexibility—will require extensive collaboration between Washington and the private sector. It will also take time and money. Here again, a well-developed strategy is essential. Congress should therefore direct the executive branch to produce a National Advanced Manufacturing Strategy, in keeping with recommendations from the Pentagon's supply-chain resiliency task force[24] and a bipartisan 2019 bill called the Global Economic Security Strategy.[25] This would serve as an answer to Made in China 2025, laying out how to reduce our dependence on Chinese supply chains and revitalize American manufacturing. While many details will need to be fleshed out, a few elements for such a strategy are worth highlighting.

In the early stages of the decoupling process, we should think strategically about which goods should be produced in which places. This means taking inventory of the products most salient to national security—determining which high-tech and vital goods must be produced domestically, which can safely be sourced from an Allied Industrial and Innovation Base, and which goods can still be imported from the global market, including from authoritarian states like China. It's impractical to think that American companies are prepared to bring back to the U.S. the production of every computer, server, and mobile device as well as everything that *connects* to a computer—every camera, every keyboard, every mouse and microphone, and every USB key. But according to Diogo Monica, a leading cybersecurity architect, we don't have to. Instead, he told me, "We can reshore the *right* components" and ensure that others can be easily inspected and audited. This would help build a "minimum viable industrial capacity," sufficient not simply to meet a national emergency but to protect our back-end and wage a long-term competition with China.

For example, since high-performing microchips are indispensable to everything from artificial intelligence to cell phones, a potential initial area of focus could be the production of semiconductors and microchips. Bipartisan legislation by Senators John Cornyn and Mark Warner to create a tax credit for constructing semiconductor factories—the appropriately named Creating Helpful Incentives to Produce Semiconductors (CHIPS) for America Act[26]—is an encouraging sign. So is an Intel proposal for a joint semiconductor foundry with the Pentagon,[27] and the Taiwan Semiconductor Manufacturing Company's agreement to construct a $12 billion facility in Arizona, with the company's chairman citing state and federal subsidies as "a key factor in TSMC's decision to set up a fab[rication plant] in the

U.S."[28] More such investments will be necessary, in the semiconductor industry and others.

Next, there must be a shared commitment—by both the public and the private sectors—to *build* again. For too long, some of tech's brightest minds have fixated on convenience and entertainment, developing apps to disrupt laundry or expedite pizza delivery rather than tackling existential crises. As COVID bore down on the United States, Marc Andreessen, the venture capitalist and Silicon Valley godfather, wrote a widely read blog post lamenting "our widespread inability to build." He called for "aggressive investment in new products, in new industries, in new factories, in new science, in big leaps forward," and concluded that "building is how we reboot the American dream."[29] It is time for tech to take up that challenge—for instance, with more venture capital directed toward advanced manufacturing processes and robotics that would enable us to creatively reshore American industry.

The federal government should stand ready to help. A National Infrastructure Bank—proposed in Congress many times—could establish a public-private entity to spur investment in everything from railways to smart grids. Such legislation has included provisions to "bolster manufacturing in the United States" and promote "economic connectivity," and could be expanded to explicitly include priorities like establishing a national 5G network.[30] Instead of fifty-eight manufacturing-related programs across eleven agencies, a standalone National Institute of Manufacturing—modeled on the National Institutes of Health, as Michigan senator Gary Peters has proposed—could be created to implement a national manufacturing strategy.[31] The government should also greatly increase funding for small businesses, focusing on the same strategically vital industries China has emphasized in its Made in China 2025 initiative.

The tax code also provides ways to renew American industry. For example, we might extend the R&D tax credit to earlier-stage manufacturing research, targeting sectors where China threatens America's edge (as the U.S.-China Economic and Security Review Commission has suggested).[32] Robert Atkinson, the Information Technology and Innovation Foundation president, has floated the idea of a 45 percent Competitiveness Tax Credit for businesses that invest in R&D, skills training, and setting global standards.[33] We should also reform "quarterly capitalism," as many have advocated.[34] By revising the definition of "long-term" investments—taxing investments sold in the first few years as regular income, with a sliding scale that reduces tax rates each subsequent year—we could incentivize shareholders and executives to prioritize bigger projects with higher risk.

A final key element of any industrial policy should involve clustering together hubs of production and innovation. Although policymakers' natural instincts—and political incentives—might push them to spread reshoring investments across the country, some of America's most innovative global hubs have been successful because they are geographically concentrated: Wall Street, Hollywood, Silicon Valley, the Motor City. Geographically concentrated regional hubs unlock network effects that allow them to become growth engines for their state and the rest of the country.

Much like magnets, these hubs attract talented individuals from around the world who self-select to relocate closer to their industry's center of gravity. This clustering of specialized expertise increases the connections between participants of the ecosystem, allowing them to match problems and solutions more quickly than elsewhere. This was the rationale behind more than a dozen manufacturing hubs the Obama administration established, in cities from Detroit, Michigan[35] to Knoxville, Tennessee.[36]

Future efforts should continue to focus on building hubs in the industrial Midwest—for instance in my father's native Ohio—which has been hardest hit by deindustrialization but retains deep manufacturing expertise. A number of notable efforts—including Mark Kvamme and Chris Olsen's Drive Capital, former AOL CEO Steve Case's Rise of the Rest fund, and J. D. Vance's Narya, a venture capital firm, Naryafund—have begun to incubate a Silicon Valley start-up culture in struggling midwestern communities, defying the narrative that says only Silicon Valley can reap the gains of the tech revolution. While the vast majority of tech growth remains concentrated in a handful of big cities,[37] tech investment in middle America has tripled to more than $20 billion over the past decade,[38] leading to talk of a "Silicon Prairie." With the right investments and attention, the government and the private sector could build new high-tech manufacturing centers, simultaneously securing our back-end and enhancing our competitiveness. One day, perhaps, Obama's question to Jobs will be answered by iPhones that say "Designed in Cupertino, Assembled in Youngstown."

Invest in Innovation

Americans are accustomed to being the unquestioned global leader in technology. Over the past half century, however, government R&D spending has declined in both relative and real terms. As a percentage of the federal budget, investment in R&D has dropped from nearly 12 percent (about $400 billion) to about 3 percent ($150 billion).[39] The half trillion that the U.S. public and private sectors spend annually on R&D seems substantial. Yet China, with R&D expenditures growing at more than 17 percent annually, is poised to top the United States by the end of the decade.[40] Notably, about 84 percent of China's R&D focuses on experimental technologies, compared to 63 percent in the United States.[41] While the United States remains at the forefront of technologies like artificial intelligence for now,[42] it is no longer a given that future cutting-edge advances will originate in America.

Simply put, winning the Gray War will require massive new investments in American innovation. Here Silicon Valley has a vital role to play. As government investment has fallen over the decades, corporate R&D has filled the vacuum. The private sector accounts for more than two-thirds of American R&D.[43] Much of that spending comes from tech's biggest names; together, Google, Apple, Amazon, Facebook, and Microsoft spend more on R&D in a single quarter ($29 billion in the first quarter of 2020) than the entire annual budget of NASA.[44] Through initiatives like X—Google's "moonshot factory"—tech firms should continue to ramp up their investments in breakthrough technologies. One of the benefits of bigness is having the resources to focus on so-called blue sky research, where real-world applications may not be immediately obvious. If tech giants are going to remain hugely profitable and influential, they have a reciprocal responsibility to devote substantial resources to pushing technological progress forward.

At the same time, the U.S. government should once again lead the way in R&D. MIT economists Jonathan Gruber and Simon Johnson propose spending an additional $100 billion annually—an 80 percent increase—to match the roughly $250 billion we spent on R&D in the 1980s.[45] This additional funding could be spread across institutions like the Defense Advanced Research Projects Agency, the National Science Foundation, National Laboratories, a new National Institute of Manufacturing, regional hubs, and university grants. It sounds like a lot of money to spend—until you realize that the return on investment might be an additional four million American jobs.

It's not enough to merely increase R&D funding, however. These additional investments should be targeted to the unique needs of the Gray War. This means placing a particular emphasis on next-generation technologies like 5G (or even 6G), artificial intelligence, and quantum computing. The National Quantum Initiative Act of 2018, designed to strengthen quantum R&D investment and coordination, is a heartening indication that the federal government is beginning to take these cutting-edge technologies seriously. In addition, the Trump administration's 2021 budget proposed investing roughly

$2.2 billion in artificial intelligence and quantum computing, an increase of almost a third from the previous year.[46] This is a decent start, but still well short of the $25 billion annually proposed in the Center for a New American Security's blueprint for an "American AI Century,"[47] or the president's Council of Advisors on Science and Technology recommendation to grow federal AI investment tenfold over the next ten years.[48]

Staff "America's Team"

In Silicon Valley, your company is the people who make up the company. No matter how good your technology or your ideas might be, your success hinges on the talent of your team. The same is true of the United States as a whole. If the United States is going to outcompete China's growing tech dominance, we need to staff the team with a skilled and innovative workforce.

Some of the brightest minds and greatest technical talent anywhere in the world still reside right here in the United States. But the rest of the world offers stiff competition. In 2015, American teenagers only scored around the international average in math and science. Over the past decade and a half, the United States produced 10 percent of global science and engineering bachelor's degrees; China produced 22 percent.[49] The number of patent applications in China is now more than double the number in the United States.[50] Meanwhile, there are not enough Americans with the requisite skills to fill growing fields like computer science and electrical engineering.[51]

There is a tremendous need for greater investment in science, technology, engineering, and math (or STEM) education. Just as the launch of Sputnik spurred the passage of the National Defense Education Act, the Gray War demands that we dramatically grow our pool of advanced scientists and engineers. This doesn't mean neglecting the liberal arts: for one thing, we'll need philosophy majors to help us think through how to use AI and other advanced technologies ethically. But it does mean we should think about what the marketplace—and our country—needs to win a conflict fought with algorithms and artificial intelligence.

Where we fall short the most—and where China excels—is in producing a large supply of workers with highly specific technical training. In a 2019 survey by the National Association of Manufacturers, almost three in four manufacturing employers cited "the inability to attract and retain a quality workforce" as their most significant business challenge.[52] This has led to the so-called trade skills gap, which has left vital manufacturing roles such as machinery and welding unfilled. In fact, Apple's Tim Cook has explained that tech companies flock to China not because of the low cost of labor—many other countries now manufacture goods more cheaply—but because China possesses such a high concentration of precision technical skills. "In the U.S., you could have a meeting of tooling engineers and I'm not sure we could fill the room," Cook observed. "In China, you could fill multiple football fields."[53]

If America is going to compete in the decades ahead, Washington must acknowledge these realities and invest in low-cost, skill-based workforce training in vital industries. One proposal, for example, is to have the National Science Foundation create STEM Retraining Boards to link workers to opportunities for reskilling and continuing education.[54] While "learn to code" has come to be derided as an out-of-touch panacea, it is worth considering how we might use technology, like virtual reality, to help workers transition into technical careers. Many of these occupations don't even require a four-year STEM degree. This won't necessarily bring back all the jobs lost to China or elsewhere. But focusing training on high-tech manufacturing jobs can help prepare a workforce that attracts new, potentially higher-paying jobs to the United States and reduces our back-end reliance on China.

Put Out the Welcome Sign for the World's Best and Brightest

Staffing the team also entails overhauling the immigration system. Immigration might be controversial among some Americans, but its value is an article of faith in the tech industry. Each year roughly 40 percent of Stanford graduate engineering degrees are awarded to international students.[55] According to MacroPolo, more than two-thirds of top AI researchers in the United States earned their undergraduate degrees abroad—and the majority of China's best AI graduates study, work, and live in the United States.[56] Over half of the twenty-five most valuable tech companies have at least one founder who is an immigrant or the child of immigrants.[57] Elon Musk emigrated from South Africa. Sundar Pichai and Satya Nadella emigrated from India. Sergey Brin emigrated from Russia. Steve Jobs was the son of a Syrian immigrant. If the United States is a nation of immigrants, Silicon Valley may well be the capital of our immigrant nation.[*]

For years, however, our immigration system has made it exceedingly difficult to attract the world's top talent. Ask anyone at a tech company, and they can tell you stories of green cards delayed, work visas in limbo, and brilliant engineers turned away due to byzantine and archaic immigration laws. The Trump administration's nativist policies only exacerbated this dynamic. Every year from 2016 to 2020, the United States admitted 43,000 fewer legal immigrants (on average) than the year before.[58] Over the course of the Trump administration, legal immigration was cut nearly in half.[59] Using the coronavirus as a pretext, Trump even suspended work visas, including the H-1B visas for skilled workers on which most tech companies rely,[60] and which have been capped at 85,000 since 1990.[61]

---

[*] While we tend to focus on "high-skilled" immigration, Silicon Valley was likewise built by "low-skilled" workers who assembled many of the tech industry's best-known products. In the 1980s, the Immigration and Naturalization Service estimated that perhaps a quarter of Silicon Valley workers were undocumented.

If we want to attract the best minds to our shores, America needs to put out the welcome sign once more. To start, that means significantly raising, if not removing entirely, the H-1B cap, which is typically met within the first week applicants can file for a visa.[62] As is often said in Silicon Valley, instead of training and then chasing away top students, we should be stapling green cards to university diplomas.

Yet training international students has begun to raise serious concerns—in particular, fears that the Chinese government is sending students to the United States to "steal" advances in sensitive dual-use technologies. In 2020, the Trump administration canceled the visas of roughly 3,000 Chinese students in the United States who had previously studied at universities tied to the Chinese military[63] (less than 1 percent of the 370,000 or so Chinese students in the United States).[64] Senator Tom Cotton has proposed banning Chinese students from studying certain fields entirely. "If Chinese students want to come here and study Shakespeare and the *Federalist Papers*," he said, "that's what they need to learn from America. They don't need to learn quantum computing."[65]

But such a draconian approach risks closing our doors to some of the world's best researchers and encouraging anti-Asian xenophobia. As Lisa Li, a Johns Hopkins–trained Chinese engineer, put it, "Sacrificing international students is killing the goose that lays the golden egg. It will eventually destroy the future competitiveness of America."[66] According to a 2020 survey by a Chinese education company, the United States for the first time is no longer the top-choice destination for Chinese students, having been surpassed by the UK.[67]

To be sure, there are valid security concerns. China *does* mine Western universities for research, a strategy the People's Liberation Army calls "picking flowers in foreign lands to make honey in China."[68] Its "Thousand Talents" program seeks to recruit top American researchers to China. In 2020, the Department of Justice charged Yanqing Ye, a Boston University student who hid her affiliation with the Chinese military, with acting as a foreign agent.[69] During the Cold War, it would have been absurd for U.S. colleges and universities to train Soviet scientists in missile technology. Why would we train China's artificial intelligence researchers during the Gray War?

At the same time, it is clearly in America's national interest to attract bright Chinese students—especially because so many of them remain in the United States and contribute to American society after they graduate. (In fact, nine out of ten Chinese doctoral students stay at least five years after graduation.)[70] If implemented with the right safeguards, proactively denying China's technology and military sectors from its most talented minds is in America's long-term strategic interest. Moreover, as the United States challenges the autocrats, our openness and tolerance serve as a critical source of American "soft power." In fact, a 2020 Stanford study found that "Chinese students who study in the United States are more predisposed to favor liberal democracy than their peers in China," while "anti-Asian discrimination significantly reduces their belief that political reform is desirable for China and increases their support for authoritarian rule."[71]

The key is to avoid shutting off the flow of Chinese students to the United States, while also limiting the ability of the small number of students involved in malicious activities to make inroads. This could mean, as the U.S.-China Economic and Security Review Commission recommends, creating a higher education advisory board within the FBI to evaluate the issue and regularly "review the adequacy of protections for sensitive technologies and research."[72] It will also mean that U.S. universities will need to cooperate closely with the government to ensure targeted screening of Chinese students, without engaging in careless, xenophobic restrictions.

We should not ignore the potential for damaging espionage that saps our technological edge. But neither can we abandon the American ideals that have made us strong.

Reimagine Tech's Role

Strengthen Cooperation Between the Hill and the Valley

In 2017, I recall attending a meeting on disinformation at a prominent think tank. The meeting took place in DC, a few thousand miles
from Silicon Valley—and it showed. The twenty or so people assembled were extremely bright and competent members of the DC
establishment. But I was struck by how superficial their understanding of the technological issues were. It underscored that for all the
linkages between Silicon Valley and Washington—from political
fundraisers to federal funding—there simply aren't sufficient channels for communicating between coasts. If the Hill and the Valley
are like a couple in a bad marriage, we're in desperate need of some
particularly good couples counseling.

To further these exchanges, the United States government should
set up a formal mechanism for collaboration—the U.S. Trust and
Safety Agency mentioned earlier. (I've had the privilege to brain-
storm with a number of senators, including Cory Booker and Richard Blumenthal, on legislation ideas to do just that.) Such an agency
would be based in the Bay Area, becoming the federal government's
outpost in the tech industry, almost like a kind of National Lab. It
would be staffed by government officials and technical experts, continuously watching for emerging civilian technologies, stress-testing
ways dual-use technology could be weaponized by malicious actors,
and serving as a liaison to CFIUS as it evaluates foreign tech transactions. This Trust and Safety Agency would likewise study and survey companies whose supply chains expose them to risks from the
Chinese government. The agency would submit regular reports to
Congress, including recommendations for new laws to account for
new technologies.

A final element of a U.S. Trust and Safety Agency would be an
Information Sharing and Analysis Center, or ISAC, building on the

provision for a Social Media Data and Threat Analysis Center that was authorized in the 2020 National Defense Authorization Act. Much like the Centers for Disease Control gathers information on potential pandemics, this bicoastal observatory would gather information on actors that threaten the integrity of our networks. This agency might liaise with or absorb some of the functions of institutions like the Department of Homeland Security's Cybersecurity and Infrastructure Security Agency and the National Cybersecurity and Communications Integration Center, which do important work but are hampered by their distance from Silicon Valley (though CISA does have a Bay Area office). It would include penalties—such as the Federal Trade Commission levying substantial fines for "unfair and deceptive practices"—to ensure that companies like Google, Facebook, and Twitter are sharing that information with the federal government.

For such entities to work, however, we must also do more to cultivate personnel with ties to both worlds. While countless former DC staffers have transitioned to the West Coast, the reverse is less typical. John Doerr, the prominent venture capitalist, somewhat famously left his firm to serve for several months in the Senate as "Capital Hill's highest-net-worth summer intern."[73] Other fellowships have sought to expose technologists to the workings of government. For instance, New America's TechCongress program offers fellowships to both new graduates and midcareer technologists interested in learning more about policymaking while advising members of Congress on tech issues. Already, TechCongress fellows have helped to investigate Cambridge Analytica abuses and uncover Russian attacks on congressional email accounts.[74] Significantly expanding programs like this would infuse Washington with greater tech savvy and help repair and reinforce the critical relationship between the Hill and the Valley.

Encourage Industry-Based Innovations and Experiments

Google has a concise mission statement: "Our company mission is to organize the world's information and make it universally accessible and useful."[75] Nowhere in those sixteen words does it say that Google is responsible "to provide for the common defense." The United States Constitution grants that power to Congress. It is the job of our government to protect the American people. It's the job of tech companies to innovate and build products that Americans want.

Given the centrality of their platforms to the Gray War, however, tech companies cannot fully abdicate responsibility for national security. They have a duty to ensure that their users are interacting with information that is organic, authentic, and safe. Even as platforms have made some encouraging strides since 2016, much more must be done to limit the spread of disinformation campaigns by foreign actors.

While social media platforms can't stop people from believing disinformation, they can offer as much truthful context as possible. That means combating "bad" speech not by shutting it down but by giving users more information that is accurate. For instance, in 2020, Facebook and Twitter began labeling the accounts of foreign officials and—crucially—state-supported foreign media organizations.[76] Tweets from RT now carry a label that says "Russia state-affiliated media." The *Global Times* is rightly tagged as "China state-affiliated media." Platforms have moved, fitfully, toward labeling disinformation about critical subjects—like voting or the coronavirus pandemic—and directing users to accurate information. Google searches likewise bring up "Knowledge" panels offering high-level, objective information on the subject being googled, while Google News has elevated a sidebar fact-checking topics in the news.[77] Some emerging social networks, like Telepath, have even begun assigning trust scores to publishers and showing where they're factually inaccurate.[78] Platforms could also implement a "circuit-breaker" (as proposed by the Forum on Information & Democracy) that temporarily halts the spread of viral content until it can be properly fact-checked.[79]

Tech companies should also continue to develop better tools to identify and remove inauthentic content. For instance, as bots become more believable, we'll need more sophisticated natural language processing to detect if accounts are posting in unnatural increments or using suspicious syntax. To combat manipulated images and video, social media platforms should likewise invest in deepfake detection. Qualcomm has begun incorporating sophisticated photo and video verification tools into its smartphone chips, making it easier to determine if content originating on its phones has been manipulated.[80] Blockchain technology could allow every image to carry with it a log of any alterations made to the content. Other technologies are being developed that could determine if a video is being broadcast live or not.[81]

Big Is Not Necessarily Bad

Clearly, the tech industry has a critical role to play in addressing the front-end conflict raging on its platforms. This may very well entail new regulation from Washington, in addition to whichever new policies companies voluntarily adopt. What will not necessarily help win the Gray War, however, is a wholesale breaking up of Big Tech. The decision to break up America's most successful technology companies is enormously consequential for the U.S. economy and American national security. It is not a decision that should be political or decided based on vague accusations or the whims of public polling. A decision of this significance should be carefully considered against tangible evidence of consumer harm—evidence that a breakup would be the right remedy to address the harm, and that the benefits of a breakup wouldn't outweigh the costs. That is why, as we refocus on promoting American competitiveness in the face of China's growing economic might, we need an *enlightened* antitrust policy.

Opponents of the tech industry's bigness typically cite a litany of alleged harms. We're told that tech giants like Google and Facebook are weakening market competition by monopolizing tech talent, putting mom-and-pop shops out of business, and stifling start-ups. Or that a behemoth like Amazon is unfairly operating as both a marketplace and a market participant, thereby denying consumers better products or lower prices. Critics warn of powerful tech titans buying off members of Congress, hoarding data that violates our privacy and gives them an unfair advantage over other companies, or making decisions about their platforms that can single-handedly shift an election. "Today's big tech companies have too much power—too much power over our economy, our society, and our democracy,"[82] Senator Elizabeth Warren, a leading advocate for breaking up Big Tech, has charged. In October 2020, the Department of Justice sued Google, alleging that the company was "unlawfully maintaining monopolies through anticompetitive and exclusionary practices in the search and search advertising markets."[83] About a month later, the Federal Trade Commission and nearly every state attorney general sued Facebook for anti-competitive practices.[84]

There are kernels of truth to these arguments. Social media companies have at times been irresponsible with the mind-boggling amount of personal data they possess. They have the potential to wield immense influence when it comes to our elections. Some technology companies have in some instances acquired potential rivals, as when Facebook purchased Instagram.

Yet this is only part of the story. Dominance is ephemeral. What's big today can be small tomorrow—just ask onetime giant IBM. In 1965, corporations in the S&P 500 Index held their place in the index for an average of thirty-three years; by 1990, the average tenure had shrunk to twenty years. By 2026, that number is expected to dwindle to just fourteen years.[85] In just six years, Shopify, an Amazon competitor, went from being a relatively small e-commerce player valued at just over $1 billion,[86] to being worth over $184 billion.[87] As Mark Zuckerberg pointed out in his congressional testimony in

July 2020, "Of the ten most valuable companies a decade ago, only three still make that list today." "And if you look at where the top technology company has come from," he continued, "a decade ago the vast majority were American. Today almost half are Chinese."[88] To be sure, Zuckerberg has become a controversial figure in many political circles, but regardless of what one thinks of him personally, certain facts are true even if he believes them.

Tom Wheeler, the former Federal Communications Commission chairman, has taken on this debate, arguing that the best way to compete with China is to "be more competitive at home"—an appealing framing hard to dispute at first glance.[89] The only issue is this argument is entirely based on the erroneous idea that the U.S. is not currently competitive at home. Everywhere you look, there are hungry start-ups nipping at the heels of lumbering legacy companies. According to one venture capitalist I know, more start-ups are getting funded, at higher valuations, than at any point in the last twenty years. And this observation is overwhelmingly supported by the data: venture capital investments in the United States reached record levels in 2019 and 2020, exceeding over 10,000 deals totaling more than $130 billion.[90] Ten thousand deals. Worth over $130 billion. Can anyone seriously argue these numbers are indicative of a consolidated market void of new participants?

This is hardly a picture of scrappy start-ups crushed by digital goliaths. Indeed—even as investors become more selective—89 percent of start-ups say they were able to successfully raise capital in 2019.[91] While start-up executives cite "access to talent" as a key challenge, they largely attribute this to shortcomings with our immigration and education systems rather than a few companies monopolizing the best engineers. All in all, once you dispassionately focus on the hard evidence, it's hard to argue that Big Tech companies prevent new start-ups from emerging on the supply side of the market, and it's equally hard to define a concrete form of "consumer harm" on the demand side of the market, given that most tech products are typically free. So, one has to ask: If the evidence doesn't actually substantiate a lack of competition on the supply side of the market (the ability for new start-ups to raise capital and enter the market), and if it doesn't show clear abuses on the demand side (for example, consumer harms, such as price gauging), what exactly is the evidence-based case for breaking up Big Tech?

The common thread in these critiques seems to be an instinctive discomfort with the size, and more specifically the market cap, of these companies. However, *big is not inherently bad*. As noted earlier, the vast majority of technological R&D today comes from the private sector, with the core businesses of big companies often subsidizing research in less profitable areas. Break up Alphabet and you might lose Verily, an outgrowth of Google's X that funds medical research and innovations—including, for instance, expanding COVID testing.

It's true that, because there are so few powerful platforms, a single point of failure can have dramatic impact. Such was the case with underestimating the impact of Russian interference in the 2016 election. But tech behemoths can afford expensive safeguards against foreign interference or intrusions in ways smaller companies cannot. By consolidating so much power and data in a single place, Big Tech's platforms have made themselves bigger targets. They've also potentially made themselves *harder* targets. For example, Google's Trust and Safety team alone now counts over 1,100 full-time experts around the world tasked with protecting its products from abuse and ensuring the company's global policies are working as intended. This doesn't include the countless other teams working on cybersecurity-related issues, or part-time content reviewers. As of July 2020, Facebook similarly employed a total of over 35,000 people working on all issues related to safety and security across the company.[92] Large technology companies across the spectrum of different industries are investing significant resources to build scalable systems and new technologies to automatically detect and prevent activity ranging from wire fraud and money laundering to the dissemination of deep-fakes and forgeries.

Moreover, what's big domestically isn't necessarily big internationally. In the United States, Amazon is unavoidable; in China, it's negligible, with less than 1 percent of the e-commerce market, which is dominated by Alibaba.[93] In Europe, Amazon makes up less than 10 percent of online retail sales.[94] Tencent surpassed Facebook's market capitalization in July of 2020.[95] Today, tech companies operate in a global marketplace—an important and necessary consideration in any credible assessment of "market dominance." As we've seen, the American tech industry's Chinese competitors receive no shortage of state support and subsidies, and the benefits they derive in China can then be used to expand elsewhere around the globe. If we break up Facebook or Google and make them less competitive with Baidu or Tencent globally, that's a lousy outcome—for American consumers and for all the small-*d* democrats caught in the Gray War.

Relative platform dominance, at the global level, is central to competing with China and winning the Gray War. The country that will ultimately be home to the world's most dominant platforms will control technological choke points in systems critical to the functioning of modern daily life. It will also have the world's most advanced intelligence capabilities and will be best positioned to shape global norms on foreign interference and election integrity, human rights, free speech and privacy, and the protection of intellectual property. Given China's habit of melding its private companies with its state objectives, a world in which China's platforms are dominant would likely be a world in which the national sovereignty of democracies would be eroded and undermined.

This doesn't mean that the U.S. government should artificially inflate or protect the dominance of U.S. tech companies; it simply means that artificially breaking them up would have serious and real consequences for national security. The solution is to regulate responsibly, based on evidence of actual harm to consumers and with an eye toward ensuring that the American technology ecosystem can compete head-to-head with China's. It's perfectly reasonable to write new rules around whether and how companies are allowed to act as both a marketplace and a participant in that marketplace. If compelling evidence emerged that a company abused its position as a marketplace to unfairly favor its own position, it could be reasonable to expect that to be treated as an "unfair and deceptive practice" under the Federal Trade Commission Act, and for the company to be fined. It remains unproven that breaking up the entire company would remedy such practices. It is also important to appreciate that if we object to Amazon being allowed to sell Amazon-branded products on the Amazon marketplace platform, we would need to object to CVS and Walmart selling their own brands, which they already do. The Federal Trade Commission should be empowered with the resources and tools to discourage anti-competitive practices causing consumer harm when a violation is substantiated by evidence.

Finally, scholars like Vanderbilt Law School's Ganesh Sitaraman have suggested that "the government could require technology companies to make their data available in interoperable formats."[96] These proposals are not new: criticisms of Big Tech for its hoarding of data led directly to Facebook's allowing third-party developers greater access to its trove in the late 2000s and early 2010s. And then Cambridge Analytica happened. If the government required tech companies to open up access to their data to third-party developers, who would ensure that it didn't fall into the wrong hands? Who would be responsible for making that judgment call? How would the implementation of such judgment calls be operationalized and enforced at scale against thousands and thousands of developers requesting access every single day? What happens when the wrong call is made? Proposals to force technology companies to open up access to their data come with serious and significant questions that need to be answered in order for any of this to be viable in the real world.

The bottom line is that these companies may need additional regulation; but winning the Gray War also means we cannot pretend that there aren't real, undeniable strategic benefits to having globally dominant U.S. companies vis-à-vis China's national—and increasingly global—champions. After all, as a report from the China Strategy Group put it: "In addition to the scenario of two distinct digital worlds is that of a single digital world in which the governing standards and norms do not reflect democratic values (that is, a world in which China has 'won' the internet)."[97] The real harm to consumers and everyday citizens would be far greater if that scenario were to materialize, and averting it should be a top policy priority. If the trust-busters do encounter unethical or anti-competitive behavior, the responsibility is on them to prove why breaking up the company is the right remedy—as opposed to levying multibillion-dollar fines or other penalties. Regulators should be prepared to answer how a series of smaller companies will leave our country better off when it comes to cybersecurity or privacy. Likewise, it's time for Big Tech to use the benefits of bigness to support the U.S. government's battle against the autocrats, rather than courting them as lucrative markets.

Strengthen Digital Citizenship

Learn to Discern

"Information is like a product," the narrator says in Ukrainian, over footage of shoppers mindlessly placing groceries in their carts. "It can be of poor quality, incomplete, and even harmful. So what do you consume—high quality? Or just whatever looks good? Be cautious; check your information."[98] The Ukrainian public service announcement was sponsored by a nonprofit called IREX as part of its Learn to Discern initiative.

From Ukraine to the United States, too many people shovel information into their heads like they're packing a shopping cart full of junk food. The greatest challenge in the front-end battle isn't the growing sophistication of Russian trolls. The biggest vulnerability we face is *ourselves*. It's our own easily manipulated minds and willingness to blithely believe and share what we see online. As we've seen, too many Americans, including supposed digital natives in younger generations, unquestioningly take dubious and divisive messages at face value.

If we have any hope of winning the front-end fight, we'll need a major national commitment to basic online literacy. Every American reading a blog or a Facebook post should be interrogating the information they come across. *Is this source credible, or is it an anonymous Twitter account with sixteen followers? Does this grainy video really show ballots being stolen? That photo seems too good to be true—what if it's a deepfake?* In short, we, too, must learn to discern.

The IREX initiative in Ukraine is a case in point. IREX spent more than a year and a half training 15,000 Ukrainians to spot disinformation, in a country so battered by Kremlin propaganda and oligarch-owned outlets that less than a quarter of the population trusts the media.[99] The results were notable. Participants spoke of "a fog lifting" as they found new confidence in their ability to think critically about the news they were consuming. Learn to Discern participants were more likely than the general population to accurately identify fake news and more likely to cross-check information with other sources. This greater perceptiveness persisted even a year and a half after the training. Not only that, but participants shared what they'd learned with another 90,000 people, spreading digital literacy among their family, friends, coworkers, and neighbors.[100]

Other countries have tried education to combat disinformation. Perhaps the most successful example is Finland, which has long been targeted by propaganda from its Russian neighbor. Ever since 2014, Finnish students have received a remarkably thorough education in detecting and debunking disinformation. Math students learn how statistics can be manipulated. Art classes teach how images are used to deceive. History courses study the propaganda of the past. And the Finns start early; even children's fairy tales offer an opportunity to scrutinize why one shouldn't trust cunning tricksters like a fox.[101] Thanks to this intense focus on defeating disinformation, Finns rank at the top of all Europeans in their ability to resist fake news.[102] Russian trolls appear to have largely given up on interfering in Finland's elections.[103]

There's no reason Americans cannot be as discerning as Finns. In fact, a handful of states—from Washington to Rhode Island—have put forward bipartisan legislation to promote greater digital literacy.[104] Programs like the Poynter Institute's MediaWise initiative, funded in part by Google, have done valuable work teaching Americans "How to sort fact from fiction online."[105] Yet many of these efforts remain voluntary, underfunded, and incomplete.

As part of prioritizing the defense of digital democracy, we need strong statewide standards across the nation to promote digital literacy and combat disinformation. These standards could be modeled on Finland's comprehensive and integrated curriculum. A number of universities have likewise offered classes, such as the University of Washington's INFO 270/BIOL 270, also known as Calling Bullshit: Data Reasoning in a Digital World.[106] Courses like this should be mandatory for every college freshman. When nearly half of Americans can't identify all three branches of government and around one in five can't name a single First Amendment right,[107] education to combat disinformation should also entail greater instruction in civics. As Joshua Yaffa, a *New Yorker* Moscow correspondent, observes, "If you don't know how government actually works, you're more likely to believe in conspiratorial versions of its doings."[108]

To ensure that digital literacy filters beyond schools, students should be encouraged to share what they've learned—especially with those family members most susceptible to sharing conspiracy-filled Facebook posts. Since older users have been shown to be more likely to fall prey to disinformation,[109] programs like Poynter's MediaWise for Seniors should be expanded. The ex-FBI counterintelligence official Clint Watts and disinformation researcher Tim Hwang have proposed that during high-stakes moments like our elections, journalists and other well-trained community leaders can serve as "disinformation field medics" to monitor and push back on digital falsehoods.[110] These efforts should be supplemented with public awareness campaigns similar to the one run by IREX in Ukraine. The National Highway Traffic Safety Administration's Click It or Ticket campaign led to a measurable increase in seat belt use[111]; done right, perhaps a Click It and Check It campaign could encourage more skeptical analysis of online news consumption.

Based on what I saw combating disinformation at Google, all of us can do more to become better consumers and sharers of information. Here are some useful dos and don'ts:

Dos:

- Check the source. Is it truly independent? Does it have a track record of accuracy? Or is it an anonymous Twitter account started a week earlier?
- Check the source's source. Sometimes even friends or verified accounts can credulously share disinformation. Take the time to see where they got their information before sharing it yourself.
- Compare with other sources. Cross-checking information is one of the best ways to distinguish fact from fiction—especially if something strikes you as surprising.
- Read and share authoritative sources. There's a reason the *New York Times* and the BBC are a lot more accurate than a blog with inconsistent grammar. Serious news organizations invest tremendous time and resources into getting the story right, and they can be held accountable when they fall short.

Whenever possible, rely on sources that uphold rigorous standards of accuracy.

- Check your own biases. Human beings seek out information that confirms what they already believe. Disinformation plays on that tendency. Before you share a seemingly outrageous article or tweet, take a beat and add a dose of skepticism.

Don'ts

- Don't click on the first link you see. Thanks to techniques like firehosing, the top-ranked search result isn't necessarily from the most credible source.
- Don't share without reading. Headlines can be sensationalist or misleading. Reading the full article provides useful context for determining the veracity of the information.
- Don't trust something just because you see it repeated everywhere. Trolls and bots intentionally try to amplify disinformation as much as possible. "Trending" doesn't necessarily mean truthful.
- Don't believe your own eyes. With deepfakes and their low-budget cousins, "cheapfakes," even images and video can be doctored. If something seems too good to be true, it probably is.
- Don't "RT" RT. Twitter and Facebook now label sources like RT and Xinhua because they are funded by foreign governments. When you retweet and amplify our adversaries, you're doing their work for them.

"We all know, don't get into a car with a stranger," Congressman (and former CIA officer) Will Hurd has said. So "why are you listening to a stranger on social media?"[112] In the battle for those six inches inside our heads, better digital literacy is the defense we need.

Break Out of Hyper-Partisan Bubbles

Yet even greater digital literacy won't overcome one of the greatest challenges we face—our willingness to believe any information that comes from our own tribe or filter bubble. One 2018 study demonstrated that we're more likely to trust people from our own political group even when it comes to completely unrelated tasks like sorting shapes.[113]

This poses several challenges. On the front-end, partisanship and polarization accelerate the spread of fake news. That too-good-to-be-true quote certainly *sounds* like something a Republican would say, you might think, as you click Retweet and send a mistruth zinging through cyberspace. More broadly, our corrosive politics have hampered our ability to put forward a unified front against the autocrats. How can the federal government invest in job training or overhaul our immigration system—policies that would allow us to compete with China—when our two major political parties spend so much time fighting that we can barely keep the lights on?

There is no simple solution to America's toxic political climate. Advocates have suggested structural reforms like ranked-choice voting and nonpartisan commissions to draw the lines of legislative districts. Others have proposed some form of national service to help break down barriers in race, class, and political affiliation. It's even been suggested that we handcuff new Democratic and Republican members of Congress together for a year to force them to learn to get along—an idea that is as impractical as it is tempting.

However, no structural reform or policy can substitute for just reaching out to one another. Too often we allow ourselves to believe oversimplified, black-and-white narratives about each other. The truth is, Democrats aren't all raging socialists and Republicans aren't all selfish and evil. To paraphrase Aaron Burr in my favorite musical, people aren't easily divided into sinners or saints. Life is about nuance. Once we realize that, we can learn to listen. Sometimes, as Keith and I have found, we can even love each other.

The key, I've learned in my own marriage, is to appreciate that in most cases we want the same things—like healthier Americans and a healthier planet—and then look for areas of agreement. While we have different views of guns, for example, Keith and I agree that reducing gun violence should be a priority. Because Keith sees technology as a solution to many social problems, he's open to restrictions such as Bluetooth-enabled firearms that are locked unless you're in proximity to someone else with a gun. Similarly, while Keith feels strongly about freedom of speech and believes tech companies shouldn't be in the business of limiting content—except in the narrow case of foreign governments deliberately deceiving American audiences under the guise of being independent journalists—I've persuaded him that cracking down on disinformation is important and necessary.

I won't pretend it's easy, but there is cause for hope. In an era of bitter partisanship, the imperative of meeting the China challenge is being widely embraced across the political spectrum. When John Ratcliffe, Trump's outgoing director of National Intelligence, called China "the greatest threat to America today, and the greatest threat to democracy and freedom world-wide since World War II,"[114] Representative Adam Schiff, the chairman of the House intelligence committee, agreed that China "is an area of substantial bipartisan agreement, and a challenge we must rise to meet."[115]

Even as Congress remains deeply divided and gridlocked, bills are regularly introduced by both parties—whether Senator Mitt Romney's STRATEGIC Act[116] or Senator Schumer's Endless Frontier Act[117]—with the goal of pushing back on China's aggression and investing in American competitiveness. The Secure and Trusted Communications Networks Act of 2019, which prohibits using federal funds to buy telecom equipment from companies like Huawei, passed Congress unanimously.[118] Legislation tightening the screws on China for its abuses in Hong Kong was approved with just a single dissenting vote.[119] The Pacific Deterrence Initiative, intended to offer a regional approach to China's designs, likewise received overwhelming bipartisan support. At a time when observers despair at the idea of Washington getting anything done, framing policy in terms of meeting the threat from the Chinese Communist Party may offer a road map for making progress on issues ranging from manufacturing to the military. In the same way that the threat of the Soviet Union galvanized our nation, the challenge posed by China is an opportunity for us to come together to meet a common adversary.

Epilogue

In 2019, German chancellor Angela Merkel addressed the graduating class of Harvard University. Merkel was born less than a decade after the end of World War II. She grew up in East Germany, in the shadow of the Berlin Wall that divided her from members of her own family. Yet only thirty years after the end of the Cold War, Merkel stood as the leader of a unified Germany, the unofficial leader of the European Union, speaking to students whose grandparents had faced hers on the battlefield only a few generations before. Given the course of her own country over the past three-quarters of a century, Merkel's message to the graduates was perhaps unsurprising: "Nothing has to remain as it is," she said. "What seems fixed and unchanging can in fact change."[1]

I find myself thinking about that sentiment often. Studying the Gray War, the future can appear bleak. Reading the steady stream of news about increasingly devious Russian front-end tactics, we might assume that there's simply no way to combat the viral spread of disinformation. When China's leaders make yet another eye-popping investment in the technology sector or lay out another ten-year plan, it's not hard to envision the world slipping under the influence of an autocratic surveillance state. The solutions we do come up with can feel insufficient and incomplete.

It can be easy to imagine that we will lose this war. It can be easy, at times, to lose hope.

But this story is not finished. History didn't end in 2016 any more than it did in 1989. China is not fated to eclipse the United States and dominate the world. Nor is the United States guaranteed to sustain its position of global leadership without breaking a sweat. For all the lightning-fast algorithms and terabytes of data, all the cables and satellites and semiconductors, there may be no greater force in this fight than the power of human agency. We have the power to choose.

So in spite of it all, I am genuinely optimistic. Hard as it may be to believe at times, there are few countries better equipped to win the Gray War than the United States. The country I idolized as a young kid in France may have been an idealized America. But only somewhat. Despite all its shortcomings, all the narratives of American decline, the United States retains enormous reservoirs of resilience and resourcefulness. Our raucous, messy, contradictory system— which can feel so frustrating when Beijing rapidly reorients all of China around a bold agenda—is the same decentralized framework that empowered a handful of college dropouts to build an Internet empire. The open and pluralistic society that allows disinformation to take root is also what allows us to push our government to take the authoritarian threat more seriously. Welcoming strangers to our shores brings with it risks; it also brought us Google and Apple.

We likely won't move as quickly or as decisively as the authoritarians; that's the nature of democracies. Finding our footing in this fight will no doubt involve the usual foot-dragging and partisan strife. But winning the war is within our power.

The culminating foreign policy question of this decade is whether the free world should meet this threat by submission or resistance.

Indeed, the deepening bipartisan consensus on the seriousness of the China challenge offers encouraging signs of an awakening of sorts on this issue. So do the Biden administration's early moves. President Biden has appointed high-level cybersecurity officials to the White House[2] and ordered a review of supply-chain vulnerabilities.[3] The Biden Commerce Department is moving forward with a Trump administration rule that will ban technology transactions deemed detrimental to national security.[4] Secretary of State Tony Blinken has echoed his predecessor Mike Pompeo in acknowledging the atrocities taking place in Xinjiang as a genocide,[5] with President Biden raising these human rights violations in his first call with President Xi.[6]

While Americans should never underestimate the power and efficiency of authoritarian regimes like China, they should also never succumb to crises of confidence and paralysis. The central source of China's hubris is the size of its population, which—the theory goes— ensures its eventual ascendance as the world's largest economy. This theory omits the power of ideas and the basic instincts of human nature. As Winston Churchill once prophetically observed:

You see these dictators on their pedestals, surrounded by the bayonets of their soldiers and the truncheons of their police. On all sides they are guarded by masses of armed men, cannons, aeroplanes, fortifications, and the like—they boast and vaunt themselves before the world, yet in their hearts there is unspoken fear. They are afraid of words and thoughts; words spoken abroad, thoughts stirring at home—all the more powerful because forbidden—terrify them. A little mouse of thought appears in the room, and even the mightiest potentates are thrown into panic. They make frantic efforts to bar our thoughts and words; they are afraid of the workings of the human mind. Cannons, aeroplanes, they can manufacture in large quantities; but how are they to quell the natural

promptings of human nature, which after all these centuries
of trial and progress has inherited a whole armoury of potent
and indestructible knowledge?[7]

Dictators, Churchill concluded, are "all strong without" and "all weak within." He was right then and still is. The United States remains in control of its own destiny. We are still "young, scrappy, and hungry," still home to "the crazy ones." Whenever we're tempted to think decline is our destiny, we should remember: the Soviets may have beat us into outer space, but American boots were the first to set foot on the moon.

A new American moment, and a safer world for democracy, online and off-, is within reach; but time can no longer be taken for granted. The 2020s will be a decisive decade for the global configuration of power. China believes it is winning the Gray War and its path to global ascendance is already preordained. If America allows China to win, democracy and the rule of law may be remembered as, in the words of Bob Kagan, "an anomaly in the history of human existence."[8] Americans wrote the lines of code that unleashed both creativity and conflict over the past half century. The future, too, remains ours to rewrite.

Acknowledgments

This book originated as an effort to make sense of cascading geopolitical events affecting the technology industry. The Trust and Safety and Policy teams across the technology industry deserve credit and recognition for grappling with these complex events in an increasingly politicized environment. Whatever the shortcomings of this book may be, they would have been far greater without hours of conversations with many friends and colleagues: Trae Stephens, Daniel Gross, Diogo Monica, and Tamir Pardo.

I owe a great deal of gratitude to my friends and former colleagues at Google that have enriched, challenged, and expanded my thinking on technology policy issues over the years: David Graff, Reese Pecot, Paul Haahr, Ian Goodfellow, Lavanya Mahendran, Vijay Padmanabhan, Beth Tsai, Michelle Chang, David Price, Erin Simon, Richard Gingras, Paul Shaw, Clement Wolf, Lara Levin, Maggie Shiels, Sean Casey, Jeff Lazarus, Jen Granito, Andrew Trabulsi, Peter Burke, Ardan Arac, Dan Cary, and Robin Dua. I have also benefited from many conversations with friends across the tech industry: Sam Altman, Peter Thiel, Jason Calacanis, David Sacks, Michael Solona,

Erik Torenberg, Delian Asparouhov, Alex MacCaw, Joshua Buckley, Clara Tsao, and Nick Lovrien.

I want to thank my current and former colleagues from Brookings, Stanford, and CSIS, whose work have directly and indirectly helped shape many of the concepts in this book (and revisit many others): Tarun Chhabra, Rush Doshi, Tanvi Madan, Michael McFaul, Andrew Grotto, Alex Stamos, Renee DiResta, Eileen Donahoe, Daphne Keller, and Jim Lewis. I offer special thanks to Tom Wright, Bruce Jones, Hal Brands, Zev Karlin-Neumann, and Terry Szuplat for reading several chapters and offering invaluable stylistic and substantive advice.

Ben Loehnen, my editor at Avid Reader Press (Simon & Schuster), has been a constant reservoir of editorial insight. Working with him has been a true pleasure from start to finish. Carolyn Kelly also provided timely and able assistance in the preparation of the manuscript. The book would have no doubt been very different without the feedback of Suzanne Gluck and Jay Mandel, my outstanding literary agents at WME.

My greatest debt of gratitude is to my husband, Keith Rabois. This book is the product of his love, encouragement, and intellectual audacity. It is to him that I owe the most.

Notes

Prologue

1 Elizabeth Dwoskin, Adam Entous, and Craig Timberg, "Google uncovers Russian-bought ads on YouTube, Gmail and other platforms," *Washington Post,* October 9, 2017, https://www.washingtonpost.com/news/the-switch/wp/2017/10/09/google-uncovers-russian-bought-ads-on-youtube-gmail-and-other-platforms/.

2 Adrian Chen, "The Agency," *New York Times,* June 2, 2015, https://www.nytimes.com/2015/06/07/magazine/the-agency.html.

3 "Security and disinformation in the U.S. 2016 election: What we found," Google, October 30, 2017, https://storage.googleapis.com/gweb-uniblog-publish-prod/documents/google_US2016election_findings_1_zm64A1G.pdf.

4 Patrick Hoge, "S.F. struck by love / Cupid's big bow gets rise out of passers-by," *SF Gate,* January 27, 2012, https://www.sfgate.com/news/article/S-F-struck-by-love-Cupid-s-big-bow-gets-rise-2751612.php.

5 Robert McMillan, "Inside Google's Team Fighting to Keep Your Data Safe From Hackers," *Wall Street Journal,* January 23, 2019, wsj.com/articles/inside-googles-team-battling-hackers-11548264655.

6 "'#hillaryhealth' typed query," Twitter, https://twitter.com/search?q=%23hillaryhealth&src=typed_query.

7 "'hillary founded isis' typed query," Twitter, https://twitter.com/search?q=hillary%20founded%20isis&src=typed_query.

8 Jacob Ogles, "Senate Intelligence Committee says Russian meddling targeted Marco Rubio, Jeb Bush in 2016." *Florida Politics,* October 9, 2019, https://floridapolitics.com/archives/307822-senate-intelligence-committee-russian-meddling-targeted-marco-rubio-jeb-bush-in-2016/.

9 Jill Lepore, "Party Time," *New Yorker,* September 10, 2007, https://www.newyorker.com/magazine/2007/09/17/party-time.

10 "About COVID-19," Centers for Disease Control and Prevention,

September 1, 2020, https://www.cdc.gov/coronavirus/2019-ncov
/cdcresponse/about-COVID-19.html.

11 Finbarr Bermingham and Cissy Zhou, "Coronavirus: China and US in 'new Cold War' as relations hit lowest point in 'more than 40 years,' spurred on by pandemic," *South China Morning Post*, May 5, 2020, https://www.scmp.com/economy/china-economy/article/3082968 /coronavirus-china-us-new-cold-war-relations-hit-lowest-point.

12 Chris Buckley and Steven Lee Myers, "From 'Respect' to 'Sick and Twisted': How Coronavirus Hit U.S.-China Ties," *New York Times*, May 15, 2020, https://www.nytimes.com/2020/05/15/world/asia /coronavirus-china-united-states-cold-war.html.

13 Hal Brands and Jake Sullivan, "China Has Two Paths to Global Domination," *Foreign Policy*, May 22, 2020, https://foreignpolicy.com /2020/05/22/china-superpower-two-paths-global-domination-cold -war/.

14 David E. Sanger, "Russian Hackers Broke Into Federal Agencies, U.S. Officials Suspect," *New York Times*, December 13, 2020, https:// www.nytimes.com/2020/12/13/us/politics/russian-hackers-us-gov ernment-treasury-commerce.html.

15 Tarun Chhabra, "The China challenge, democracy, and U.S. grand strategy," Brookings Institution, https://www.brookings.edu/wp-con tent/uploads/2019/02/FP_20190311_us_grand_strategy_chhabra .pdf.

16 Hans Morgenthau, *Politics Among Nations: The Struggle for Power and Peace* (New York: Knopf, 1948), 137.

17 Raphael Cohen, "It's time to drop 'competition' from US defense strategy," *The Hill*, May 17, 2021, https://thehill.com/opinion /national-security/553787-its-time-to-drop-competition-from-us-de fense-strategy.

18 Office of the U.S. Trade Representative, "Findings of the Investigation into China's Acts, Policies, and Practices Related to Technology Transfer, Intellectual Property, and Innovation Under Section 301 of the Trade Act of 1974," March 22, 2018, https://ustr.gov/sites/de fault/files/Section%20301%20FINAL.PDF.

19 "Prepared Statement of Gen (Ret) Keith B. Alexander on the Future of Warfare before the Senate Armed Services Committee," November 3, 2015, https://www.armed-services.senate.gov/imo/media/doc /Alexander_11-03-15.pdf.

20 Christopher Wray, "The Threat Posed by the Chinese Government and the Chinese Communist Party to the Economic and National Security of the United States," Federal Bureau of Investigation, July 7, 2020, https://www.fbi.gov/news/speeches/the-threat-posed-by -the-chinese-government-and-the-chinese-communist-party-to-the -economic-and-national-security-of-the-united-states.

21 "Chapter 1: U.S.-China Trade and Economic Relations," U.S.-China Economic and Security Review Commission, https://www.uscc.gov /sites/default/files/Annual_Report/Chapters/Chapter%201%20 U.S.-China%20Economic%20and%20Trade%20Relations.pdf.

22 "Salt Lake City, Utah," United States Census Bureau, https://www .census.gov/quickfacts/saltlakecitycityutah.

23 David E. Sanger and Emily Schmall, "China Appears to Warn India: Push too Hard and the Lights Could Go Out," *New York Times*, February 28, 2021, https://www.nytimes.com/2021/02/28/us/politics /china-india-hacking-electricity.html.

24 Ibid.

25 Paul Simao and Josh Horwitz, "NBA stirs U.S. hornet's nest, faces China backlash over Hong Kong tweet," Reuters, October 6, 2019, https://www.reuters.com/article/us-china-basketball-nba/nba-stirs -u-s-hornets-nest-faces-china-backlash-over-hong-kong-tweet-idUS KCN1WL04T.

26 Wayne Ma, "Marriott Employee Roy Jones Hit 'Like.' Then China Got Mad," *Wall Street Journal*, March 3, 2018, https://www.wsj.com /articles/marriott-employee-roy-jones-hit-like-then-china-got-mad -1520094910.

27 "COVID-19: China Medical Supply Chains and Broader Trade Issues," Congressional Research Service, December 23, 2020, https:// crsreports.congress.gov/product/pdf/R/R46304.

28 "Zoom Video Communications, Inc.," U.S. Securities and Exchange Commission, January 31, 2020, https://investors.zoom.us/static-files /09a01665-5f33-4007-8e90-de02219886aa.

29 Betsy Woodruff Swan, "State report: Russian, Chinese and Iranian disinformation narratives echo one another," *Politico*, April 21, 2020, https://www.politico.com/news/2020/04/21/russia-china-iran-disin- formation-coronavirus-state-department-193107.

30 Yuval Harari, "Read Yuval Harari's blistering warning to Davos in full," World Economic Forum, January 24, 2020, https://www.weforum .org/agenda/2020/01/yuval-hararis-warning-davos-speech-future -predications/.

31 Chris Brose, *The Kill Chain: Defending America in the Future of High-Tech Warfare* (New York: Hachette, 2020), xii.

32 Jane Zhang, "China created a unicorn every 3.8 days in 2018," *South China Morning Post*, January 27, 2019, https://www.scmp.com /tech/start-ups/article/2183717/china-created-unicorn-every-38 -days-2018.

33 John Adams, "To Thomas Jefferson from John Adams, 6 December 1787," Founders Online, https://founders.archives.gov/documents /Jefferson/01-12-02-0405.

34 Josh Constine, "AOL Instant Messenger is shutting down after

20 years," *TechCrunch*, October 6, 2017, https://techcrunch.com /2017/10/06/aol-instant-messenger-shut-down/.

35 Angus King, "CSC Final Report," Cyberspace Solarium Commission, March 2020, https://www.solarium.gov/report.

36 Sir Winston S. Churchill, *Never Give In! The Best of Winston Churchill's Speeches* (New York: Hyperion, 2003), 126.

37 KQED News Staff, "Dramatic Photos of 1906 San Francisco Earthquake Aftermath," KQED, April 18, 2014, https://www.kqed.org /news/133039/dramatic-photos-of-1906-san-francisco-earthquake -aftermath.

38 Ken Miguel, "The Earthquake Effect: Bridging the Faults—The catastrophic fall and slow rise of the Bay Bridge after Loma Prieta," ABC 7 News, October 18, 2019, https://abc7news.com/loma-prieta -earthquake-1989-san-francisco-quake/5609358/.

Introduction: IN THE HEART OF THE EMPIRE

1 "Route from Marseille, France, to Vaux-sur-Seine, 78740, France," Google Maps, https://www.google.com/maps/dir/Marseille,+France /78740+Vaux-sur-Seine,+France/@46.1310127,1.3555 829,7z/data=!3m1!4b1!4m14!4m13!1m5!1m1!1s0x12c9bf4344d a5333:0x40819a5fd970220!2m2!1d5.36978!2d43.296482!1m5!1 m1!1s0x47e68d213a86a2c1:0x40b82c3688c3660!2m2!1d1.9650 47!2d49.009778!3e0.

2 "Holocaust survivor developed real estate," *Toledo Blade*, September 9, 2003, https://www.toledoblade.com/news/deaths/2003/09/09 /Holocaust-survivor-developed-real-estate/stories/200309090018.

3 "About Us," Bellevue Investors, https://bellevueinvestors.com /about.

4 "About," GWU Elliott School of International Affairs, https://elliott .gwu.edu/about.

5 *Entrepreneur* Staff, "Peter Thiel Commencement Speech, Hamilton College, May 2016 (Transcript)," *Entrepreneur*, May 23, 2016, https://www.entrepreneur.com/article/276303.

6 "Think Different. Steve Jobs narrated version," The Crazy Ones, http://www.thecrazyones.it/spot-en.html.

7 Lev Grossman, "Person of the Year 2010: Mark Zuckerberg," *Time*, December 15, 2010, http://content.time.com/time/specials/pack ages/article/0,28804,2036683_2037183_2037185,00.html.

8 *Forbes* Staff, "America's Best Entrepreneurs: *Forbes*' Annual Ranking of the Best Small Companies in America," *Forbes*, October 17, 2012, https://www.forbes.com/sites/forbespr/2012/10/17/americas-best -entrepreneurs-forbes-annual-ranking-of-the-best-small-companies -in-america/?sh=7c5a86af9857.

9 Harrison Weber, "Airbnb officially closes its $475 million mega-

round," *VentureBeat*, August 1, 2014, https://venturebeat.com/2014/08/01/airbnb-officially-closes-its-475-million-mega-round/.

10 Josh Ong, "Uber announces UberPool, a carpooling experiment with 40% lower prices than UberX," *The Next Web News*, August 6, 2014, https://thenextweb.com/insider/2014/08/06/uber-announces-uberpool-carpooling-experiment-40-lower-prices-uberx/.

11 Ananya Bhattacharya, "Fitbit is now worth $4.1 billion after IPO," CNN Money, June 25, 2015, https://money.cnn.com/2015/06/17/investing/fitbit-ipo/index.html.

12 Quentin Hardy, "Palantir, a Silicon Valley Start-Up, Raises Another $880 Million," *New York Times* Business, Innovation, Technology, Society, December 23, 2015, https://bits.blogs.nytimes.com/2015/12/23/palantir-a-silicon-valley-start-up-raises-another-880-million/.

13 Katie Benner, "The 'Unicorn' Club, Now Admitting New Members," *New York Times*, August 23, 2015, https://www.nytimes.com/2015/08/24/technology/the-unicorn-club-now-admitting-new-members.html.

14 Maeve Duggan, "Mobile Messaging and Social Media 2015," Pew Research Center, August 19, 2015, https://www.pewresearch.org/internet/2015/08/19/mobile-messaging-and-social-media-2015/.

15 Jonathan Allen and Amie Parnes, *HRC: State Secrets and the Rebirth of Hillary Clinton* (New York: Random House, 2014).

16 Veronica Toney, "Complete guest list for the state dinner in honor of Chinese President Xi Jinping," *Washington Post*, September 25, 2015, https://www.washingtonpost.com/news/reliable-source/wp/2015/09/25/complete-guest-list-for-the-state-dinner-in-honor-of-chinese-president-xi-jinping/.

17 Robinson Meyer, "The Secret Startup That Saved the Worst Website in America," *The Atlantic*, July 9, 2015, https://www.theatlantic.com/technology/archive/2015/07/the-secret-startup-saved-healthcare-gov-the-worst-website-in-america/397784/.

18 David Dayen, "The Android Administration," *The Intercept*, April 22, 2016, https://theintercept.com/2016/04/22/googles-remarkably-close-relationship-with-the-obama-white-house-in-two-charts/; Brody Mullins, "Google Makes Most of Close Ties to White House," *Wall Street Journal*, March 24, 2015, https://www.wsj.com/articles/google-makes-most-of-close-ties-to-white-house-1427242076.

19 Andrew Orlowski, "Revealed: The revolving door between Google and the US govt—in pictures," *The Register*, April 29, 2016, https://www.theregister.com/2016/04/29/google_transparency_project/; "Our Offices," Google, https://about.google/intl/en_us/locations/?region=north-america&office=mountain-view.

20 "Keith Rabois," Founders Fund, https://foundersfund.com/team/keith-rabois/.

21 "GeoQuant," *Medium*, https://medium.com/@GeoQuant.
22 ABC News, "FULL TEXT: Khizr Khan's Speech to the 2016 Democratic National Convention," ABC News, August 1, 2016, https://abcnews.go.com/Politics/full-text-khizr-khans-speech-2016-democratic-national/story?id=41043609.
23 Mary McNamara, "The hug that will go down in history," *Los Angeles Times*, July 28, 2016, https://www.latimes.com/politics/la-na-pol-obama-clinton-hug-20160728-snap-story.html.
24 Christopher Allen, "User Clip: Hillary Clinton Breaks the Glass Ceiling," C-SPAN, August 1, 2016, https://www.c-span.org/video/?c4616537/user-clip-hillary-clinton-breaks-glass-ceiling.
25 Tom Hamburger and Karen Tumulty, "WikiLeaks releases thousands of documents about Clinton and internal deliberations," *Washington Post*, July 22, 2016, https://www.washingtonpost.com/news/post-politics/wp/2016/07/22/on-eve-of-democratic-convention-wikileaks-releases-thousands-of-documents-about-clinton-the-campaign-and-internal-deliberations/.
26 Rebecca Shabad, "Donald Trump: I hope Russia finds Hillary Clinton's emails," CBS News, July 27, 2016, https://www.cbsnews.com/news/donald-trump-i-hope-russia-finds-hillary-clintons-emails/.
27 David A. Fahrenthold, "Trump recorded having extremely lewd conversation about women in 2005," *Washington Post*, October 8, 2016, https://www.washingtonpost.com/politics/trump-recorded-having-extremely-lewd-conversation-about-women-in-2005/2016/10/07/3b9ce776-8cb4-11e6-bf8a-3d26847eeed4_story.html.
28 Aaron Sharockman, "On Oct. 7, the Access Hollywood tape comes out. One hour later, WikiLeaks starts dropping my emails," PolitiFact, December 18, 2016, https://www.politifact.com/factchecks/2016/dec/18/john-podesta/its-true-wikileaks-dumped-podesta-emails-hour-afte/.
29 "Hillary Clinton has a 91% chance to win," *New York Times*, October 18, 2016, https://www.nytimes.com/newsgraphics/2016/10/18/presidential-forecast-updates/newsletter.html.
30 "World's Most Admired Companies 2016," *Fortune*, 2016, https://fortune.com/worlds-most-admired-companies/2016/.
31 Alexis C. Madrigal, "The Tower at the Heart of the Tech Boom," *The Atlantic*, November 19, 2017, https://www.theatlantic.com/technology/archive/2017/11/picturing-the-tech-boom/545114/.

Chapter 1: THE ORIGINS OF THE GRAY WAR

1 Dan Frommer, "Google's parent company Alphabet added almost 5,000 employees last quarter, and now has more than 85,000," *Vox*, April 23, 2018, https://www.vox.com/2018/4/23/17272502/googl-alphabet-google-q1-earnings-2018-headcount.

2 Seth Fiegerman, "Google posts its first $100 billion year," CNN Money, February 1, 2018, https://money.cnn.com/2018/02/01/tech nology/google-earnings/index.html.

3 Madeline Farber, "Google Tops Apple as the World's Most Valuable Brand," *Fortune*, February 2, 2017, https://fortune.com/2017/02/02 /google-tops-apple-brand-value/.

4 Dana Bash, "Hillary Clinton calls Donald Trump to concede election," CNN Politics, https://www.cnn.com/videos/politics/2016/11 /09/hillary-clinton-calls-donald-trump-to-concede-election-bash-sot .cnn.

5 Charles II, "By the King, a proclamation. To restrain the spreading of false news," 1688, https://ota.bodleian.ox.ac.uk/repository/xmlui /bitstream/handle/20.500.12024/A87488/A87488.html?sequence= 5&isAllowed=y.

6 Craig Silverman and Lawrence Alexander, "How Teens in the Balkans Are Duping Trump Supporters With Fake News," *BuzzFeed News*, November 3, 2016, https://www.buzzfeednews.com/article /craigsilverman/how-macedonia-became-a-global-hub-for-pro-trump -misinfo#.fu2okXaeKo.

7 Kurt Wagner, "Mark Zuckerberg says it's 'crazy' to think fake news stories got Donald Trump elected," *Recode*, November 11, 2016, https://www.vox.com/2016/11/11/13596792/facebook-fake-news -mark-zuckerberg-donald-trump.

8 Amit Singhal, "'Revenge porn' and Search," Google Public Policy Blog, June 19, 2015, https://publicpolicy.googleblog.com/2015/06 /revenge-porn-and-search.html.

9 P. W. Singer and Emerson T. Brooking, *LikeWar: The Weaponization of Social Media* (New York: First Mariner Books, 2019), 27.

10 Katie Hafner and Matthew Lyon, *Where Wizards Stay Up Late: The Origins of the Internet* (New York: Simon & Schuster Paperbacks, 1996), 153.

11 Singer and Brooking, *LikeWar*, 35.

12 Singer and Brooking, *LikeWar*, 35; Andrew Blum, *Tubes: A Journey to the Center of the Internet* (New York: HarperCollins, 2012), e-book 99.

13 Johnny Ryan, *A History of the Internet and the Digital Future* (London: Reaktion Books Ltd, 2010), 78.

14 Ibid., 77.

15 Singer and Brooking, *LikeWar*, 36.

16 Ibid., 58.

17 Connie Loizos, "One-Fifth of Americans: We're Online 'Almost Constantly,'" *TechCrunch*, December 8, 2015, https://techcrunch .com/2015/12/08/one-fifth-of-americans-were-online-almost -constantly/?guccounter=1&guce_referrer=aHR0cHM6Ly93d3cu

Z29vZ2xlLmNvbS8&guce_referrer_sig=AQAAAHyI8D7LmH-g
_AbPhYoztCSNVDK5Nj1h1kDTdPQhczfj—ayPdyeFhT47kBv
UQCERoUbcya4zQVsh26cS0P8NP_nI2JSKE1KBvSXqVg_i1CgAy
5BAYQJIwEiLNkhZB3p5vYe2KyhOF0Zwx3Go1Yzoeq-KK6ajyC
68ErjgCCOO1ma.

18 Hafner and Lyon, *Where Wizards Stay Up Late*, 236.

19 John P. Carlin, *Dawn of the Code War: America's Battle Against Russia, China, and the Rising Global Cyber Threat* (New York: Hachette, 2018), e-book, 59.

20 Fred Kaplan, *Dark Territory: The Secret History of Cyber War* (New York: Simon & Schuster Paperbacks, 2016), 2.

21 Carlin, *Dawn of the Code War*, e-book, 160–161.

22 "Timeline: The U.S. Government and Cybersecurity," *Washington Post*, May 16, 2003, https://www.washingtonpost.com/wp-dyn/articles/A50606-2002Jun26.html.

23 Carlin, *Dawn of the Code War*, e-book, 161.

24 Ibid.

25 Brad Smith, *Tools and Weapons: The Promise and the Peril of the Digital Age* (New York: Penguin Random House, 2019), 23.

26 Singer and Brooking, *LikeWar*, 38.

27 Walter Isaacson, *The Innovators: How a Group of Hackers, Geniuses, and Geeks Created the Digital Revolution* (New York: Simon & Schuster Paperbacks, 2014), 411.

28 Singer and Brooking, *LikeWar*, 39.

29 Ibid.

30 Carlin, *Dawn of the Code War*, e-book, 162–163.

31 "The Reaction to that First Spam," Brad Templeton, May 4, 1978, https://www.templetons.com/brad/spamreact.html#reaction.

32 Carlin, *Dawn of the Code War*, e-book, 153.

33 Ibid., 181.

34 Ibid., 104.

35 Ibid., 106.

36 William M. Arkin, "Sunrise, Sunset," *Washington Post*, March 29, 1999, https://www.washingtonpost.com/wp-srv/national/dotmil/arkin032999.htm.

37 Arkin, "Sunrise, Sunset."

38 "Route from Berlin, Germany, to Saint-Germain-en-Laye, France," Google Maps, https://www.google.com/maps/dir/Berlin,+Germany/Saint-Germain-en-Laye,+France/@50.617891,3.2648464,6z/data=!3m1!4b1!4m14!4m13!1m5!1m1!1s0x47a84e373f035901:0x42120465b5e3b70!2m2!1d13.404954!2d52.5200066!1m5!1m1!1s0x47e66206d8924985:0x40b82c3688c3840!2m2!1d2.093761!2d48.898908!3e0.

39 Vladimir Putin, *First Person: An Astonishingly Frank Self-Portrait by Russia's President* (New York: Perseus, 2000), 76.

40 Ibid., 79.

41 Chris Bowlby, "Vladimir Putin's formative German years," BBC, March 27, 2015, https://www.bbc.com/news/magazine-32066222.

42 Ibid.

43 Ibid.

44 Evan Osnos, David Remnick, and Joshua Yaffa, "Trump, Putin, and the New Cold War," *New Yorker,* February 24, 2017, https://www.newyorker.com/magazine/2017/03/06/trump-putin-and-the-new-cold-war.

45 Henry Foy, "'We need to talk about Igor': the rise of Russia's most powerful oligarch," *Financial Times,* March 1, 2018, https://www.ft.com/content/dc7d48f8-1c13-11e8-aaca-4574d7dabfb6; Guy Chazan, "A Trusted Ally of Putin, Miller Vaults From Obscurity to Gazprom's Helm," *Wall Street Journal,* June 1, 2001, https://www.wsj.com/articles/SB991339427925984520.

46 Joshua Yaffa, "Putin's Shadow Cabinet and the Bridge to Crimea," *New Yorker,* May 22, 2017, https://www.newyorker.com/magazine/2017/05/29/putins-shadow-cabinet-and-the-bridge-to-crimea.

47 "Duo get life for Anna Politkovskaya murder," BBC, June 9, 2014, https://www.bbc.com/news/world-europe-27760498.

48 Osnos, Remnick, and Yaffa, "Trump, Putin, and the New Cold War."

49 "Russia opposition politician Boris Nemtsov shot dead," BBC, February 28, 2015, https://www.bbc.com/news/world-europe-31669061.

50 Matthew Kaminski, "Notable & Quotable: The Man Vladimir Putin Fears Most," *Wall Street Journal,* July 18, 2013, https://www.wsj.com/articles/SB10001424127887323309404578614210222799482.

51 Andrey Kozenko, "Navalny poisoning: Kremlin critic recalls near-death Novichok torment," BBC, October 7, 2020, https://www.bbc.com/news/world-europe-54434082.

52 "Putin: Soviet collapse a 'genuine tragedy,'" NBC News, April 25, 2005, http://www.nbcnews.com/id/7632057/ns/world_news/t/putin-soviet-collapse-genuine-tragedy/#.XrwLDBNKihd.

53 Paul Lewis, "CONFLICT IN THE BALKANS; RUSSIA A BARRIER TO NATO AIR STRIKE," *New York Times,* February 9, 1994, https://www.nytimes.com/1994/02/09/world/conflict-in-the-balkans-russia-a-barrier-to-nato-air-strike.html.

54 "What is NATO?," NATO, https://www.nato.int/nato-welcome/index.html.

55 Osnos, Remnick, and Yaffa, "Trump, Putin, and the New Cold War."

56 "Soviet Active Measures in the 'Post-Cold War' Era 1988–1991," Intellit, http://intellit.muskingum.edu/russia_folder/pcw_era/exec_sum.htm.

57 Thomas Rid, *Active Measures: The Secret History of Disinformation and Political Warfare* (New York: Farrar, Straus and Giroux, 2020), 330.

58 Osnos, Remnick, and Yaffa, "Trump, Putin, and the New Cold War."

59 Douglas Selvage and Christopher Nehring, "Operation 'Denver': KGB and Stasi Disinformation regarding AIDS," *Sources and Methods*, July 22, 2019, https://www.wilsoncenter.org/blog-post/opera tion-denver-kgb-and-stasi-disinformation-regarding-aids.

60 David Brennan, "Chinese State Media Pushes Conspiracy Theory That Coronavirus Escaped From Maryland Military Base," *Newsweek*, May 12, 2020, https://www.newsweek.com/chinese -state-media-pushes-conspiracy-theory-coronavirus-escaped-mary land-military-base-1503345.

61 Rid, *Active Measures*, 313.

62 Thomas Rid, "Disinformation: A Primer in Russian Active Measures and Influence Campaigns," Senate Committee on Intelligence, March 30, 2017, https://www.intelligence.senate.gov/sites/default/files /documents/os-trid-033017.pdf.

63 Clint Watts, *Messing with the Enemy: Surviving in a Social Media World of Hackers, Terrorists, Russians, and Fake News* (New York: HarperCollins, 2018), e-book, 141.

64 David Sanger, *The Perfect Weapon: War, Sabotage, and Fear in the Cyber Age* (New York: Penguin Random House, 2018), 157.

65 Andrei Soldatov and Irina Borogan, *The Red Web: The Struggle Between Russia's Digital Dictators and the New Online Revolutionaries* (New York: Perseus, 2015), 54.

66 Carlin, *Dawn of the Code War*, e-book, 192–193.

67 Joshua Davis, "Hackers Take Down the Most Wired Country in Europe," *Wired*, August 21, 2007, https://www.wired.com/2007/08 /ff-estonia/; Christian Lowe, "Kremlin loyalist says launched Estonia cyber-attack," Reuters, March 13, 2009, https://www.reuters.com /article/us-russia-estonia-cyberspace/kremlin-loyalist-says-launched -estonia-cyber-attack-idUSTRE52B4D820090313.

68 Osnos, Remnick, and Yaffa, "Trump, Putin, and the New Cold War."

69 Sanger, *The Perfect Weapon*, 20.

70 Ibid.

71 "Tiananmen Square: What happened in the protests of 1989?," BBC, June 4, 2019, https://www.bbc.com/news/world-asia-48445934.

72 Javier C. Hernandez, "30 Years After Tiananmen, 'Tank Man' Remains an Icon and a Mystery," *New York Times*, June 3, 2019, https://www.nytimes.com/2019/06/03/world/asia/tiananmen-tank -man.html.

73 Evan Osnos, *Age of Ambition: Chasing Fortune, Truth, and Faith in the New China* (New York: Farrar, Straus and Giroux, 2014), 145.

74 Barb Darrow, "New Node.js blocked by Great Firewall of China," GigaOm, December 5, 2011, https://gigaom.com/2011/12/05/new -node-js-blocked-by-great-firewall-of-china/.

75 Hal Brands, interview with author, April 24, 2020.

76 Seymour Martin Lipset, *Political Man: The Social Bases of Politics* (Baltimore: Johns Hopkins University Press, 1981), 31.

77 Osnos, *Age of Ambition*, 150.

78 Ibid., 25.

79 Ana Swanson, "How China used more cement in 3 years than the U.S. did in the entire 20th Century," *Washington Post*, March 24, 2015, https://www.washingtonpost.com/news/wonk/wp/2015/03/24/how-china-used-more-cement-in-3-years-than-the-u-s-did-in-the-entire-20th-century/.

80 Charles Ball, "China: a dense, striving organism," Boston.com, June 15, 2008, http://archive.boston.com/travel/getaways/asia/articles/2008/06/15/china_a_dense_striving_organism/.

81 "GDP per capita (current US$)," World Bank, https://data.worldbank.org/indicator/NY.GDP.PCAP.CD?locations=CN.

82 Martin Jacques, *When China Rules the World: The End of the Western World and the Birth of a New Global Order* (New York: Penguin Books, 2012), 18.

83 Ibid.

84 H. R. McMaster, "How China Sees the World," *The Atlantic*, May 2020, https://www.theatlantic.com/magazine/archive/2020/05/mcmaster-china-strategy/609088/.

85 Ibid.

86 Hal Brands and Jake Sullivan, "China Has Two Paths to Global Domination," *Foreign Policy*, May 22, 2020, https://foreignpolicy.com/2020/05/22/china-superpower-two-paths-global-domination-cold-war/.

87 Ibid.

88 Singer and Brooking, *LikeWar*, 95.

89 Ibid.

90 Ibid.

91 Ibid., 51.

92 William J. Clinton, "Remarks at the Paul H. Nitze School of Advanced International Studies," The American Presidency Project, March 8, 2000, https://www.presidency.ucsb.edu/documents/remarks-the-paul-h-nitze-school-advanced-international-studies.

93 Singer and Brooking, *LikeWar*, 97.

94 Qiao Liang and Wang Xiangsui, "Unrestricted Warfare," Cryptome, January 18, 2000, http://www.cryptome.org/cuw.htm.

95 "Neither war nor peace," *The Economist*, January 25, 2018, https://www.economist.com/special-report/2018/01/25/neither-war-nor-peace.

96 Carlin, *Dawn of the Code War*, e-book, 200.

97 Osnos, *Age of Ambition*, 30.

98 Sanger, *The Perfect Weapon*, 18.

99 Ibid.

100 James Glanz and John Markoff, "Vast Hacking by a China Fearful of the Web," *New York Times*, December 4, 2010, https://www.nytimes.com/2010/12/05/world/asia/05wikileaks-china.html?_r=2&hp.

101 Carlin, *Dawn of the Code War*, e-book, 323.

102 Ibid., 324.

103 Ben Buchanan, *The Hacker and the State: Cyber Attacks and the New Normal of Geopolitics* (Cambridge, MA: Harvard University Press, 2020), 90.

104 Andrew Jacobs and Miguel Helft, "Google, Citing Attack, Threatens to Exit China," *New York Times*, January 12, 2010, www.nytimes.com/2010/01/13/world/asia/13beijing.html?mcubz=1.

105 Marc Fisher, "In Tunisia, act of one fruit vendor sparks wave of revolution through Arab world," *Washington Post*, March 26, 2011, https://www.washingtonpost.com/world/in-tunisia-act-of-one-fruit-vendor-sparks-wave-of-revolution-through-arab-world/2011/03/16/AFjfsueB_story.html.

106 Ian Black, "WikiLeaks cables: Tunisia blocks site reporting 'hatred' of first lady," *The Guardian*, December 7, 2010, https://www.theguardian.com/world/2010/dec/07/wikileaks-tunisia-first-lady.

107 "Protesters with a sign that says 'Ben Ali, get lost' in French," Wikipedia, January 14, 2011, https://en.wikipedia.org/wiki/Tunisian_Revolution#/media/File:Tunisia_Unrest_-_VOA_-_Tunis_14_Jan_2011_(3).jpg.; Amira Aleya-Sghaier, "The Tunisian Revolution: The Revolution of Dignity," Taylor Francis Online, May 29, 2012, https://www.tandfonline.com/doi/abs/10.1080/21520844.2012.675545.

108 Aleya-Sghaier, "The Tunisian Revolution."

109 Jennifer Metz, "Social Media Plays Role in Toppling Tunisian President," ABC News, January 14, 2011, https://abcnews.go.com/International/tunisian-president-pushed-power-country-rocked-riots/story?id=12617025.

110 "Tunisia: President Zine al-Abidine Ben Ali forced out," BBC, January 15, 2011, https://www.bbc.com/news/world-africa-12195025.

111 "Tunisia assembly passes new constitution," BBC, January 27, 2014, https://www.bbc.com/news/world-africa-25908340.

112 Mark LeVine, "Tunisia: How the US got it wrong," *Al Jazeera*, January 16, 2011, https://www.aljazeera.com/opinions/2011/1/16/tunisia-how-the-us-got-it-wrong/.

113 Matt Richtel, "Egypt Cuts off Most Internet and Cell Service," *New York Times*, January 28, 2011, https://www.nytimes.com/2011/01/29/technology/internet/29cutoff.html.

114 Maeve Shearlaw, "Egypt five years on: was it ever a 'social media revolution'?," *The Guardian*, January 25, 2016, https://www.the

guardian.com/world/2016/jan/25/egypt-5-years-on-was-it-ever-a
-social-media-revolution.

115 Edmund Blair and Samia Nakhoul, "Egypt protests topple Mubarak
after 18 days," Reuters, February 10, 2011, https://www.reuters.com
/article/us-egypt/egypt-protests-topple-mubarak-after-18-days-idUS
TRE70O3UW20110211.

116 Alexia Tsotsis, "Libya Follows Egypt's Lead, Starts Shutting off Internet Services," *TechCrunch*, February 18, 2011, https://techcrunch
.com/2011/02/18/reports-libya-follows-egypts-lead-starts-shutting
-off-internet-services/.

117 Michael Birnbaum, "NATO launches largest airstrike against Gaddafi
regime," *Washington Post*, May 23, 2011, https://www.washington
post.com/world/french-officials-france-and-britain-to-use-attack-he
licopters-in-libya/2011/05/23/AFTF909G_story.html.

118 Tim Gaynor and Taha Zargoun, "Gaddafi caught like 'rat' in a drain,
humiliated and shot," Reuters, October 21, 2011, https://www.re
uters.com/article/us-libya-gaddafi-finalhours/gaddafi-caught-like
-rat-in-a-drain-humiliated-and-shot-idUSTRE79K43S20111021.

119 Andrew Sullivan, "The Revolution Will Be Twittered," *The Atlantic*,
June 13, 2009, https://www.theatlantic.com/daily-dish/archive/2009
/06/the-revolution-will-be-twittered/200478/.

120 Hillary Clinton, "Remarks on Internet Freedom," U.S. Department
of State, January 21, 2010, https://2009-2017.state.gov/secretary
/20092013clinton/rm/2010/01/135519.htm.

121 Alexia Tsotsis, "To Celebrate the #Jan25 Revolution, Egyptian Names
His Firstborn 'Facebook,'" *TechCrunch*, February 20, 2011, https://
techcrunch.com/2011/02/19/facebook-egypt-newborn/.

122 Osnos, *Age of Ambition*, 219.

123 Michael McFaul, "Russia as It Is," *Foreign Affairs*, August 2018,
https://www.foreignaffairs.com/articles/russia-fsu/2018-06-14/rus
sia-it.

124 Osnos, Remnick, and Yaffa, "Trump, Putin, and the New Cold
War."

125 Reuters Staff, "Russia's Putin disgusted by Gaddafi death images,"
Reuters, October 26, 2011, https://www.reuters.com/article/libya
-gaddafi-putin/russias-putin-disgusted-by-gaddafi-death-images
-idUSR4E7K701B20111026.

126 Julia Ioffe, "What Putin Really Wants," *The Atlantic*, February 2018,
https://www.theatlantic.com/magazine/archive/2018/01/putins
-game/546548/.

127 "Vladimir Putin Claims the Internet Is 'A CIA Project,'" NBC News,
April 24, 2014, https://www.nbcnews.com/storyline/ukraine-crisis
/vladimir-putin-claims-internet-cia-project-n88766.

128 Kurt Andersen, "The Protester," *Time*, December 14, 2011, http://con

tent.time.com/time/specials/packages/printout/0,29239,2101745
_2102132_2102373,00.html.

129 Michael Schwirtz and David M. Herszenhorn, "Voters Watch Polls in Russia, and Fraud Is What They See," *New York Times*, December 5, 2011, https://www.nytimes.com/2011/12/06/world/europe /russian-parliamentary-elections-criticized-by-west.html.

130 David M. Herszenhorn and Ellen Barry, "Putin Contends Clinton Incited Unrest Over Vote," *New York Times*, December 8, 2011, https://www.nytimes.com/2011/12/09/world/europe/putin-ac cuses-clinton-of-instigating-russian-protests.html.

131 Singer and Brooking, *LikeWar*, 87.

132 Osnos, Remnick, and Yaffa, "Trump, Putin, and the New Cold War."

133 "Questia," Gale, https://www.questia.com/library/journal/1P3-3936 791341/the-value-of-science-is-in-the-foresight.

134 Andrey Kurkov, "Ukraine's revolution: Making sense of a year of chaos," BBC, November 21, 2014, https://www.bbc.com/news/world -europe-30131108.

135 Vitaly Shevchenko, "'Little green men' or 'Russian invaders'?," BBC, March 11, 2014, https://www.bbc.com/news/world-europe-26 532154.

136 Szabolcs Panyi, "Orbán is a tool in Putin's information war against the West," Index, April 2, 2017, https://index.hu/english/2017/02 /04/orban_is_a_tool_for_putin_in_his_information_war_against _the_west/.

137 Singer and Brooking, *LikeWar*, 204.

138 Chen, "The Agency."

139 Buchanan, *The Hacker and the State*, 195–196.

140 Andrew Chatzky and James McBride, "China's Massive Belt and Road Initiative," Council on Foreign Relations, January 28, 2020, https://www.cfr.org/backgrounder/chinas-massive-belt-and-road -initiative.

141 Charles Clover, Sherry Fei Ju, and Lucy Hornby, "China's Xi hails Belt and Road as 'project of the century,'" *Financial Times*, May 14, 2017, https://www.ft.com/content/88d584a2-385e-11e7-821a-6027 b8a20f23.

142 Andrew Kitson and Kenny Liew, "China Doubles Down on Its Digi-tal Silk Road," Reconnecting Asia, November 14, 2019, https://recon nectingasia.csis.org/analysis/entries/china-doubles-down-its-digital -silk-road/.

143 "Made in China 2025," Center for Strategic and International Stud-ies, June 1, 2015, https://www.csis.org/analysis/made-china-2025.

144 Sarah Cook, "China's Cyber Superpower Strategy: Implementa-tion, Internet Freedom Implications, and U.S. Responses," Free-dom House, September 28, 2018, https://freedomhouse.org/article

/chinas-cyber-superpower-strategy-implementation-internet-freedom
-implications-and-us.

145 "Civil-Military Fusion: The Missing Link Between China's Technological and Military Rise," Council on Foreign Relations, January 29, 2018,
https://www.cfr.org/blog/civil-military-fusion-missing-link-between
-chinas-technological-and-military-rise.

146 "National Intelligence Law of the People's Republic," Chinese People's
National Congress Network, Brown University, https://cs.brown.edu
/courses/csci1800/sources/2017_PRC_NationalIntelligenceLaw.pdf.

147 "Tweet from @gerryshih," Twitter, July 15, 2020, https://twitter.com
/gerryshih/status/1283590815466455040?s=20; Xi Jinping, "The
leadership of the Chinese Communist Party is the most essential feature of socialism with Chinese characteristics," *Quishi*, July 15, 2020,
http://www.qstheory.cn/dukan/qs/2020-07/15/c_1126234524.htm.

148 Carlin, *Dawn of the Code War*, e-book, 437.

149 Ibid., 468–469.

150 Ibid., 485.

151 Ellen Nakashima, "Confidential report lists U.S. weapons system designs compromised by Chinese cyberspies," *Washington Post*, May
27, 2013, https://www.washingtonpost.com/world/national-security
/confidential-report-lists-us-weapons-system-designs-compromised
-by-chinese-cyberspies/2013/05/27/a42c3e1c-c2dd-11e2-8c3b
-0b5e9247e8ca_story.html.

152 Sanger, *The Perfect Weapon*, 100.

153 "FACT SHEET: President Xi Jinping's State Visit to the United
States," The White House, September 25, 2015, https://obama
whitehouse.archives.gov/the-press-office/2015/09/25/fact-sheet
-president-xi-jinpings-state-visit-united-states.

154 "Member of Sophisticated China-Based Hacking Group Indicted
for Series of Computer Intrusions, Including 2015 Data Breach of
Health Insurer Anthem Inc. Affecting Over 78 Million People," U.S.
Department of Justice, May 9, 2019, https://www.justice.gov/opa
/pr/member-sophisticated-china-based-hacking-group-indicted
-series-computer-intrusions-including.

155 Carlin, *Dawn of the Code War*, e-book, 618.

156 Sanger, *The Perfect Weapon*, 114.

157 Ibid.

158 Jason Chaffetz, Mark Meadows, and Will Hurd, "The OPM Data
Breach: How the Government Jeopardized Our National Security for
More than a Generation," Committee on Oversight and Government
Reform, September 7, 2016, https://republicans-oversight.house
.gov/wp-content/uploads/2016/09/The-OPM-Data-Breach-How
-the-Government-Jeopardized-Our-National-Security-for-More-than
-a-Generation.pdf.

159 Carlin, *Dawn of the Code War*, e-book, 393–395.

160 Ibid., 403.

161 Buchanan, *The Hacker and the State*, 163.

162 Ibid., 168.

163 Sanger, *The Perfect Weapon*, 136.

164 "Jenny Jun, Scott LaFoy, and Ethan Sohn, "North Korea's Cyber Operations: Strategy and Responses," Center for Strategic and International Studies, https://csis-website-prod.s3.amazonaws.com /s3fs-public/legacy_files/files/publication/151216_Cha_NorthKoreas CyberOperations_Web.pdf.

165 Ibid.

166 Buchanan, *The Hacker and the State*, 173.

167 Carlin, *Dawn of the Code War*, e-book, 552.

168 Buchanan, *The Hacker and the State*, 179.

169 Kelsey McKinney, "The 8 most embarrassing revelations from the Sony hack," *Vox*, December 12, 2014, https://www.vox.com/2014 /12/12/7377685/sony-hack-drama.

170 Sanger, *The Perfect Weapon*, 142.

171 Ibid., 141.

172 Ibid., 144.

173 Aaron Sorkin, "The Sony Hack and the Yellow Press," *New York Times*, December 14, 2014, https://www.nytimes.com/2014/12/15 /opinion/aaron-sorkin-journalists-shouldnt-help-the-sony-hackers .html.

174 Watts, *Messing with the Enemy*, e-book, 149.

175 Sanger, *The Perfect Weapon*, 172.

176 Osnos, Remnick, and Yaffa, "Trump, Putin, and the New Cold War."

177 Sanger, *The Perfect Weapon*, 173.

178 Buchanan, *The Hacker and the State*, 217.

179 Sanger, *The Perfect Weapon*, 174.

180 Ibid., 205

181 Ibid., 193.

182 Ibid., 193.

183 Rid, *Active Measures*, 379

184 Buchanan, *The Hacker and the State*, 225, 229.

185 Jeff Stein, "What 20,000 pages of hacked WikiLeaks emails teach us about Hillary Clinton," *Vox*, October 20, 2016, https://www.vox .com/policy-and-politics/2016/10/20/13308108/wikileaks-podesta -hillary-clinton.

186 Singer and Brooking, *LikeWar*, 143–144.

187 Mike Isaac and Daisuke Wakabayashi, "Russian Influence Reached 126 Million Through Facebook Alone," *New York Times*, October 30, 2017, https://www.nytimes.com/2017/10/30/technology/face book-google-russia.html.

188 John D. Gallacher and Marc W. Heerdink, "Measuring the Effect of Russian Internet Research Agency Information Operations in Online Conversations," *Defence Strategic Communications* 6 (Spring 2019): 155–198, doi 10.30966/2018.RIGA.6, https://www.stratcomcoe .org/jd-gallacher-m-w-heerdink-measuring-effect-russian-internet -research-agency-information-operations.

189 Jane Mayer, "How Russia Helped Swing the Election for Trump," *New Yorker,* September 24, 2018, https://www.newyorker.com /magazine/2018/10/01/how-russia-helped-to-swing-the-election -for-trump.

190 "2016 November General Election Turnout Rates," United States Elections Project, September 5, 2018, http://www.electproject.org /2016g.

191 Philip Bump, "Donald Trump will be president thanks to 80,000 people in three states," *Washington Post*, December 1, 2016, https:// www.washingtonpost.com/news/the-fix/wp/2016/12/01/donald -trump-will-be-president-thanks-to-80000-people-in-three-states/.

192 Steven T. Dennis and Ben Brody, "Russian Operative Said 'We Made America Great' After Trump's Win," *Bloomberg,* October 8, 2019, https://www.bloomberg.com/news/articles/2019-10-08/senate-in telligence-panel-warns-russian-meddling-continues.

Chapter 2: THE SOFTWARE WAR ON THE FRONT-END OF YOUR SCREEN

1 Gary Shteyngart, "'Out of My Mouth Comes Unimpeachable Manly Truth,'" *New York Times*, February 18, 2015, https://www.nytimes .com/2015/02/22/magazine/out-of-my-mouth-comes-unimpeach able-manly-truth.html.

2 "Trump transition: Who is General 'Mad Dog' Mattis?," BBC, December 2, 2015, https://www.bbc.com/news/world-us-canada-38056197.

3 "VOA Through the Years," VOA Public Relations, April 3, 2017, https://www.insidevoa.com/a/3794247.html; "History," Radio Free Europe, https://pressroom.rferl.org/history.

4 Robert W. Chandler, *War of Ideas: The U.S. Propaganda Campaign in Vietnam* (New York: Westview Press, 1981), 3, 29.

5 Rid, *Active Measures*, 12.

6 Stephen Kinzer, *All the Shah's Men: An American Coup and the Roots of Middle East Terror* (Hoboken, NJ: Wiley, 2003), 5–6.

7 Onora O'Neill, "Shoot the messenger," *The Guardian*, May 1, 2002, https://www.theguardian.com/comment/story/0,3604,707820,00 .html.

8 Michiko Kakutani, review of David Shenk, *"Data Smog": Created by Overload of Information, New York Times,* July 8, 1997, https://ar chive.nytimes.com/www.nytimes.com/books/97/07/06/daily/data -book-review.html.

9 Niraj Chokshi, "That Wasn't Mark Twain: How a Misquotation Is Born," *New York Times*, April 26, 2017, https://www.nytimes.com /2017/04/26/books/famous-misquotations.html.

10 Soroush Vosoughi, Deb Roy, and Sinan Aral, "The Spread of True and False News Online," MIT Initiative on the Digital Economy, http:// ide.mit.edu/sites/default/files/publications/2017%20IDE%20Re search%20Brief%20False%20News.pdf.

11 Craig Silverman, "This Analysis Shows How Viral Fake Election News Stories Outperformed Real News On Facebook," *BuzzFeed News*, November 16, 2016, https://www.buzzfeednews.com/article /craigsilverman/viral-fake-election-news-outperformed-real-news -on-facebook#.sf9JbwppAm.

12 Jamie Susskind, *Future Politics: Living Together in a World Transformed by Tech* (New York: Oxford University Press, 2018), 230.

13 Brooke Donald, "Stanford researchers find students have trouble judging the credibility of information online," Stanford News and Media, November 22, 2016, https://ed.stanford.edu/news/stanford -researchers-find-students-have-trouble-judging-credibility-informa tion-online.

14 Joel Breakstone, Mark Smith, and Sam Wineburg, "Students' Civic Online Reasoning," Stanford, https://stacks.stanford.edu /file/druid:gf151tb4868/Civic%20Online%20Reasoning%20Na tional%20Portrait.pdf.

15 Matt McKinney, "'If it's going viral, it must be true': Hampton Roads kids struggle with fake news, teachers say," *Virginian-Pilot*, November 28, 2016, https://www.pilotonline.com/news/education/article _4a785dfb-3dd3-5229-9578-c4585adfefb4.html.

16 Yosh Halberstam and Brian Knight, "Homophily, Group Size, and the Diffusion of Political Information in Social Networks: Evidence from Twitter," National Bureau of Economic Research, November 2014, https://www.nber.org/system/files/working_papers/w20681 /w20681.pdf.

17 Zeynep Tufekci, "YouTube, the Great Radicalizer," *New York Times*, March 10, 2018, https://www.nytimes.com/2018/03/10/opinion /sunday/youtube-politics-radical.html.

18 "The Flat Earth Society," Facebook, https://www.facebook.com/Flat EarthToday/.

19 Singer and Brooking, *LikeWar*, 126.

20 Steven Levy, "'Hackers' and 'Information Wants to Be Free,'" *Medium*, November 21, 2014, https://medium.com/backchannel/the -definitive-story-of-information-wants-to-be-free-a8d95427641c# .y7d0amvr3.

21 Michael M. Grynbaum, "Right-Wing Media Uses Parkland Shooting as Conspiracy Fodder," *New York Times*, February 20, 2018, https://

www.nytimes.com/2018/02/20/business/media/parkland-shooting
-media-conspiracy.html.

22 Jennifer Kavanagh and Michael D. Rich, "Truth Decay: An Initial Exploration of the Diminishing Role of Facts and Analysis in American Public Life," RAND Corporation, 2018, https://www.rand.org/pubs/research_reports/RR2314.html.

23 Indictment, U.S. Department of Justice, 18 U.S.C. §§ 2,371, 1349, 1028A, https://www.justice.gov/opa/press-release/file/1035562/download.

24 Chen, "The Agency."

25 Renee DiResta, Kris Shaffer, Becky Ruppel, "The Tactics & Tropes of the Internet Research Agency," *Disinformation Report*, https://disinformationreport.blob.core.windows.net/disinformation-report/NewKnowledge-Disinformation-Report-Whitepaper.pdf.

26 Sanger, *The Perfect Weapon*, 182.

27 Indictment, U.S. Department of Justice, 18 U.S.C. §§ 2,371, 1349, 1028A.

28 Chen, "The Agency."

29 Rid, *Active Measures*, 408–409.

30 Jim Rutenberg, "RT, Sputnik and Russia's New Theory of War," *New York Times*, September 13, 2017, https://www.nytimes.com/2017/09/13/magazine/rt-sputnik-and-russias-new-theory-of-war.html.

31 Rid, *Active Measures*, 400.

32 "Did Russia Influence Brexit?," Center for Strategic and International Studies, July 21, 2020, https://www.csis.org/blogs/brexit-bits-bobs-and-blogs/did-russia-influence-brexit.

33 Matthew Field and Mike Wright, "Russian trolls sent thousands of pro-Leave messages on day of Brexit referendum, Twitter data reveals," *The Telegraph*, October 17, 2018, https://www.telegraph.co.uk/technology/2018/10/17/russian-iranian-twitter-trolls-sent-10-million-tweets-fake-news/.

34 Indictment, U.S. Department of Justice, 18 U.S.C. §§ 2,371, 1349, 1028A.

35 Rid, *Active Measures*, 402.

36 DiResta, Shaffer, and Ruppel, "The Tactics & Tropes of the Internet Research Agency."

37 Sanger, *The Perfect Weapon*, 201.

38 Indictment, U.S. Department of Justice, 18 U.S.C. §§ 2,371, 1349, 1028A.

39 Rid, *Active Measures*, 401.

40 DiResta, Shaffer, and Ruppel, "The Tactics & Tropes of the Internet Research Agency," October 2019, https://digitalcommons.unl.edu/cgi/viewcontent.cgi?article=1003&context=senatedocs.

41 Franklin Foer, "Putin Is Well on His Way to Stealing the Next Elec-

tion," *The Atlantic*, June 2020, https://www.theatlantic.com/maga
zine/archive/2020/06/putin-american-democracy/610570/.

42 DiResta, Shaffer, and Ruppel, "The Tactics & Tropes of the Internet
Research Agency."

43 Ibid.

44 Ibid.

45 Ibid.

46 Ibid.

47 Ibid.

48 Ibid.

49 "Russian Active Measures Campaigns and Interference in the 2016
U.S. Election," Select Committee on Intelligence, https://www.intel
ligence.senate.gov/sites/default/files/documents/Report_Volume2
.pdf.

50 DiResta, Shaffer, and Ruppel, "The Tactics & Tropes of the Internet
Research Agency."

51 Ibid.

52 Ibid.

53 Indictment, U.S. Department of Justice, 18 U.S.C. §§ 2,371, 1349,
1028A.

54 Sanger, *The Perfect Weapon*, 186.

55 Claire Allbright, "A Russian Facebook page organized a protest in
Texas. A different Russian page launched the counterprotest," *Texas
Tribune*, November 1, 2017, https://www.texastribune.org/2017
/11/01/russian-facebook-page-organized-protest-texas-different-rus
sian-page-l/.

56 DiResta, Shaffer, and Ruppel, "The Tactics & Tropes of the Internet
Research Agency."

57 Indictment, U.S. Department of Justice, 18 U.S.C. §§ 2,371, 1349,
1028A; Frank Cerabino, "Local Trump supporters shrug off being
paid and played by Russians," *Palm Beach Post*, February 23, 2018,
https://www.palmbeachpost.com/news/local-trump-supporters
-shrug-off-being-paid-and-played-russians/3WCytHAHy3PodLVe
PU1PMK/.

58 Tony Romm, "Zuckerberg: Standing For Voice and Free Expression,"
Washington Post, October 17, 2019, https://www.washingtonpost
.com/technology/2019/10/17/zuckerberg-standing-voice-free-ex
pression/.

59 Romm, "Zuckerberg."

60 Byron Tau and Deepa Seetharaman, "Senators Press Tech Officials
Over Missed Signs of Russia Influence," *Wall Street Journal*, October 31, 2017, https://www.wsj.com/articles/senators-press-tech-offi
cials-over-missed-signs-of-russia-influence-1509489592.

61 Ben Gomes, "Our latest quality improvements for Search," Google,

April 25, 2017, https://blog.google/products/search/our-latest-qual
ity-improvements-search/.

62 Danny Sullivan, "Google now handles at least 2 trillion searches per
year," *Search Engine Land*, May 24, 2016, https://searchengineland
.com/google-now-handles-2-999-trillion-searches-per-year-250247.

63 "Google News policies," Google, https://support.google.com/news
/publisher-center/answer/6204050?hl=en.

64 Mark Bergen, "Google Changes Rules to Purge News That Masks
Country of Origin," *Bloomberg*, December 15, 2017, https://www
.bloomberg.com/news/articles/2017-12-15/google-changes-rules
-to-purge-news-that-masks-country-of-origin?fbclid=IwAR2QcDy
7IheQLYz5T-aNntaP61k-BFaxucM6yLZSExgQHSPfJwpDJthEyIQ.

65 Raymond Wong, "Google's taking another big step to stop the spread
of fake news," *Mashable*, December 17, 2017, https://mashable
.com/2017/12/17/google-news-no-hiding-country-origin-stop-fake
-news/?fbclid=IwAR2XOal9c41fBx0dvkI1roYZYJgkn7G87r0P86ir
eEOrNVHE96wF8cgobi0#t67OIbjrsmqX.

66 David Sacks, "The Speech Cartel," *Medium*, January 16, 2021,
https://davidsacks.medium.com/the-speech-cartel-b3f5555f7787.

67 Indictment, U.S. Department of Justice, 18 U.S.C. §§ 2,371, 1349,
1028A.

68 "The Cambridge Analytica Files," *The Guardian*, https://www
.theguardian.com/news/series/cambridge-analytica-files;   Matthew
Rosenberg, Nicholas Confessore, and Carole Cadwalladr, "How
Trump Consultants Exploited the Facebook Data of Millions," *New
York Times*, March 17, 2018, https://www.nytimes.com/2018/03/17
/us/politics/cambridge-analytica-trump-campaign.html.

69 Brittany Kaiser, *Targeted: The Cambridge Analytica Whistleblower's
Inside Story of How Big Data, Trump, and Facebook Broke Democracy and How It Can Happen Again* (New York: HarperCollins,
2019), 78.

70 Singer and Brooking, *LikeWar*, 61.

71 Hannes Grassegger and Mikael Krogerus, "The Data That Turned the
World Upside Down," *Vice*, January 28, 2017, https://www.vice.com
/en_us/article/mg9vvn/how-our-likes-helped-trump-win.

72 Grassegger and Krogerus, "The Data That Turned the World Upside
Down."

73 Paul Grewal, "Suspending Cambridge Analytica and SCL Group
From Facebook," Facebook, March 17, 2018, https://about.fb.com
/news/2018/03/suspending-cambridge-analytica/.

74 "FTC Imposes $5 Billion Penalty and Sweeping New Privacy Re-
strictions on Facebook," Federal Trade Commission, July 24, 2019,
https://www.ftc.gov/news-events/press-releases/2019/07/ftc-im
poses-5-billion-penalty-sweeping-new-privacy-restrictions.

75 "ICO investigation into use of personal information and political influence," Information Commissioner's Office, October 2, 2020, https://ico.org.uk/media/action-weve-taken/2618383/20201002_ico-o-ed-l-rtl-0181_to-julian-knight-mp.pdf.

76 "ICO investigation into use of personal information and political influence."

77 Craig Timberg, Tony Romm, and Elizabeth Dwoskin, "Zuckerberg apologizes, promises reform as senators grill him over Facebook's failings," *Washington Post*, April 10, 2018, https://www.washingtonpost.com/business/technology/2018/04/10/b72c09e8-3d03-11e8-974f-aacd97698cef_story.html.

78 Drew Harwell, "Facebook is now in the data-privacy spotlight. Could Google be next?," *Washington Post*, April 11, 2018, https://www.washingtonpost.com/news/the-switch/wp/2018/04/11/facebook-is-now-in-the-data-privacy-spotlight-could-google-be-next/.

79 Nellie Bowles and Sheera Frenkel, "Facebook and Twitter Plan New Ways to Regulate Political Ads," *New York Times*, May 24, 2018, https://www.nytimes.com/2018/05/24/technology/twitter-political-ad-restrictions.html.

80 Sheera Frenkel and Matthew Rosenberg, "Top Tech Companies Met With Intelligence Officials to Discuss Midterms," *New York Times*, June 25, 2018, https://www.nytimes.com/2018/06/25/technology/tech-meeting-midterm-elections.html.

81 Sheera Frenkel and Nicholas Fandos, "Facebook Identifies New Influence Operations Spanning Globe," *New York Times*, August 21, 2018, https://www.nytimes.com/2018/08/21/technology/facebook-political-influence-midterms.html.

82 Michael Wines and Julian E. Barnes, "How the U.S. Is Fighting Russian Election Interference," *New York Times,* August 2, 2018, https://www.nytimes.com/2018/08/02/us/politics/russia-election-interference.html.

83 Kent Walker, "Supporting election integrity through greater advertising transparency," Google, May 4, 2018, https://blog.google/topics/public-policy/supporting-election-integrity-through-greater-advertising-transparency/.

84 "Update to Misrepresentation policy (September 2020)," Google, July 2020, https://support.google.com/adspolicy/answer/9991401?hl=en&ref_topic=29265.

85 Kirill Meleshevich and Bret Schafer, "Online Information Laundering: The Role of Social Media," Alliance for Securing Democracy, January 2018, https://securingdemocracy.gmfus.org/wp-content/uploads/2018/06/InfoLaundering_final-edited.pdf.

86 Anton Troianovski, "A former Russian troll speaks: 'It was like being in Orwell's world,'" *Washington Post*, February 17, 2018, https://

www.washingtonpost.com/news/worldviews/wp/2018/02/17/a-for
mer-russian-troll-speaks-it-was-like-being-in-orwells-world/.

87 Laura Sydell, "We Tracked Down a Fake-News Creator in the Sub-
urbs. Here's What We Learned," NPR, November 23, 2016, https://
www.npr.org/sections/alltechconsidered/2016/11/23/503146770
/npr-finds-the-head-of-a-covert-fake-news-operation-in-the-suburbs.

88 Ben Schreckinger, "How Russia Targets the U.S. Military," *Politico*,
June 12, 2017, https://www.politico.com/magazine/story/2017/06
/12/how-russia-targets-the-us-military-215247.

89 Singer and Brooking, *LikeWar*, 112.

90 Ibid., Singer and Brooking, 141.

91 "Fake Accounts," Facebook, https://transparency.facebook.com
/community-standards-enforcement#fake-accounts.

92 "Former Russian Troll Describes Night Shift as 'Bacchanalia,'"
Moscow Times, October 27, 2017, https://www.themoscowtimes
.com/2017/10/27/former-russian-troll-describes-night-shift-as
-bacchanalia-a59398.

93 Meleshevich and Schafer, "Online Information Laundering: The Role
of Social Media."

94 Ben Collins and Joseph Cox, "Jenna Abrams, Russia's Clown Troll
Princess, Duped the Mainstream Media and the World," *Daily Beast*,
November 3, 2017, https://www.thedailybeast.com/jenna-abrams-rus
sias-clown-troll-princess-duped-the-mainstream-media-and-the-world.

95 Patrick Kingsley and Richard Pérez-Peña, "In Poisoning of Sergei
Skripal, Russian Ex-Spy, U.K. Sees Cold War Echoes," *New York
Times*, March 6, 2018, https://www.nytimes.com/2018/03/06
/world/europe/uk-russian-spy-counterterrorism.html.

96 "Home," Salisbury Cathedral, https://www.salisburycathedral.org
.uk/; "Anthony Daniels," IMDb, https://www.imdb.com/name/nm
0000355/.

97 Kingsley and Pérez-Peña, "In Poisoning of Sergei Skripal, Russian
Ex-Spy, U.K. Sees Cold War Echoes."

98 Michael Schwirtz, "Top Secret Russian Unit Seeks to Destabilize
Europe, Security Officials Say," *New York Times*, October 8, 2019,
https://www.nytimes.com/2019/10/08/world/europe/unit-291
55-russia-gru.html.

99 Kingsley and Pérez-Peña, "In Poisoning of Sergei Skripal, Russian
Ex-Spy, U.K. Sees Cold War Echoes."

100 William Booth, "Theresa May: 'Highly likely' Russia responsible
for spy's poisoning by nerve agent," *Washington Post*, May 12,
2018, https://www.washingtonpost.com/world/theresa-may-says
-highly-likely-russia-is-responsible-for-spys-poisoning/2018/03/12
/7baa6d22-25f4-11e8-a227-fd2b009466bc_story.html.

101 Singer and Brooking, *LikeWar*, 107.

102 Watts, *Messing with the Enemy*, e-book, 92.
103 Jim Rutenberg, "Larry King, the Russian Media and a Partisan Land-scape," *New York Times*, September 18, 2016, https://www.nytimes.com/2016/09/19/business/media/moscow-joins-the-partisan-media-landscape-with-familiar-american-faces.html.
104 Hunter Walker and Michael Isikoff, "FBI document cache sheds light on inner workings of Russia's U.S. news (and propaganda) net-work," Yahoo! News, October 13, 2017, https://news.yahoo.com/fbi-document-cache-sheds-light-inner-workings-russias-u-s-news-propaganda-network-172317008.html.
105 Singer and Brooking, *LikeWar*, 107.
106 Ibid.
107 "Home," RT, https://www.rt.com/.
108 Watts, *Messing with the Enemy*, e-book, 93.
109 "Anatomy of an Info-War: How Russia's Propaganda Machine Works, and How to Counter It," StopFake, May 19, 2015, https://www.stopfake.org/en/anatomy-of-an-info-war-how-russia-s-propaganda-machine-works-and-how-to-counter-it/.
110 Finian Cunningham, "Who Gains From Poisoning a Russian Exile in Britain?," *Sputnik News*, March 8, 2018, https://sputniknews.com/columnists/201803081062350153-who-gains-from-poisonings-russian-ex-spy-uk/.
111 "UK intelligence may be complicit in Skripal's poisoning—ex-FSB head," RT, March 13, 2018, https://www.rt.com/news/421123-uk-complicit-skripal-poisoning/.
112 "Russian Ex-Spy's Poisoning Seems Like Ploy to Derail UK-Russia Ties—Analysts," *Sputnik News*, March 13, 2018, https://sputniknews.com/analysis/201803131062492854-russia-spy-poisoning-bilateral-relations/.
113 "US Had Access to Substance Allegedly Used to Poison Skripal Since 1999—Report," *Sputnik News*, March 14, 2018, https://sputniknews.com/world/201803141062510743-skripal-case-novichok-us-uzbekistan/.
114 Ruptly, "Russia: UK may have orchestrated attack on Skripal's daughter—FM official," YouTube, March 21, 2018, https://www.youtube.com/watch?v=RsM-MCKhMWw.
115 Ruptly, "Russia: Skripal was of 'zero value' to Moscow—Peskov *EXCLUSIVE*," YouTube, March 22, 2018, https://www.youtube.com/watch?v=UhAjHvIWbSE.
116 "'We're not agents': UK's suspects in Skripal case talk exclusively with RT's editor-in-chief," RT, September 13, 2018, https://www.rt.com/news/438350-petrov-boshirov-interview-simonyan/.
117 Susskind, *Future Politics: Living Together in a World Transformed by Tech*, 95.

118 Michael Golebiewski, "Where Missing Data Can Easily Be Exploited," Data & Society 2008, https://datasociety.net/wp-content /uploads/2019/11/Data-Voids-2.0-Final.pdf.

119 "County, City to Hold Observances of Two-Year Anniversary of Wildfires," Sonoma County, October 7, 2019, https://sonomacounty .ca.gov/CAO/Press-Releases/Observances-of-Two-Year-Anniver sary-of-Wildfires/.

120 Dale Kasler, "Wine country wildfire costs now top $9 billion, costliest in California history," *Sacramento Bee*, https://www.sacbee.com /news/california/fires/article188377854.html.

121 Niraj Chokshi, "How the California Wildfire Was Falsely Pinned on an Immigrant," *New York Times*, October 20, 2017, https://www .nytimes.com/2017/10/20/us/wildfire-immigrant-breitbart.html.

122 Chriss W. Street, "ICE Detainer Issued for Suspected Wine Country Arsonist in Sonoma Jail," *Breitbart*, October 17, 2017, https://www .breitbart.com/local/2017/10/17/ice-detainer-issued-for-suspected -wine-country-arsonist-in-sonoma-jail/.

123 Kate Conger, Davey Alba and Mike Baker, "False Rumors That Activists Set Wildfires Exasperate Officials," *New York Times*, September 10, 2020, https://www.nytimes.com/2020/09/10/us /antifa-wildfires.html.

124 Audra D. S. Burch and Patricia Mazzei, "Death Toll Is at 17 and Could Rise in Florida School Shooting," *New York Times*, February 14, 2018, https://www.nytimes.com/2018/02/14/us/parkland -school-shooting.html.

125 Matthew Yglesias, "The Parkland conspiracy theories, explained," *Vox*, February 22, 2018, https://www.vox.com/policy-and-politics /2018/2/22/17036018/parkland-conspiracy-theories.

126 Geoff Brumfiel, "As an American Tragedy Unfolds, Russian Agents Sow Discord Online," NPR, February 16, 2018, https://www.npr .org/sections/thetwo-way/2018/02/16/586361956/as-an-american -tragedy-unfolds-russian-agents-sow-discord-online.

127 Margaret E. Roberts, *Censored: Distraction and Diversion Inside China's Great Firewall* (Princeton, NJ: Princeton University Press, 2018), 6.

128 Ibid.

129 Gary King, Jennifer Pan, and Margaret E. Roberts, "How the Chinese Government Fabricates Social Media Posts for Strategic Distraction, not Engaged Argument," Harvard, April 9, 2017, https://gking.har vard.edu/files/gking/files/50c.pdf.

130 Marc Faddoul, Guillaume Chaslot, and Hany Farid, "A longitudinal analysis of YouTube's promotion of conspiracy videos," UC–Berkeley, March 6, 2020, https://farid.berkeley.edu/downloads/publications /arxiv20.pdf.

131 Renee DiResta, "The Digital Maginot Line," Ribbonfarm, November 28, 2018, https://www.ribbonfarm.com/2018/11/28/the-digital-maginot-line/.

132 Mark Scott and Laurens Cerulus, "Russian groups targeted EU election with fake news, says European Commission," *Politico*, June 14, 2019, https://www.politico.eu/article/european-commission-disinformation-report-russia-fake-news/.

133 Davey Alba and Sheera Frenkel, "Russia Tests New Disinformation Tactics in Africa to Expand Influence," *New York Times*, October 30, 2019, https://www.nytimes.com/2019/10/30/technology/russia-facebook-disinformation-africa.html.

134 Michael Schwirtz and Sheera Frenkel, "In Ukraine, Russia Tests a New Facebook Tactic in Election Tampering," *New York Times*, March 29, 2019, https://www.nytimes.com/2019/03/29/world/europe/ukraine-russia-election-tampering-propaganda.html.

135 Alba and Frenkel, "Russia Tests New Disinformation Tactics in Africa to Expand Influence."

136 Ibid.

137 Davey Alba, "How Russia's Troll Farm Is Changing Tactics Before the Fall Election," *New York Times*, March 29, 2020, https://www.nytimes.com/2020/03/29/technology/russia-troll-farm-election.html.

138 "America has always been hinged on hard-working people," UMD Archive, September 23, 2016, https://archive.mith.umd.edu/irads/items/show/8941.html.

139 Alba, "How Russia's Troll Farm Is Changing Tactics Before the Fall Election."

140 Ibid.

141 Ibid.

142 Nicole Perlroth, "A Conspiracy Made in America May Have Been Spread by Russia," *New York Times*, June 15, 2020, https://www.nytimes.com/2020/06/15/technology/coronavirus-disinformation-russia-iowa-caucus.html.

143 Joseph Menn, "Russian-backed organizations amplifying QAnon conspiracy theories, researchers say," Reuters, August 24, 2020, https://www.reuters.com/article/us-usa-election-qanon-russia/russian-backed-organizations-amplifying-qanon-conspiracy-theories-researchers-say-idUSKBN25K13T.

144 Nicole Perlroth, "A Conspiracy Made in America May Have Been Spread by Russia."

145 Andy Greenberg, "Hackers broke into real news sites to plant fake stories," *Wired*, July 29, 2020, https://www.wired.com/story/hackers-broke-into-real-news-sites-to-plant-fake-stories-anti-nato/.

146 Charles Davis, "'Grassroots' Media Startup Redfish Is Supported by the Kremlin," *Daily Beast*, June 19, 2018, https://www.the

dailybeast.com/grassroots-media-startup-redfish-is-supported-by
-the-kremlin.

147 Albert Shuldiner, "Declaratory Ruling," Federal Communications
Commission, May 29, 2020, https://docs.fcc.gov/public/attachments
/DA-20-568A1.pdf.

148 "Assessment on U.S. Defense Implications of China's Expanding Global Access," U.S. Department of Defense, December 2018,
https://media.defense.gov/2019/Jan/14/2002079292/-1/-1/1/EX
PANDING-GLOBAL-ACCESS-REPORT-FINAL.PDF.

149 Neil MacFarquhar, "Playing on Kansas City Radio: Russian Propaganda," *New York Times*, February 13, 2020, https://www.nytimes
.com/2020/02/13/us/russian-propaganda-radio.html.

150 Renee DiResta, Carly Miller, Vanessa Molter, John Pomfret, and
Glenn Tiffert, "Telling China's Story: The Chinese Communist Party's
Campaign to Shape Global Narratives," 2020, https://fsi-live.s3.us
-west-1.amazonaws.com/s3fs-public/sio-china_story_white_paper
-final.pdf.

151 DiResta, Miller, Molter, Pomfret, and Tiffert, "Telling China's Story:
The Chinese Communist Party's Campaign to Shape Global Narratives."

152 Craig Silverman and Jane Lytvynenko, "Reddit Has Become a Battle-
ground of Alleged Chinese Trolls," *BuzzFeed News*, March 14, 2019,
https://www.buzzfeednews.com/article/craigsilverman/reddit-coor
dinated-chinese-propaganda-trolls.

153 Kate Conger, "Twitter Removes Chinese Disinformation Campaign,"
New York Times, June 11, 2020, https://www.nytimes.com/2020
/06/11/technology/twitter-chinese-misinformation.html?action=
click&module=Alert&pgtype=Homepage.

154 Conger, "Twitter Removes Chinese Disinformation Campaign."

155 Jeff Horwitz, "'Live' Facebook Protest Videos Drew Millions of
Views, but Some Footage Was Years Old," *Wall Street Journal*,
June 2, 2020, https://www.wsj.com/articles/live-facebook-protest
-videos-drew-millions-of-views-but-some-footage-was-years-old
-11591118628.

156 DiResta, Miller, Molter, Pomfret, and Tiffert, "Telling China's Story:
The Chinese Communist Party's Campaign to Shape Global Narratives."

157 Tereza Dvorakova, "HispanTV: Iran's Attempts to Influence the
Spanish Speaking World," Radio Farda, April 19, 2020, https://
en.radiofarda.com/a/hispantv-iran-s-attempts-to-influence-the-span
ish-speaking-world-/30564208.html.

158 Carly Nyst and Nick Monaco, "State-Sponsored Trolling," 2018,
http://www.iftf.org/fileadmin/user_upload/images/DigIntel/IFTF
_State_sponsored_trolling_report.pdf.

159 Ibid.

160 Ibid.

161 Ibid.

162 "Chinese and Russian Foreign Ministry Spokespersons Held Consultations and Agreed to Cooperate in Combating Disinformation," Ministry of Foreign Affairs of the People's Republic of China, https://www.fmprc.gov.cn/mfa_eng/wjbxw/t1800619.shtml.

163 Joel Schectman, Raphael Satter, Christopher Bing, and Joseph Menn, "Exclusive: Microsoft believes Russians that hacked Clinton targeted Biden campaign firm—sources," Reuters, September 10, 2020, https://www.reuters.com/article/us-usa-election-cyber-biden-exclusive-idUSKBN2610I4.

164 Sean Lyngaas, "Industry alert pins state, local government hacking on suspected Russian group," CyberScoop, October 19, 2020, https://www.cyberscoop.com/russia-temp-isotope-election-security-mandiant/.

165 David Corn, "Giuliani and the New York Post Are Pushing Russian Disinformation. It's a Big Test for the Media," *Mother Jones*, October 14, 2020, https://www.motherjones.com/politics/2020/10/giuliani-and-the-new-york-post-are-pushing-russian-disinformation-its-a-big-test-for-the-media/.

166 Karen Kornbluh, "New Study by Digital New Deal Finds Engagement with Deceptive Outlets Higher on Facebook Today Than Run-up to 2016 Election," The German Marshall Fund of the United States, October 12, 2020, https://www.gmfus.org/blog/2020/10/12/new-study-digital-new-deal-finds-engagement-deceptive-outlets-higher-facebook-today.

167 Jordan Schneider, "China's Hopeless Twitter Influence Operations," China Talk, October 29, 2020, https://chinatalk.substack.com/p/chinas-hopeless-twitter-influence.

168 "Chinese people showing interest in US presidential election for laughs, comicalness," *Global Times*, May 11, 2020, https://www.globaltimes.cn/content/1205864.shtml.

169 "Joint Statement from Elections Infrastructure Government Coordinating Council and the Election Infrastructure Sector Coordinating Executive Committees," CISA, November 12, 2020, https://www.cisa.gov/news/2020/11/12/joint-statement-elections-infrastructure-government-coordinating-council-election.

170 David E. Sanger and Nicole Perlroth, "Trump Fires Christopher Krebs, Official Who Disputed Election Fraud Claims," *New York Times*, November 17, 2020, https://www.nytimes.com/2020/11/17/us/politics/trump-fires-christopher-krebs.html.

171 "#PROTECT2020 RUMOR VS. REALITY," CISA, https://www.cisa.gov/rumorcontrol.

172 Julian E. Barnes and David E. Sanger, "Iran and Russia Seek to Influence Election in Final Days, U.S. Officials Warn," *New York Times*, October 21, 2020, https://www.nytimes.com/2020/10/21/us/politics/iran-russia-election-interference.html.

173 Ellen Nakashima, "Cyber Command has sought to disrupt the world's largest botnet, hoping to reduce its potential impact on the election," *Washington Post*, October 9, 2020, https://www.washingtonpost.com/national-security/cyber-command-trickbot-disrupt/2020/10/09/19587aae-0a32-11eb-a166-dc429b380d10_story.html.

174 Ellen Nakashima, "U.S. undertook cyber operation against Iran as part of effort to secure the 2020 election," *Washington Post*, November 3, 2020, https://www.washingtonpost.com/national-security/cybercom-targets-iran-election-interference/2020/11/03/aa0c9790-1e11-11eb-ba21-f2f001f0554b_story.html.

175 Nakashima, "U.S. undertook cyber operation against Iran as part of effort to secure the 2020 election."

176 "New Steps to Protect the US Elections," Facebook, September 3, 2020, https://about.fb.com/news/2020/09/additional-steps-to-protect-the-us-elections/.

177 Adam Rawnsley, "Putin's Troll Farm Busted Running Sprawling Network of Facebook Pages," *Daily Beast*, September 25, 2020, https://www.thedailybeast.com/putins-troll-farm-busted-running-sprawling-network-of-facebook-pages.

178 Shirin Ghaffary, "Facebook is finally cracking down on QAnon," *Vox*, August 19, 2020, https://www.vox.com/recode/2020/8/19/21376166/facebook-qanon-take-down-groups-conspiracy-theory.

179 Vijaya Gadde and Kayvon Beykpour, "Additional steps we're taking ahead of the 2020 US Election," Twitter, October 9, 2020, https://blog.twitter.com/en_us/topics/company/2020/2020-election-changes.html.

180 Vijaya Gadde and Kayvon Beykpour, "An update on our work around the 2020 US Elections," Twitter, November 12, 2020, https://blog.twitter.com/en_us/topics/company/2020/2020-election-update.html.

181 Nick Statt, "YouTube defends choice to leave up videos with false election claims," *The Verge*, November 12, 2020, https://www.theverge.com/2020/11/12/21562910/youtube-2020-election-trump-misinformation-fake-news-recommendations.

182 Jason Murdock, "Parler Tops App Store Charts As Conservatives Flock to Site After Biden Victory Over Trump," *Newsweek*, November 9, 2020, https://www.newsweek.com/parler-tops-app-store-ios-android-charts-conservatives-twitter-biden-trump-election-1545921.

183 Tweet from @ewong, Twitter, December 9, 2020, https://twitter.com/ewong/status/1336742141264072705?s=11.

184 Patrick Murray, "National: More Americans Happy About Trump

Loss Than Biden Win," Monmouth University, November 18, 2020, https://www.monmouth.edu/polling-institute/documents/mon mouthpoll_us_111820.pdf/.

185 Sheera Frenkel, "The Rise and Fall of the 'Stop the Steal' Facebook Group," *New York Times*, November 5, 2020, https://www.nytimes .com/2020/11/05/technology/stop-the-steal-facebook-group.html.

186 Kate Conger, "Twitter Has Labeled 38% of Trump's Tweets Since Tuesday," *New York Times*, November 5, 2020, https://www.nytimes .com/2020/11/05/technology/donald-trump-twitter.html.

187 Jeff Jones, "In Election 2020, how did the media, electoral process fare? Republicans, Democrats disagree," Knight Foundation, December 7, 2020, https://knightfoundation.org/articles/in-election -2020-how-did-the-media-electoral-process-fare-republicans-demo crats-disagree/.

Chapter 3: THE HARDWARE WAR ON THE BACK-END OF YOUR DEVICE

1 Jon Stewart, "Headlines—Internet," *The Daily Show*, July 12, 2006, http://www.cc.com/video-clips/uo1ore/the-daily-show-with-jon -stewart-headlines-internet.

2 Ibid.

3 Keith Johnson and Elias Groll, "The Improbable Rise of Huawei," *Foreign Policy*, April 3, 2019, https://foreignpolicy.com/2019/04/03 /the-improbable-rise-of-huawei-5g-global-network-china/.

4 Johnson and Groll, "The Improbable Rise of Huawei."

5 Cheng Ting-Fang and Lauly Li, "China can make it," *Nikkei Asian Review*, September 16, 2019, https://lp.asia.nikkei.com/lp/nl_cam paign/pdf/20190912_Huaweis_Battle_Plan.pdf.

6 Johnson and Groll, "The Improbable Rise of Huawei."

7 "Our Philosophy," Huawei, https://huawei.eu/who-we-are/our-phi losophy.

8 Alan Taylor, "Photos of Huawei's European-Themed Campus in China," *The Atlantic*, May 13, 2019, https://www.theatlantic.com /photo/2019/05/photos-of-huaweis-european-themed-campus-in -china/589342/.

9 Mike Murphy, "Take a tour of Huawei's sprawling, spectacular new European-themed R&D campus," *MarketWatch*, May 23, 2019, https:// www.marketwatch.com/story/take-a-tour-of-huaweis-sprawling -spectacular-new-european-themed-rd-campus-2019-05-23.

10 David Lumb, "Huawei has built the Disneyland of tech R&D," *TechRadar*, August 20, 2019, https://www.techradar.com/news /huawei-has-built-the-disneyland-of-tech-randd.

11 Lucy Fisher, "CIA warning over Huawei," *The Times*, April 20, 2019, https://www.thetimes.co.uk/article/cia-warning-over-huawei-rz6x c8kzk.

12 Ryan Mcmorrow, "Huawei a key beneficiary of China subsidies that US wants ended," *Phys*, May 30, 2019, https://phys.org/news /2019-05-huawei-key-beneficiary-china-subsidies.html.

13 Chuin-Wei Yap, "State Support Helped Fuel Huawei's Global Rise," *Wall Street Journal*, December 25, 2019, https://www.wsj.com/ar ticles/state-support-helped-fuel-huaweis-global-rise-11577280736.

14 Alberto F. De Toni, *International Operations Management: Lessons in Global Business* (New York: Gower Publishing, 2011), 128.

15 Johnson and Groll, "The Improbable Rise of Huawei."

16 Isaac Stone Fish, "Opinion: Even if Trump trusts Huawei, here's why America shouldn't," *Washington Post*, July 5, 2019, https://www .washingtonpost.com/opinions/2019/07/05/even-if-trump-trusts -huawei-heres-why-america-shouldnt/.

17 Mike Rogers and C. A. Dutch Ruppersberger, "Investigative Report on the U.S. National Security Issues Posed by Chinese Telecommu- nications Companies Huawei and ZTE," U.S. House of Represen- tatives, October 8, 2012, https://republicans-intelligence.house.gov /sites/intelligence.house.gov/files/documents/huawei-zte%20inves tigative%20report%20(final).pdf.

18 "The Security of 5G," House of Commons Committees, October 8, 2020, https://committees.parliament.uk/publications/2877/docu ments/27899/default/.

19 Tweet by @MartignRasser, Twitter, April 18, 2021, https://twitter .com/MartijnRasser/status/1383769537829502979.

20 "Chinese Telecommunications Conglomerate Huawei and Subsid- iaries Charged in Racketeering Conspiracy and Conspiracy to Steal Trade Secrets," U.S. Department of Justice, February 13, 2020, https://www.justice.gov/opa/pr/chinese-telecommunications-con glomerate-huawei-and-subsidiaries-charged-racketeering.

21 Jim Morris, "Canadian extradition judge deals Huawei CFO legal blow," Associated Press, October 9, 2020, https://apnews.com /article/technology-business-beijing-meng-wanzhou-vancouver-b8 b1162c4aabe02c96a527e13eed167a.

22 Johnson and Groll, "The Improbable Rise of Huawei."

23 Jonathan Stearns, "Pelosi Warns Europe That Huawei Represents Chinese State Police," *Bloomberg*, February 17, 2020, https://www .bloomberg.com/news/articles/2020-02-17/pelosi-warns-europe -that-huawei-represents-chinese-state-police.

24 Anna Fifield, "China's Huawei says it has long prepared for a U.S. assault," *Washington Post*, May 21, 2019, https://www .washingtonpost.com/world/asia_pacific/chinas-huawei-says-it -has-long-prepared-for-americas-assault/2019/05/21/04b29c60 -7bc2-11e9-b1f3-b233fe5811ef_story.html.

25 Joe Ngai, Kevin Sneader, and Cecilia Ma Zecha, "China's One Belt,

One Road: Will it reshape global trade?," McKinsey, July 19, 2016, https://www.mckinsey.com/featured-insights/china/chinas-one-belt-one-road-will-it-reshape-global-trade.

26 Logan Pauley and Hamza Shad, "Gwadar: Emerging Port City or Chinese Colony?," *The Diplomat*, October 5, 2018, https://the diplomat.com/2018/10/gwadar-emerging-port-city-or-chinese-colony/.

27 Laura Zhou, "How a Chinese investment boom is changing the face of Djibouti," *South China Morning Post*, https://www.scmp.com/news/china/diplomacy-defence/article/2087374/how-chinese-investment-boom-changing-face-djibouti.

28 Ernesto Londoño, "From a Space Station in Argentina, China Expands Its Reach in Latin America," *New York Times*, July 28, 2018, https://www.nytimes.com/2018/07/28/world/americas/china-latin-america.html.

29 Jonathan E. Hillman, "The Imperial Overreach of China's Belt and Road Initiative," *Wall Street Journal*, October 1, 2020, https://www.wsj.com/articles/the-imperial-overreach-of-chinas-belt-and-road-initiative-11601558851.

30 Chatzky and McBride, "China's Massive Belt and Road Initiative."

31 "The Digital Silk Road: Expanding China's Digital Footprint," Eurasia Group, April 8, 2020, https://www.eurasiagroup.net/files/up load/Digital-Silk-Road-Expanding-China-Digital-Footprint.pdf.

32 Maria Abi-Habib, "China's 'Belt and Road' Plan in Pakistan Takes a Military Turn," *New York Times*, December 19, 2018, https://www.nytimes.com/2018/12/19/world/asia/pakistan-china-belt-road-mili tary.html.

33 Charles Duhigg and Keith Bradsher, "How the U.S. Lost Out on iPhone Work," *New York Times*, January 21, 2012, https://www.nytimes.com/2012/01/22/business/apple-america-and-a-squeezed-middle-class.html?referringSource=articleShare.

34 Duhigg and Bradsher, "How the U.S. Lost Out on iPhone Work."

35 Reade Pickert, "Manufacturing Is Now Smallest Share of U.S. Economy in 72 Years," *Bloomberg*, October 29, 2019, https://www.bloomberg.com/news/articles/2019-10-29/manufacturing-is-now-smallest-share-of-u-s-economy-in-72-years.

36 Thomas C. Mahoney and Susan Helper, "Next-Generation Supply Chains," MForesight, July 18, 2017, http://mforesight.org/projects-events/supply-chains/.

37 Heather Long, "U.S. has lost 5 million manufacturing jobs since 2000," CNN Business, March 29, 2016, https://money.cnn.com/2016/03/29/news/economy/us-manufacturing-jobs/index.html.

38 Duhigg and Bradsher, "How the U.S. Lost Out on iPhone Work."

39 Jon Chavez, "Major magic not enough to keep restaurant open," *To-*

ledo Blade, July 8, 2010, https://www.toledoblade.com/local/2010
/07/08/Major-magic-not-enough-to-keep-restaurant-open.html.

40 Federica Cocco, "Most US manufacturing jobs lost to technology, not trade," *Financial Times,* December 2, 2016, https://www.ft.com /content/dec677c0-b7e6-11e6-ba85-95d1533d9a62.

41 Kai-Fu Lee, *AI Superpowers: China, Silicon Valley, and the New World Order* (New York: Houghton Mifflin Harcourt, 2018), e-book, 207.

42 Duhigg and Bradsher, "How the U.S. Lost Out on iPhone Work."

43 Robert Spalding, *Stealth War: How China Took Over While America's Elite Slept* (New York: Portfolio, 2019), 37.

44 "Assessing and Strengthening the Manufacturing and Defense Industrial Base and Supply Chain Resiliency of the United States," U.S. Department of Defense, September 2018, https://media .defense.gov/2018/Oct/05/2002048904/-1/-1/1/ASSESSING -AND-STRENGTHENING-THE-MANUFACTURING-AND%20 DEFENSE-INDUSTRIAL-BASE-AND-SUPPLY-CHAIN-RESIL IENCY.PDF.

45 Yichi Zhang, "European Chamber Report Cautions Against the Negative Aspects of China Manufacturing 2025," European Chamber, March 7, 2017, https://www.europeanchamber.com.cn/en/press -releases/2532.

46 "Attorney General William P. Barr Delivers Remarks on China Policy at the Gerald R. Ford Presidential Museum," U.S. Department of Justice, July 16, 2020, https://www.justice.gov/opa/speech/attorney -general-william-p-barr-delivers-remarks-china-policy-gerald-r-ford -presidential.

47 Xio Cen, Vyacheslav Fos, and Wei Jiang, "A Race to Lead: How Chinese Government Interventions Shape the Sino-US Production Competition," SSRN, April 15, 2020, https://poseidon01.ssrn.com /delivery.php?ID=9940201230000981060890670180781080101 1 604506706009502811009908110302212010802003110101806 3 099111026042034105115029092095007023029066004033083 0 010771260990080290741230770220500210260081090870270 94 122023020116003006076127014003109086115004109072096 02 2087&EXT=pdf.

48 "Assessing and Strengthening the Manufacturing and Defense Industrial Base and Supply Chain Resiliency of the United States."

49 John Adams, "Remaking American Security," Alliance for American Manufacturing, May 2013, https://www.americanmanufacturing.org /wp-content/uploads/2017/03/RemakingAmericanSecurityExecu tiveSummary-1.pdf.

50 Dion Rabouin, "Coronavirus has disrupted supply chains for nearly 75% of U.S. companies," *Axios,* March 11, 2020, https://www.axios

.com/coronavirus-supply-chains-china-46d82a0f-9f52-4229-840a
-936822ddef41.html.

51 "No improvement in China's rare earths ban," *Japan Times*, October 13, 2010, https://www.japantimes.co.jp/news/2010/10/13/national /no-improvement-in-chinas-rare-earths-ban/.

52 Ainissa Ramirez, "Where to Find Rare Earth Elements," PBS, April 2, 2013, https://www.pbs.org/wgbh/nova/article/rare-earth-elements -in-cell-phones/.

53 "Assessing and Strengthening the Manufacturing and Defense Industrial Base and Supply Chain Resiliency of the United States."

54 Jordan Robertson and Michael Riley, "The Big Hack: How China Used a Tiny Chip to Infiltrate U.S. Companies," *Bloomberg*, October 4, 2018, https://www.bloomberg.com/news/features/2018-10-04/the-big -hack-how-china-used-a-tiny-chip-to-infiltrate-america-s-top-companies.

55 Ibid.

56 Ibid.

57 Ibid.

58 Mara Hvistendahl, "The friendly Mr Wu," *The Economist*, February 25, 2020, https://www.1843magazine.com/features/the-friendly -mr-wu.

59 Thomas Brewster, "Exclusive: Warning Over Chinese Mobile Giant Xiaomi Recording Millions of People's 'Private' Web and Phone Use," *Forbes*, April 30, 2020, https://www.forbes.com/sites /thomasbrewster/2020/04/30/exclusive-warning-over-chinese-mo bile-giant-xiaomi-recording-millions-of-peoples-private-web-and -phone-use/?sh=707cb72d1b2a.

60 "South America-1 (Sam-1)," Submarine Cable Map, March 2001, https://www.submarinecablemap.com/#/submarine-cable/south -america-1-sam-1.

61 Andrew Blum, *Tubes*, e-book, 116, 125.

62 "Internet Exchange Points," Data Center Map, https://www.datacen termap.com/ixps.html.

63 John Watkins Brett, *On the Origin and Progress of the Oceanic Electric Telegraph: With a Few Facts, and Opinions of the Press* (London: Nassau Steam Press, 1858), 66.

64 "History and Achievements," Global Marine, https://globalmarine .co.uk/about-us/history-achievements/.

65 Adam Satariano, "How the Internet Travels Across Oceans," *New York Times*, March 10, 2019, https://www.nytimes.com/interactive /2019/03/10/technology/internet-cables-oceans.html.

66 "Submarine Cable 101," TeleGeography, https://www2.telegeogra phy.com/submarine-cable-faqs-frequently-asked-questions.

67 "Submarine Cable Map," Submarine Cable Map, https://www.sub marinecablemap.com/#/submarine-cable/seamewe-3.

68 Jeremy Page, Kate O'Keeffe, and Rob Taylor, "America's Undersea Battle With China for Control of the Global Internet Grid," *Wall Street Journal*, March 12, 2019, https://www.wsj.com/articles/u-s -takes-on-chinas-huawei-in-undersea-battle-over-the-global-internet -grid-11552407466.

69 Satariano, "How the Internet Travels Across Oceans."

70 John Hendel and Betsy Woodruff Swan, "Justice Department opposes Google, Facebook cable link to Hong Kong," *Politico*, June 17, 2020, https://www.politico.com/news/2020/06/17/justice-department -hong-kong-google-facebook-cable-326688.

71 Page, O'Keeffe, and Taylor, "America's Undersea Battle With China for Control of the Global Internet Grid."

72 Ibid.

73 Ibid.

74 Chris C. Demchak and Yuval Shavitt, "China's Maxim—Leave No Access Point Unexploited: The Hidden Story of China Telecom's BGP Hijacking," *Military Cyber Affairs*, 2018, https://scholarcom mons.usf.edu/mca/vol3/iss1/7/.

75 Winston Qiu, "Global Marine Group Fully Divests Stake in Hua-wei Marine Networks," Submarine Cable Networks, June 6, 2020, https://www.submarinenetworks.com/en/vendors/huawei-marine /global-marine-completes-sale-of-30-stake-in-huawei-marine-net works-for-85-million.

76 Hendel and Swan, "Justice Department opposes Google, Facebook cable link to Hong Kong."

77 Justin Sherman, "Senate Report Finds Poor Executive Branch Over-sight of Chinese State-Owned Telecoms," *Lawfare* (blog), June 17, 2020, https://www.lawfareblog.com/senate-report-finds-poor-execu tive-branch-oversight-chinese-state-owned-telecoms.

78 Marissa Fessenden, "This is the First Detailed Public Map of the U.S. Internet Infrastructure," *Smithsonian Magazine*, September 23, 2015, https://www.smithsonianmag.com/smart-news/first-detailed -public-map-us-internet-infrastructure-180956701/.

79 Winston Qiu, "China-Myanmar International (CMI) Terrestrial Cable Launches for Service," Submarine Cable Networks, November 15, 2014, https://www.submarinenetworks.com/news/china-myanmar -international-cmi-terrestrial-cable-launches-for-service.

80 "Terrestrial Cable Resource," China Mobile International, https:// www.cmi.chinamobile.com/en/terrestrial-cable.

81 Ibid.

82 Kitson and Liew, "China Doubles Down on Its Digital Silk Road."

83 Tom Stroup, "Comments of the Satellite Industry Association," Federal Communications Commission, December 6, 2019, https:// ecfsapi.fcc.gov/file/12062609405024/SIA%20Regulatory%20

Fees%20FNPRM%20Comments%20with%20attachment%20 6%20Dec%202019%20(002).pdf.

84 Mariella Moon, "SpaceX is requesting permission to launch 30,000 more Starlink satellites," Yahoo! Money, October 16, 2019, https:// money.yahoo.com/2019-10-16-spacex-30-000-starlink-satellites .html.

85 Jose Del Rosario, "NSR Reports China's Ambitious Constellation of 300 Small Satellites in LEO," *Satnews*, March 8, 2018, http://www .satnews.com/story.php?number=257303683.

86 Ben Westcott, "China's GPS rival Beidou is now fully operational after final satellite launched," CNN, June 24, 2020, https://www.cnn .com/2020/06/24/tech/china-beidou-satellite-gps-intl-hnk/index .html.

87 Trefor Moss, "China's 'One Belt, One Road' Takes to Space," *Wall Street Journal*, December 28, 2016, https://blogs.wsj.com/chinareal time/2016/12/28/chinas-one-belt-one-road-takes-to-space/.

88 Westcott, "China's GPS rival Beidou is now fully operational after final satellite launched."

89 Jiang Jie, "Nation considers space-based 'Silk Road of satellites' to provide data services," *Global Times*, May 31, 2015, http://www.glo baltimes.cn/content/924600.shtml.

90 "AIMS Data Centre," Data Center Map, February 2, 2009, https:// www.datacentermap.com/malaysia/kuala-lumpur/aims-data-centre _connectivity.html.

91 Prachi Bhardwaj, "Fiber optic wires, servers, and more than 550,000 miles of underwater cables: Here's what the internet actually looks like," *Business Insider*, June 23, 2018, https://www.businessinsider .com/how-internet-works-infrastructure-photos-2018-5#as-it-travels -any-information-transferred-over-the-web-arrives-at-internet-data -servers-which-live-in-data-centers-around-the-world-in-2008-an-es timated-95-trillion-gigabytes-passed-in-and-out-of-the-worlds-servers -but-more-on-those-later-2.

92 Brady Gavin, "How Big Are Gigabytes, Terabytes, and Petabytes?," *How-to Geek*, May 25, 2018, https://www.howtogeek.com/353116 /how-big-are-gigabytes-terabytes-and-petabytes/.

93 John Roach, "Under the sea, Microsoft tests a datacenter that's quick to deploy, could provide internet connectivity for years," *Microsoft News*, June 5, 2018, https://news.microsoft.com/features/under-the -sea-microsoft-tests-a-datacenter-thats-quick-to-deploy-could-pro vide-internet-connectivity-for-years/.

94 "Data Centers Locations," Google, https://www.google.com/about /datacenters/locations/.

95 "The Data Center Mural Project," Data Center Murals, https://data centermurals.withgoogle.com/.

96 Jake Brutlag, "Speed Matters," *Google AI Blog*, June 23, 2009, https://ai.googleblog.com/2009/06/speed-matters.html.

97 Yuxi Wei, "Chinese Data Localization Law: Comprehensive but Ambiguous," Henry M. Jackson School of International Studies, February 7, 2018, https://jsis.washington.edu/news/chinese-data-localization-law-comprehensive-ambiguous/.

98 Shan Li, "China Expands Its Cybersecurity Rulebook, Heightening Foreign Corporate Concerns," *China Technology News*, October 6, 2018, http://www.technologynewschina.com/2018/10/china-expands-its-cybersecurity.html.

99 Rita Liao, "Tibet to become China's data gateway to South Asia," *TechCrunch*, June 8, 2020, https://techcrunch.com/2020/06/08/tibet-to-become-chinas-data-gateway-to-south-asia/.

100 Abigail Opiah, "China Mobile International launches first European data centre," Capacity Media, December 20, 2019, https://www.capacitymedia.com/articles/3824709/china-mobile-international-launches-first-european-data-centre.

101 Max Bearak, "In strategic Djibouti, a microcosm of China's growing foothold in Africa," *Washington Post*, December 30, 2019, https://www.washingtonpost.com/world/africa/in-strategic-djibouti-a-microcosm-of-chinas-growing-foothold-in-africa/2019/12/29/a6e664ea-beab-11e9-a8b0-7ed8a0d5dc5d_story.html.

102 Angus Grigg, "Huawei data centre built to spy on PNG," *Financial Review*, August 11, 2020, https://www.afr.com/companies/telecommunications/huawei-data-centre-built-to-spy-on-png-20200810-p55k7w.

103 Henrik Frystyk, "The Internet Protocol Stack," W3, July 1994, https://www.w3.org/People/Frystyk/thesis/TcpIp.html.

104 David Kelly, "The 'China Solution': Beijing responds to Trump," *The Interpreter*, February 17, 2017, https://www.lowyinstitute.org/the-interpreter/china-solution-beijing-responds-trump.

105 Hal Brands, "China's Global Influence Operation Goes Way Beyond the WHO," *Bloomberg*, March 31, 2020, https://www.bloomberg.com/opinion/articles/2020-03-31/china-s-influence-operation-goes-beyond-who-taiwan-and-covid-19.

106 Bonnie Bley, "The New Geography of Global Diplomacy: China Advances as the United States Retreats," *Foreign Affairs*, November 27, 2019, https://www.foreignaffairs.com/articles/china/2019-11-27/new-geography-global-diplomacy.

107 "In the UN, China uses threats and cajolery to promote its worldview," *The Economist*, December 7, 2019, https://www.economist.com/china/2019/12/07/in-the-un-china-uses-threats-and-cajolery-to-promote-its-worldview.

108 Yaroslav Trofimov, Drew Hinshaw, and Kate O'Keeffe, "How China Is Taking Over International Organizations, One Vote at a Time,"

Wall Street Journal, September 29, 2010, https://www.wsj.com/arti cles/how-china-is-taking-over-international-organizations-one-vote -at-a-time-11601397208.

109 Hilary McGeachy, "Us-China Technology Competition: Impacting a Rules-Based Order," United States Studies Centre, May 2, 2019, https://www.ussc.edu.au/analysis/us-china-technology-competition -impacting-a-rules-based-order.

110 Tom Miles, "Huawei allegations driven by politics not evidence: U.N. telecoms chief," Reuters, April 5, 2019, https://www.reuters.com /article/us-usa-china-huawei-tech-un/huawei-allegations-driven-by -politics-not-evidence-u-n-telecoms-chief-idUSKCN1RH1KN.

111 Kong Wenzheng, "ITU vows to join hands with China," *China Daily*, April 24, 2019, http://www.chinadaily.com.cn/a/201904/24 /WS5cbfbb1aa3104842260b7f2f.html.

112 Madhumita Murgia and Anna Gross, "Inside China's controversial mission to reinvent the internet," *Financial Times*, March 27, 2020, https://www.ft.com/content/ba94c2bc-6e27-11ea-9bca-bf503995cd6f.

113 Anna Gross and Madhumita Murgia, "China and Huawei propose re-invention of the internet," *Financial Times*, March 27, 2020, https:// www.ft.com/content/c78be2cf-a1a1-40b1-8ab7-904d7095e0f2.

114 Emily de La Bruyére and Nathan Picarsic, "China's next plan to dominate international tech standards," *TechCrunch*, April 11, 2020, https://techcrunch.com/2020/04/11/chinas-next-plan-to-dominate -international-tech-standards/.

115 Graham Webster and Paul Triolo, "Translation: China Proposes 'Global Data Security Initiative,'" New America, September 7, 2020, https://www.newamerica.org/cybersecurity-initiative/digichina/blog /translation-chinese-proposes-global-data-security-initiative/.

116 David Wertime, "Death of trade deal with China could be 'October surprise,'" *Politico*, September 10, 2020, https://www.politico.com /newsletters/politico-china-watcher/2020/09/10/phase-one-deal -death-could-be-october-surprise-trade-china-trump-490274.

117 Katrina Trinko, "Huawei's Role in the 'Chinese Espionage Enter-prise,'" *Daily Signal*, February 19, 2020, https://www.dailysignal.com /2020/02/19/huaweis-role-in-the-chinese-espionage-enterprise/.

118 Chris Hoffman, "What is 5G, and How Fast Will It Be?," *How-To Geek*, January 3, 2020, https://www.howtogeek.com/340002/what -is-5g-and-how-fast-will-it-be/.

119 Tom Wheeler, "If 5G Is So Important, Why Isn't It Secure?," *New York Times*, January 21, 2019, https://www.nytimes.com/2019/01 /21/opinion/5g-cybersecurity-china.html.

120 Karen Campbell, "The 5G economy: How 5G technology will contrib-ute to the global economy," IHS Economics, January 2017, https://cdn .ihs.com/www/pdf/IHS-Technology-5G-Economic-Impact-Study.pdf.

121 Johnson and Groll, "The Improbable Rise of Huawei."

122 Arjun Kharpal, "Huawei overtakes Samsung to be No. 1 smartphone player in the world thanks to China as overseas sales drop," CNBC, July 29, 2020, https://www.cnbc.com/2020/07/30/huawei-overtakes-samsung-to-be-no-1-smartphone-maker-thanks-to-china.html.

123 Johnson and Groll, "The Improbable Rise of Huawei."

124 Dan Strumpf, "Huawei Workers Return After Coronavirus, But CEO Sees Financial Hit," *Wall Street Journal*, March 25, 2020, https://www.wsj.com/articles/huawei-workers-return-after-coronavirus-but-ceo-sees-financial-hit-11585149231.

125 Johnson and Groll, "The Improbable Rise of Huawei."

126 Daniel Van Boom, "Huawei starts research on 6G internet," CNET, August 14, 2019, https://www.cnet.com/news/huawei-starts-research-on-6g-internet/.

127 "The fight with Huawei means America can't shape tech rules," *The Economist*, April 23, 2020, https://www.economist.com/united-states/2020/04/23/the-fight-with-huawei-means-america-cant-shape-tech-rules.

128 Hugo Yen, David Simpson, and Lindsey Gorman, "Tech Factsheets for Policymakers," Harvard Kennedy School Belfer Center, 2020, https://www.belfercenter.org/sites/default/files/files/publication/5G_2.pdf.

129 Yawen Chen and Se Young Lee, "China slams U.S. blacklisting of Huawei as trade tensions rise," Reuters, May 16, 2019, https://www.reuters.com/article/us-usa-trade-china-huawei/china-slams-u-s-blacklisting-of-huawei-as-trade-tensions-rise-idUSKCN1SM0NR.

130 Dan Strumpf, "Huawei Struggles to Get Along Without Google," *Wall Street Journal*, May 12, 2020, https://www.wsj.com/articles/huawei-struggles-to-get-along-without-google-11589277481.

131 David Ljunggren, "Canada has effectively moved to block China's Huawei from 5G, but can't say so," Reuters, August 25, 2020, https://www.reuters.com/article/us-canada-huawei-analysis/canada-has-effectively-moved-to-block-chinas-huawei-from-5g-but-cant-say-so-idUSKBN25L26S.

132 Johnson and Groll, "The Improbable Rise of Huawei."

133 Charlotte Graham-McLay, "New Zealand Fears Fraying Ties With China, Its Biggest Customer," *New York Times*, February 14, 2019, https://www.nytimes.com/2019/02/14/world/asia/new-zealand-china-huawei-tensions.html.

134 Supantha Mukherjee and Helena Soderpalm, "Sweden bans Huawei, ZTE from upcoming 5G networks," Reuters, October 20, 2020, https://www.reuters.com/article/sweden-huawei-int/sweden-bans-huawei-zte-from-upcoming-5g-networks-idUSKBN2750WA.

135 Supantha Mukherjee and Helena Soderpalm, "Huawei ousted from

heart of EU as Nokia wins Belgian 5G contracts," Reuters, October 9, 2020, https://www.reuters.com/article/us-orange-nokia-security-5g-idUSKBN26U0YY.

136 "France won't ban Huawei, but encouraging 5G telcos to avoid it: report," Reuters, July 5, 2020, https://www.reuters.com/article/us-france-huawei-5g/france-wont-ban-huawei-but-encouraging-5g-telcos-to-avoid-it-report-idUSKBN2460TT.

137 "Italy considering whether to exclude Huawei from 5G: report," Reuters, July 8, 2020, https://www.reuters.com/article/us-huawei-italy/italy-considering-whether-to-exclude-huawei-from-5g-report-idUSKBN2491C1.

138 "A Huawei Turning Point," *Wall Street Journal*, October 2, 2020, https://www.wsj.com/articles/a-huawei-turning-point-11601680165.

139 Pablo Gorondi, "Hungary says Huawei to help build its 5G wireless network," Associated Press, November 5, 2019, https://apnews.com/688e48fac84a4eeca73fdb5e17732c5f.

140 Kitson and Liew, "China Doubles Down on Its Digital Silk Road."

141 Paul Adepoju, "Gabon and Congo test 5G," IT Web, December 2, 2019, https://itweb.africa/content/Pero3qZxZ3a7Qb6m.

142 "China's ZTE, local telecom firm start 5G technology trial in Uganda," Xinhua, January 18, 2020, http://www.xinhuanet.com/english/2020-01/18/c_138716219.htm.

143 "Venezuela's Maduro promises 5G, new satellite with Chinese tech," BNamericas, July 1, 2019, bnamericas.com/en/news/venezuelas-maduro-promises-5g-new-satellite-with-chinese-tech.

144 Trinko, "Huawei's Role in the 'Chinese Espionage Enterprise.'"

145 "National Strategy to Secure 5G of the United States of America," The White House, March 2020, file:///C:/Users/MY%20PC/Downloads/835776.pdf.

146 "The Clean Network," U.S. Department of State, https://2017-2021.state.gov/the-clean-network/index.html.

147 "William M. (Mac) Thornberry National Defense Authorization Act for Fiscal Year 2021," U.S. House of Representatives, December 2020, https://docs.house.gov/billsthisweek/20201207/CRPT-116hrpt617.pdf.

148 Michael Schuman, "How Xi Jinping Blew It," *The Atlantic*, November 19, 2020, https://www.theatlantic.com/international/archive/2020/11/chinas-missed-opportunity/617136/.

149 "Xi Says Economy Can Double as China Lays Out Ambitious Plans," *Bloomberg*, November 3, 2020, https://www.bloomberg.com/news/articles/2020-11-03/china-s-xi-says-economy-can-double-in-size-by-2035.

150 "The Regional Comprehensive Economic Partnership: Status and Re-

cent Developments," Congressional Research Service, November 19, 2020, https://crsreports.congress.gov/product/pdf/IN/IN11200.

151 Campbell Kwan, "15 Asia Pacific countries sign world's largest free trade agreement," ZDNet, November 16, 2020, https://www.zdnet .com/article/15-asia-pacific-countries-sign-worlds-largest-free-trade -agreement/.

152 Sophie Dirven and Miriam Garcia Ferrer, "Key elements of the EU-China Comprehensive Agreement on Investment," European Commission, December 30, 2020, https://ec.europa.eu/commission /presscorner/detail/en/IP_20_2542.

153 Finbarr Bermingham, "China tried to punish European states for Huawei bans by adding eleventh-hour rule to EU investment deal," *South China Morning Post*, January 8, 2021, https://www.scmp.com /economy/china-economy/article/3116896/china-tried-punish-euro pean-states-huawei-bans-adding.

154 Toru Tsunashima, "China rises as world's data superpower as internet fractures," *Nikkei Asia*, November 24, 2020, https://asia.nikkei .com/Spotlight/Century-of-Data/China-rises-as-world-s-data-super power-as-internet-fractures.

155 Dan Strumpf, "U.S. vs. China in 5G: The Battle Isn't Even Close," *Wall Street Journal*, November 9, 2020, https://www.wsj.com/ar ticles/u-s-vs-china-in-5g-the-battle-isnt-even-close-11604959200.

156 "Forecast 2025: China Adjusts Course," MacroPolo, October 2020, https://macropolo.org/wp-content/uploads/2020/10/china2025 -final.pdf.

157 Ellen Nakashima and Souad Mekhennet, "U.S. officials planning for a future in which Huawei has a major share of 5G global networks," *Washington Post*, April 1, 2019, https://www.washingtonpost.com /world/national-security/us-officials-planning-for-a-future-in-which -huawei-has-a-major-share-of-5g-global-networks/2019/04/01 /2bb60446-523c-11e9-a3f7-78b7525a8d5f_story.html.

Chapter 4: THE FUTURE OF NATIONAL SOVEREIGNTY IS TECH, NOT TROOPS

1 David E. Sanger and Emily Schmall, "China Appears to Warn India: Push too Hard and the Lights Could Go Out," *New York Times*, February 28, 2021, https://www.nytimes.com/2021/02/28/us/politics /china-india-hacking-electricity.html?referringSource=article Share.

2 Emma Graham-Harrison, "China's Communist party ran campaign to discredit BBC, thinktank finds," *The Guardian*, March 4, 2021, https://www.theguardian.com/world/2021/mar/04/chinas-commu nist-party-ran-campaign-to-discredit-bbc-thinktank-finds.

3 Ibid.

4 Shen Lu, "I helped build ByteDance's censorship machine," *Proto-*

col, February 18, 2021, https://www.protocol.com/china/i-built-byte dance-censorship-machine?utm_campaign=post-teaser&utm_con tent=8gi0rq1u.

5 Robert Kagan, *The Jungle Grows Back* (New York: Penguin Random House, 2018), 4

6 Amy Thomson and Stephanie Bodoni, "Google CEO Thinks AI Will Be More Profound Change Than Fire," *Bloomberg Quint*, January 22, 2020, https://www.bloombergquint.com/davos-world-economic -forum-2020/google-ceo-thinks-ai-is-more-profound-than-fire.

7 Hal Brands, "China's Foreign Policy Weapons: Technology, Coercion, Corruption," *Bloomberg*, January 24, 2021, bloomberg.com/opinion /articles/2021-01-25/china-s-geopolitical-weapons-technology-coer cion-corruption.

8 Rob Wile, "A Venture Capital Firm Just Named an Algorithm to Its Board of Directors—Here's What It Actually Does," *Business In-sider*, May 13, 2014, https://www.businessinsider.com/vital-named -to-board-2014-5.

9 Lee, *AI Superpowers*, e-book, 36.

10 Pedro Domingos, *The Master Algorithm: How the Quest for the Ul-timate Learning Machine Will Remake Our World* (New York: Basic Books, 2015), 10.

11 Lee, *AI Superpowers*, e-book, 8.

12 "Once again, a neural net tries to name cats," AI Weirdness, https:// aiweirdness.com/post/185339301987/once-again-a-neural-net-tries -to-name-cats.

13 Miles Brundage, *The Malicious Use of Artificial Intelligence: Fore-casting, Prevention, and Mitigation*, Arxiv, February 2010, https:// arxiv.org/pdf/1802.07228.pdf.

14 "Vision: Transform the DoD Through Artificial Intelligence," U.S. Department of Defense Chief Information Officer, https://dodcio .defense.gov/About-DoD-CIO/Organization/JAIC/.

15 James Vincent, "Putin says the nation that leads in AI 'will be the ruler of the world,'" *The Verge*, September 4, 2017, https://www .theverge.com/2017/9/4/16251226/russia-ai-putin-rule-the-world.

16 Lee, *AI Superpowers*, e-book, 224.

17 Benjamin Romano, "Amid Global Race for A.I. Talent, China's Ten-cent Sets Up Seattle Lab," *Xconomy*, December 14, 2017, https:// xconomy.com/seattle/2017/12/14/amid-global-race-for-a-i-talent -chinas-tencent-sets-up-seattle-lab/.

18 Lee, *AI Superpowers*, e-book, 162–163.

19 Tom Simonite, "China is catching up to the US in AI Research—Fast," *Wired*, March 13, 2019, https://www.wired.com/story/china -catching-up-us-in-ai-research/.

20 James Vincent, "China is about to overtake America in AI research,"

The Verge, March 14, 2019, https://www.theverge.com/2019/3/14/18265230/china-is-about-to-overtake-america-in-ai-research.

21 Lee, *AI Superpowers*, e-book, 143.

22 Ibid., x.

23 Eric Rosenbach and Katherine Mansted, "The Geopolitics of Information," Harvard Kennedy School Belfer Center, May 28, 2019, https://www.belfercenter.org/publication/geopolitics-information.

24 Anna Funder, *Stasiland: True Stories from Behind the Berlin Wall* (London: Granta, 2003), 57. Excerpt from Brad Smith & Carol Ann Browne, "Tools and Weapons," Apple Books, https://books.apple.com/us/book/tools-and-weapons/id1455068611.

25 Lee, *AI Superpowers*, e-book, 130.

26 "Beijing police have covered every corner of the city with video surveillance system," *People China*, October 5, 2015, http://en.people.cn/n/2015/1005/c90000-8958235.html.

27 Josh Chin and Liza Lin, "China's all-seeing surveillance state is reading its citizens' faces," *Strait Times*, July 8, 2017, http://www.straittimes.com/opinion/chinas-all-seeing-surveillance-state-is-reading-its-citizens-faces.

28 Ross Andersen, "The Panopticon Is Already Here," *The Atlantic*, September 2020, https://www.theatlantic.com/magazine/archive/2020/09/china-ai-surveillance/614197/.

29 Lee, *AI Superpowers*, e-book, 94.

30 James Vincent, "Watch Jordan Peele use AI to make Barack Obama deliver a PSA about fake news," *The Verge*, April 17, 2018, https://www.theverge.com/tldr/2018/4/17/17247334/ai-fake-news-video-barack-obama-jordan-peele-buzzfeed.

31 Daniel Gross, interview with author, May 1, 2020.

32 Vincent, "Watch Jordan Peele use AI to make Barack Obama deliver a PSA about fake news."

33 "Kenya election: Fake CNN and BBC news reports circulate," BBC, July 29, 2017, https://www.bbc.com/news/world-africa-40762796.

34 Gianluca Mezzofiore, "No, Emma Gonzalez did not tear up a photo of the Constitution," CNN, March 26, 2018, https://www.cnn.com/2018/03/26/us/emma-gonzalez-photo-doctored-trnd/index.html.

35 Ady Barkan, "Opinion: I speak with a computerized voice. Republicans used it to put words in my mouth," *Washington Post*, September 2, 2020, https://www.washingtonpost.com/opinions/2020/09/02/ady-barkan-op-ed-scalise-video/.

36 Max Fisher, "Syrian hackers claim AP hack that tipped stock market by $136 billion. Is it terrorism?," *Washington Post*, April 23, 2013, https://www.washingtonpost.com/news/worldviews/wp/2013/04/23/syrian-hackers-claim-ap-hack-that-tipped-stock-market-by-136-billion-is-it-terrorism/.

37 Jane Lytvynenko, "Thousands of Women Have No Idea a Telegram Network Is Sharing Fake Nude Images of Them," *BuzzFeed News*, October 20, 2020, https://www.buzzfeednews.com/article/jane lytvynenko/telegram-deepfake-nude-women-images-bot.

38 Yonah Jeremy Bob, "How is Bar Refaeli connected to a plot to discredit Robert Mueller?," *Jerusalem Post*, November 1, 2018, https://www.jpost.com/international/how-is-bar-refaeli-connected-to-a -plot-to-discredit-robert-mueller-570866.

39 Adam Rawnsley, "Right-Wing Media Outlets Duped by a Middle East Propaganda Campaign," *Daily Beast*, July 7, 2020, https://www .thedailybeast.com/right-wing-media-outlets-duped-by-a-middle-east -propaganda-campaign.

40 Ben Collins and Brandy Zadrozny, "How a fake persona laid the groundwork for a Hunter Biden conspiracy deluge," NBC News, October 29, 2020, https://www.nbcnews.com/tech/security/how -fake-persona-laid-groundwork-hunter-biden-conspiracy-deluge -n1245387.

41 Kashmir Hill and Jeremy White, "Designed to Deceive: Do These People Look Real to You?," *New York Times*, November 21, 2020, https://www.nytimes.com/interactive/2020/11/21/science/artificial -intelligence-fake-people-faces.html.

42 Robert Chesney and Danielle Keats Citron, "Deep Fakes: A Looming Challenge for Privacy, Democracy, and National Security," SSRN, July 14, 2018, https://poseidon01.ssrn.com/delivery.php?ID=42207 31030081270801071240810690000880500130550190190541130 25080123110095098127113089026006024040028056016073101 11300106911311206104305904402806910110410211110511008 10130201250830650110040921021190890730810070851220870 68074077123124065106126030010022&EXT=pdf.

43 Ashley Rodriguez, "Microsoft's AI millennial chatbot became a racist jerk after less than a day on Twitter," *Quartz*, March 24, 2016, https://qz.com/646825/microsofts-ai-millennial-chatbot-became-a -racist-jerk-after-less-than-a-day-on-twitter/; Smith, *Tools and Weapons*, 255.

44 Will Knight, "An AI that writes convincing prose risks mass-producing fake news," *Technology Review*, February 14, 2019, https://www.technologyreview.com/s/612960/an-ai-tool-auto-gener ates-fake-news-bogus-tweets-and-plenty-of-gibberish/.

45 Vinod Khosla, "An AI that writes convincing prose risks mass-producing fake news," *Medium*, September 12, 2017, https://me dium.com/@vkhosla/ai-scary-for-the-right-reasons-185bee8c6daa.

46 Richard Fontaine and Kara Frederick, "The Autocrat's New Tool Kit," *Wall Street Journal*, March 15, 2019, https://www.wsj.com /articles/the-autocrats-new-tool-kit-11552662637.

47 Davey Alba, "How Russia's Troll Farm Is Changing Tactics Before the Fall Election," *New York Times*, March 29, 2020, https://www.nytimes.com/2020/03/29/technology/russia-troll-farm-election.html.

48 Henry A. Kissinger, "How the Enlightenment Ends," *The Atlantic*, June 2018, https://www.theatlantic.com/magazine/archive/2018/06/henry-kissinger-ai-could-mean-the-end-of-human-history/559124/.

49 Tamir Pardo, interview with author, August 6, 2018.

50 Diogo Monica, interview with author, May 13, 2020.

51 Katie Hunt and CY Xu, "China 'employs 2 million to police internet,'" CNN, October 7, 2013, https://www.cnn.com/2013/10/07/world/asia/china-internet-monitors/index.html.

52 Paul Mozur and Don Clark, "China's Surveillance State Sucks Up Data. U.S. Tech Is Key to Sorting It," *New York Times*, November 22, 2020, https://www.nytimes.com/2020/11/22/technology/china-intel-nvidia-xinjiang.html.

53 Andersen, "The Panopticon Is Already Here."

54 Paul Mozur, "One Month, 500,000 Face Scans: How China Is Using A.I. to Profile a Minority," *New York Times*, April 14, 2019, https://www.nytimes.com/2019/04/14/technology/china-surveillance-artificial-intelligence-racial-profiling.html.

55 Andersen, "The Panopticon Is Already Here."

56 Drew Harwell and Eva Dou, "Huawei tested AI software that could recognize Uighur minorities and alert police, report says," *Washington Post*, December 8, 2020, https://www.washingtonpost.com/technology/2020/12/08/huawei-tested-ai-software-that-could-recognize-uighur-minorities-alert-police-report-says/.

57 Anna Fifield, "TikTok's owner is helping China's campaign of repression in Xinjiang, report finds," *Washington Post*, November 28, 2019, https://www.washingtonpost.com/world/tiktoks-owner-is-helping-chinas-campaign-of-repression-in-xinjiang-report-finds/2019/11/28/98e8d9e4-119f-11ea-bf62-eadd5d11f559_story.html.

58 Andersen, "The Panopticon Is Already Here."

59 Anna Fifield, "As repression mounts, China under Xi Jinping feels increasingly like North Korea," *Washington Post*, September 28, 2020, https://www.washingtonpost.com/world/asia_pacific/china-muslims-xinjiang-north-korea-repression/2020/09/28/ad2fefd8-f316-11ea-8025-5d3489768ac8_story.html.

60 Scott Simon, "China Suppression of Uighur Minorities Meets U.N. Definition of Genocide, Report Says," NPR, July 4, 2020, https://www.npr.org/2020/07/04/887239225/china-suppression-of-uighur-minorities-meets-u-n-definition-of-genocide-report-s.

61 Allison Gordon, "13-ton shipment of human hair, likely from Chinese prisoners, seized," CNN, July 2, 2020, https://www.cnn.com/2020/07/02/us/china-hair-uyghur-cpb-trnd/index.html.

62 Muyi Xiao, Haley Willis, Christoph Koettl, Natalie Reneau, and Drew Jordan, "China Is Using Uighur Labor to Produce Face Masks," *New York Times*, July 19, 2020, https://www.nytimes.com/2020/07/19/world/asia/china-mask-forced-labor.html.

63 Ben Westcott and Rebecca Wright, "First independent report into Xinjiang genocide allegations claims evidence of Beijing's 'intent to destroy' Uyghur people," CNN, March 9, 2021, https://www.cnn.com/2021/03/09/asia/china-uyghurs-xinjiang-genocide-report-intl-hnk/index.html.

64 Singer and Brooking, *LikeWar.*

65 Bill Gertz, *Deceiving the Sky: Inside Communist China's Drive for Global Supremacy* (New York: Encounter Books, 2019), 87.

66 Rosie Perper, "Chinese dog owners are being assigned a social credit score to keep them in check—and it seems to be working," *Business Insider*, October 26, 2018, https://www.businessinsider.com/china-dog-owners-social-credit-score-2018-10#.

67 Gertz, *Deceiving the Sky,* 86.

68 Andersen, "The Panopticon Is Already Here."

69 Paul Mozur, "With Hacks and Cameras, Beijing's Electronic Dragnet Closes on Hong Kong," *New York Times*, August 25, 2020, https://www.nytimes.com/2020/08/25/technology/hong-kong-national-security-law.html.

70 Yan Zhao and Su Xinqi, "Hongkongers scrub social media after security law," *Asia Times*, July 3, 2020, https://asiatimes.com/2020/07/hongkongers-scrub-social-media-after-security-law/.

71 Paul Mozur, Jonah M. Kessel, and Melissa Chan, "Made in China, Exported to the World: The Surveillance State," *New York Times*, April 24, 2019, https://www.nytimes.com/2019/04/24/technology/ecuador-surveillance-cameras-police-government.html.

72 Megha Rajagopalan, "Facial Recognition Technology Is Facing a Huge Backlash in the US. But Some of the World's Biggest Tech Companies Are Trying to Sell It in the Gulf," *BuzzFeed News*, May 29, 2019, https://www.buzzfeednews.com/article/meghara/dubai-facial-recognition-technology-ibm-huawei-hikvision.

73 Amit Katwala, "Why China's perfectly placed to be quantum computing's superpower," *Wired*, November 14, 2010, https://www.wired.co.uk/article/quantum-computing-china-us.

74 Charles Riley, "Google claims its quantum computer can do the impossible in 200 seconds," CNN, October 23, 2019, https://www.cnn.com/2019/10/23/tech/google-quantum-supremacy-scn/index.html.

75 Jack Nicas, "Does the F.B.I. Need Apple to Hack Into iPhones?,"

New York Times, January 17, 2020, https://www.nytimes.com/2020 /01/17/technology/fbi-iphones.html.

76 Jeanne Whalen, "The quantum revolution is coming, and Chinese scientists are at the forefront," *Washington Post*, August 18, 2019, https://www.washingtonpost.com/business/2019/08/18/quantum -revolution-is-coming-chinese-scientists-are-forefront/.

77 Katwala, "Why China's perfectly placed to be quantum computing's superpower."

78 "Emerging Military Technologies: Background and Issues for Congress," Congressional Research Service, November 10, 2020, https:// crsreports.congress.gov/product/pdf/R/R46458.

79 Bethany Allen-Ebrahimian, "Estonia warns of 'silenced world dominated by Beijing,'" *Axios*, February 17, 2021, https://www.axios.com /estonia-warns-of-silenced-world-dominated-by-beijing-09e54843 -6b45-491a-9bfd-e880f6f14795.html.

80 Edward Wong, "'Doctor Strange' Writer Says China-Tibet Remarks Don't Represent Marvel," *New York Times*, April 29, 2016, https:// www.nytimes.com/2016/04/29/world/asia/doctor-strange-tilda -swinton-china-tibet.html.

81 Lucas Shaw, "Fearing Chinese Censors, Paramount Changes 'World War Z' (Exclusive)," *The Wrap*, March 31, 2013, https://www .thewrap.com/fearing-chinese-censors-paramount-changes-world -war-z-exclusive-83316/.

82 Sam Byford, "Apple pulls podcast apps in China after government pressure," *The Verge*, June 11, 2020, https://www.theverge.com /2020/6/11/21287436/pocket-casts-castro-china-apple-govern ment-pressure.

83 "Former Boeing Engineer Convicted of Economic Espionage in Theft of Space Shuttle Secrets for China," U.S. Department of Justice, July 16, 2009, https://www.justice.gov/opa/pr/former-boeing-engineer -convicted-economic-espionage-theft-space-shuttle-secrets-china.

84 Roberts, *Censored Distraction and Diversion Inside China's Great Firewall*, 178.

85 "2016 Wisconsin Results," *New York Times*, August 1, 2017, https:// www.nytimes.com/elections/2016/results/wisconsin.

86 Cynthia McFadden, William M. Arkin, and Kevin Monahan, "Russians penetrated U.S. voter systems, top U.S. official says," NBC News, February 7, 2018, https://www.nbcnews.com/politics/elec tions/russians-penetrated-u-s-voter-systems-says-top-u-s-n845721.

87 Fontaine and Frederick, "The Autocrat's New Tool Kit."

88 Dean Takahashi, "SoftBank believes 1 trillion connected devices will create $11 trillion in value by 2025," *VentureBeat*, October 16, 2018, https://venturebeat.com/2018/10/16/softbank-believes-1-tril lion-connected-devices-will-create-11-trillion-in-value-by-2025/.

89 Carlin, *Dawn of the Code War*, e-book, 756.
90 Paul Tullis, "The US military is trying to read minds," *Technology Review*, October 16, 2019, https://www.technologyreview.com/2019/10/16/132269/us-military-super-soldiers-control-drones-brain-computer-interfaces/.
91 "Elon Musk's Neuralink puts computer chips in pigs' brains in bid to cure diseases," NBC News, August 29, 2020, https://www.nbcnews.com/tech/tech-news/elon-musk-s-neuralink-puts-computer-chips-pigs-brains-bid-n1238782.
92 Lora Kolodny, "Former Google CEO predicts the internet will split in two—and one part will be led by China," CNBC, September 20, 2018, https://www.cnbc.com/2018/09/20/eric-schmidt-ex-google-ceo-predicts-internet-split-china.html.
93 Rose Wong, "There May Soon Be Three Internets. America's Won't Necessarily Be the Best," *New York Times*, October 15, 2018, https://www.nytimes.com/2018/10/15/opinion/internet-google-china-balkanization.html.
94 Tweet from @wolfejosh, Twitter, June 9, 2019, https://twitter.com/wolfejosh/status/1137731248015794176/photo/1.
95 Rongbin Han, *Contesting Cyberspace in China: Online Expression and Authoritarian Resilience* (New York: Columbia University Press, 2018), 101.
96 "Huawei's deep roots put Africa beyond reach of US crackdown," KrAsia, August 17, 2020, https://kr-asia.com/huaweis-deep-roots-put-africa-beyond-reach-of-us-crackdown.
97 "Assessment on U.S. Defense Implications of China's Expanding Global Access," U.S. Department of Defense, December 2018, https://media.defense.gov/2019/Jan/14/2002079292/-1/-1/1/EXPANDING-GLOBAL-ACCESS-REPORT-FINAL.PDF.
98 Eric Schmidt, *The New Digital Age: Transforming Nations, Businesses, and Our Lives* (New York: Vintage, 2014), 111.
99 "Exporting Repression? China's Artificial Intelligence Push into Africa," Council on Foreign Relations, December 17, 2018, https://www.cfr.org/blog/exporting-repression-chinas-artificial-intelligence-push-africa.
100 Adrian Shahbaz, "The Rise of Digital Authoritarianism," Freedom House, https://freedomhouse.org/report/freedom-net/2018/rise-digital-authoritarianism.
101 Ghalia Kadiri, "A Addis-Abeba, le siège de l'Union africaine espionné par Pékin," *Le Monde*, January. 26, 2018, https://www.lemonde.fr/afrique/article/2018/01/26/a-addis-abeba-le-siege-de-l-union-africaine-espionne-par-les-chinois_5247521_3212.html.
102 Joe Parkinson, Nicholas Bariyo, and Josh Chin, "Huawei Technicians Helped African Governments Spy on Political Opponents,"

Wall Street Journal, August 15, 2019, https://www.wsj.com/articles /huawei-technicians-helped-african-governments-spy-on-political -opponents-11565793017.

103 Yuval Harari, "Read Yuval Harari's blistering warning to Davos in full," World Economic Forum, January 24, 2020, https://www.we forum.org/agenda/2020/01/yuval-hararis-warning-davos-speech -future-predications/.

104 Vincent, "Watch Jordan Peele use AI to make Barack Obama deliver a PSA about fake news."

Chapter 5: THE HILL AND THE VALLEY

1 "Transcript with Rep. Cicilline," Rev, https://www.rev.com/transcript -editor/shared/_FX24Jlb75YkV0wn0tdgEzn7hr3YnKHiYFR aJHC36c puN8-hRZCoC _eanIZkNRqAAoCUFtC 5429 mmv3rvjnTX3PpTLo?loadFrom=PastedDeeplink&ts=16474.82.

2 Laura Hautala, "Tech titans face video glitches in congressional tes-timony," CNET, July 29, 2020, https://www.cnet.com/news/tech -titans-face-video-glitches-in-congressional-testimony/.

3 Elizabeth Culliford, "Bezos' snack, room ratings and 'the net': Key online moments from tech hearing," Reuters, July 29, 2020, https://www.reuters.com/article/us-usa-tech-congress-memes-id USKCN24U341.

4 "Transcript with Rep. Cicilline."

5 Ibid.

6 Ibid.

7 Sanger, *The Perfect Weapon*, xi.

8 Noah Smith, "Interview: Marc Andreessen, VC and tech pioneer," Substack, June 22, 2021, https://noahpinion.substack.com/p/inter view-marc-andreessen-vc-and.

9 Margaret O'Mara, *The Code: Silicon Valley and the Remaking of America* (New York: Penguin Press, 2019), 15.

10 Ibid., 18.

11 Ibid., 36.

12 "Tech-Politik: Historical Perspectives on Innovation, Technology, and Strategic Competition," Center for Strategic and International Studies, December 19, 2019, https://www.csis.org/analysis/tech -politik-historical-perspectives-innovation-technology-and-strategic -competition.

13 O'Mara, *The Code*, 24.

14 Liz Jacobs, "GPS, lithium batteries, the internet, cellular technol-ogy, airbags: A Q&A about how governments often fuel innovation," *TED Blog*, October 28, 2013, https://blog.ted.com/qa-mariana-maz zucato-governments-often-fuel-innovation/.

15 "Technology and National Security: Maintaining America's Edge,"

Aspen Institute, February 7, 2019, https://www.aspeninstitute.org /publications/technology-and-national-security-maintaining-ameri cas-edge/.

16 David B. Green, "This Day in Jewish History, 1998: Two Computer Scientists Who Disagreed on Everything Found Google," *Haaretz*, September 4, 2015, https://www.haaretz.com/jewish/2-computer -scientists-found-google-1.5394903.

17 "Technology and National Security: Maintaining America's Edge."

18 "(U) Review of the Unauthorized Disclosures of Former National Security Agency Contractor Edward Snowden," U.S. House of Representatives, September 15, 2016, https://fas.org/irp/congress/2016 _rpt/hpsci-snowden.pdf.

19 Heather Kelly, "Protests against the NSA spring up across U.S.," CNN, July 5, 2013, https://www.cnn.com/2013/07/04/tech/web /restore-nsa-protests/.

20 James Gordon Meek, Luis Martinez, and Alexander Mallin, "Intel Heads: Edward Snowden Did 'Profound Damage' to U.S. Security," ABC News, January 29, 2014, https://abcnews.go.com/Blotter/in tel-heads-edward-snowden-profound-damage-us-security/story?id= 22285388.

21 John R. Schindler, "The Real Ed Snowden Is a Patsy, a Fraud and a Kremlin-Controlled Pawn," *Observer*, September 19, 2016, https:// observer.com/2016/09/the-real-ed-snowden-is-a-patsy-a-fraud-and -a-kremlin-controlled-pawn/.

22 Smith, *Tools and Weapons*, 17.

23 Jon Evans, "Dear America, Would You Please Give Edward Snowden His Medal of Freedom Already?," *TechCrunch*, August 2, 2014, https://techcrunch.com/2014/08/02/the-rorschach-rashomon/.

24 Kwame Opam, "Google engineers issue 'fuck you' to NSA over surveillance scandal," *The Verge*, November 6, 2013, https://www .theverge.com/2013/11/6/5072924/google-engineers-issue-fuck -you-to-nsa-over-surveillance-scandal.

25 Sanger, *The Perfect Weapon*, 84.

26 Matt Stevens, "San Bernardino shooting updates," *Los Angeles Times*, December 9, 2015, https://www.latimes.com/local/lanow/la -me-ln-san-bernardino-shooting-live-updates-htmlstory.html.

27 Peter Bergen, "What explains the biggest U.S. terror attack since 9/11?," CNN, December 5, 2015, https://www.cnn.com/2015/12/04 /opinions/bergen-san-bernardino-terror-attack-explain/index.html.

28 Sanger, *The Perfect Weapon*, 91.

29 Ibid., 97.

30 Andrea Peterson, "Here's how the clash between the NSA Director and a senior Yahoo executive went down," *Washington Post*, February 23, 2015, https://www.washingtonpost.com/news/the-switch

/wp/2015/02/23/heres-how-the-clash-between-the-nsa-director
-and-a-senior-yahoo-executive-went-down/?arc404=true.

31 "CBS News poll: Americans split on unlocking San Bernardino shooter's iPhone," CBS News, March 18, 2016, https://www.cb snews.com/news/cbs-news-poll-americans-split-on-unlocking-san -bernardino-shooters-iphone/.

32 Brian Hall, "Silicon Valley—Making the World a Better Place," YouTube, April 26, 2019, https://www.youtube.com/watch?v=B8C5sjjhsso.

33 Jon Swartz, "Here are the major brands that have pulled ads from Facebook," *MarketWatch*, July 17, 2020, https://www.marketwatch .com/story/here-are-the-major-brands-that-have-pulled-ads-from -facebook-2020-06-30.

34 "Stifling Free Speech: Technological Censorship and the Public Discourse," Committee on the Judiciary, April 10, 2019, https://www .judiciary.senate.gov/meetings/stifling-free-speech-technological -censorship-and-the-public-discourse.

35 Veronica Stracqualursi, "Republican Devin Nunes sues Twitter, users over attacks," CNN, June 9, 2019, https://www.cnn.com/2019/03 /19/politics/devin-nunes-twitter-lawsuit/index.html.

36 Josh Hawley, "Senators Hawley and Cruz Ask FTC to Investigate Tech Censorship Practices, Make Findings Public," Josh Hawley: U.S. Senator for Missouri, July 15, 2019, https://www.hawley.senate.gov /senators-hawley-and-cruz-ask-ftc-investigate-tech-censorship-prac tices-make-findings-public.

37 "Preventing Online Censorship," The White House, May 28, 2020, https://www.federalregister.gov/documents/2020/06/02/2020 -12030/preventing-online-censorship.

38 "Navigator Daily Tracker," Global Strategy Group, June 4, 2020, https://navigatorresearch.org/wp-content/uploads/2020/06/Navi gating-Coronavirus-Full-Topline-F06.11.20.pdf.

39 Tony Romm, "Congress has battled airlines, banks, tobacco and baseball. Now it's preparing to clash with Big Tech," *Washington Post*, July 27, 2020, https://www.washingtonpost.com/technology /2020/07/27/congress-tech-hearing/.

40 Loren DeJonge Schulman, Alexandra Sander, and Madeline Christian, "The Rocky Relationship Between Washington and Silicon Valley," Copia, https://copia.is/wp-content/uploads/2017/07/CO PIA-CNAS-Rocky-Relationship-Between-Washington-And-Silicon -Valley.pdf.

41 John Perry Barlow, "A Declaration of the Independence of Cyberspace," Electronic Frontier Foundation, February 8, 1996, https:// www.eff.org/cyberspace-independence.

42 Amy Zegart and Kevin Childs, "The Divide Between Silicon Valley and Washington Is a National Security Threat," *The Atlantic*, Decem-

ber 13, 2018, https://www.theatlantic.com/ideas/archive/2018/12
/growing-gulf-between-silicon-valley-and-washington/577963/.

43 Angus Loten, "Older IT Workers Left Out Despite Tech Talent
Shortage," *Wall Street Journal*, November 25, 2019, https://www
.wsj.com/articles/older-it-workers-left-out-despite-tech-talent-short
age-11574683200?mod=rsswn.

44 Greg Baumann, "Silicon Valley age discrimination: If you've experienced it, say something," *Silicon Valley Business Journal*, January
5, 2015, https://www.bizjournals.com/sanjose/news/2015/01/05
/silicon-valley-age-discrimination-if-youve.html.

45 Joe Lazauskas, "Is 27 the Tech World's New Middle Age?," *Fast Company*, September 15, 2015, https://www.fastcompany.com/3051030
/is-27-the-tech-worlds-new-middle-age.

46 "Policy, Data, Oversight," U.S. Office of Personnel Management,
September 2017, https://www.opm.gov/policy-data-oversight/data
-analysis-documentation/federal-employment-reports/reports-publi
cations/full-time-permanent-age-distributions/.

47 "Demography of Article III Judges, 1789-2020," Federal Judicial
Center, https://www.fjc.gov/history/exhibits/graphs-and-maps/age
-and-experience-judges#_ftn7.

48 "Membership of the 116th Congress: A Profile," Congressional Research Service, December 17, 2020, https://fas.org/sgp/crs/misc
/R45583.pdf.

49 "Membership of the 116th Congress."

50 "116th Congress House Committee Chairs," Quorum, https://www
.quorum.us/data-driven-insights/democrat-committee-chairs/.

51 Tweet from @shl, Twitter, July 29, 2020, https://twitter.com/shl
/status/1288535357919596544?s=20.

52 "Membership of the 116th Congress."

53 Michael Gold, "Senators Had a Lot to Say About Facebook. That
Hasn't Stopped Them From Using It," *New York Times*, April 12,
2018, https://www.nytimes.com/2018/04/12/us/politics/facebook
-senators-usage.html.

54 Ibid.

55 "Transcript with Rep. Cicilline."

56 Andy Greenberg, "The Senate's Draft Encryption Bill Is 'Ludicrous,
Dangerous, Technically Illiterate,'" *Wired*, April 8, 2016, https://
www.wired.com/2016/04/senates-draft-encryption-bill-privacy
-nightmare/.

57 Kim Zetter, "Of Course Congress Is Clueless about Tech—It Killed
Its Tutor," *Wired*, April 21, 2016, https://www.wired.com/2016/04
/office-technology-assessment-congress-clueless-tech-killed-tutor/.

58 "FAQ," Thiel Fellowship, https://www.thielfellowship.org/faq/.

59 "Organization and Management of the Department of Defense," Di-

rectorate for Organizational Policy, March 2019, https://fas.org/irp /agency/dod/org-man.pdf.

60 Melissa Mittelman, "Why GitHub Finally Abandoned Its Bossless Workplace," *Bloomberg*, September 6, 2016, https://www.bloom berg.com/news/articles/2016-09-06/why-github-finally-abandoned -its-bossless-workplace.

61 Christo Petrov, "50 Gmail Statistics to Show How Big It Is in 2020," TechJury, March 19, 2021, https://techjury.net/blog/gmail -statistics/#gref.

62 Adam Robinson, "Want to Boost Your Bottom Line? Encourage Your Employees to Work on Side Projects," *Inc.*, March 12, 2018, https://www.inc.com/adam-robinson/google-employees-dedicate -20-percent-of-their-time-to-side-projects-heres-how-it-works.html.

63 Letter from employees to Google CEO Sundar Pichai, April 2018, *New York Times*, https://static01.nyt.com/files/2018/technology /googleletter.pdf; Daisuke Wakabayashi and Scott Shane, "Google Will Not Renew Pentagon Contract That Upset Employees," *New York Times*, June 1, 2018, https://www.nytimes.com/2018/06/01 /technology/google-pentagon-project-maven.html.

64 Wakabayashi and Shane, "Google Will Not Renew Pentagon Contract That Upset Employees."

65 Letter from employees to Google CEO Sundar Pichai.

66 Kate Conger, "Google Plans Not to Renew Its Contract for Project Maven, a Controversial Pentagon Drone AI Imaging Program," *Gizmodo*, June 1, 2018, https://gizmodo.com/google-plans -not-to-renew-its-contract-for-project-mave-1826488620?rev= 1527878336532&utm_campaign=socialflow_gizmodo_twitter&utm _source=gizmodo_twitter&utm_medium=socialflow.

67 "Artificial Intelligence at Google: Our Principles," Google AI, https:// ai.google/principles.

68 Ryan Gallagher, "Google China Prototype Links Searches to Phone Numbers," *The Intercept*, September 14, 2018, https://theintercept .com/2018/09/14/google-china-prototype-links-searches-to-phone -numbers/.

69 Harper Neidig, "Pence calls on Google to end censored search engine for China," *The Hill*, October 4, 2018, https://thehill.com/policy /technology/409980-pence-calls-on-google-to-end-censored-search -engine-for-china.

70 Caroline O'Donovan, "Google Employees Are Quitting Over the Company's Secretive China Search Project," *BuzzFeed News*, September 13, 2018, https://www.buzzfeednews.com/article/caroline odonovan/google-project-dragonfly-employees-quitting.

71 Tom McKay, "Google Exec Tells Senate That Project Dragonfly Has Been 'Terminated,'" *Gizmodo*, July 16, 2019, https://gizmodo.com

/google-exec-tells-senate-that-project-dragonfly-has-been-183643 2810.

72 Albert J. Baime, *Arsenal of Democracy: FDR, Detroit, and an Epic Quest to Arm an America at War* (New York: Houghton Mifflin Harcourt, 2014), 73.

73 Ibid., 85.

74 Arthur Herman, *Freedom's Forge: How American Business Produced Victory in World War II* (New York: Random House, 2013), 249.

75 Lee, *AI Superpowers*, e-book, 348.

76 Smith, *Tools and Weapons*, 11.

77 Adam Satariano, "The World's First Ambassador to the Tech Industry," *New York Times*, September 3, 2019, https://www.nytimes.com /2019/09/03/technology/denmark-tech-ambassador.html.

78 Esmy Jimenez, "'We Won't Build It': Northwest Tech Workers Struggle With Company Ties to Immigration Enforcement," Northwest Public Broadcasting, January 14, 2020, https://www.nwpb.org/2020 /01/14/we-wont-build-it-northwest-tech-workers-struggle-with -company-ties-to-immigration-enforcement/.

79 Michael Steinberger, "Does Palantir See too Much?," *New York Times*, October 23, 2020, https://www.nytimes.com/interactive /2020/10/21/magazine/palantir-alex-karp.html.

80 Alex Karp, "Opinion: I'm a tech CEO, and I don't think tech CEOs should be making policy," *Washington Post*, September 5, 2019, https://www.washingtonpost.com/opinions/policy-decisions-should -be-made-by-elected-representatives-not-silicon-valley/2019/09/05 /e02a38dc-cf61-11e9-87fa-8501a456c003_story.html.

81 Trae Stephens, "The Ethics of Defense Technology Development: An Investor's Perspective," *Medium*, December 4, 2019, https://medium .com/@traestephens/the-ethics-of-defense-technology-development -an-investors-perspective-45c71bf6e6af.

82 Michael Brown and Pavneet Singh, "China's Technology Transfer Strategy: How Chinese Investments in Emerging Technology Enable a Strategic Competitor to Access the Crown Jewels of U.S. Innovation," Defense Innovation Unit Experimental, January 2018, https:// admin.govexec.com/media/diux_chinatechnologytransferstudy_jan _2018_(1).pdf.

83 Faith Karimi and Michael Pearson, "The 13 states that still ban same-sex marriage," CNN, February 13, 2015, https://www.cnn.com/2015 /02/13/us/states-same-sex-marriage-ban/index.html.

84 "Suicide Facts," Suicide Awareness Voices of Education, https://save .org/about-suicide/suicide-facts/.

85 Jamie Wareham, "Map Shows Where It's Illegal to Be Gay—30 Years Since WHO Declassified Homosexuality As Disease," *Forbes*, May 17, 2020, www.forbes.com/sites/jamiewareham/2020/05/17

/map-shows-where-its-illegal-to-be-gay-30-years-since-who-declassi
fied-homosexuality-as-disease/#5d42c32e578a.

86 Adam Taylor, "Ramzan Kadyrov says there are no gay men in
Chechnya—and if there are any, they should move to Canada," *Washington Post*, July 15, 2017, https://www.washingtonpost.com/news
/worldviews/wp/2017/07/15/ramzan-kadyrov-says-there-are-no
-gay-men-in-chechnya-and-if-there-are-any-they-should-move-to
-canada/.

87 Wareham, "Map Shows Where It's Illegal to Be Gay—30 Years Since
WHO Declassified Homosexuality As Disease."

88 Jethro Mullen and Steven Jiang, "Chinese firm buys gay dating app
Grindr," CNN, January 12, 2016, https://money.cnn.com/2016/01
/12/technology/grindr-china-beijing-kunlun-tech-deal/index.html.

89 Simon Elegant, "The Love That Dares to Speak Its Name—Discreetly,"
Time, January 13, 2018, http://content.time.com/time/world/article
/0,8599,1703180,00.html.

90 Peter Moskowitz, "Grindr user 'outed North Dakota politician in retaliation for anti-gay vote,'" *The Guardian*, April 28, 2015, https://
www.theguardian.com/us-news/2015/apr/28/north-dakota-politi
cian-randy-boehning-outed-grindr-nude-photos.

91 Echo Wang and Carl O'Donnell, "Exclusive: Behind Grindr's doomed
hookup in China, a data misstep and scramble to make up," Reuters,
May 22, 2019, https://www.reuters.com/article/us-usa-china-grindr
-exclusive/exclusive-behind-grindrs-doomed-hookup-in-china-a
-data-misstep-and-scramble-to-make-up-idUSKCN1SS10H.

92 Echo Wang, Alexandra Alper, and Chibuike Oguh, "Exclusive:
Winning bidder for Grindr has ties to Chinese owner," Reuters, June
2, 2020, https://www.reuters.com/article/us-grindr-m-a-sanvicente
-exclusive/exclusive-winning-bidder-for-grindr-has-ties-to-chinese
-owner-idUSKBN2391AI.

93 Geoffrey A. Fowler, "Is it time to delete TikTok? A guide to the rumors and the real privacy risks," *Washington Post*, July 13, 2020,
https://www.washingtonpost.com/technology/2020/07/13/tiktok
-privacy/.

94 Craig Chapple, "TikTok Crosses 2 Billion Downloads After Best
Quarter for Any App Ever," *Sensor Tower Blog*, April 29, 2020,
https://sensortower.com/blog/tiktok-downloads-2-billion.

95 Fowler, "Is it time to delete TikTok? A guide to the rumors and the
real privacy risks."

96 Ibid.

97 Mike Isaac and Karen Weise, "Amazon Backtracks From Demand
That Employees Delete TikTok," *New York Times*, July 10, 2020,
https://www.nytimes.com/2020/07/10/technology/tiktok-amazon
-security-risk.html.

98 Fowler, "Is it time to delete TikTok? A guide to the rumors and the real privacy risks."

99 Salvador Rodriguez, "TikTok insiders say social media company is tightly controlled by Chinese parent," CNBC, June 25, 2021, https:// www.cnbc.com/2021/06/25/tiktok-insiders-say-chinese-parent -bytedance-in-control.html.

100 Ibid.

101 Georgia Wells, Shan Li, and Liza Lin, "TikTok, Once an Oasis of Inoffensive Fun, Ventures Warily Into Politics," *Wall Street Journal*, July 8, 2020, https://www.wsj.com/articles/tiktok-ventures-warily -into-politics-and-finds-complications-11594224268.

102 Wells, Li, and Lin, "TikTok, Once an Oasis of Inoffensive Fun, Ventures Warily Into Politics."

103 Ursula Perano, "TikTok executive says app used to censor content critical of China," *Axios*, November 7, 2020, https://www.axios .com/tiktok-censor-content-privacy-app-uighur-c4badd9d-a44f -4568-8cbc-af664f6bf78b.html.

104 Tanya Basu, "This girl's TikTok "makeup" video went viral for discussing the Uighur crisis," *Technology Review*, November 27, 2019, https://www.technologyreview.com/2019/11/27/65030/feroza-aziz -tiktok-makeup-video-went-viral-for-discussing-the-uighur-crisis/.

105 Eva Xiao, "TikTok Users Gush About China, Hoping to Boost Views," *Wall Street Journal*, June 17, 2020, https://www.wsj.com /articles/tiktok-users-gush-about-china-hoping-to-boost-views -11592386203.

106 "The TikTok War," *Stratechery*, July 14, 2020, https://stratechery .com/2020/the-tiktok-war/.

107 Sherisse Pham, "TikTok could threaten national security, US lawmakers say," CNN, October 25, 2019, https://www.cnn.com/2019 /10/25/tech/tiktok-national-security/index.html.

108 Chen Du, "Exclusive: ByteDance Cuts Domestic Engineers' Data Access to TikTok, Other Overseas Products," *PingWest*, June 7, 2020, https://en.pingwest.com/a/6875.

109 Paul Mozur, "TikTok to Withdraw From Hong Kong as Tech Giants Halt Data Requests," *New York Times*, July 6, 2020, https://www.ny times.com/2020/07/06/technology/tiktok-google-facebook-twitter -hong-kong.html.

110 Cecilia Kang, Lara Jakes, Ana Swanson, and David McCabe, "TikTok Enlists Army of Lobbyists as Suspicions Over China Ties Grow," *New York Times*, July 15, 2020, https://www.nytimes.com /2020/07/15/technology/tiktok-washington-lobbyist.html?smid=tw -nytpolitics&smtyp=cur.

111 Monica Chin, "TikTok reduces India staff after long-standing countrywide ban," *The Verge*, February 3, 2021, https://www.theverge

.com/2021/2/2/22262940/tiktok-leaves-india-ban-app-china-gov ernment-security-privacy.

112 "AliExpress: India continues to ban China apps amid standoff," BBC, November 25, 2020, https://www.bbc.com/news/world-asia-india -55068372.

113 Emily Schmall, "India bans TikTok, other Chinese apps amid border standoff," ABC News, April 29, 2021, https://abcnews.go.com /Technology/wireStory/india-bans-tiktok-chinese-apps-amid-border -standoff-71625376.

114 "Addressing the Threat Posed by TikTok, and Taking Additional Steps to Address the National Emergency With Respect to the Information and Communications Technology and Services Supply Chain," The White House, August 6, 2020, https://www.federalregister.gov /documents/2020/08/11/2020-17699/addressing-the-threat-posed-by -tiktok-and-taking-additional-steps-to-address-the-national-emergency.

115 Kim Lyons, "TikTok confirms it will sue the Trump administration," *The Verge,* August 22, 2020, https://www.theverge.com/2020/8/22 /21397131/tiktok-lawsuit-president-trump-china-ban-executive-order.

116 Roslyn Layton, "The Clock Is Ticking On TikTok," *Forbes*, August 5, 2020, https://www.forbes.com/sites/roslynlayton/2020/08/05/the -clock-is-ticking-on-tiktok.

117 Ana Swanson, David McCabe, and Erin Griffith, "Trump Approves Deal Between Oracle and TikTok," *New York Times*, September 19, 2020, https://www.nytimes.com/2020/09/19/technology/trump-oracle -and-tiktok.html.

118 "Walmart Statement About Potential Investment in and Commercial Agreements with TikTok Global," Walmart, September 19, 2020, https://web.archive.org/web/20200920114627/https://corporate .walmart.com/newsroom/2020/09/19/walmart-statement-about -potential-investment-in-and-commercial-agreements-with-tiktok -global.

119 "Home," Defense Innovation Unit, https://www.diu.mil/.

120 Jennings Brown, "Weird Tooth Phone Wins Millions in Pentagon Funding," *Gizmodo*, September 12, 2018, https://gizmodo.com /weird-tooth-phone-wins-millions-in-pentagon-funding-1829004364.

121 Brown and Singh, "China's Technology Transfer Strategy."

122 Katy Stech Ferek, "Rubio Seeks Security Review of Chinese Bid for GNC," *Wall Street Journal*, September 10, 2020, https://www.wsj .com/articles/rubio-seeks-security-review-of-chinese-bid-for-gnc -11599775144.

123 "Annual Report to Congress," Committee on Foreign Investment in the United States, 2019, https://home.treasury.gov/system/files/206 /CFIUS-Public-Annual-Report-CY-2019.pdf.

124 Foer, "Putin Is Well on His Way to Stealing the Next Election."

125 Tom Warren, "Zoom admits it doesn't have 300 million users, corrects misleading claims," *The Verge*, April 30, 2020, https://www.theverge.com/2020/4/30/21242421/zoom-300-million-users-incorrect-meeting-participants-statement.

126 Micah Lee and Yael Grauer, "Zoom Meetings Aren't End-to-End Encrypted, Despite Misleading Marketing," *The Intercept*, March 31,2020, https://theintercept.com/2020/03/31/zoom-meeting-encryption/.

127 Charlie Wood, "Zoom admits calls got 'mistakenly' routed through China," *Business Insider*, April 6, 2020, https://www.businessinsider.com/china-zoom-data-2020-4?amp.

128 Gerry Shih, "Zoom censors video talks on Hong Kong and Tiananmen, drawing criticism," *Washington Post*, June 11, 2020, https://www.washingtonpost.com/world/asia_pacific/zoom-censors-video-talks-on-hong-kong-and-tiananmen-drawing-criticism/2020/06/11/0197dc94-ab90-11ea-a43b-be9f6494a87d_story.html.

129 Ibid.

130 Tweet from @LizEconomy, Twitter, June 11, 2020, https://twitter.com/lizeconomy/status/1271108849332781062.

131 "Improving Our Policies as We Continue to Enable Global Collaboration," Zoom, June 11, 2020, https://blog.zoom.us/improving-our-policies-as-we-continue-to-enable-global-collaboration/.

132 "Zoom Video Communications, Inc.," U.S. Securities and Exchange Commission, January 31, 2020.

133 Leah MarieAnn Klett, "China: Police arrest Christians participating in Zoom Easter worship service," *Christian Post*, April 17, 2020, https://www.christianpost.com/news/china-police-arrest-christians-participating-in-zoom-easter-worship-service.html.

134 Joseph Kahn, "Yahoo helped Chinese to prosecute journalist," *New York Times*, September 8, 2005, https://www.nytimes.com/2005/09/08/business/worldbusiness/yahoo-helped-chinese-to-prosecute-journalist.html.

Chapter 6: WINNING THE GRAY WAR

1 "CyCon 2019 brought together 645 participants from 47 countries and 5 continents," *Baltic Times*, June 7, 2019, https://www.baltictimes.com/cycon_2019_brought_together_645_participants_from_47_countries_and_5_continents/.

2 Hillary Rodham Clinton, "Economic Statecraft," U.S. Department of State, October 14, 2011, https://2009-2017.state.gov/secretary/20092013clinton/rm/2011/10/175552.htm.

3 Richard Haass, "A Cold War With China Would Be a Mistake," *Wall Street Journal*, May 7, 2020, https://www.wsj.com/articles/dont-start-a-new-cold-war-with-china-11588860761.

4 Dan Coats, "Opinion: There's no Cold War with China—and if there were, we couldn't win," *Washington Post*, July 28, 2020, https://www.washingtonpost.com/opinions/2020/07/28/new-cold-war-between-us-china-is-dangerous-myth/.

5 Graham Allison, "The Thucydides Trap: Are the U.S. and China Headed for War?," *The Atlantic*, September 24, 2015, https://www.theatlantic.com/international/archive/2015/09/united-states-china-war-thucydides-trap/406756/.

6 Cui Tiankai, "China and the U.S. Should Reset Their Relationship," *Politico*, July 30, 2020, https://www.politico.com/news/magazine/2020/07/30/us-china-relationship-reset-387515.

7 "China's countermeasures ready for prolonged 'war' with US: Global Times editorial," *Global Times*, May 15, 2020, https://www.globaltimes.cn/content/1188494.shtml.

8 H. E. Xi Jinping, "Full Text of Xi Jinping keynote at the World Economic Forum," CGTN TV, January 17, 2017, https://america.cgtn.com/2017/01/17/full-text-of-xi-jinping-keynote-at-the-world-economic-forum.

9 Zhou Xin, "Xi Jinping calls for 'new Long March' in dramatic sign that China is preparing for protracted trade war," *South China Morning Post*, May 21, 2019, https://www.scmp.com/economy/china-economy/article/3011186/xi-jinping-calls-new-long-march-dramatic-sign-china-preparing.

10 "Exclusive: Internal Chinese report warns Beijing faces Tiananmen-like global backlash over virus," Reuters, May 4, 2020, https://www.reuters.com/article/us-health-coronavirus-china-sentiment-ex/exclusive-internal-chinese-report-warns-beijing-faces-tiananmen-like-global-backlash-over-virus-idUSKBN22G19C.

11 Yi-Zheng Lian, "Trump Is Wrong About TikTok. China's Plans Are Much More Sinister," *New York Times*, September 17, 2020, https://www.nytimes.com/2020/09/17/opinion/tiktok-china-strategy.html?referringSource=articleShare.

12 Lidia Kelly, "Australia says China ignores calls to ease trade tension," Reuters, May 17, 2020, https://www.reuters.com/article/us-health-coronavirus-australia-china-idUSKBN22T041.

13 Carl J. Friedrich and Zbigniew K. Brzezinski, *Totalitarian Dictatorship and Autocracy* (Cambridge, MA: Harvard University Press, 1965), 354.

14 Mitt Romney, "Opinion: Mitt Romney: America is awakening to China. This is a clarion call to seize the moment," *Washington Post*, April 23, 2020, https://www.washingtonpost.com/opinions/global-opinions/mitt-romney-covid-19-has-exposed-chinas-utter-dishonesty/2020/04/23/30859476-8569-11ea-ae26-989cfce1c7c7_story.html.

15 Catie Edmondson, "Senate Democrats Present $350 Billion Strategy to Counter China," *New York Times*, September 17, 2020, https://www.nytimes.com/2020/09/17/us/politics/democrats-china-strategy.html.

16 Pete Buttigieg, "VIDEO: "America and the World in 2054: Reimagining National Security For a New Era," Democracy in Action, June 11, 2019, https://www.democracyinaction.us/2020/buttigieg/buttigiegpolicy061119foreign.html.

17 Ursula Perano, "Debate night: What the candidates are saying on China," *Axios*, June 28, 2019, https://www.axios.com/debate-night-what-the-candidates-are-saying-on-china-a530a78a-d7e6-462c-b172-7d17e463d9f3.html.

18 Mike Gallagher, "Yes, America Is in a Cold War With China," *Wall Street Journal*, June 7, 2020, https://www.wsj.com/articles/yes-america-is-in-a-cold-war-with-china-11591548706.

19 Chhabra, "The China challenge, democracy, and U.S. grand strategy."

20 Arthur Waldron, "The Chamberlain trap," *New Criterion*, September 2017, https://newcriterion.com/issues/2017/9/the-chamberlain-trap-8757.

21 Anthony Adamthwaite, *The Making of the Second World War* (New York: Routledge, 1989), 62.

22 Laura Silver, Kat Devlin, and Christine Huang, "Americans Fault China for Its Role in the Spread of COVID-19," Pew Research Center, July 30, 2020, https://www.pewresearch.org/global/2020/07/30/americans-fault-china-for-its-role-in-the-spread-of-covid-19/.

23 "Russia," Gallup, https://news.gallup.com/poll/1642/russia.aspx.

24 Jeffrey Goldberg, "Why Obama Fears for Our Democracy," *The Atlantic*, November 16, 2020, https://www.theatlantic.com/ideas/archive/2020/11/why-obama-fears-for-our-democracy/617087/.

25 "Remarks by the President at the United States Coast Guard Academy Commencement," The White House, May 20, 2015, https://obamawhitehouse.archives.gov/the-press-office/2015/05/20/remarks-president-united-states-coast-guard-academy-commencement.

26 "2014 Climate Change Adaptation Roadmap," U.S. Department of Defense, https://www.acq.osd.mil/eie/downloads/CCARprint_wForward_e.pdf.

27 "The Paris Agreement," United Nations Framework Convention on Climate Change, https://unfccc.int/process-and-meetings/the-paris-agreement/the-paris-agreement.

28 Mike Pompeo, "Keynote Address at the Ministerial to Advance Religious Freedom," July 18, 2019, https://2017-2021.state.gov/secretary-of-state-michael-r-pompeo-keynote-address-at-the-ministerial-to-advance-religious-freedom/index.html.

29 "National Cyber Strategy of the United States of America," The

White House, September 2018, https://trumpwhitehouse.archives
.gov/wp-content/uploads/2018/09/National-Cyber-Strategy.pdf.

30 "Washington's Farewell Address 1796," The Avalon Project, https://
avalon.law.yale.edu/18th_century/washing.asp.

31 "William M. (Mac) Thornberry National Defense Authorization Act
for Fiscal Year 2021."

32 "Keynote Remarks by Assistant Secretary Feddo at the American
Conference Institute's Sixth National Conference on CFIUS," U.S.
Department of the Treasury, July 15, 2020, https://home.treasury.gov
/news/press-releases/sm1067.

33 Danny Crichton, "The US is formalizing Team Telecom rules to restrict foreign ownership of internet and telecom assets," *TechCrunch*,
April 6, 2020, https://techcrunch.com/2020/04/06/the-u-s-is-for
malizing-team-telecom-rules-to-restrict-foreign-ownership-of-inter
net-and-telecom-assets/.

34 "NATO will defend itself," NATO, August 27, 2019, https://www
.nato.int/cps/en/natohq/news_168435.htm?selectedLocale=en.

35 Steven Hill, "NATO and the International Law of Cyber Defence,"
SSRN, November 3, 2020, https://poseidon01.ssrn.com/delivery.php
?ID=72308912110508408407700206808101202301803103506400
80380641010260040980871170000660940370260341111230610
01010120109125013083108105082056047035112070116022113124
09102806004100209700407903112710809311007108300608207
0020105071025105124095026070067064102&EXT=pdf.

36 "What is NATO?"

37 Shruti Srivastava and Isabel Reynolds, "Japan, India and Australia to
Seek Supply Chain Pact," *Bloomberg*, August 21, 2020, https://www
.bloomberg.com/news/articles/2020-08-21/japan-india-and-austra
lia-are-said-to-seek-supply-chain-pact.

38 Pranshu Verma, "In Wake of Recent India-China Conflict, U.S. Sees
Opportunity," *New York Times*, October 3, 2020, https://www.ny
times.com/2020/10/03/world/asia/india-china-trump.html?refer
ringSource=articleShare.

39 Sanjeev Miglani, "U.S. says 'Quad' nations ready to work with others
for free, open Indo-Pacific," Yahoo! News, October 12, 2020, https://
news.yahoo.com/u-says-quad-nations-ready-171308007.html.

40 Derek Grossman, "The Quad Is Poised to Become Openly Anti-
China Soon," *RAND Blog*, July 28, 2020, https://www.rand.org
/blog/2020/07/the-quad-is-poised-to-become-openly-anti-china
-soon.html.

41 "Alexander Hamilton's Final Version of the Report on the Subject of
Manufactures," Founders Online, December 5, 1791, https://founders
.archives.gov/documents/Hamilton/01-10-02-0001-0007.

42 Keith Johnson and Robbie Gramer, "The Great Decoupling," *Foreign*

Policy, May 14, 2020, https://foreignpolicy.com/2020/05/14/china -us-pandemic-economy-tensions-trump-coronavirus-covid-new-cold -war-economics-the-great-decoupling/.

43 Michael A. Witt, "Prepare for the U.S. and China to Decouple," *Harvard Business Review*, June 26, 2020, https://hbr.org/2020/06 /prepare-for-the-u-s-and-china-to-decouple.

44 "Trump again raises idea of decoupling economy from China," Reuters, September 15, 2020, https://www.reuters.com/article/us -usa-trump-china/trump-again-raises-idea-of-decoupling-economy -from-china-idUSKBN25Y1V9.

45 Jacky Wong, "Beijing Still Wants Microchips Made in China," *Wall Street Journal*, April 17, 2020, https://www.wsj.com/articles/beijing -still-wants-microchips-made-in-china-11587125377.

46 Joseph S. Nye Jr. and Condoleezza Rice, "The Struggle for Power: U.S.-China Relations in the 21st Century," Aspen Institute, 2020, https://assets.aspeninstitute.org/content/uploads/2020/01/The StruggleForPower.pdf?_ga=2.61349548.1878621097.1579623448 -1739069731.1574791461.

47 Lucy Fisher, "Downing Street plans new 5G club of democracies," *The Times*, May 29, 2020, https://www.thetimes.co.uk/article /downing-street-plans-new-5g-club-of-democracies-bfnd5wj57.

48 Jakob Hanke Vela and David M. Herszenhorn, "EU seeks anti-China alliance on tech with Biden," *Politico*, November 30, 2020, https:// www.politico.eu/article/eu-seeks-anti-china-alliance-on-tech-with -joe-biden/.

49 Daniel Kliman, Ben FitzGerald, Kristine Lee, and Joshua Fitt, "Forging an Alliance Innovation Base," Center for a New Ameri- can Security, 2020, https://s3.amazonaws.com/files.cnas.org/docu ments/CNAS-Report-Alliance-Innovation-Base-Final.pdf?mtime= 20200329174909; "Gross domestic spending on R&D," OECD, https://data.oecd.org/rd/gross-domestic-spending-on-r-d.htm.

50 Michèle A. Flournoy, "Testimony before the U.S.-China Economic and Security Review Commission: The Chinese View of Strategic Competition with the United States," U.S.-China Economic and Se- curity Review Commission, June 24, 2020, https://www.uscc.gov /sites/default/files/2020-06/Flournoy_Testimony.pdf.

51 "The Trump administration wants a US-China commercial split," *The Economist*, August 13, 2020, https://www.economist.com /business/2020/08/13/the-trump-administration-wants-a-us-china -commercial-split; Apjit Walia, "The coming Tech Wall and the covid dilemma," DB Research, https://www.dbresearch.com/PROD/RPS _EN-PROD/PROD0000000000507995/The_coming_Tech_Wall _and_the_covid_dilemma.pdf.

52 Kim Lyons, "Apple starts making first flagship iPhone in India,"

The Verge, July 25, 2020, https://www.theverge.com/2020/7/25/21338436/apple-iphone11-india-foxconn-china.

53 Lauly Li and Cheng Ting-Fang, "Inside the US campaign to cut China out of the tech supply chain," *Nikkei Asia,* October 7, 2020, https://asia.nikkei.com/Spotlight/The-Big-Story/Inside-the-US-campaign-to-cut-China-out-of-the-tech-supply-chain.

54 Huileng Tan, "Coronavirus outbreak in China spurs supply chain shifts that began during trade war," CNBC, February 20, 2020, https://www.cnbc.com/2020/02/20/coronavirus-outbreak-spurs-supply-chain-shifts-started-by-us-china-trade-war.html.

55 Huileng Tan, "There will be a 'massive' shuffling of supply chains globally after coronavirus shutdowns," CNBC, March 20, 2020, https://www.cnbc.com/2020/03/20/coronavirus-shocks-will-lead-to-massive-global-supply-chain-shuffle.html.

56 "Attorney General William P. Barr Delivers the Keynote Address at the Department of Justice's China Initiative Conference," U.S. Department of Justice, February 6, 2020, https://www.justice.gov/opa/speech/attorney-general-william-p-barr-delivers-keynote-address-department-justices-china.

57 Matt Kapko, "Huawei Dominates Nokia, Ericsson, Dell'Oro Says," SDX Central, December 3, 2020, https://www.sdxcentral.com/articles/news/huawei-dominates-nokia-ericsson-delloro-says/2020/12/.

58 "National Security Senators Introduce Bipartisan Legislation to Develop 5G Alternatives to Huawei," Mark R. Warner, January 14, 2020, https://www.warner.senate.gov/public/index.cfm/2020/1/national-security-senators-introduce-bipartisan-legislation-to-develop-5g-alternatives-to-huawei.

59 Trinko, "Huawei's Role in the 'Chinese Espionage Enterprise.'"

60 "Advancing Digital Connectivity in the Indo-Pacific Region," USAID, https://www.usaid.gov/sites/default/files/documents/1861/USAID_DCCP_Fact_Sheet_080719f.pdf.

61 "Digital Connectivity and Cybersecurity Partnership," U.S. Department of State, https://2017-2021.state.gov/digital-connectivity-and-cybersecurity-partnership/index.html.

62 Nakirfai Tobor, "Kenya secures $173 million from Huawei for data center," *iAfrikan*, April 30, 2019, https://www.iafrikan.com/2019/04/30/kenya-has-secured-666-million-from/.

63 "The New Big Brother: China and Digital Authoritarianism," Committee on Foreign Relations, July 21, 2020, https://www.foreign.senate.gov/imo/media/doc/2020%20SFRC%20Minority%20Staff%20Report%20-%20The%20New%20Big%20Brother%20-%20China%20and%20Digital%20Authoritarianism.pdf.

64 "Testimony before the U.S.-China Economic and Security Review

Commission," Center for a New American Security, January 25, 2018, https://www.uscc.gov/sites/default/files/Kliman_USCC%20 Testimony_20180119.pdf.

65 "Index W," Theodore Roosevelt Association, https://theodore roosevelt.org/content.aspx?page_id=22&club_id=991271&module _id=339551&actr=4.

66 Eamon Barrett, "Intel's decline makes rival chipmaker TSMC the world's 10th most valuable company," *Fortune*, July 28, 2020, https://fortune.com/2020/07/28/intel-7nm-delay-tsmc-stock -shares-worlds-tenth-most-valuable-company/.

67 Sherisse Pham, "Taiwan chip maker TSMC's $12 billion Arizona factory could give the US an edge in manufacturing," CNN, May 15, 2020, https://www.cnn.com/2020/05/15/tech/tsmc-arizona-chip -factory-intl-hnk/index.html.

68 Eamon Barrett, "Semiconductors are a weapon in the U.S.-China trade war. Can this chipmaker serve both sides?," *Fortune*, August 10, 2020, https://fortune.com/2020/08/10/us-china-trade-war -semiconductors-chips-tsmc-chipmakers/.

69 "Chipmaker TSMC eyeing expansion of planned Arizona plant -sources," Reuters, May 4, 2021, https://www.reuters.com/tech nology/chipmaker-tsmc-eyeing-expansion-planned-arizona-plant -sources-2021-05-04/.

70 Steven Lee Myers and Javier C. Hernandez, "With a Wary Eye on China, Taiwan Moves to Revamp Its Military," *New York Times*, August 30, 2020, https://www.nytimes.com/2020/08/30/world/asia /taiwan-china-military.html.

71 Ibid.

72 David Wertime, "Former intel officers: U.S. must update its thinking on Taiwan," *Politico*, October 8, 2020, https://www.politico.com /newsletters/politico-china-watcher/2020/10/08/former-intel-offi cers-were-thinking-about-taiwan-wrong-taipei-beijing-washington -conflict-490547.

73 Brad Lendon, "The US is standing firm with Taiwan, and it's making that point very clear," CNN, September 2, 2020, https://www.cnn .com/2020/09/02/asia/china-taiwan-us-analysis-intl-hnk/index .html.

74 Paula Hancocks and Ben Westcott, "Taiwan risks being caught up in the power struggle between the United States and China," CNN, August 15, 2020, https://edition.cnn.com/2020/08/14/asia/taiwan -tsai-trump-azer-china-intl-hnk/index.html.

75 "50 U.S. senators call for talks on trade agreement with Taiwan," Reuters, October 1, 2020, https://www.reuters.com/article/us-usa -taiwan-china-idUSKBN26M7HL.

76 David R. Stilwell, "The United States, Taiwan, and the World: Part-

ners for Peace and Prosperity," U.S. Department of State, August 31, 2020, https://2017-2021.state.gov/The-United-States-Taiwan-and -the-World-Partners-for-Peace-and-Prosperity/index.html.

77 "Tiffany Introduces Bill to Scrap 'One China Policy,' Resume Normal Ties with Taiwan," Congressman Tom Tiffany, September 17, 2020, https://tiffany.house.gov/media/press-releases/tiffany-introduces -bill-scrap-one-china-policy-resume-normal-ties-taiwan; John Bolton, "Revisit the 'One-China Policy,'" *Wall Street Journal*, January 16, 2017, https://www.wsj.com/articles/revisit-the-one-china-policy-14846 11627.

78 "U.S. Relations With Taiwan," U.S. Department of State, August 31, 2018, https://www.state.gov/u-s-relations-with-taiwan/.

79 Richard Haass and David Sacks, "American Support for Taiwan Must Be Unambiguous," *Foreign Affairs*, September 2, 2020, https:// www.foreignaffairs.com/articles/united-states/american-support -taiwan-must-be-unambiguous.

80 Michèle A. Flournoy, "How to Prevent a War in Asia," *Foreign Affairs*, June 18, 2020, https://www.foreignaffairs.com/articles/united -states/2020-06-18/how-prevent-war-asia.

81 "AliExpress: India continues to ban China apps amid standoff."

82 Joshua R. Fattal, "FARA on Facebook: Modernizing the Foreign Agents Registration Act to Address Propagandists on Social Media," SSRN, July 10, 2019, https://papers.ssrn.com/sol3/papers.cfm? abstract_id=3416925.

83 Nakashima, "Cyber Command has sought to disrupt the world's largest botnet, hoping to reduce its potential impact on the election."

84 Garrett M. Graff, "The Man Who Speaks Softly—and Commands a Big Cyber Army," *Wired*, October 13, 2020, https://www.wired.com /story/general-paul-nakasone-cyber-command-nsa/.

85 King, "CSC Final Report."

86 "Cybersecurity Supply/Demand Heat Map," CyberSeek, https:// www.cyberseek.org/heatmap.html.

87 Ibid.

88 "The New Big Brother."

Chapter 7: A *SPUTNIK* MOMENT

1 "Sputnik: The Beep Heard Round the World, the Birth of the Space Age," NASA, October 2, 2007, https://www.nasa.gov/multimedia /podcasting/jpl-sputnik-20071002.html.

2 Paul Dickson, *Sputnik: The Shock of the Century* (Nebraska: University of Nebraska Press, 2019), 1.

3 "National Defense Education Act," History, Art & Archives, U.S.

House of Representatives, August 21, 1958, https://history.house
.gov/HouseRecord/Detail/15032436195.

4 "HR. 13247. National Defense Education Act [of 1958]," GovTrack,
August 22, 1958, https://www.govtrack.us/congress/votes/85-1958
/s300.

5 Dickson, *Sputnik*, 1.

6 O'Mara, *The Code*, (93).

7 Dickson, *Sputnik*, 1.

8 "Hr 13247. National Defense Education Act of 1958," RT, June 12,
2013, https://www.rt.com/news/putin-rt-interview-full-577/.

9 Rutenberg, "RT, Sputnik and Russia's New Theory of War."

10 Chester E. Finn Jr., "A Sputnik Moment for U.S. Education," Hoover
Institution, December 8, 2010, https://www.hoover.org/research
/sputnik-moment-us-education.

11 Robert Hockett, "America's digital Sputnik moment," *The Hill*, May
12, 2020, https://thehill.com/opinion/technology/497427-americas
-digital-sputnik-moment.

12 "Dunford: US Faces 'Sputnik Moment' in Space Race Competition,"
Military.com, September 9, 2019, https://www.military.com/daily
-news/2019/09/09/dunford-us-faces-sputnik-moment-space-race
-competition.html.

13 Barack Obama, "Remarks by the President in State of Union Address,"
The White House, January 25, 2011, https://obamawhitehouse.ar
chives.gov/the-press-office/2011/01/25/remarks-president-state
-union-address.

14 Charles S. Clark, "Reinventing Government—Two Decades Later,"
Government Executive, April 26, 2013, https://www.govexec.com
/management/2013/04/what-reinvention-wrought/62836/.

15 "President Donald J. Trump Announces the White House Office of
American Innovation (OAI)," The White House, March 27, 2017,
https://trumpwhitehouse.archives.gov/briefings-statements/presi
dent-donald-j-trump-announces-white-house-office-american-innova
tion-oai/.

16 "President Obama Announces proposal to reform, reorganize and
consolidate Government," The White House, January 13, 2012,
https://obamawhitehouse.archives.gov/the-press-office/2012/01/13
/president-obama-announces-proposal-reform-reorganize-and-con
solidate-gov.

17 Jonathan Sallet and Sean Pool, "Rewiring the Federal Government
for Competitiveness," Center for American Progress, January 2012,
https://cdn.americanprogress.org/wp-content/uploads/issues
/2012/01/pdf/dwwsp_competitiveness.pdf?_ga=2.261902414
.2137670932.1602748894-321124460.1602748894.

18 Kurt M. Campbell and Rush Doshi, "The China Challenge Can Help

America Avert Decline," *Foreign Affairs*, December 3, 2020, https://www.foreignaffairs.com/articles/china/2020-12-03/china-challenge-can-help-america-avert-decline.

19 Robert D. Atkinson, "The Case for a National Industrial Strategy to Counter China's Technological Rise," Information Technology and Innovation Foundation, April 13, 2020, https://itif.org/publications/2020/04/13/case-national-industrial-strategy-counter-chinas-technological-rise.

20 Duhigg and Bradsher, "How the U.S. Lost Out on iPhone Work."

21 Henry Farrell and Abraham L. Newman, "Weaponized Interdependence: How Global Economic Networks Shape State Coercion," *MIT Press Direct*, July 1, 2019, https://www.mitpressjournals.org/doi/full/10.1162/isec_a_00351.

22 Joe Stephens and Carol D. Leonnig, "Solyndra Scandal," *Washington Post*, December 25, 2011, https://www.washingtonpost.com/politics/specialreports/solyndra-scandal/.

23 Jared Bernstein, "The Time for America to Embrace Industrial Policy Has Arrived," *Foreign Policy*, July 22, 2020, https://foreignpolicy.com/2020/07/22/industrial-policy-jobs-climate-change/.

24 "Assessing and Strengthening the Manufacturing and Defense Industrial Base and Supply Chain Resiliency of the United States."

25 "S. 2826—Global Economic Security Strategy of 2019," Congress, November 7, 2019, https://www.congress.gov/bill/116th-congress/senate-bill/2826.

26 "S. 3933—CHIPS for America Act," Congress, June 10, 2020, https://www.congress.gov/bill/116th-congress/senate-bill/3933?q=%7B%22search%22%3A%5B%22CHIPS+for+America+act%22%5D%7D&s=1&r=1.

27 Asa Fitch, Kate O'Keeffe, and Bob Davis, "Trump and Chip Makers Including Intel Seek Semiconductor Self-Sufficiency," *Wall Street Journal*, May 11, 2020, https://www.wsj.com/articles/trump-and-chip-makers-including-intel-seek-semiconductor-self-sufficiency-11589103002.

28 Debby Wu, "TSMC Scores Subsidies and Picks Site for $12 Billion U.S. Plant," *Bloomberg*, June 8, 2020, https://www.bloomberg.com/news/articles/2020-06-09/tsmc-confident-of-replacing-any-huawei-orders-lost-to-u-s-curbs.

29 Marc Andreessen, "It's Time to Build," Andreessen Horowitz, https://a16z.com/2020/04/18/its-time-to-build/.

30 "H.R.6422—National Infrastructure Bank Act of 2020," Congress, March 31, 2020, https://www.congress.gov/bill/116th-congress/house-bill/6422/text.

31 "Peters Announces Proposal to Establish a National Institute of Manufacturing, Make Manufacturing Policy a Major National

Focus," Gary Peters, June 18, 2019, https://www.peters.senate.gov /newsroom/press-releases/peters-announces-proposal-to-establish -a-national-institute-of-manufacturing-make-manufacturing-policy -a-major-national-focus.

32 "Section 2: Emerging Technologies and Military-Civil Fusion: Artificial Intelligence, New Materials, and New Energy," U.S.-China Economic and Security Review Commission, https://www.uscc.gov /sites/default/files/2019-11/Chapter%203%20Section%202%20 -%20Emerging%20Technologies%20and%20Military-Civil%20 Fusion%20-%20Artificial%20Intelligence,%20New%20Materials, %20and%20New%20Energy.pdf.

33 Atkinson, "The Case for a National Industrial Strategy to Counter China's Technological Rise."

34 Hillary Clinton, "Moving beyond quarterly capitalism," *Medium*, July 24, 2015, https://medium.com/hillary-for-america/moving-beyond -quarterly-capitalism-7abec53733f6.

35 "President Obama Announces Two New Public-Private Manufacturing Innovation Institutes and Launches the First of Four New Manufacturing Innovation Institute Competitions," The White House, February 25, 2014, https://obamawhitehouse.archives.gov /the-press-office/2014/02/25/president-obama-announces-two-new -public-private-manufacturing-innovation.

36 "FACT SHEET: President Obama Announces New Manufacturing Innovation Hub in Knoxville, Tennessee," The White House, January 9, 2015, https://obamawhitehouse.archives.gov/the-press-office /2015/01/09/fact-sheet-president-obama-announces-new-manufac turing-innovation-hub-kn.

37 Mark Muro, "No matter which way you look at it, tech jobs are still concentrating in just a fe1w cities," Brookings Institution, March 3, 2020, https://www.brookings.edu/research/tech-is-still-concentrating/.

38 Mae Rice, "The Tech Industry Has Outgrown the Bay Area," Built In, May 13, 2020, https://builtin.com/founders-entrepreneurship /mighty-middle-report.

39 "R&D as Percent of the Federal Budget," Budget of the U.S. Government Fiscal Year 2021, American Association for the Advancement of Science, https://www.aaas.org/sites/default/files/2020-05/Budget.png.

40 Kliman, FitzGerald, Lee, and Fitt, "Forging an Alliance Innovation Base."

41 Beethika Khan, Carol Robbins, and Abigail Okrent, "The State of U.S. Science and Engineering 2020," National Center for Science and Engineering Statistics, January 15, 2020, https://ncses.nsf.gov /pubs/nsb20201/global-r-d.

42 Daniel Castro, Michael McLaughlin, and Eline Chivot, "Who Is Winning the AI Race: China, the EU or the United States?," Center for

Data Innovation, August 19, 2019, https://www.datainnovation.org /2019/08/who-is-winning-the-ai-race-china-the-eu-or-the-united -states/.

43 "U.S. Research and Development Funding and Performance: Fact Sheet," Congressional Research Service, January 24, 2020, https:// fas.org/sgp/crs/misc/R44307.pdf.

44 Christopher Mims, "Not Even a Pandemic Can Slow Down the Biggest Tech Giants," *Wall Street Journal*, May 23, 2020, https://www .wsj.com/articles/not-even-a-pandemic-can-slow-down-the-biggest -tech-giants-11590206412.

45 Jonathan Gruber and Simon Johnson, *Jump-Starting America: How Breakthrough Science Can Revive Economic Growth and the American Dream* (New York: Hachette, 2019), e-book.

46 Sara Castellanos, "White House Plans to Boost AI, Quantum Funding by 30%," *Wall Street Journal*, August 14, 2020, https://www.wsj .com/articles/white-house-plans-to-boost-ai-quantum-funding-by -30-11597420800.

47 Martijn Rasser, Megan Lamberth, Ainikki Riikonen, Chelsea Guo, Michael Horowitz, and Paul Scharre, "The American AI Century: A Blueprint for Action," Center for a New American Security, December 17, 2019, https://www.cnas.org/publications/reports/the-american -ai-century-a-blueprint-for-action.

48 "Recommendations for Strengthening American Leadership in Industries of the Future," President's Council of Advisors on Science and Technology, June 2020, https://science.osti.gov/-/media/_/pdf /about/pcast/202006/PCAST_June_2020_Report.pdf?la=en&hash= 019A4F17C79FDEE5005C51D3D6CAC81FB31E3ABC.

49 "Overview of the State of the U.S. S&E Enterprise in a Global Context," National Science Foundation, https://www.nsf.gov/statistics/2018/nsb20181/report/sections/overview/workers-with-s-e skills.

50 Jane Croft, "China plays catch-up with Europe and US in patents filing race," *Financial Times*, July 9, 2019, https://www.ft.com/content /8ecf7464-8d05-11e9-b8cb-26a9caa9d67b.

51 "Charting a Course for Success: America's Strategy for Stem Education," National Science and Technology Council, December 2018, https://www.energy.gov/sites/prod/files/2019/05/f62/STEM-Education-Strategic-Plan-2018.pdf.

52 "2019 1st Quarter Manufacturers' Outlook Survey," National Association of Manufacturers, https://www.nam.org/2019-1st-quarter -manufacturers-outlook-survey/.

53 Glenn Leibowitz, "Apple CEO Tim Cook: This Is the No. 1 Reason We Make iPhones in China (It's Not What You Think)," *Inc.*, December 21, 2017, https://www.inc.com/glenn-leibowitz/apple

-ceo-tim-cook-this-is-number-1-reason-we-make-iphones-in-china -its-not-what-you-think.html.

54 "Recommendations for Strengthening American Leadership in Industries of the Future."

55 O'Mara, *The Code*, 389.

56 "The Global AI Talent Tracker," MacroPolo, https://macropolo.org /digital-projects/the-global-ai-talent-tracker/.

57 Sara Salinas, "Mary Meeker just presented 294 slides on the future of the internet—read them here," CNBC, May 30, 2018, https://www .cnbc.com/2018/05/30/mary-meekers-internet-trends-2018.html.

58 Ruchir Sharma, "The Comeback Nation," *Foreign Affairs*, May 2020, https://www.foreignaffairs.com/articles/united-states/2020-03-31 /comeback-nation.

59 Stuart Anderson, "Trump Cuts Legal Immigrants By Half and He's Not Done Yet," *Forbes*, July 21, 2020, https://www.forbes.com/sites /stuartanderson/2020/07/21/trump-cuts-legal-immigrants-by-half -and-hes-not-done-yet/#4446d3f46168.

60 "Suspension of Entry of Immigrants Who Present a Risk to the United States Labor Market During the Economic Recovery Following the 2019 Novel Coronavirus Outbreak," The White House, April 22, 2020, https://www.federalregister.gov/documents/2020/04/27 /2020-09068/suspension-of-entry-of-immigrants-who-present-a -risk-to-the-united-states-labor-market-during-the.

61 Laura Collins and Matthew Denhart, "Policy Recommendations: Modernizing Immigration for Today's Realities," George W. Bush Presidential Center, November 26, 2018, https://www.bushcenter .org/publications/articles/2019/policy-recommendations/immigra tion.html.

62 Ibid.

63 Edward Wong and Julian E. Barnes, "U.S. to Expel Chinese Graduate Students With Ties to China's Military Schools," *New York Times*, May 28, 2020, https://www.nytimes.com/2020/05/28/us/politics /china-hong-kong-trump-student-visas.html.

64 "Fast Facts 2020," Open Doors, https://opendoorsdata.org/fast _facts/fast-facts-2019/.

65 Benjamin Fearnow, "GOP Senator Tom Cotton Says Chinese Students Should Be Banned From Studying Science at U.S. Colleges," *Newsweek*, April 26, 2020, https://www.newsweek.com/gop-sen ator-tom-cotton-says-chinese-students-should-banned-studying-sci ence-tech-us-colleges-1500282.

66 Paul Mozur and Cade Metz, "A U.S. Secret Weapon in A.I.: Chinese Talent," *New York Times*, June 9, 2020, https://www.nytimes.com /2020/06/09/technology/china-ai-research-education.html?refer ringSource=articleShare.

67 David Wertime, "Earth to Washington and Beijing: It's not all about you," *Politico*, September 24, 2020, https://www.politico.com/newsletters/politico-china-watcher/2020/09/24/earth-to-washington-and-beijing-its-not-all-about-you-un-general-assembly-covid-covax-europe-asia-rise-490418.

68 Alex Joske, "Picking flowers, making honey," Australian Strategic Policy Institute, October 30, 2018, https://www.aspi.org.au/report/picking-flowers-making-honey.

69 "Harvard University Professor and Two Chinese Nationals Charged in Three Separate China Related Cases," U.S. Department of Justice, January 28, 2020, https://www.justice.gov/opa/pr/harvard-university-professor-and-two-chinese-nationals-charged-three-separate-china-related.

70 Mozur and Metz, "A U.S. Secret Weapon in A.I."

71 Yingjie Fan, Jennifer Pan, Zijie Shao, and Yiqing Xu, "How Discrimination Increases Chinese Overseas Students' Support for Authoritarian Rule," SSRN, June 29, 2020, https://papers.ssrn.com/sol3/papers.cfm?abstract_id=3637710.

72 "Comprehensive List of the Commission's Recommendations," U.S.-China Economic and Security Review Commission, https://www.uscc.gov/sites/default/files/2019-11/2019%20Recommendations%20to%20Congress.pdf.

73 O'Mara, *The Code*, 304.

74 "About Us," TechCongress, https://www.techcongress.io/about-us.

75 "About," Google, https://about.google/.

76 Guy Rosen, Katie Harbath, Nathaniel Gleicher, and Rob Leathern, "Helping to Protect the 2020 US Elections," Facebook, October 21, 2019, https://about.fb.com/news/2019/10/update-on-election-integrity-efforts/; "New labels for government and state-affiliated media accounts," Twitter Blog, August 6, 2020, https://blog.twitter.com/en_us/topics/product/2020/new-labels-for-government-and-state-affiliated-media-accounts.html.

77 "How Google Fights Disinformation," Google Blog, February 2019, https://www.blog.google/documents/37/How_Google_Fights_Disinformation.pdf.

78 Sara Perez, "Hands on with Telepath, the social network taking aim at abuse, fake news and, to some extent, 'free speech,'" *TechCrunch*, October 11, 2020, https://techcrunch.com/2020/10/11/hands-on-with-telepath-the-social-network-taking-aim-at-abuse-fake-news-and-to-some-extent-free-speech/.

79 "Working Group on Infodemics," Forum on Information & Democracy, November 2020, https://informationdemocracy.org/wp-content/uploads/2020/11/ForumID_Report-on-infodemics_101120.pdf.

80 Olivia Solon, "Qualcomm announces photo verification tool," NBC

News, October 15, 2020, https://www.nbcnews.com/tech/security /qualcomm-announces-photo-verification-tool-n1243550.

81 Brundage, *The Malicious Use of Artificial Intelligence.*

82 Elizabeth Warren, "Here's how we can break up Big Tech," *Medium*, March 8, 2019, https://medium.com/@teamwarren/heres-how-we -can-break-up-big-tech-9ad9e0da324c.

83 "Justice Department Sues Monopolist Google for Violating Antitrust Laws," U.S. Department of Justice, October 20, 2020, https://www .justice.gov/opa/pr/justice-department-sues-monopolist-google-vio lating-antitrust-laws.

84 "FTC Sues Facebook for Illegal Monopolization," Federal Trade Commission, December 9, 2020, https://www.ftc.gov/news-events /press-releases/2020/12/ftc-sues-facebook-illegal-monopolization.

85 Mark J. Perry, "Only 52 US companies have been on the Fortune 500 since 1955, thanks to the creative destruction that fuels economic prosperity," American Enterprise Institute, May 22, 2019, https:// www.aei.org/carpe-diem/only-52-us-companies-have-been-on-the -fortune-500-since-1955-thanks-to-the-creative-destruction-that-fu els-economic-prosperity/.

86 Kia Kokalitcheva, "This is the latest $1 billion tech company to IPO," *Fortune*, May 20, 2015, https://fortune.com/2015/05/20/shopify -ipo-pricing/.

87 Y Charts, Shopify Market Cap, https://ycharts.com/companies /SHOP/market_cap.

88 "Mark Zuckerberg Opening Statement Transcript Antitrust Hearing July 29," Rev, July 29, 2020, https://www.rev.com/blog/transcripts/mark -zuckerberg-opening-statement-transcript-antitrust-hearing-july-29.

89 Tom Wheeler, "Digital competition with China starts with compe-tition at home," Brookings Institution, April 2020, https://www .brookings.edu/research/digital-competition-with-china-starts-with -competition-at-home/.

90 "US Venture Capital Investment Surpasses $130 Billion in 2019 for Second Consecutive Year," PitchBook, January 14, 2020, https:// pitchbook.com/media/press-releases/us-venture-capital-investment -surpasses-130-billion-in-2019-for-second-consecutive-year.

91 "2020 Global Startup Outlook," Silicon Valley Bank, https://www .svb.com/globalassets/library/uploadedfiles/content/trends_and _insights/reports/startup_outlook_report/suo_global_report_2020 -final.pdf.

92 Mark Zuckerberg, "Hearing Before the United States House of Rep-resentatives," Subcommittee on Antitrust, Commercial, and Admin-istrative Law, July 29, 2020, https://docs.house.gov/meetings/JU /JU05/20200729/110883/HHRG-116-JU05-Wstate-ZuckerbergM -20200729.pdf.

93 Jeff Desjardins, "China's home-grown tech giants are dominating their US competitors," *Business Insider*, February 7, 2018, https://www.businessinsider.com/chinas-home-grown-tech-giants-are-dominating-their-us-competitors-2018-2.

94 Tugba Sabanoglu, "Global market share of Amazon 2020, by region," Statista, December 1, 2020, https://www.statista.com/statistics/1183515/amazon-market-share-region-worldwide/.

95 Arjun Kharpal, "China's Tencent is now bigger than Facebook after adding around $200 billion to its value this year," CNBC, July 29, 2020, https://www.cnbc.com/2020/07/29/tencent-is-now-bigger-than-facebook-after-shares-surged-this-year.html.

96 Ganesh Sitaraman, "Too Big to Prevail: The National Security Case for Breaking Up Big Tech," *Foreign Affairs*, March 2020, https://www.foreignaffairs.com/articles/2020-02-10/too-big-prevail.

97 "Asymmetric Competition: A Strategy for China & Technology," China Strategy Group, https://assets.documentcloud.org/documents/20463382/final-memo-china-strategy-group-axios-1.pdf.

98 "IREX Ukraine public service announcement for the Citizen Media Literacy Project (Ukrainian)," YouTube, February 26, 2016, https://www.youtube.com/watch?v=QEEnme-miW4&feature=youtu.be.

99 "Impact Study on Citizens' Ability to Detect Disinformation 1.5 Years After Completing a News Media Literacy Program," IREX, https://www.irex.org/resource/impact-study-citizens-ability-detect-disinformation-15-years-after-completing-news-media.

100 Erin Murrock, Joy Amulya, Mehri Druckman, and Tetiana Liubyva, "Winning the war on state-sponsored propaganda," IREX, https://www.irex.org/sites/default/files/node/resource/impact-study-media-literacy-ukraine.pdf.

101 Jon Henley, "How Finland starts its fight against fake news in primary schools," *The Guardian*, January 29, 2020, https://www.theguardian.com/world/2020/jan/28/fact-from-fiction-finlands-new-lessons-in-combating-fake-news.

102 "The Media Literacy Index 2019: Just think about it," Open Society Institute–Sofia, November 29, 2019, https://osis.bg/?p=3356&lang=en.

103 Eliza Mackintosh, "Finland is winning the war on fake news. What it's learned may be crucial to Western democracy," CNN, https://edition.cnn.com/interactive/2019/05/europe/finland-fake-news-intl/.

104 Ryan J. Foley, "Efforts grow to help students evaluate what they see online," Associated Press, December 30, 2017, https://apnews.com/64b5ce49f58940eda86608f3eac79158.

105 "MediaWise," Poynter Institute, https://www.poynter.org/mediawise/.

106 Carl T. Bergstrom and Jevin West, "Calling Bullshit: Data Reasoning in a Digital World," https://www.callingbullshit.org/syllabus.html.

107 "Amid Pandemic and Protests, Civics Survey Finds Americans Know More of Their Rights," Annenberg Public Policy Center, September 14, 2020, https://www.annenbergpublicpolicycenter.org/pandemic-protests-2020-civics-survey-americans-know-much-more-about-their-rights/.

108 Joshua Yaffa, "Is Russian Meddling as Dangerous as We Think?," *New Yorker*, September 7, 2020, https://www.newyorker.com/magazine/2020/09/14/is-russian-meddling-as-dangerous-as-we-think.

109 Nir Grinberg, Kenneth Joseph, Lisa Friedland, Briony Swire-Thompson, and David Lazer, "Fake news on Twitter during the 2016 U.S. presidential election," *Science* 363 (January 2019): 374–378, https://science.sciencemag.org/content/363/6425/374.full.

110 Clint Watts and Tim Hwang, "Opinion: Deepfakes are coming for American democracy. Here's how we can prepare," *Washington Post*, September 10, 2020, https://www.washingtonpost.com/opinions/2020/09/10/deepfakes-are-coming-american-democracy-heres-how-we-can-prepare/.

111 "Analyzing the First Years of the Ticket or Click It Mobilizations," National Highway Traffic Safety Administration, January 2010, https://www.nhtsa.gov/staticfiles/nti/pdf/811232.pdf.

112 David Salvo, "How to Respond to Russia's Attacks on Democracy," Alliance for Securing Democracy, January 12, 2018, https://securingdemocracy.gmfus.org/how-to-respond-to-russias-attacks-on-democracy/.

113 Joseph Marks, Eloise Copland, Eleanor Loh, Cass R. Sunstein, and Tali Sharot, "Epistemic spillovers: Learning others' political views reduces the ability to assess and use their expertise in nonpolitical domains," *Science Direct*, October 19, 2018, https://www.sciencedirect.com/science/article/pii/S0010027718302609.

114 John Ratcliffe, "China Is National Security Threat No. 1," *Wall Street Journal*, December 3, 2020, https://www.wsj.com/articles/china-is-national-security-threat-no-1-11607019599.

115 Warren P. Strobel and Dustin Volz, "U.S. Boosts China Spying Budget to Meet Growing Economic, National-Security Threat," *Wall Street Journal*, December 3, 2020, https://www.wsj.com/articles/u-s-boosts-china-spying-budget-to-meet-growing-economic-national-security-threat-11607037778.

116 "Romney, Risch, Gardner, Young Introduce Landmark Legislation to Compete with China," Mitt Romney, July 22, 2020, https://www.romney.senate.gov/romney-risch-gardner-young-introduce-landmark-legislation-compete-china.

117 "With the Support of New York's Leading Tech Innovators, Schumer Announces Bipartisan Endless Frontier Act, Bolstering U.S. Leadership in Scientific Research & Innovation, Dramatically Increase

Investment in Building New Tech Hubs in Upstate NY," Charles E. Schumer, May 28, 2020, https://www.schumer.senate.gov/newsroom /press-releases/with-the-support-of-new-yorks-leading-tech-innova tors-schumer-announces-bipartisan-endless-frontier-act-bolstering -us-leadership-in-scientific-research-and-innovation-dramatically-in crease-investment-in-building-new-tech-hubs-in-upstate-ny.

118 "H.R. 4998—Secure and Trusted Communications Networks Act of 2019," Congress, November 8, 2019, https://www.congress.gov/bill /116th-congress/house-bill/4998/actions.

119 "Hong Kong Human Rights and Democracy Act of 2019," *Congressional Record* 165, no. 186, Congress, November 20, 2019, https:// www.congress.gov/congressional-record/2019/11/20/house-section /article/H9100-1.

Epilogue

1 Angela Merkel, "Commencement Address at Harvard University," American Rhetoric, May 30, 2019, https://www.americanrhetoric .com/speeches/angelamerkelharvardcommencementenglish.htm.

2 Eric Geller, "Biden poised to pick Obama-era security veterans for 3 top cyber roles," *Politico*, January 22, 2021, https://www.politico .com/news/2021/01/22/biden-cybersecurity-appointments-461394.

3 Kevin Liptak, "Biden orders review on cracks in critical supply chains," CNN, February 24, 2021, https://www.cnn.com/2021/02 /24/politics/biden-executive-order-review-supply-chains/index.html.

4 John D. McKinnon, "U.S. to Impose Sweeping Rule Aimed at China Technology Threats," *Wall Street Journal*, February 26, 2021, https:// www.wsj.com/articles/u-s-to-impose-sweeping-rule-aimed-at-china -technology-threats-11614362435.

5 Humeyra Pamuk and David Brunnstrom, "New U.S. secretary of state favors cooperation with China despite genocide of Uighurs," Reuters, January 27, 2021, https://www.reuters.com/article/us-usa -china-blinken/new-u-s-secretary-of-state-favors-cooperation-with -china-despite-genocide-of-uighurs-idUSKBN29W2RC.

6 "Readout of President Joseph R. Biden, Jr. Call with President Xi Jinping of China," The White House, February 10, 2021, https://www .whitehouse.gov/briefing-room/statements-releases/2021/02/10 /readout-of-president-joseph-r-biden-jr-call-with-president-xi-jin ping-of-china/.

7 Winston Churchill, "The Lights Are Going Out, 1938," America's National Churchill Museum, October 16, 1938, https://www.na tionalchurchillmuseum.org/the-lights-are-going-out.html.

8 Robert Kagan, *The Jungle Grows Back* (New York: Penguin Random House, 2018), 4.

INDEX

ABOUT THE AUTHOR

JACOB HELBERG is a senior adviser at the Stanford University Center on Geopolitics and Technology and an adjunct fellow at the Center for Strategic and International Studies (CSIS). Helberg is also the cochair of the Brookings Institution China Strategy Initiative. From 2016 to 2020, he led Google's internal global product policy efforts to combat disinformation and foreign interference, including policy and enforcement processes against state-backed foreign interference, misinformation, and actors undermining election integrity. Helberg studied international affairs at The George Washington University and received his master of science in cybersecurity risk and strategy from New York University.